Communicating in Public

Speaking and Listening

Robert N. Bostrom

Burgess Publishing
A Division of Burgess International Group, Inc.

Publisher: *Brete C. Harrison*
Editor: *Barbara Pickard*
Production Manager: *Larry Lazopoulos*
Assistant Editor: *Elizabeth Assefnia*
Editorial Assistants: *Yvette Schnoeker-Shorb
    and Sandy Tradewell*
Photo Research: *Carolyn Chandler*
Interior Design: *Detta Penna*
Cover Design and Illustration: *Tim Blakey*
Art: *Ben Turner Graphics*
Composition: *Jonathan Peck Typographers*
Printing/Binding: *Burgess Printing*

Copyright © 1988, by Burgess Publishing, a division of The Burgess International Group, Inc.

All rights reserved. No part of this book may be reproduced or transmitted in any form or by any means—electronic or mechanical, including photocopying, recording, or any information storage and retrieval system—without permission in writing by the publisher.

Library of Congress Cataloging-in-Publication Data

Bostrom, Robert N.
Communicating in public: speaking and listening
Bibliography: p.
Includes index.
1. Public speaking. 2. Oral communication.
3. Listening. 4. Persuasion (Rhetoric) I. Title.
PN4121.B592 1988 808.5'1 87-31469
ISBN 0-8087-4981-1

Printed in the United States of America
J I H G F E

Address book orders to:
Burgess Publishing
A Division of The Burgess International Group, Inc.
7110 Ohms Lane
Edina, Minnesota 55435

Burgess Publishing
A Division of The Burgess International Group, Inc.
7110 Ohms Lane
Edina, Minnesota 55435

Communicating in Public

Speaking and Listening

Contents

Preface xv

Part One Introductory Principles 1

Chapter One
Introduction 3

Communication and Public Speaking 5
    Communication 5
    Public Speaking 7
    Functional Aspects of Public Speaking 8
Misconceptions about Speech 9
    Misconception 1: Good Speech and "Success" 9
    Misconception 2: Good Speaking Requires a Good "Performance" 10
    Misconception 3: Good Writers Are Usually Good Speakers 10
    Misconception 4: Speakers Are Active, Listeners Are Passive 11
Why Study Speech? 11
    Human Communication: The Essential Process 11
    Speech and a Democratic Society 12
    Speech and Liberal Education 13
    Speech and Personal Growth 13

Improving Speaking Ability   14
     Practice in Speaking   14
     Adapting to Communicative Environments   15
Summary   15
On Your Own   15
Suggestions for Further Reading   16

Chapter Two
The Principles of Communication   17

Fundamental Characteristics of Communication   18
     Interaction   18
     Symbols   19
     Purpose   20
The Inner Environment   20
     Percepts   21
     Language   22
     Schemas   23
     Affects   24
How Communication Works   25
     Relaying   25
     Externalizing   26
     Stimulating   27
     Activating   29
Communicative Public Speaking   31
     When to Use the Oral Channel   31
     Advantages of the Oral Channel   32
Summary   35
On Your Own   36
Suggestions for Further Reading   36

Chapter Three
Receiving Messages: Listening   37

How Does Listening Work   38
     Selection   38
     Retention   41
     Interpretation   42
Improving Listening Ability   44
     Improving Efficiency   46
     Listening Constructively   46
     Listening Objectively   46
Evaluation and Listening   47
     Ethical Issues   47
     Listening to Your Classmates   48

Listening and Life   49
A Listening Checklist   50
Summary   50
On Your Own   51
Suggestions for Further Reading   51

Chapter Four
Managing Communication Apprehension   53

Nature of Communication Apprehension   54
    State or Trait?   57
Dealing with Apprehension   58
    Building Experience   58
    Controlling Tension   58
    Making Thorough Preparation   59
    Thinking Positively   60
    Tactics to Avoid   60
Summary   61
On Your Own   61
Suggestions for Further Reading   61

Part Two   Preparing the Speech   63

Chapter Five
Getting Started: The First Speech   65

Choosing a Topic   66
    Looking Within: Yourself As a Resource   66
    Looking Without: The Audience   67
Preparing the First Speech   68
Methods of Spoken Presentation   70
    Manuscript Speeches   70
    Memorized Speeches   70
    Extemporaneous Speeches   71
    Impromptu Speeches   71
Practicing Your First Speech   72
Delivering Your First Speech   72
Listening to Beginning Speeches   73
Summary   73
On Your Own   74
Suggestions for Further Reading   74

Chapter Six
Audience Analysis   75

The Importance of Audience Analysis   77
    Audiences and Selective Listening   78
    Empathzing with Audiences   80
    The "Electronic Audience"   80
Demographic Audience Analysis   80
    Gender   80
    Age   81
    Educational Level   81
    Economic Status   82
    Racial, Ethnic, or Cultural Background   82
    Attitudes   82
    Group Membership   82
    Political Groups   84
    Religious Groups   84
Situational Audience Analysis   84
Audience Checklist   85
Summary   87
On Your Own   87
Suggestions for Further Reading   88

Chapter Seven
Choosing a Topic   89

Methods of Classifying Purpose   90
Determining the General Purpose of the Speech   91
    Setting and Audience   91
    Traditional Speech Purposes   91
    Traditional Purposes and Communicative Functions   93
Determining Specific Purpose   95
    Ethical Issues   96
Choosing a Topic   97
    Sources of Topics   97
    Narrowing the Topic   100
Speech Purpose, Topic Choice, and Listening   102
    Hidden Agendas   102
    Topic Choice and Source Credibility   102
Summary   104
On Your Own   104
Suggestions for Further Reading   104

Chapter Eight
Materials: Finding Content for the Speech   105

Firsthand Information: Your Own Resources   106
    Experience   107
    Ideas   107
    Emotions as Resources   110
    Personal Background   110
    Secondhand Materials—Research   111
    Interviews   111
    Libraries   112
    Current Events   115
    Computer Databases   115
Selecting Materials—Speech Composition   116
    Adding New Perceptions   116
    Changing Concepts and Language   117
    Altering Affects   118
Listening for Content in Speeches   120
    Listening for the "Big Picture"   120
    Note-taking   120
Summary   121
On Your Own   121
Suggestions for Further Reading   122

Chapter Nine
Organizing the Speech   123

Rationales for Organization   124
    Formalistic Patterns   124
    Following the Audience's Thought Sequences   125
    Aiding Retention   125
    Increasing the Audience's Understanding   126
Types of Organization   126
    Chronological Order   127
    Spatial Organization   127
    Logical Plans   127
Problem-Solving Organization   128
    Cause-Effect Order   129
Introductions and Conclusions   129
    Introductions   129
    Conclusions   130
Outlining   130
    Heading System   131
    Outlines as Aids to Delivery   134
    Transitions: Speaking in "Outline" Terms   135

Listening and Organization 135
    Reorganizing What You Hear 136
    Note-taking 137
Summary 137
On Your Own 137
Suggestions for Further Reading 137

Part Three Presenting the Speech   141

Chapter Ten
Language and the Speech   143

Language and Communication: Basic Elements 144
    Social Signalling 144
    Mediated Responses 146
The Study of Language 148
    Abstract and Concrete Words 148
    Intensity 149
    Multiple Interpretation of Words 151
Using Language Effectively 152
    Using Precise Language 152
    Avoiding Overworked Words 153
    Adapting Your Language to the Audience and Situation 153
    Avoiding Verbosity 153
    Avoiding Sexist Language 154
    Choosing Vivid and Colorful Words 154
Listening and Language 155
    Diagnose Your Language Habits 155
    Language as Memory Aids 156
Summary 156
On Your Own 157
Suggestions for Further Reading 157

Chapter Eleven
Delivery: Nonverbal Elements   159

Nonverbal Communication 160
    Nature of Nonverbal Communication 160
Putting Nonverbal Communication to Work: Delivery 163
    Using Your Body 163
    Using Your Voice 166
    Vocal Cues and "Personality" 170

Listening and Delivery: Decoding Nonverbal Messages   170
Summary   170
On Your Own   171
Suggestions for Further Reading   172

Chapter Twelve
Audio and Visual Elements   173

Attention   174
    Selective Perception and Attention   174
    Psychophysical Attention Factors   175
Creating Effective Visual Aids   176
    Demonstrations   177
    Chalkboard   178
    Diagrams   179
Using Audiovisual Equipment   180
    Audio Equipment   180
    Visual Equipment   182
Listening and Video Aids   183
Summary   184
On Your Own   184
Suggestions for Further Reading   184

Part Four Specific Speaking Tasks   187

Chapter Thirteen
Information and Informative Speaking   189

What is Information?   191
    The Measurement of Information   191
    Informative Communication   193
Successful Informative Speaking   195
    The Demonstration   195
    Explanations or Briefings   196
    Self-Disclosure   198
    Statistical Presentations   200
A Sample Informative Speech   202
Listening to Informative Speaking   206
    Significance   206
    Retention   206
    Note-taking   206

Summary   207
On Your Own   207
Suggestions for Further Reading   208

Chapter Fourteen
Persuasive Communication   209

Definitions of Persuasion   210
    Persuasion and Action   210
    Attitudes and Behavioral Intentions   212
    Persuasion or Coercion?   213
How Does Persuasion Work?   214
    Credibility   218
Constructing the Persuasive Speech   220
    Evidence   220
    Organization   221
    Problem-Solution   222
    Stimulating—Arousing Audiences   222
Listening to Persuasion   224
    Propaganda Techniques   224
Summary   226
On Your Own   227
Suggestions for Further Reading   227

Chapter Fifteen
Logic and Reasoning   229

The Logic Schema   230
    Audiences and Logic   231
Working with Logic in Speaking   232
    Process of Reasoning   232
    Traditional Forms of Reasoning   233
    Toulmin's Model of Reasoning   236
Summary   239
On Your Own   240
Suggestions for Further Reading   240

Chapter Sixteen
Speaking in Specialized Settings   241

Speaking in Small Groups   242
    Group Purpose   242
    Group Dynamics   244

>   Participation and Group Influence   245
>   Speaking in Organizational Settings   246
>   Communication Networks   246
>   Positional Relationships   247
>   Speaking at Special Occasions   250
>   Speech of Welcome   251
>   Dedication Speeches   251
>   Introductions   252
>   Nominating Speeches   252
>   Apology   253
>   Summary   254
>   On Your Own   254
>   Suggestions for Further Reading   255

Appendix   Sample Speeches   257

Bibliography   337

Glossary   347

Index   357

Preface

This book is based on a few very simple ideas about teaching and learning in the basic public speaking course: first, students truly enjoy learning to speak well publicly; second, they enjoy learning about the *process* while they learn speaking skills; and third, listening is an important partner in the process of speaking, not just a supplemental activity to be dealt with briefly.

Hard work and practice is required to learn new skills, whatever the discipline. Public speaking is no exception. Beyond the time and effort required, however, there is an element of good fun here not always present in other courses. In public speaking we get to express ourselves about things that concern us, that are important to our community and nation, and that deserve thinking about. Few other skills courses involve so much that is positive. Teaching this course has always been fun; taking the course, while admittedly a different experience, can be just as much fun.

The second notion stems from my admittedly traditionalist perspective as a college teacher. While I enjoy "advancing the frontiers of knowledge" as much as the next researcher, I really enjoy passing on some of that knowledge to my students. Most college students want to know *why* things work and *how* they can be changed. Learning often becomes an addiction, and each new learning experience stimulates yet another.

Obviously, then, this book is aimed at the introductory public speaking course in which a substantial amount of communicative content is an integral part of the course. It is a joy to see students learn to speak well. It is also a joy to see them learn about speech—an academic discipline with its roots in the great ideas of Western civilization and its future bright. What this means is that this book is equally devoted to teaching about speech, as well as telling about effective practice on the platform.

The third idea involves the integration of speaking and listening as simultaneous mechanisms that make communication work. Listening is not something we can cover in a chapter and then forget. To stress both speaking and listening means to keep listening at the forefront throughout the book. For example, in Chapter 14, Persuasive Communication, you will see a section called "listening to persuasion," which discusses propaganda.

Many times, books are organized into artificial sections or modules that often get in the way of teaching and learning. To afford a measure of flexibility, the book is only generally organized into four parts, and chapters may be juxtaposed to suit individual tastes.

Chapters One through Four in the first part of the book cover introductory principles. The material necessary for the minimal set of activities is presented. It is typical in textbooks of this kind to include one chapter entitled "communication theory" and then go on to emphasize public speaking exclusively. Here an integrated view of communication is presented, beginning with a comprehensive model and proceeding to analysis of communicative functions, including specialized chapters on listening and communication apprehension. The integration of these functions into the process of public speaking presented here is unique.

In the second part, *Preparing the Speech,* the focus is on constructing the first speech. By using a fictitious student, Mary, the chapters on topic selection, audience analysis, research, and organization are made more immediate and relevant. This continuing case example demonstrates the steps involved in preparing a speech. (Mary's sample speech is presented in Chapter Thirteen, together with the outline, research materials, and practice suggestions.)

The third part, *Presenting the Speech,* Chapters Ten through Twelve, concentrates on language choice, nonverbal elements, and audio and visual aids.

Part Four, *Specific Speaking Tasks,* covers specialized topics where the student is introduced to more advanced study of the process of speaking and listening. This includes analysis of informative and persuasive speaking, logic and reasoning, and unique presentation settings.

To aid and support learning, each chapter contains an opening list of key terms, objectives, and preview paragraphs which bridge previous chapters to upcoming material. Chapter summaries recap and direct students to use what they have learned, followed by a series of questions or activities, *On Your Own,* that provide direct applications of chapter content. Each chapter closes with a list of suggested readings to expand student horizons.

Within each chapter, frequent use of interesting and informative examples and speech excerpts makes contemporary communication theory accessible to beginning students and contributes to overall readability. A good many of the examples and illustrations in this book are drawn from organizational settings, partly because of my long experience as a consultant to the business community and partly to emphasize the modern trend toward applications of communication.

To expand on the speech excerpts found in the book, an appendix contains nine full length speeches for use and critique. A comprehensive glossary, cross-referenced to terms where they are first introduced in the text, supplies the student with an active resource to learning and retention. A full bibliography provides additional assistance to the student.

To enhance student learning and instruction, a number of supplements complement the book: a study guide/workbook, *Things To Do,* an instructor's manual, and a computerized examination package, *Test One.*

Things To Do, a study guide/workbook by Enid Waldhart, Mary Helen Brown, and the author, provides an active review of central terms and concepts from the text, along with specific guidelines for speech preparation. It covers purpose statement, topic selection, and audience analysis and is accompanied by many useful forms for self-analysis and evaluation. The focus is on first speeches, as well as, informative and persuasive forms.

The *Instructor's Manual* by Mary Helen Brown and the author supports the teaching environment by providing sample syllabi, speech criticism forms, a communication apprehension test, teaching tips and strategies, transparency masters, and test items.

A computerized IBM PC/compatible version of the test items found in the Instructor's Manual is available to qualified adoptors using Burgess' *Test One* examination-generation software.

Obviously any book of this type is truly a cooperative endeavor. No author is capable of producing a final product in the form you see here. Along the way many reviewers have given generously of their time and advice. I would like to thank: Jan Andersen, San Diego State University; Rich Arthur, Montana State University; Martha Atkins, Iowa State University; David Branco, University of Nebraska; James Brooks, Middle Tennessee State University; John Buckley, University of Tennessee; Nancy Buerkel-Rothfuss, Central Michigan University; James Bynum, Georgia Institute of Technology; Thurston E. Doler, Oregon State University; E. Samuel Dudley, Mississippi State University; Jerry D. Feezel, Kent State University; Allen Glanzer, Glendale Community College; Ethel Glenn, University of North Carolina-Greensboro; Richard Halley, Weber State College; Gail Hankins, North Carolina State University-Raleigh; Lawrence W. Hugenberg, Youngstown State University; Jim Hughey, Oklahoma State University; Thomas Kane, University of Pittsburgh; Madeline Keaveney, California State University-Chico; Beth Le Poire, University of Arizona; Allen Merriam, Missouri Southern State College; Don B. Morlan, University of Dayton; Donovan J. Ochs, University of Iowa; Mary Pelias, Southern Illinois State University; Jack Perella, Santa Rosa Junior College; Robert Powell, California State University-Los Angeles; Sara Pyfrom, Phoenix College; Lawrence Rifkind, Georgia State University; Janene Roberts, Virginia Polytechnic Institute and State University; W. Robert Sampson, University of Wisconsin; Donald Shields, Indiana State University; Aileen L. Sundstrom, Henry Ford Community College; Anita Taylor, George Mason University; Charles Tucker, Northern Illinois University; Andrew D. Wolvin, University of Maryland; Leonard Wurthman, California State University-Northridge; Donald D. Yoder, Creighton University.

At Burgess, I would like to thank Brete Harrison for shaping the concept of the book and providing expert input about the needs of speech teachers across the country. Barbara Pickard, more than anyone, is responsible for the final design and appearance of the book, as well as for the many improvements in content. She alternately scolded and coddled me into doing a better job. Gary Brahms provided sage advice, and Elizabeth Assefnia was helpful at every stage. Larry Lazopoulos brought the many discrete ideas together into a unified whole.

The last achnowledgement is obviously the most important—but the ways in which a life partner, companion, and friend contribute toward any of the good things one does are immeasurable. Needless to say, without my wife, Ann, the book would never have been done. In every project of this type, there are times when one simply wants to quit. At such times, the kinds of relational support available is the difference between finishing a project and not. "Encouragement" is too weak a word for the debt owed here. But for now, thanks will have to do.

Robert N. Bostrom
Lexington, Kentucky
January, 1988

To Rob, who thinks,
to Erik, who acts,
and to Becky, who communicates.

Part One

Introductory Principles

One

Introduction

Speech created thought, which is the measure of the Universe.

Percy Bysshe Shelley

Key Terms

communication
interpersonal communication
mediated communication
mass communication
public speaking
extended message
performance
adaptation

Objectives

After studying this chapter, you should be able to:

1. Understand the importance of knowledge about speech to the practice of good public speaking
2. Differentiate among interpersonal, mediated, and mass communication
3. Define the process of communication
4. Contrast extended messages from shorter ones; larger audiences from smaller ones
5. Understand the role of good speech in achieving "success"
6. Know some of the reasons why speaking and writing skills are different
7. Contrast speech with performance
8. List some of the reasons why we study public speaking

Here you are in a college public speaking course, preparing to learn the ins and outs of speaking before a group. You may have visions of becoming a great orator, whose ringing phrases carry the multitude and win the day. Or you may simply want to become a more effective speaker at meetings, at work, or in class. Whatever your individual motives, enrolling in this class will give you an opportunity to acquire skills that you can use in school and in your career.

Most of us understand how important communication is in our daily lives; modern society favors those who can communicate effectively. We often have to communicate to large groups in formal ways; we usually call this activity "making a speech."

This book is designed to help you communicate more effectively in public speaking situations. One of the best ways to learn to speak is simply to make speeches, but a general knowledge of the principles of public speaking is also vital to the process. Just as beginning aviators must attend "ground school" before learning to fly in the air, you can consider this book as a "ground school" of speech.

The study of public speaking has a long tradition in higher education. In ancient Greece and Rome, schools were organized around public discourse. The Greeks and Romans felt that well-educated people should speak well in public. Partly because of this classical influence, college students have been studying public speaking for centuries, attempting to gain skill and confidence.

We must be careful, however, not to overemphasize speech as a means to achieve success. Some popular courses in public speaking stress the desire to "win friends and influence people" and guarantee that those who finish the courses (and pay the fees) will get ahead in the world. Fortunately, most people are not so gullible as to accept this guarantee at face value. To succeed in any profession requires ability and hard work. Good communication is a vital part of success but certainly not the only part.

> *In 1975, the Kroger corporation (a large Midwestern food chain) felt that their corporation was not well understood by the average shopper and instituted "Speak Out," a program in which corporation executives were urged to seek opportunities to speak to community groups. At the same time, Kroger provided expert help in public speaking for any participant in the program. As the executives' abilities in public speaking increased, their confidence and skill in general corporate activities also increased, and today many of the original participants in the "Speak Out" program have moved up to very important positions in the Kroger management. Many of these executives attribute at least part of this success to their abilities in public communication. "It was a great confidence builder," said one, "and helps you organize your materials and ideas."*

It is true that successful people are usually better speakers than unsuccessful ones. In addition, the skills involved in good speaking carry over into many other activities, such as organizing written material and interpreting information. Learning to speak well also helps you improve your self-confidence. Though success in oral communication and success in general are often linked, good speaking is important in many other ways.

Communication And Public Speaking

We have been using the terms *public speaking* and *communication* rather loosely up to now. Though many people use these terms as if they meant the same thing, they are quite different. Before we go any further, let's compare these two activities.

Communication

The term **communication** has been applied to many processes, from the chemical interaction of nerve cells to the production of television commercials (Pierce, 1961). Human communication, of course, is a more specific activity. Here is a widely accepted definition of communication:

> **Human communication is purposeful interaction between at least two persons, principally through the use of verbal and nonverbal symbols.**

Even though this is more restrictive than some definitions, it still includes a great many activities. When you write to a friend, listen to a traffic report on the radio, make a plane reservation, or discuss current affairs, you are involved in communication.

As you might have guessed, there are many different kinds of communication, but some researchers have pointed out three basic types: interpersonal, mediated, and mass communication (Dominick, 1983). Each form is distinguished by the manner in which the messages are delivered and by the number of receivers involved.

Basic Forms of Communication
- Face-to-Face (Interpersonal)
    - Dyadic (One-to-one)
    - Small Groups
    - Larger Groups
- Mediated
    - Writing
    - Audio
    - Video
    - Telex
    - Computers

    Mass
      Newspapers
      Magazines
      Radio
      Television
      Cable

  Special Settings
    Organizational
    Political
    Intercultural
    Technical
    International
    Instructional

  Interpersonal communication takes place when the participants are in direct contact, that is, when they can see, hear, or touch each other. A friendly conversation or an interview with a professor are examples of interpersonal communication. *Mediated communication* occurs when some mechanical device is interposed between participants. The telephone, a public address system, or a letter all use some mechanical means to "mediate" the message. *Mass communication* happens when a very large number of receivers are involved, usually more than a thousand. Newspapers, magazines, radio, and television are all examples of mass communication.

During his term as governor of California, Jerry Brown had enormous public appeal and relied on public speaking as an important part of the democratic process. (© *Kent Reno/ Jeroboam, Inc.*)

Introductory Principles

Each of these three types of communication can take place in a variety of settings, depending on the desired goal. For example, political communication uses interpersonal (face-to-face campaigning on the street and in shopping centers), mediated (telephone calls by campaign workers), and mass communication (television and radio commercials) to influence voters. Organizational communication (communication in business settings) is accomplished through face-to-face interactions, small group meetings, written memos and computer messages.

Because these activities are so different, you may wonder why we use the word *communication* to describe all of them. In fact, all of these diverse behaviors have a common element: *interactive behavior between human beings through use of language*.

Public speaking fits into this general definition but has its own rules and characteristics. Let's look at some of these in the next section.

Public Speaking

Public speaking is a specialized form of communication. It is not mediated or mass communication, which would seem to place it in the "interpersonal" category. However, most communication researchers define interpersonal communication as one-to-one, or "dyadic." Miller and Steinberg (1975), for example, state that interpersonal communication depends on psychological principles rather than sociological or cultural principles. This means that interpersonal communication takes place at the level of the individual rather than a larger group. Obviously, this restriction excludes public speaking.

So, while public speaking usually takes place in a face-to-face setting as other interpersonal communication does, it differs from most interpersonal communication in three important ways: in size of group involved, the nature of the message, and in the formality of the occasion.

Though there is no set rule on size, a group of eight persons or more is usually considered to be "public" in the sense that it is no longer a small group. However, Winans (1938) illustrates the folly of trying to make hard and fast rules about size.

> *Here comes a man who has seen a great race, or has been in a battle, or perhaps is excited by his new invention, or on fire with enthusiasm for a cause. He begins to talk with a friend on the street. Others join them, five, ten, twenty, a hundred. Interest grows. He lifts his voice that all may hear; but the crowd wishes to hear and see the speaker better. "Get up on this truck!" they cry; and he mounts the truck and goes on with his story or his plea.*
>
> *A private conversation has become a public speech; but under the circumstances imagined it is thought of only as conversation, an enlarged conversation. It does not seem abnormal, but quite the natural thing.*
>
> *When does the converser become the speechmaker? When ten persons gather? Fifty? Or is it when he gets up on the truck? There is, of course, no point at which we can say the change has taken place.*

As the example points out, we cannot set an arbitrary point at which one is "really" engaged in public speaking. A presentation to a school board, for example, might only have six or seven listeners but still be "public" in its essence.

The nature of the message is another determinant of public speaking. In public speaking, the message is usually planned ahead of time and is longer than interpersonal communication. While it is true that occasionally we plan our interpersonal messages, typically we do not. In addition, the extended messages in public speaking are typically aimed at specific social or organizational goals.

The third important characteristic of public speaking is the formality of the occasion. Public speaking occurs in meetings, proceedings, and hearings: The speech delivered after dinner or the sales manager's introduction of the "fall line" are examples. We use speeches for Bar-Mitzvahs, for the opening of shopping centers, and for graduation exercises.

Communication, then, is interactive human behavior that takes place in many different settings and is of many different types. Public speaking is a special type of interpersonal communication where one person presents an extended message to a larger group in a formal situation.

Functional Aspects of Public Speaking

In the excitement of formal situations, large groups, and extended messages, speakers often forget that their central purpose is communication and that these face-to-face situations offer many advantages that mediated communication does not. One of the advantages of public speaking is that it can use some of the elements of good interpersonal communication, particularly when the speech has a clear, specific purpose. Consider the following public speaking situations all of which have a specific purpose.

- A social worker explaining the food stamp program to a group of welfare mothers
- A football coach going over a new play with the team
- A lifeguard at a municipal pool explaining the rules to a newly formed swim club
- A teacher advocating a new reading program before the local school board
- An army officer giving instructions to a unit before a training exercise
- A student testifying before the city council concerning parking problems
- A personnel supervisor showing new employees how to use the company's cash register system

All of these situations have several common elements: Each was an example of *one* individual presenting an *extended message* to a *large group* of other individuals. In addition, certain agreed-upon *rules* contribute to an element of *formality* in these occasions:

1. Some mutual goal or purpose is assumed, whether organizational or societal.

Introductory Principles

2. Minimal structure and role expectations divide the group into one "source" (speaker) and many "receivers" (listeners).
3. The receivers assume that the source has some expertise.
4. The receivers assume specific preparation on the part of the source.
5. The receivers don't talk as much as the source.

The most important characteristic common to all these examples is that the speeches had *functions* in the course of everyday events in the lives of all the persons concerned and were part of some larger framework of group activity or group goals. These functions are not necessarily lofty aspirations or calls to arms but are usually ordinary, everyday organizational tasks.

The fact that good public speaking is often used to accomplish routine tasks, however, should not obscure the fact that learning public speaking technique has many other rewards. As you will see later in this course and in your career, this skill leads to better attainment of personal development and organizational goals.

As we go about our daily lives, we often use oral communication as described above: the one-to-many "talk" that is an integral part of our organizational and social tasks. This type of functional, useful communication will be the model for the kind of public speaking that we will study in this book.

Misconceptions About Speech

Sometimes we form a mistaken first impression about a person, a college course, or an everyday situation that affects all our subsequent impressions. Since such misconceptions can interfere with our ability to know, we need to take a moment and examine them. There are a surprising number of common misconceptions about public speaking.

Misconception 1: Good Speech and "Success"

Sometimes the desire for success is used to justify the manipulation of others. Unscrupulous persons use speech in this way, but most of them are successful only in the short run. As soon as receivers discover the manipulation, their perception of the source is altered drastically. For example, imagine that a state legislator advocates the adoption of an expensive system of pollution control for cities in the state. Later it is discovered that the legislator owns a company that manufactures these systems. At that point, we would certainly change our opinion of the legislator. Although the message might have been successful at first, it has considerably less impact once the listeners find they cannot trust the legislator.

In a later chapter we will examine *credibility*, which is the receiver's perception of the source, usually based on competence, familiarity, and other factors. One important part of credibility is the perception of the source's motive. If receivers believe that the source's motive is primarily selfish, receivers have difficulty in accepting the source's ideas. There are many ethical reasons why we should not use

Introduction ■ ■ ■ 9

communicative skill for self-aggrandizement, but the loss of credibility is one of the most practical.

So, while good speech may help you in your job or in other aspects of your life, no amount of good speaking will assist the person who consistently puts personal motives above the organization or society. In short, while good public speaking can certainly contribute to your success, the desire for *personal* success may interfere with good communication.

Misconception 2: Good Speaking Requires a Good "Performance"

This misconception arises when we confuse speaking and acting. Of course, performance skills are important for speakers: Voice, movement, and "presence" all contribute to successful speaking. Yet many feel these factors are the most important aspect of public speaking and that, if one can "perform," one is automatically a good speaker. Ronald Reagan's political success has often been attributed to his abilities as an actor, but many people forget that he spent a great deal of time learning to be a good public speaker as well.

Good public speaking and *performance* have different goals. A good performance produces a response of appreciation or enjoyment—an "aesthetic" response. Often we say that a good performance "entertains" us. Even though public speaking has elements of entertainment, its principal goals are *understanding* and *action*. We will return to the question of goals in Chapter Two.

"Giving a show" often interferes with real communication. One reason is that a show doesn't allow for much feedback. Feedback is the interaction of speaker and listener, in which the speaker receives messages from the listener and vice versa. Feedback is vital in conversations, only slightly less important in informal and formal public speaking, but least important in acting. Good speakers *adapt* to their audiences in ways that actors cannot do.

> Eileen returned from a conference on health care delivery systems, where she had been a featured speaker on malpractice. "I was speaking for only a few minutes," she said later, "when I discovered that the audience didn't care about malpractice costs. They wanted to know more about more effective understanding between doctor and patient. I threw out everything I prepared and described the new research we were doing."

Misconception 3: Good Writers Are Usually Good Speakers

We have all heard of highly skilled writers who are also excellent public speakers. Mark Twain was as good on the lecture platform as he was with the written word. Tom Wicker, a columnist for the *New York Times*, is also an excellent speaker. However, the two sets of skills do not always coincide. Many distinguished writers are lost on the lecture platform. Similarly, many effective speakers are terrible writers. Unfortunately, much of our educational system is predicated on the notion that the study of writing automatically gives students skill in oral communication. Most research in this area shows that there is little relationship between speaking skill and writing skill.

The interactive and adaptive qualities of good oral communication are the principal reasons why we cannot assume that writing skill always transfers into speaking skill. A written script may help in preparing a speech, but the give-and-take of good public speaking requires a different set of skills. When a speech is too firmly fixed, the speaker often becomes wooden and unable to respond to audience feedback or changes in the speaking situation.

Misconception 4: Speakers Are Active, Listeners Are Passive

In most public speaking situations, the speaker talks more than the listeners, but this doesn't mean that listeners are passive.

Many of us are accustomed to sitting back and relaxing when we listen to a speech. Unfortunately that is the best way to guarantee that the speech will fail. Listeners need to involve themselves in the situation to the same degree as the speaker. Although, the listener's activity is primarily cognitive and the activity of the speaker is physical, both speaker and listener must work at the job. Many people imagine a speech as a one-way process—speakers pouring information into listeners, as if they were pouring gasoline into a car. The communication process simply doesn't work that way. If the listener just sits like a car, passively waiting to be filled with information, the listener may find that the tank has not really been filled.

These and other misconceptions about speech have prevented many of us from taking speech as seriously as we should. In this book we take the approach that you communicate while you speak *and* listen.

Why Study Speech?

Why should we study speech? What is so important about being able to speak to a group? It is important for several reasons.

Human Communication: The Essential Process

Public speaking is a significant part of the process we call communication. Communication occupies most of our waking hours and usually mediates most activities that we consider to be important. Indeed, many anthropologists define us as "the communicating animal," implying that our very humanity is determined by communicative activity. Studying public speaking contributes to our understanding of one of humanity's most vital activities, and by extension, gives us insight into human nature.

We communicate in at least four general ways: speaking, listening, writing, and reading. More subtle messages can also be communicated using our bodies. In addition, the advent of technological methods of communication have drastically altered the ways in which we communicate and even the ways in which we think about communication. The print and electronic media rely on basic principles of

Introduction ■ ■ ■ 11

Thrust into the forefront of the public arena after Anwar Sadat's assassination, Jihan Sadat has shown remarkable skill as a lecturer, teacher, and advocate of women's rights in Third World countries. (© UPI/Bettmann Newsphotos)

speech communication that are learned in interpersonal interactions. For example, when Diane Sawyer of CBS News brings us news of the world, she uses her voice, her facial expression, clear language, and precise organization—all characteristics of a good short speech. Many of the principles that she uses for effective communication are the same as the ones you will learn in this course.

Speech and a Democratic Society

A democratic form of government is based on the free exchange of ideas. To make government responsive to the people, the people need to express themselves, not only at election time, but to government officials at all times (see Figure 1-1). One of the first acts of a new totalitarian government is suppressing the freedom of expression for its citizens. When the Nazis came to power in Germany in 1933, the ability of German citizens to express themselves was seriously curtailed. When many countries boycotted the 1980 Olympics in Moscow, Soviet citizens were not told that this action had resulted from their government's intervention in Afghanistan, and many of them still do not know that their government took this action.

Both private and governmental institutions depend on communication as an important part of the problem-solving process. For this to work, however, all of us need to take our responsibilities seriously and strive to become well-informed citizens. More large companies are recognizing that it is good business to involve employees in the decision-making processes in their organizations. This "democratization" is resulting in better management decisions, better employee morale, and better productivity.

This trend is not confined only to business. Schools are more interested

12 ■ ■ ■ Introductory Principles

Figure 1.1

Communication and Politics

> When Walter Mondale is asked why Ronald Reagan defeated him so decisively in the 1984 Presidential campaign (Mondale carried only Minnesota, his home state, and the District of Columbia), he frankly admits, "I fundamentally mishandled my case to the American people."
>
> Mondale concedes that he failed to emphasize the positive side of his message and couldnot approach Reagan in the technique of communication, even though, he says, "I was essentially correct on the fundamental issues."
>
> He believes strongly that, in future electins, the Democrats "must find a candidate who, in addition to being right on the issues and stating them correctly, can master this modern challenge of communication in this huge country of ours."
>
> Many voters believe politicians often are elected not on the basis of fundamental issues but on personality, communication skills and name identification. Which is why Walter Cronkite, Gregory Peck, Bob Hope, Eddie Albert, Warren Beatty, and Charlton Heston all have been urged in the past to run for political office. Bob Hope used to joke that if he hadn't been born overseas (in Eltham, England, in 1903), he might have run for President and, with luck, been elected.

in what their students have to say, churches are more responsive to their congregations' attitudes, and even in the military, the generals are listening to enlisted men.

Yet this opening of communication lines cannot be effective unless everyone involved is able to listen responsibly and effectively and to express themselves often and well. Conflict in any society is inevitable, and some method must be found for resolving it peacefully. Communication is one of the best methods.

Speech and Liberal Education

Public speaking is an important part of everyone's education. Its study has its roots in the work of history's most renowned thinkers. Statesmen and philosophers of ancient Greece and Rome, for example, wrote at length about speech and public speaking. The Greek philosopher, Aristotle, devoted his famous work, *Rhetoric*, to the topic. Cicero, one of Rome's most influential statesmen, wrote thoughtful analyses of the interaction between effective communication and public life. Other important thinkers and philosophers, such as Shakespeare, Ben Jonson, Erasmus, John Milton, Booker T. Washington, Edmund Burke, Karl Marx, George Bernard Shaw, Susanne Langer, John Dewey, Margaret Mead, and B. F. Skinner, have all contributed to our knowledge of speech communication. The study of good speech is closely connected to the study of fundamental truths of human behavior, and in order to understand speech we must study human nature.

The skills used in preparing a speech—gathering information, selecting and analyzing it, and using logical relationships—are also valuable aspects of a well-rounded education.

Speech and Personal Growth

The ability to express oneself simply and directly has an important influence on one's general outlook on life. Shyness and insecurity prevent many of us from participating in successful interpersonal interactions. On the other hand, the confidence that comes from knowing we have the ability to speak well can carry over into other tasks. Former football star Gayle Sayers recalls his first public speaking experiences.

> I remember the first speech I made in class. It was terrible, just terrible. I think it was the worst experience of my life. I struggled through it, and Tom Hendricks (the instructor) struggled through it with me. In fact, he struggled through the whole semester with me. But by the time it was over, I had improved. I mean, I wasn't great, but there was quite a contrast.

Those who have seen Sayers as an articulate spokesman in television commercials might have a hard time imagining him as an awkward student in public speaking class! As Sayers demonstrates, however, general growth in confidence is an important outcome of improved public speaking. In addition, good interpersonal communication is often considered one of the essentials of a good life (Katriel and Phillipsen, 1981).

Increasing one's speaking skills usually enhances one's listening skills. The ability to understand others is vital to the establishment of any personal relationship. No one can exist without friends, loved ones, or some kind of social contact. All of these relationships can benefit from increased skill in communication.

Improving Speaking Ability

In order to improve your speaking performance, it is essential to understand the *why* of the process, which involves gaining a knowledge of communication principles, such as persuasion, language, organization, and listening. Familiarity with these aspects of public speaking will help you in this course and even more in your personal and professional life. In effect, this knowledge will enable you to become your own speech teacher.

Practice in Speaking

A vital part of your study of public speaking consists of actual practice in writing and delivering speeches and in listening to them. Speeches need to be carefully planned, which means studying the topic, gathering material, organizing the material, and practicing delivery. Listening well involves analysis, comparison, and evaluation. Each of these steps requires physical and mental activities.

It should come as no surprise to learn that in this speech course you will be expected to make speeches. What may surprise you is the *type* of speeches and exercises you will be assigned. Professor Hugh Seabury of the University of Iowa was fond of pointing out that when we learn how to play golf, we do not practice "slicing into the slough," nor do we compete against professional golfers. Instead, we learn, by a careful succession of steps, how to hold the club, swing, and hit the ball. Similarly, in public speaking, we must proceed from simple activities to more complex ones, relying on *directed practice* for our improvement.

Adapting to Communicative Environments

Another essential element for good speech is the ability to adapt to different communicative *settings*. Speaking can take place in small organizations and large; before small and large groups; in formal and informal settings; and before many different types of people.

Summary

Public speaking is a practical, everyday activity that involves both speaker and listener. Its success depends on dynamic interaction between sender and receiver and on their ability to communicate with one another. This ability can be acquired through diligent study and practice. The acquisition of the skills necessary for communicative, functional speaking and effective listening is the purpose of the public speaking course.

In this chapter we have examined the processes of communication and public speaking and have explored some of the reasons for learning to speak and listen well. We have discussed several misconceptions about public speaking: (1) good speech is studied solely to achieve success, (2) good speaking requires a good performance, (3) good writers are always good speakers, and (4) speakers are active while listeners are passive.

Some important reasons for studying speech are tied to our social and personal growth: (1) communication is a basic human activity, (2) good speech is essential for a democratic society, (3) speech is an important part of education, and (4) speech is a vital part of our personal growth. Our general plan for studying speech includes not only learning about the communicative process but also practicing fundamental communication principles and learning to adapt to communicative environments.

Finally the give and take with your classmates and instructor and the realization that you have actually affected them can provide a great deal of satisfaction and enjoyment.

On Your Own

1. Think about the last speech you attended. Did you enjoy it? Why or why not? Could you have listened better? List the reasons you did or didn't enjoy yourself.
2. Decide whether you prefer speaking or listening. What does this tell you about yourself? Explain why you feel as you do.
3. Find an advertisement for a "self-improvement" speech course. What do they promise? How do they propose to achieve it? Call them up and ask how they proceed and how much the course costs.
4. Think about various political figures. Are all of them good speakers? Good listeners? Why or why not? List some of the characteristics of a good politician.
5. List your own personal goals for this class. How do they fit into your career plans?

Introduction ■ ■ ■ 15

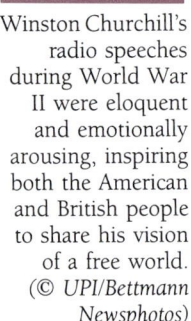

Winston Churchill's radio speeches during World War II were eloquent and emotionally arousing, inspiring both the American and British people to share his vision of a free world. (© UPI/Bettmann Newsphotos)

Suggestions For Further Reading

Berlo, D. 1960. *The processes of communication.* New York: Holt, Rinehart, and Winston.

Bormann, E. 1980. *Communication theory.* New York: Holt, Rinehart, and Winston.

Dominick, J. 1983. *The dynamics of mass communication.* Reading, Mass.: Addison-Wesley.

Fisher, B. 1987. *Interpersonal communication: The pragmatics of human relationships.* New York: Random House.

Wolvin, A., and C. Coakley. 1985. *Listening.* Dubuque: Wm. C. Brown.

Two

Principles of Communication

It is the concentration on communication that will produce something really new under the sun, rather than the ancient recourse to violence.

J. A. Harris

Key Terms

interaction
language
purpose
inner environment
outer environment
percept
schema
affect
relay
externalize
stimulate
activate

Objectives

After studying this chapter, you should be able to:

1. Differentiate between communicative and noncommunicative interactions
2. Recognize the essential elements in communication
3. Identify typical human interactions
4. Show how purpose is vital to communication
5. Describe percepts, affects, language, and schemas
6. Explain the differences among relaying, externalizing, stimulating, and activating
7. Recognize appropriate situations where public speaking is required
8. List the advantages and disadvantages of the oral channel

In Chapter One, we learned that communication is typically classified into interpersonal, mediated, and mass communication and that it takes place in a variety of settings. Though public speaking is interpersonal in the sense that it is usually conducted in face-to-face settings, it is quite different from other interpersonal processes in that it is done before a larger group, uses extended messages, and usually occurs in formal settings.

Because you will be called on to speak in many different settings and circumstances and on many different topics, you should understand the general principles involved in human communication. Knowing how communication works will help you adapt to new communicative tasks. In this chapter, we will study these principles, exploring what communication is, how it works, and how it can be improved. Then we will apply these principles to speaking and listening.

Studying communication is complicated by the fact that the word *communication* is typically used in many different ways. Journalists, advertisers, political candidates, government agencies, diplomats, friends, neighbors, husbands, wives, lovers, and friends all assume that they are communicating. When we use the same word to describe both television commercials and sex, however, the word loses its precision.

Unfortunately, the experts are not much help in this regard. Stephen Littlejohn (1983) found at least fifteen different ways that experts use the word *communication*. To avoid confusion, we need to define this term and agree on how it will be used in this book. In the next section, we will construct such a definition and examine its principle elements.

Fundamental Characteristics of Communication

Let's review our definition of communication:

Human communication is purposeful interaction between at least two persons principally through the use of verbal and nonverbal symbols.

Our first task is to examine each element of this definition—interaction, symbols, and purpose. Understanding each element is vital to full understanding of the process and to improving our communication skills.

Interaction

Interaction involves *interdependent* behavior; during true interaction one response follows another in a cyclical, back-and-forth pattern. Interaction is probably best illustrated by game-playing. In chess, for example, each player's moves are determined by the moves of the other; neither player can ignore the other's moves and still be playing chess. Similarly, in social interactions, our responses should depend on the responses of the other person. If they do not, the interaction rapidly disintegrates.

Some experts contend that all human interaction is communicative (Watzlawick, Bevan and Jackson, 1967). Most experts, however, believe that interaction alone is not enough to qualify as true communication. For example, a tennis game or driving in traffic is interactive behavior but would not qualify as communication in the true sense of the term. Conversely, a conversation can be interactive without being communicative.

CARMEN:	Hey, how're you doing?
ESCAMILLIO:	Not bad. Yourself?
CARMEN:	Can't complain. Looks like another nice day.
ESCAMILLIO:	Yep. Could use some rain, though.
CARMEN:	My flowers are drooping.
ESCAMILLIO:	Well, I have to get rolling. Let's do lunch.
CARMEN:	Fantastic. I'll call you.
ESCAMILLIO:	Sometime next week.
CARMEN:	Okay. See you.
ESCAMILLIO:	See you.

The above interchange could be described as interactive but not as communicative because there has been no change in the inner environments of either Carmen or Escamillio; the exchange is superficial. Automatic, ritual verbal interactions are not considered communicative.

Michael Motley (1987) has pointed out that, in addition to being interactive, communication, besides using language, must have a "fidelity" characteristic. Fidelity refers to the degree of faithfulness the communication has to its purpose. In other words, did the communication accomplish what it set out to accomplish? Did it succeed?

Let's apply these characteristics and see what makes interactions truly communicative.

Symbols

Encoding and decoding—the use of symbols—occurs whenever a sound, a letter, or a sign stands for something else. When symbols are formally organized we call them *language*.

We think in symbols, and, by manipulating them, can express our thoughts, feelings, and complex ideas. Language can be universal or private; it can be spoken, written, or gestural. Human use of symbols is not limited to familiar language but also includes numbers, abstract concepts, visual images, and complex rules.

Symbols and language are so important to communication and to public speaking that we will devote an entire chapter to their use (Chapter Ten). Most

Principles of Communication ■ ■ ■ 19

importantly, when we say that communication can only be accomplished with symbols, we rule out interactions that do not use symbols, such as standing in line, interpersonal "distance," and "power dressing."

Purpose

Motley's second characteristic of communication, "fidelity," simply means that communication is either effective or ineffective. The only way that we can judge quality is to compare the actual communication to its *purpose*. This is not as easy as it sounds. Purpose, or intent, is one of the most important elements of the communication process (Bowers and Bradac, 1982). An example may make this clearer:

> Joanne was a young woman working in a large computing center. She had been studying a new software installation and was scheduled to present her recommendation to her supervisor. Normally Joanne dressed casually at work, sometimes wearing jeans, and seldom wearing makeup. On the day of the presentation, however, she wore hose, heels, and lipstick. At the close of the session, Joanne's supervisor asked a question that indicated that he had missed the point of the presentation entirely. When the session was over, he asked her out for a drink after work.

Although *some* kind of communication obviously took place in the computing center, most of us would agree that this interaction was a failure, from both Joanne's point of view and the supervisor's. The only way we can judge whether or not the communication failed was in terms of Joanne's intent. In other words, if we wish to assess whether the hose and heels made the communication a failure, we can only make this judgment *if* we know Joanne's intent. This means that communication must be purposeful as opposed to random or unintentional.

Yet purpose can best be viewed in the overall context of how communication is accomplished. In the next section, we will examine the way the process of communication works.

The Inner Environment

One important problem that arises when we talk about communication is our tendency to use physical analogies. This comes from thinking of communication as an activity that manipulates physical matter rather than behavior and ideas. For example, we often speak of "transferring material" from one person to another, in the same way that food is transferred from the kitchen to the dining room. Of course, we are used to sending messages written on physical objects, such as paper or cardboard, and the material is often physically moved a great distance.

When we use oral messages, however, the situation is quite different. Nothing physical is exchanged when your roommate asks you to turn down the stereo. The message actually consists of sound waves that affect you because you know how to react to them. This process is so common that we have invented words for the "stuff" that is transferred and sometimes forget that they are only analogies for the actual process. Some of these words—*meaning, ideas,* and *thoughts*—are useful, but they do not correspond to physical objects the way a phrase like "1959 Chevrolet" does. Their principal existence is *in* our minds, and since the interiors of our minds are difficult to see, there is no real way of telling whether the transfer has occurred or not.

If physical transfer doesn't take place, what does happen when we communicate? The answer is that communication changes our *mental states*. We use words to describe the different states. For example, the word *information* can either be used to describe information in its physical form or as a fact or image stored in memory. (For a fuller discussion of information, see Chapter 13.) If a friend asks you if you "have the information" about an Eric Clapton concert, you might respond with a set of written notes about this concert: where, when, and how much tickets will cost. You might also be able to recite these facts from memory. Your friend would not care if the information existed as physical matter (on paper) or a mental state in your mind; the purpose of the communication was accomplished either way. Frequently, the mental state makes for more interesting information. If someone asked you the definition of *soccer,* you might present something similar to the dictionary definition, but you would also be correct if you said, "In Mexico, soccer is a way of life."

These inner states are both the sources and end products of communication. Four important states are useful for our study of communication: percepts, language, schemas, and affects. Since they are thought of as occurring internally, the word *intrapersonal* is often used to describe them.

Percepts

Our outer environment is composed of millions of ordinary things, such as houses, cars, trees, and coffee cups. These become "real" whenever we perceive them. It might surprise you to learn that we don't perceive everything in our environment. In fact, the perceptual system is quite selective about what it "lets in." However, once our senses perceive something and record it in the memory, we form a *percept,* which is an impression of an object formed by the senses.

You have many such percepts in your conscious and unconscious memory. As an illustration, close your eyes and try to remember your last pizza. Most of us can "see" it, and often we can "smell" it as well. This is recreated experience, the result of the perceptual process. Now close your eyes again and try to think of a vicious, blue fighting watch-turtle. It doesn't matter that no such animal exists—you can create it in your "mind's eye" because you have stored percepts. The important point to remember is that percepts do not have direct, exact correspondences with the environmental events; they are created internally by the perceptual system.

Much of our early education focuses on language development. Here, young students learn the correct formation of letters along with their corresponding sounds. (© *Michael Markowitz, Photo/Graphic Arts*)

Language

If percepts were totally unorganized, no one would be able to use them. We organize separate and discrete elements into classes or groups, depending on our experiences and our culture. For example, you have seen trees—pine trees, oak trees, little trees, and big trees—your whole life. You clump all these separate experiences into one classification, sometimes automatically. These classifications are then associated with words and symbols; when you say "tree," everyone knows what you mean. Learning to do this is usually called "concept learning" and takes place automatically. Our culture influences our concepts in important ways, as we discuss more fully in Chapter Ten. The automatic and unconscious nature of concept formation surprises most of us. The main thing to remember about concepts is that they are percepts grouped into classes that make them easier to handle.

At an early age, most of us begin to do more with concepts than simply store them: We associate them with movements, gestures, sounds that we and others make, and finally with marks on paper. This activity is the basis of symbolizing and language. The sound "red" soon becomes associated with a class of percepts that we lump together (red apples, red cars, red leaves, and so on). In addition, we assume that others are having the same kind of perceptual experience that we are. Conceptualization is one of the most complex and interesting activities in all of human experience.

Children begin to acquire language at an early age (usually eighteen months), and then learn not only the names for things (symbols) but also grammar and other complex rules. No one really understands how we are able to learn so much at such an early age. The capacity for language acquisition is obviously biologically determined. Those of us who are studying another language can appreciate the enormous amount of information that infants apparently acquire with ease. Careful study of the language learning system could occupy us many lifetimes; for now let us simply acknowledge its central role in the mental events that we call "inner experience."

Schemas

Percepts and language are important parts of the "cognitive system" and the discipline that studies this system is called "cognitive psychology." Another important layer of the system is called the "schema" system. *Schemas* are groups of concepts and percepts and the systems we use to organize them (Sypher and Applegate, 1984).

In schema systems, associations are made that enable us to "make sense" of internal and external events. For example, if you are traveling along a highway and see a circular black object about one meter in diameter on the side of the road, you can easily identify it as a tire. You know what it is immediately, because you have an elaborate set of concepts about automobiles, travel, highways, tires, and flat tires. In other words, you have organized the concepts together into an "automobile schema," which helps you understand and act on new information. You can identify the tire's function, and probably also wonder if its presence on the road is the result of a breakdown or accident.

Let's look at another example of schemas at work. Consider the object in Figure 2-1. We may perceive this object in a number of ways, making use of concepts in whatever way we perceive it. At first we might describe it as a lightweight, high-fidelity, radio-tape player. Immediately we have invoked two concepts, "lightweight" and "high-fidelity," and might invoke others, such as "cheap" or "expensive," depending on our perception of its cost.

Someone else, however, may perceive this piece of equipment as a "blaster." The equipment is now seen in an entirely new light, one which depends on a social system for its interpretation. We now see the radio as the equipment of a skateboarder in California, or of a youth on a bicycle. A whole set of *interpretations* now accompany the "blaster," mostly associated with youthful activities. Schemas are higher-order interpretations of experience that enable us to fit our environment together in a sensible way.

To understand how schemas work, we might look at one more example.

Principles of Communication ■ ■ ■ 23

Figure 2.1

Our concepts and interpretations of a portable radio/cassette player form a schema, enabling us to find a place for this object in our environment.

Consider the way we behave in restaurants. We have a "restaurant schema" that strongly affects our behavior and our perceptions when we go out to eat. The restaurant employs hostesses, waitresses, bus boys, wine stewards, cashiers, and managers. All of us interact within the "rules" of the restaurant schema; we do not tip the cashier, for example, nor do we ask the manager to bring us more water. When we see a waitress hurrying through the tables, we interpret her destination as the kitchen rather than (say) a telephone in the lobby. Fiske and Taylor (1984) think that we probably have at least four types of schemas: *person* schemas, *self* schemas, *role* schemas, and *event* schemas. You can probably think of other ways that your experience is organized; the process is highly individualistic. Regardless of what types of schemas you accept, it is generally agreed that schemas are an important way of organizing experience. Understanding schemas is also vital for understanding communication.

Affects

In contrast to the cognitive system, which we usually associate with "knowing," other inner experiences are associated with "feeling." For example, on looking at the calendar one morning, you realize that you've forgotten your best friend's birthday. Not only do you *know* what you did, but if you're like most of us, the knowledge *upsets* you. This experience is termed affect. Another name for affect is an emotional state. Although many affects are produced by events beyond our control, sometimes the emotions in our inner environment are controlled by conscious cognitive activity. Affect is often accompanied by physiological elements, such as heart rate, pupil dilation, and so on.

24 ■■■ **Introductory Principles**

We have now examined the four basic elements of our inner environment—percepts, language, schemas, and affects. The physical world is reponsible for many of these, but other persons often influence these four elements. When this happens through the use of language, *communication* has taken place. Now we are ready to expand our definition of communication:

> **Human communication is purposeful interaction between at least two persons, principally through the use of verbal and nonverbal symbols, which affects our behavior and our inner environment— schemas, percepts, language, and affects.**

This definition now includes some notion of *how* the process works.

All communication is not the same: Sometimes percepts are the most important part, sometimes language. At another time, the understanding of a particular schema might be the crucial portion of the communication, and still another time, affective responses would be most important.

How Communication Works — (functions)

Depending on which inner state is central to the communication, we can also classify communicative acts into four categories: relaying, externalizing, stimulating, and activating. Each of these is called a *communicative function* and operates in a given social system in standard ways. Communication works slightly differently for each of the four functions.

Relaying

The simplest form of communicative activity is the relay. When one individual perceives an external event that the second person cannot, the first person can "relay" the event to the second. A *relay is a communicative act in which the source acts as a surrogate stimulus for the receiver*. For example, if a friend asks you if it is raining or not, you might look out the window and relay what you see to your friend. This process is illustrated in Figure 2-2: Person "A" takes in the environmental stimuli ($E_1 - E_n$), passes them through the percepts ($P_1 - P_n$), percept storage, language system, and schema system, and relays them to person "B." Person "B" then has a *percept* that corresponds closely to that of Person "A."

We relay constantly. When watching television, for example, we may hear the weather reporter tell us that it is 105 degrees in Phoenix. This reporter represents a link in a long chain of relayers who have been reading weather instruments, plugging data into computers, and turning on cameras. The relay form of communication, usually involving percepts, is quite simple and is used a great deal. Let's next turn to a type of communication that is more complex.

Principles of Communication ■ ■ ■ 25

Figure 2.2

The communicative act of relaying involves person "A" taking in environmental stimuli and passing the stimuli through his percept storage before relaying it to person "B."

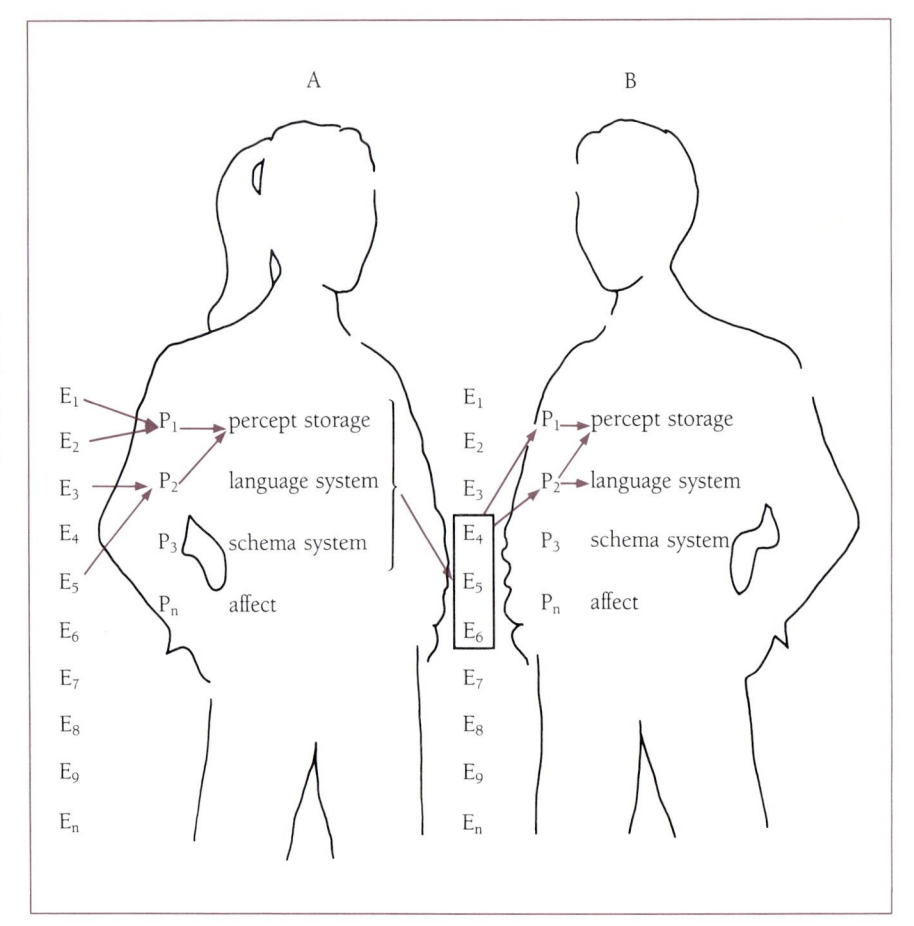

Person A:
- $E_1, E_2, E_3, E_4, E_5, E_6, E_7, E_8, E_9, E_n$
- $P_1 \rightarrow$ percept storage
- $P_2 \rightarrow$ language system
- P_3 schema system
- P_n affect

Person B:
- $E_1, E_2, E_3, E_4, E_5, E_6, E_7, E_8, E_9, E_n$
- $P_1 \rightarrow$ percept storage
- $P_2 \rightarrow$ language system
- P_3 schema system
- P_n affect

Externalizing

Often a communicator wishes to do more than simply relay events as they are perceived—sometimes an evaluation is necessary, or a comparison. Usually these secondary items are stored in our memory as parts of schema systems. This kind of communication is called *externalization* or "self-disclosure." Although externalization is quite similar to relaying, the material that is transmitted is composed not only of percepts but also of at least one schema. Suppose the weather reporter who relays the temperature in Phoenix goes on to say, "The last time I was in Phoenix it was 115 degrees. Boy was it awful! I would never live in a place like that." In this case, the reporter relays the temperature of 115 degrees but also presents an evaluation of the event. We might attribute to him a dislike of hot weather and, by extension, the Southwest. From his short statement we come to learn something personal about the weatherman as well as the temperature in Phoenix. An externalization, then, is a communicative act in which the source transmits some private portion of the inner environment, usually a schema. Political speaking is a particularly interesting example of the formal externalization. Facts or percepts may be

26 ■ ■ ■ **Introductory Principles**

used, but the principal message is an orientation toward an idea. In hearing a political speech we frequently learn more about the speaker than anything else. Figure 2-3 illustrates how externalization works. You will note that, unlike Figure 2-2, Person "A's" schema and affect systems are involved.

Stimulating

When relaying and externalizing, we set modest goals. All that is involved is the exchange of information. One transmits "facts" about the outer world; the other transmits "facts" about the inner world. The next form of communication, stimulating, is more complex.

When the receiver's affective system is activated, the receiver is said to be stirred up, or stimulated. The language, percept, and schema systems relating to emotional storage areas are utilized. In other words, *stimulation* occurs when the source relays and/or externalizes in such a way that the receiver's affective system is aroused. Typical communications of this type include "inspirational" messages,

Figure 2.3

Though similar to relaying, externalization requires person "A" to transmit a portion of his inner environment, involving the schema and affect systems, to person "B." Thus, person "B" receives not only the facts and percepts, but also an orientation towards an idea.

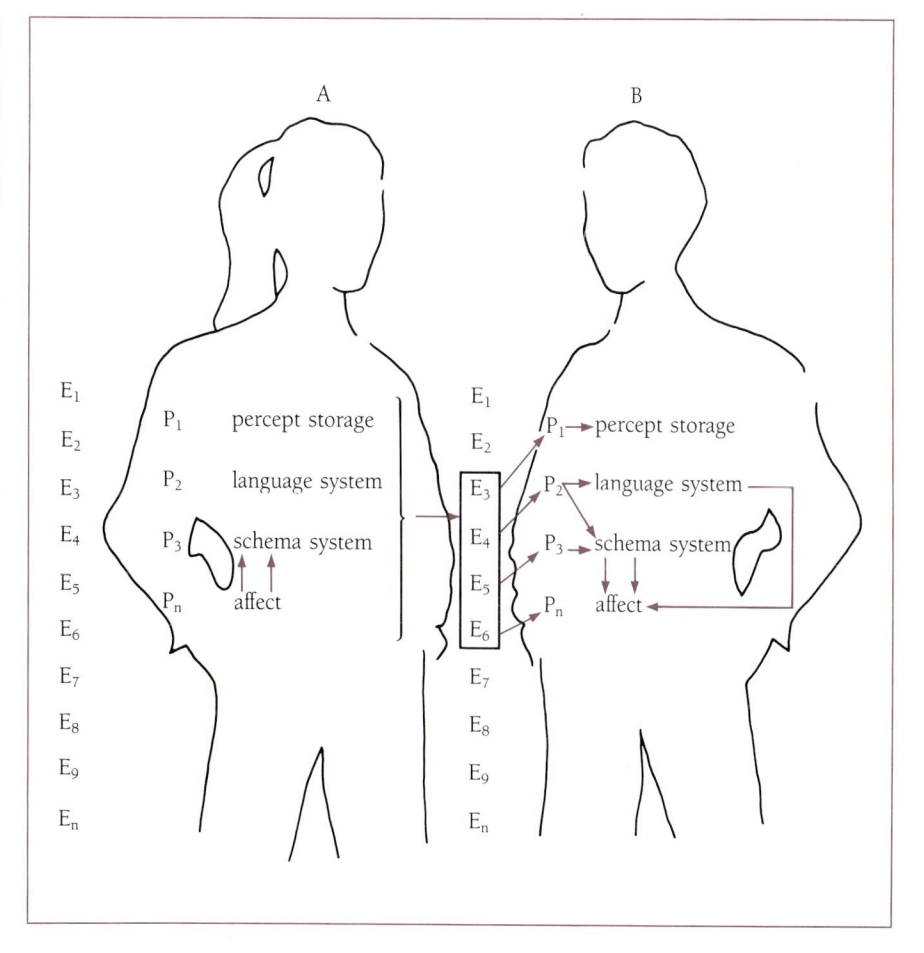

Principles of Communication ■ ■ ■ 27

"motivating" instructions ("Win one for the Gipper"), and what we usually term "commemorative" communications. This kind of communication has as its aim the appreciation of values, such as the nature of right and wrong, or the evaluation of an important event, such as the signing of the Constitution. When this is done with skill, the affective response is extremely rewarding. Figure 2-4 illustrates how stimulating takes place. Note that Person "A" (the speaker) may or may not be emotionally involved. But a good deal *more* is happening with Person "B." Affect is the *main* result.

A commemorative communication differs significantly from a pregame talk by a softball coach, but both are communications that stimulate the emotions. (Some special types of commemorative speeches are examined in Chapter Sixteen). The end product of stimulation is affect, though it may change percepts and schemas as a means of causing the stimulation.

Figure 2.4

Stimulation occurs when person "A" relays and/or externalizes in such a manner that person "B's" affective system arouses, or stimulates, her emotions. Notice that the "action" in the above figure takes place in the receiver, regardless of the transmitter's involvement.

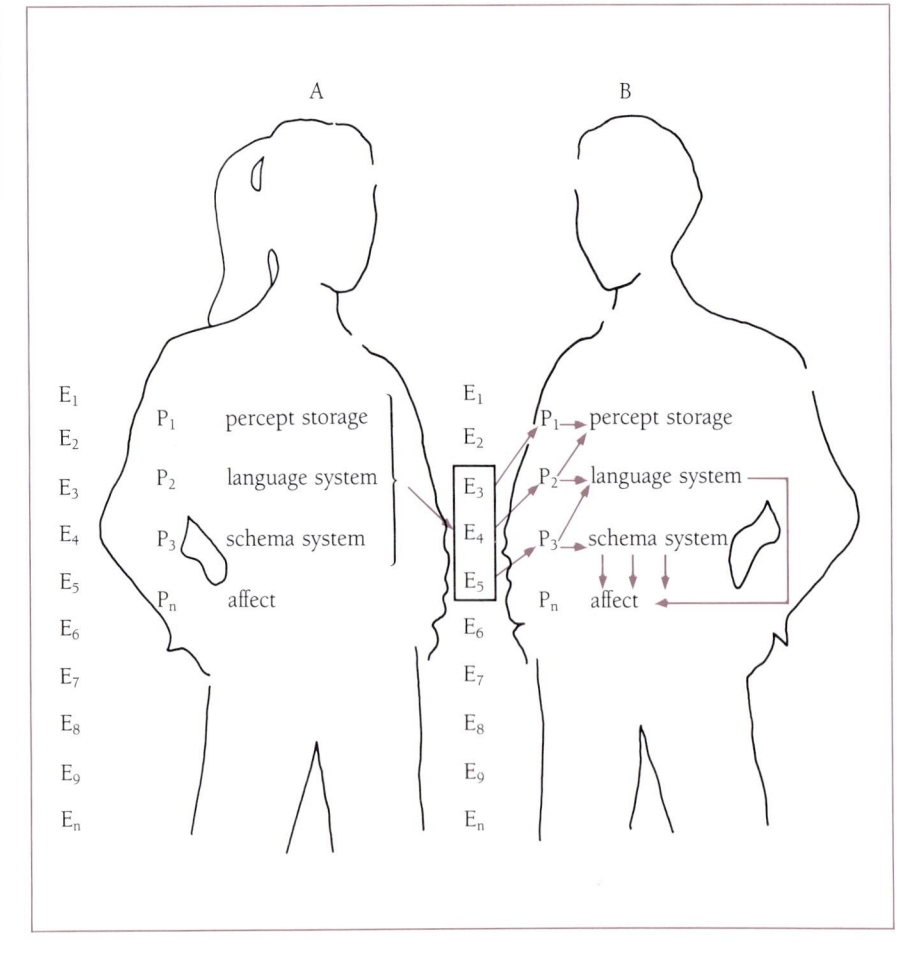

28 ■ ■ ■ Introductory Principles

Figure 2.5

Activation requires person "B," the listener/receiver, to involve her inner processes to take an action, as well as to create a change within her inner environment. This change, or action, is most often referred to as behavior.

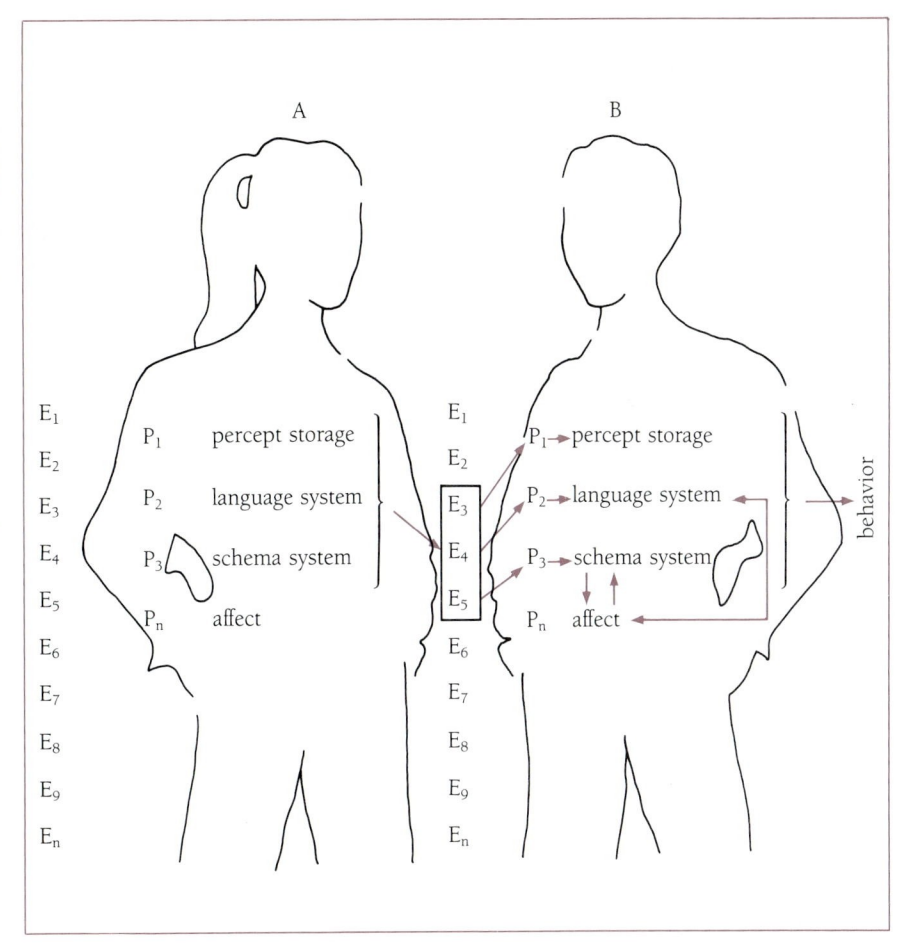

A

E_1
E_2
E_3
E_4
E_5
E_6
E_7
E_8
E_9
E_n

P_1 percept storage
P_2 language system
P_3 schema system
P_n affect

E_1
E_2
E_3
E_4
E_5
E_6
E_7
E_8
E_9
E_n

B

$P_1 \rightarrow$ percept storage
$P_2 \rightarrow$ language system
$P_3 \rightarrow$ schema system
P_n affect

behavior

Activating

As you might guess, the goal of *activation* is not only emotional involvement but also action.

It may be more typical to use the term "behavior" rather than action, but the goal is clear. Therefore, a communication that calls for action is different from those that inform and stimulate, and is called "activation." In other words, this kind of communication calls for action as well as a change in the internal environment of the listener.

Sometimes this kind of communication is called "controlling" in that it represents an attempt by the source to control the receiver in some way. This communicative act may involve stimulation, but not necessarily. Figure 2-5 illustrates an activating communication. Note that while the receiver (B) has an affective component, the speaker (A) may or may not. Now, Person "B" has put all these inner processes together, and has actually taken action based on them.

Principles of Communication   ■ ■ ■   29

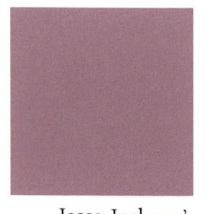

Jesse Jackson's power and charisma as a speaker has helped place him in the forefront of civil rights campaigns and the presidential race. (© Reuters/ Bettmann Newsphotos)

To make sure that we clearly understand the four communication functions, let's look at some examples.

RELAYING: "It's dark in here."
"That truck is carrying 30,000 pounds of bananas."
"There's a girl with a baby out here asking for you."

EXTERNALIZING: "My head hurts."
"I never liked Dan Rather."
"To me, all people from Muhlenberg County are odd."

STIMULATING: "Boo!"
"You are an outstanding person."
"Haven't you put on a little weight?"

ACTIVATING: "Please pass the horseradish."
"Take out your workbooks and turn to page 103."
"Come live with me and be my love."

These kinds of communications take place routinely and are usually accomplished without much thought. In addition, they do not have to be "face-to-face"; these communications would be about the same if they were mediated by the telephone or on a televised linkup. The setting that interests us the most is public speaking. It differs from ordinary interpersonal communication in many basic ways: You will remember that public speaking takes place in a larger group, uses an extended message, and contains an element of formality. Let's look at how relaying, externalizing, stimulating and activating work in a speech.

30 ▪▪▪ **Introductory Principles**

Communicative Public Speaking

First, let's review the examples of functional public speaking from Chapter One. Though none of these examples seemed to be "speeches" in the formal sense, each was an example of an extended message presented orally to a larger group.

Let's look at the first example: a social worker explaining the food stamp program to a group of twenty welfare mothers. If someone asks the social worker what she is doing, she would probably reply "explaining the program," "informing the participants," or some similar phrase. "Explaining" may cover many different communicative acts. In this example, the social worker is probably going to depend principally on the relay (passing along content). She may or may not externalize her evaluations of the program. Stimulation also may or may not be involved. Ideally, activation will be the final result, because the purpose of the explanation is to get the mothers to engage in a particular behavior (such as, dealing with food stamps correctly). The point is that by using a simple word like *explain*, people usually oversimplify a very complex communicative activity. Through oversimplification, the terminology obscures the real nature of the interaction.

In all of the examples in Chapter One, we can see that relaying, externalizing, stimulating and activating are the true end products of these communications. In none of these cases did the speaker call a group together just to socialize.

When to Use the Oral Channel

There are many available channels of communication (oral, written, printed, xeroxed, televised, and so on). How do we decide that one method is more appropriate than another? When do we use the "public speaking" channel to deliver our message?

The most obvious rationale for using any channel is efficiency. We would not use television just because we like it or we think it is fun. Efficiency should be measured by whether we get the best results for the least amount of time invested. In the social worker example, each welfare mother could have visited the social worker one at a time to receive the information. However, this method would have taken a great deal of the social worker's time. A group meeting uses significantly less of the social worker's time than individual meetings, and most organized groups assume that the client's time is less valuable than the organization's.

As another alternative, the social worker might have made copies of the message and mailed them to the mothers. People read much faster than anyone can speak, and a written record would have been made. Mailing the message also would have saved the mothers a bus ride downtown to hear the social worker. So from the mothers' point of view a mailed message would probably have been much more efficient.

Obviously, a meeting is not the only way to get a message across, but it is the most common method of presenting information in many organizations. "You may wonder why I've called you all together" is a joke to most of us, a parody of the usual company meeting. The time wasted always seems to be obvious to subordinates and never to superiors.

Principles of Communication

As a general rule, those who have organizational power tend to choose communication channels that conserve their own time and waste the time of those who have less power. Good managers recognize that communication costs—in terms of the time spent by employees and supervisors alike.

Considerations of efficiency aside, there are good reasons for using public speaking in many situations. In the next section we will look at some of the advantages of this channel, and some of the reasons why it is used.

Advantages of the Oral Channel

A speech has three advantages that a memo does not have: (1) the use of *feedback*, (2) *larger channel capacity*, and (3) the capability of using a *conversational mode*.

Feedback.

How could you persuade your parents to send you $50.00 for a weekend in the city? If you simply wrote your request in a letter, you might have a reasonable chance of getting the money, perhaps "50-50" or better, depending on your parents. On the other hand, a negative reply, written in black and white in a letter, has a certain finality to it. You might be able to improve your odds. Telephoning, for example, gives you some new options. If your parents sound reluctant, you can resort to bargaining and come down to $40.00 or even $30.00. If they are still reluctant, you might rephrase the request from an outright grant to a loan. You could even mention some of the nice things you might do for you parents when you return home!

In this instance, the oral channel is clearly more effective than writing because it provides instant *feedback*—the listener's response to the speaker's message. With access to such feedback, you can adjust your request to changes in circumstances created by the interaction. Of course, you could have put all your "bargaining chips" in the letter in the first place. However, you run the danger of settling for a $30.00 loan when you might easily have obtained an outright grant of $50.00 instead.

In formal settings, we can also make use of feedback by adjusting speech content to the immediate responses of the listeners. This illustrates the importance of *active listening* to good speaking. Without this active listening, we may as well use other methods.

Larger Channel Capacity.

The oral channel has the advantage of conveying a broader range of information than other modes of communication, such as vocal inflection, body movement, facial expression, and the like. For example, suppose that a relative of yours has been seriously injured in an accident. Would you prefer to receive the news in a telegram or in-person from a close friend? The telegram is limited to conveying factual information and cannot temper the shock, but a friend can offer sympathy, support, and friendship as well as bringing the bad news. A larger channel capacity means that you can impart more information in a shorter period of time, which in turn means that your communication is more effective.

Since the oral channel has these characteristics, you should use them. In other words,

> **if you do not intend to adapt to your receiver's reactions and if you do not intend to use the full range of your voice and body as an important part of your message, you should reconsider your reasons for making a speech.**

Let's return once more to our example of the social worker and the welfare mothers. The social worker who calls a meeting can note the ways the mothers react to the new food stamp program and their specific questions (feedback). She might also see that some mothers have particular problems that need to be addressed. She can certainly convey an overall message of sympathy, support, and caring that could not possibly be sent in a letter (larger channel capacity). If the social worker is not ready to utilize these aspects of oral communication, sending letters might be a better way to relay this information.

Speaking as Conversation.

Another benefit of the oral channel is its interactive or "conversational" nature. This is certainly not a new idea. In the 1830s, Charles Bronson Alcott (the father of Louisa May Alcott, the famous abolitionist) went on the lecture circuit with a new form of public address that he called "conversations" (Greynolds, 1972). For some unfortunate reason, his new format never caught on, and most public speakers of the era continued to thunder along with dramatic phrases and elaborate gestures. Is it realistic to call a public speech a "conversation" when one person does all the talking and the rest of the group says nothing? The answer is a qualified "yes." Despite the speaker/listener structure, most situations are interactive in much the same way conversations are.

First, in many informal speaking situations, listeners interrupt when they don't understand or need more information. In slightly more formal situations, listeners might raise their hands if they don't understand something or have a comment. Even in very formal situations, receivers react with facial expressions, posture, or movements. These messages may be intentional or unintentional, subtle or obvious.

We can say then, that *conversational public speaking* is relaxed, less formal, and has more specific references to audience reactions. Even more important, speaking with a heightened awareness of audience response leads to effective speech composition and delivery. When the medium of public speaking is used, listeners by definition have to be active, not passive. A truly conversational mode calls for effort on the part of everyone.

To summarize, good public speaking is interactive, conversational, and responsive to the needs of the receivers. We still need to keep in mind, however,

Principles of Communication

that throughout the process, speakers relay, externalize, stimulate, and activate. Let's see how these various communicative activities can be combined.

In the speech presented below, Myra, an engineer working for a large power company, has been asked by her boss to speak at the monthly meeting of a local service organization on the subject of rates. Her company has recently asked the public service commission for an increase in electric rates, and the community has reacted negatively. Myra's ostensible purpose is to inform her audience and the community about the reasons for the rate increase. As such, we would expect the speech to be primarily composed of relays. However, Myra occasionally externalizes and stimulates to give the speech continuity and impact. At the end of the speech, she attempts to activate as well.

EXTERNALIZES	Thanks for asking me here to speak today. I know that not everything we do is tremendously popular with the public, and sometimes we who work with utility corporations are seen as the bad guys. All I have to say here is that our motto is "More power to the people!" You can take it from there.
EXTERNALIZES RELAYS EXTERNALIZES	I am as concerned with utility rates as you are. All of us who work for the power company use electricity and gas, and water and other products, and pay regular rates for it. Believe me, I'd like to have lower rates, too, and I get upset when my bill goes up.
	I would like to take just a minute of your time to explain why my company needs more capital to expand our generating capacity.
RELAYS	General Utilities serves one million users in thirty-six counties in our state. We get the electricity we sell you from our generating plants, but also we buy some from a larger utility in the next state. This electricity we buy is more costly than the stuff we generate.
RELAYS	We have four coal-fired generating plants and one oil-burning plant, all of which consume millions of dollars of fuel each year.
STIMULATES	I don't know how many of you have a house with an old furnace, but if you do, you know that the older the furnace gets, the less efficient it is. In addition, older furnaces are less reliable. My neighbor has an old furnace, and last winter it broke down in February. The whole family was over at our house, and they were terrified that their pipes would freeze. Fortunately they got it fixed.
STIMULATES	Two of our coal generating plants are thirty years old. My neighbor's furnace was twenty-two years old. If we would lose these two plants at the same time next winter, we would all freeze because most of our furnaces need electricity for their blowers.

34 ■ ■ ■ **Introductory Principles**

In addition, these old plants are less than half as efficient as new ones. They take almost twice as much energy to produce one kilowatt of power than new ones. Coal is cheap now, but we have no idea how long this is going to last. If coal goes up 10 percent in cost, we would have to ask for another rate increase based on this cost alone.

In other words, we have obsolete equipment which we feel needs to be replaced. It is not reliable, and we know that it is inefficient in energy cost. We think the solution is to build a new generating plant. We want to locate it on the river so that coal can be barged in cheaply, and we want to locate it centrally so transmission won't be a problem.

RELAYS

ACTIVATES

The minimum cost of this plant will be in the neighborhood of $250 million. This will average out to around $130 per customer. Why don't you take out a pencil and see how soon we will accumulate the entire $130 per customer at the rate of $3 per month? You see, we really won't make it this way. We will borrow the money and hope that more efficient power generation will make up the difference.

STIMULATES

The alternative is to continue with our outmoded equipment, wondering when and where the breakdowns will come, squandering a precious natural resource—coal—that is irreplaceable. In addition, we are probably contributing to the acid rain problem that is plaguing the Northwest.

I hope that you can see that the proposed rate increase is a reasonable one, and that our company plans to put the money to good use, not to spend it on high salaries for our executives or for profits for our stockholders.

ACTIVATES

I hope that you see our needs—and I hope that you will support us when we ask for the new rate. We want to have enough capacity to take us into the next century, and we want to provide you as efficient, reliable, and as cheap a service as is humanly possible.

You can see how each of these communication functions are different. Some require different responses from the listeners, and some require different sorts of efforts from the speakers.

Summary

The process of communication permeates our interpersonal life, our appreciation of the arts, and our view of humanity. Not everyone agrees on a standard definition of "communication," but a workable one would include *purposefulness, language, and human interaction.* Communication uses and affects our internal environment, including percept formation and storage, concept and symbol formation, schema building, and affects. We can say that the four internal processes (percepts, language, schemas, and affects) are both the material and the end products of communication.

These internal activities are translated into relaying, externalization, stimulation, and activation. Public speaking utilizes all of these functions and often contains all four of them. Good public speaking focuses on the receivers' needs and situation; it is also interactive, and conversational. In the rest of this book, we will examine these functions in greater detail, trying to understand how they work and how we can make our communication and our speaking and listening more effective by using them.

On Your Own

1. If you have a friend who talks to his pet, interview this friend and try to understand why he does this.
2. Look for examples of using of symbols without written or spoken language. How did you decide it was a symbol? Give an example from your own behavior.
3. Recently the FCC ordered radio stations not to play records that had "drug lyrics" in them. Ask your friends if they felt more inclined to use drugs after listening to such a record. What does this indicate about stimulating communications?
4. Choose one topic (such as Yellowstone National Park) and try to catalogue its percepts in your mind. What categories did you use?
5. Distingush between relaying and activating in some routine communication act, such as a Sunday sermon or a professor's lecture. How easy was it to distinguish between the two?

Suggestions For Further Reading

Cooper, L. 1960. *Aristotle's rhetoric*. New York: Appleton-Century-Crofts.

Fiske, S., and S. Taylor. 1984. *Social cognition*. Reading, Mass.: Addison-Wesley.

Linkugel, W., R. Allen, and R. Johanneson. 1982. *Contemporary american speeches*. 5th ed. Dubuque: Kendall-Hunt.

Skinner, B. 1958. *Verbal behavior*. New York: Appleton-Century-Crofts.

Three

Receiving Messages: Listening

It takes two to speak the truth—one to speak and one to hear.

Henry David Thoreau

Key Terms

listening
selection
retention
short-term listening
rehearsal listening
long-term listening
lecture listening
interpretation
constructive listening
objective listening
evaluation
ethics
ethical communication

Objectives

After studying this chapter, you should be able to:

1. Provide examples of selective listening
2. Define the different stages in retention
3. Illustrate how short-term listening facilitates interpersonal communication
4. Explain how nonverbal elements contribute to interpretation
5. Know some of the efficiency rates of various kinds of listening
6. Enumerate the ways in which listening can be improved
7. Describe how successful communication is a joint responsibility between listener and speaker

Chapters One and Two examined the communication process, especially the ways in which communication is utilized in public speaking. We saw that communication is a purposeful, interactive process, involving at least two persons and making use of *percepts, language, schemas,* and *affects*. Public speaking uses this process when one person presents an extended preplanned message to a larger group. Speakers attempt to *relay, externalize, stimulate,* and *activate* in these situations. In each of these, the speaker has a specific purpose: in relaying, the concentration is on percepts; externalizing focuses mainly on percepts and schemas; stimulating uses percepts, schemas, and affects; and activating uses all three to bring about action. All communication uses language, whether verbal or nonverbal.

Chapters One and Two assumed that listeners had no difficulty receiving percepts, schemas, languages, and affects. In reality, the process is quite different. Even when receivers do their best, the various aspects of the message come through imperfectly.

We usually call the specific act of taking in information from an oral stimulus *listening,* and in this chapter we examine some of the ways that people listen. Listeners need to be active participants in the communication process, and in many respects, the listener's task is more difficult than the speaker's. In this chapter we will look at the way listening works and ways we can make it work better.

How Does Listening Work?

Normally we do three things when we listen: we *select* signals to take in, we *retain* the signals as part of our cognitive store, and we *interpret* the signals as part of our available information store.

Selection

We don't listen to everything that we hear. For example, at a party you might hear two different conversations at once. Hardly anyone can listen to both of them simultaneously. Usually your mind chooses one or the other and attends to it. *Selection* is the process of choosing which stimuli will be perceived. This process of selection depends heavily on our background, our attitude, our age, and our interest (Weaver, 1972). Sometimes this selection process is deliberate; more often it is unconscious. What you listen to is definitely affected by what you want to hear. Parents often say, "My children simply don't listen to me." What children do in many cases is simply select some and reject other information.

Not all selection occurs because the listener has deliberately "tuned out." Sometimes selection happens because of an unconscious attitude about the subject, or the speaker, or any one of a number of elements of the situation. All of us are easily distracted by competing stimuli.

One source of selection occurs entirely in our own minds. Most of us read at a fairly rapid rate—most college freshmen can read at least four hundred words per minute, and some can read even more rapidly. This means that we can assimilate data from language at a rapid rate. When you are called on to listen to a speech, however, you are receiving information at a much slower rate: Most speakers talk at a rate of 90 to 120 words per minute. This large discrepancy between your ability to assimilate new information and the rate that it actually gets to you can lead to problems.

Many of us adapt to the discrepancies between assimilation rate and presentation rate by daydreaming. We attend to a message for a time, assimilate it, and then think about something else. Then, in order to keep current with the speaker, the daydreamer turns back to the speech, attends to it again, and then returns to daydreaming. This natural adaptive strategy keeps most of us from getting bored. The problem arises when we daydream a while and then forget to tune back in.

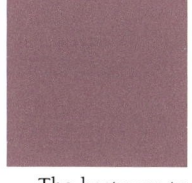

The best way to understand people is to listen to them. We must face the fact that when we succeed in "hearing a person out" our own position may become quite modified. (© Olof Kallstrom/Jeroboam)

Receiving Messages: Listening   39

Figure 3.1

Listening is an active and concentrated response to a speaker. When the listener does not work as hard as the speaker, the probability is the listener will hear a "topic" that is more interesting than the topic of the speech. Notice how the listener's thoughts wander in comparision to the speaker's words.

Speaker's Words:	Listener's Thoughts:
Now first, we need to determine what kind of grass is needed for what kind of area in your lawn. New growth is best accomplished with a kind of ryegrass, but it is not a good, permanent cover. So something should be mixed in with the ryegrass to give a permanent growth.	Gosh, grass is grass, isn't it? Ok, I guess there are some different kinds. My lawn–pooh, what a moonscape! No kind of grass is going to do well there. New growth is what I need. Ryegrass, huh? I could try that. The last stuff I put on was really a bust. He hasn't mentioned that if you don't water it, it won't grow. My water bill is a disaster as it is. Not to mention that I'll need a hose and a sprinkler.
Typical mixes that we see for sale usually contain bluegrass as the more permanent grass seed. But there are problems with bluegrass that we should be aware of. First of all, it doesn't do well in extremely hot weather. So if you plant bluegrass, you will be watering a lot. Second of all, it doesn't do well when there is a lot of shade. In other words, you need an ideal location for bluegrass.	Blue grass is what I want. I wonder why they call it "bluegrass?" They really ought to call it "greengrass." Wasn't that Esther Greenglass on Marie's swimming team? I am just sure that was her. She is far too good a swimmer for that bunch. She won the Markle Invitational last year and could qualify for the university team this year. No. It couldn't have been Esther. She's too good for that bunch. Wonder where she is going to swim this year. Marie's team really isn't going to go anywhere, that's for sure. They just don't train enough and I'm not sure they are good enough if they did train.
One type of grass that you might consider for a shady area is fescue. There are a number of types of fescue on the market, the most common of which is red fescue.	Fescue? What the heck is fescue? I'd better pay attention. Oh, it's a kind of grass. Never heard of it.

Normally, daydreaming does not interfere with attending to a speech or a lecture, but occasionally the daydreamer comes across a topic that is much more interesting than the topic of the speech. Then the listener's train of thought becomes derailed. In Figure 3.1, the listener has attended rather well up until "greengrass" suggests "Greenglass," and the subject of swimming competition replaces the subject of grasses. It takes an act of will to force the listener's attention back to the speaker.

One reason that this happens so often is that most of us have learned to *act* as if we're listening when actually we may be thinking of something entirely different. Especially in schools, we are rewarded when we "sit up, look alert, and pay attention." Skilled speakers are aware of this process and sprinkle such phrases as "This is really important," and "I think you will really want to remember this point," in their talks.

Once you understand this process, you will see how important it is to think of listening as an active, difficult task. We typically believe that the speaker

40 ■ ■ ■ **Introductory Principles**

is supposed to do all the hard work and we listeners simply sit back and take it in. However, for the whole process to work, *the listeners have to work as hard as the speaker*. This means that good listening is an active, concentrated response to the speaker.

Other problems in selection arise because of preconceived attitudes and habits that we bring to the speech. Preconceptions about the topic, the situation, or the speaker are difficult to keep under control. Suppose you attend a meeting about AIDS prevention. You might expect to hear presentations by medical researchers and sociologists. Instead, the first speaker is a minister. You might jump to the conclusion that a minister would have little to offer on this important topic. It requires a good deal of effort to swallow this preconception, construct a new schema in which the relationship of religion or ethics to AIDS can be examined, and then attend to the speech.

Retention

We retain information in several ways. *Retention* involves memory, and the types of retention vary with the type of memory used. Basically, there are three types of retention—short-term, short-term with rehearsal, and long-term—that use three different memory functions.

We use short-term listening when we don't need to keep the information very long. Many social conversations only utilize the short-term because there is no real reason to retain the information. *Short-term listening* is what we do when we retain the content for less than ninety seconds. It is usually not necessary to remember an entire speech or lecture. For example, in a typical speech the speaker might illustrate a point with an anecdote. Retention of the point is important, but retention of the anecdote may not be. All of us vary in our short-term and long-term listening ability, but short-term listening ability is not as closely related to intelligence. It is, however, closely associated with communication skill (Bostrom and Waldhart, 1980). Good communicators are almost always good short-term listeners.

What is the benefit of remembering something for that short period of time? In many interactions, short-term listening is all that is needed. In a typical conversation, the participants use short-term storage of information throughout the interaction but do not necessarily transfer everything into the long-term memory. It is important to keep the interaction going but not important to remember every detail of it.

Keeping information in a rehearsal state is another type of retention. *Rehearsal listening* occurs when you keep something in your mind consciously by repeating it to yourself. You utilize short-term rehearsal when you look up something in the telephone directory and keep repeating the number in your mind. This ability is quite different from the ability to listen and retain on the immediate short-term.

When we retain something for a long period of time, we are using *long-term memory*. Because listening for long-term retention usually occurs in lecture situations, we call this process "lecture listening." *Lecture listening* typically includes anything we retain longer than one hour. This process is much more difficult than the other two. Information must be transferred from short-term to long-term memory by conscious effort. In your lectures in other courses, you probably depend heavily on taking notes, but you can't always depend on note-taking for retention. Long-term memory is activated in numerous ways, but the most typical are association and repetition. If you can associate new data with data already in long-term memory, storage of the new data will be facilitated. If you repeat data long enough, it will usually be transferred to long-term storage.

Language is involved in all aspects of listening but is especially important in the retention phase. The assignment of meaning to incoming messages is called "decoding." When you hear the word "pin," for example, you must often decide if the object signified is utilitarian or decorative. If the speaker was not careful with pronunciation, the word might be mistakenly taken to mean a writing implement or a place where pigs are kept. All of this decoding is affected by context, which is usually linguistic in nature. Larger kinds of contexts are discussed below in terms of interpretation.

Grammar is an especially important part of decoding and is critically related to retention. The phrase "a happy, bubbly, attractive bottle of wine" is more difficult to remember than "a bottle of wine that is happy, bubbly, and attractive" (HeenWold, 1978). The noun-first position helps listeners anchor the adjectives and thus retain them better. Any words with high associational value are easier to retain than words that are strange and unfamiliar. Detailed discussion of the interaction between retention and language is presented in Chapter Ten.

Interpretation

Once we assimilate and store messages in short-term storage, we begin to interpret them. *Interpretation* is simply the process of integrating incoming material with existing schemas. We do this in at least two different ways: (1) by listening to the speaker's voice and watching bodily action, we interpret the intent of the speaker and (2) through our larger schematic structures, we arrive at what we think the message *means*.

Most of the time we listen for more than just information. People use the expanded channel capacity of speech to send more than just words. The speaker's voice, posture, and facial expressions all contribute to the interpretation of the message. In fact, the entire context of the speaking situation contributes to the meaning of the message and its reinterpretation. In other words, more than simple assimilation takes place. Interpretive listening is the process by which we detect other meaning from the larger context of the message, and involves interpretive schemas for meaning. Most of the time this works as we wish it to, but sometimes the listener invokes an interpretive schema that was not intended.

> *Recently, a local theatre group was rehearsing a production of* Music Man, *the popular musical set in Iowa at the turn of the century. The cast was assembled at the end of a scene. The director turned to the leading lady, and said "Well, you made it through the song. Congratulations. When you sang 'Goodnight, My Someone,' I really believed that you were a small-town librarian." The leading lady burst into tears and fled the rehearsal.*

Figure 3.2

Selection, retention, and interpretation occur within the receiver, or person "B." Once the receiver's short-term memory has absorbed the input, rehearsal takes place as the input moves to become part of long-term memory's schema, language, and percepts. Not all input finds it's way into long-term memory.

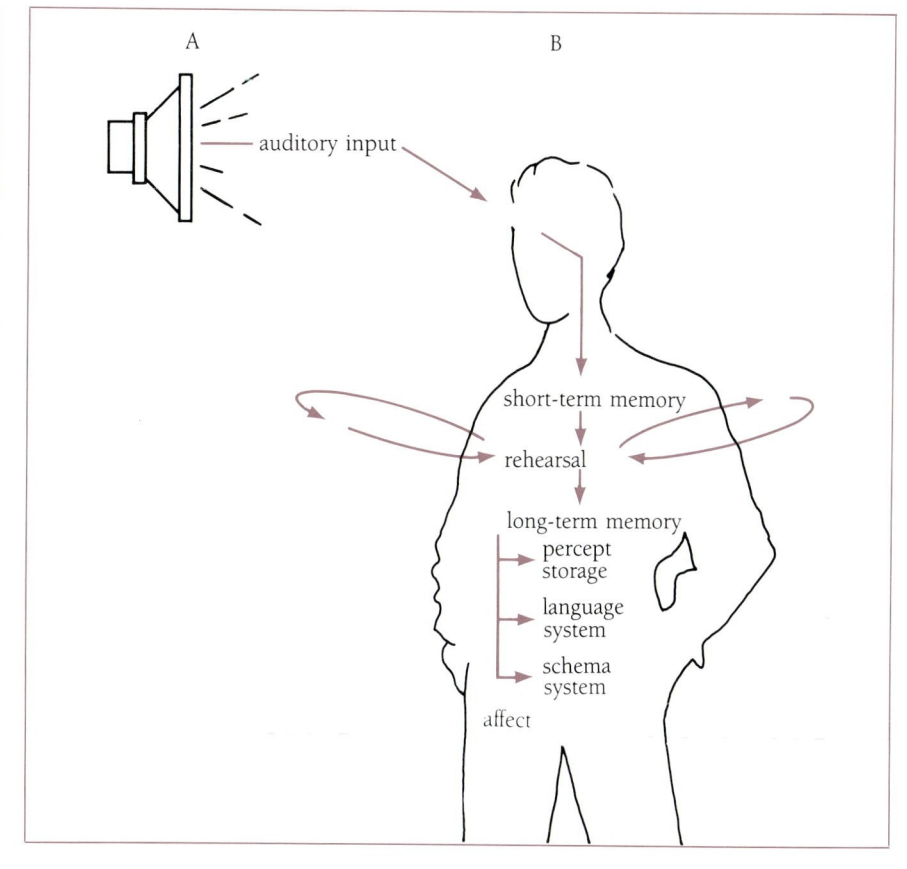

The director meant the statement as a compliment, but unfortunately said "Congratulations" with a flat, falling inflection, which made the whole statement sound sarcastic. The actress thought the director was saying that she sounded like a hick; she supplied the wrong interpretation.

Some people are much better at interpretive listening than others. Situational elements, tension, and individual expectations affect the ability to interpret vocal cues. Women are much better at this kind of listening than are men (Sypher, 1984).

The second method of interpretation involves "making sense" of the message. You will recall from Chapter Two that we have schemas for many different kinds of behavior. If we hear a friend say, "I think I'm about to lose my mind," we interpret the phrase depending on our interpersonal schema for this person. If this friend is a flighty, hyperactive, highly vocal person often given to exaggeration, we conclude that the phrase means annoyance or overwork. The same phrase coming from a person who has been undergoing serious emotional difficulties means something else entirely.

In 1987, when Russian Premier Gorbachev announced that the Soviet Union was willing to accept some of the American proposals for nuclear disarmament, many high members of the U.S. government were upset and puzzled. "They can't be serious," was a standard comment. "It's a trick," was another. The fact that the

Receiving Messages: Listening 43

Russians seemed to be saying "Yes" after years of saying "No" resulted in serious problems of interpretation. Obviously many members of our government have a "Russian schema" that colors their interpretation of messages. In other words, these listeners were *over-interpreting,* finding more meaning than may have been intended.

Now that we've explored the elements of selection, retention, and interpretation, we are ready to put them together (see Figure 3.2). Part of the speaker's auditory input flows into short-term memory, illustrating the selective process. As the short-term memory continues, rehearsal is added, and then proceeds to long-term memory, which is usually organized into schemas, language, and percepts. Clearly not all input at the beginning of the memory cycle finds its way to the end. Usually schemas do not come into play until some time has elapsed and interpretation takes place.

Improving Listening Ability

First, listening is more difficult than we realize. No speaker should assume that an audience will retain everything that is presented; nor should listeners expect it of themselves. The various kinds of listening have various retention rates; we should all be aware that none of these types of listening is very efficient. The listening research program at the University of Kentucky has discovered the following retention rates for the typical listener:

Listeners are participants in the communication process. Good listening is an active, concentrated response to the speaker. Listeners can help a speaker by appearing attentive, interested, and positive. (© Michael Markowitz, Photo/Graphic Arts)

Introductory Principles

Short-Term Listening	40%
Short-Term Listening with Rehearsal	60%
Interpretive Listening	42%
Lecture Listening	25%

In general, listening research shows that we don't retain information very well; in fact, sometimes we do it rather poorly. Note-taking improves listening somewhat, depending on the short-term ability of the listener. One reason why these efficiencies are so low is that most listeners do not take *responsibility* for the transmission. Just as speaking demands responsible preparation and ethical approaches to the task, listening also has responsibilities.

The responsibility for the success of any particular communicative act is as much the listener's as the speaker's.

Listeners can help a speaker by appearing attentive, interested, and positive. Any speaker who faces a negative, uninterested, bored audience is going to have a hard time.

In class, remember that you can help each speaker by being an active, involved listener. Whether or not the class is a success, is largely up to you. Remember that your turn is coming! With this general sense of responsibility in mind, let's look at some of the specific responsibilities of the listener.

Interpretive listening is the process of making sense of the message. The voice, the posture, and the facial expressions all contribute to the interpretation. (© Kent Reno/ Jeroboam)

Receiving Messages: Listening   45

Improving Efficiency

Good listening is no accident; those who listen well expend effort on the activity. You should listen with a purpose and have an effective listening plan. This plan should involve the diagnosis of the situation and the purpose of the speech. You should have a good idea of what you expect from this speaker and how you think this speaker is going to proceed. Then you can relate these expectations to what actually happens. Let's look at some specific steps you can take to listen more effectively.

1. *Expend some effort.* Be willing to concentrate and to resist distractions. The speaker is expending effort; you should be willing to do the same.
2. *Avoid concentrating too hard on details.* If the speaker presents statistics to prove a point, don't focus on the statistics as much as on the point itself.
3. *Create percepts of the topic being discussed.* Try to find appropriate percepts to fit the speaker's words and see if your percepts compare with the speaker's.
4. *Take notes when appropriate to increase your concentration.* However don't let note-taking interfere with your intake of the next set of points or facts.
5. *Respond overtly.* When the speaker tells a joke, respond even if you don't think the joke is hilarious. Smile, ask intelligent questions, and, if appropriate, applaud.

Listening Constructively

In addition to improving your listening efficiency, you owe it to your speakers to *listen constructively*. This process also involves a number of steps.

1. *Determine the speaker's main purpose.* If the purpose isn't immediately obvious, try to determine the speaker's goals and the direction of the speech. Compare the speech to what you would have said if you were making the same speech.
2. *Evaluate the message.* What is the speaker's attitude toward the audience? Is the speaker credible? Are the ideas adequately reported?
3. *Relate the message to your own schemas.* Can you identify with them? Why or why not? Do you need to rethink your own position? How far are you willing to go in changing the way you think?

Listening Objectively

The listener has an obligation to *listen objectively*. Let's look at the steps involved in this task.

1. *Identify your own predispositions on the topic of the speech.* Make an effort to resist these predispositions.
2. *Don't jump to conclusions.* What is your attitude toward the speaker? How does this affect the process? Have you responded this way before?
3. *Avoid emotional responses.* Everyone reacts out of fear, bias, or prejudice once

in a while. Can you recognize when you do this? If so, try to control this response.

4. *Try not to be overly influenced by the responses of other audience members.* Can you identify with them? Why or why not? Try to determine why the rest of the audience is responding the way they do and compare your reactions to them.

Evaluation and Listening

Though you should try to be as objective as possible when listening, an important part of listening is *evaluation*. We evaluate several aspects of any speaker—whether or not the speaker is successful, or good looking, and so on.

Ethical Issues

Ethics is the study of right and wrong, of good and bad. *Ethical communication* involves the greater good and transcends individual needs and rewards. You might be surprised to discover that communication is occasionally used for unethical purposes. Look at the three situations presented below.

At the high school gymnasium forty young athletes are gathered together with their parents and sweethearts for the annual football banquet. The home economics club has served a delicious dinner, and on an elevated platform at the end of the gym sit the school superintendent, the high school principal, the coach and his staff, and the featured speaker of the evening—an All-American tackle from a nearby state university. As soon as he begins, the audience squirms in embarrassment. He hesitates, mumbles, skips from one subject to another, mangles his grammar, and finally, to the relief of all, sits down. Before he drives back to the university, a local car dealer hands him an envelope containing $200, his "honorarium" for the evening.

It is a warm summer night, and a huge crowd of party members are assembled in a stadium for the final ceremony of their annual rally. They have been together for days, listening to speeches and songs, and enjoying good fellowship. For hours they have been waiting for the appearance of their leader. When he finally appears, the applause and cheers last for almost an hour. Flanked by huge banners and national symbols, the leader speaks for almost two hours. He alternates between reasonable oration and emotional frenzy, exhorting the audience to sacrifice all for the fatherland and for themselves. The party members pledge themselves to total obedience to their leader, and when he leads them into war and national disaster, they follow him with vigor and devotion.

A political candidate wishes to support a bill calling for national military service but is not sure how the electorate will react. Instead of making a statement, the candidate has a campaign worker—an associate—release a statement to the press, stating that the candidate "is considering supporting a new bill introducing national military service." Following the release of the story, there is a storm of protest, especially from young persons who are not interested in having the draft revived. The next day, the candidate says, "This was never under consideration. I have never supported the draft. I am unalterably opposed to the draft." After election to the Senate, the candidate introduces a bill funding a study of the usefulness of the draft.

The common thread running through all three real-life examples is that the sources exploited their receivers for the sources' private gains. As you read these examples, you might say to yourself, "I'd never do that," but while we recognize the deplorable ethics of these three speakers, we don't always recognize self-interest when it appears in our own speech.

One factor that makes these speeches so compelling is that in each case, the speech was successful: The athlete got his money, the dictator continued his dominance of the country, and the candidate was elected to the Senate. For some people, communication and self-interest go hand-in-hand. Yet speaking involves more than simply having an ethical goal. Ethical speech requires that the *audience's* needs be paramount in selecting the subject and material of the speech. Ethics and communication are clearly connected. Ethical behavior is as important in speech as it is in any other part of our lives. Let us next look at some of the ways that ethical issues affect speechmaking.

Speakers as "Lovers"

One researcher classifies the various ethical approaches of speakers into three groups: "rapists," "seducers," and "lovers" (Brockreide, 1972). A rapist communicator is one who uses manipulative strategies, untruthfulness, coercion, power, and other tricks to win the audience. This means that, similar to a rape victim, the receiver loses individuality and the capacity to reason.

A seducer communicator employs deceit or confusion to entice a listener into compliance. The seducer does not use force, as the rapist communicator does, but the end result is just as unethical.

The lover communicator allows the receiver to judge the value of the arguments in the speech and to accept or reject according to the listener's value system. The lover communicator is open to the possibility of the listener rejecting the ideas in the speech.

Examples of Brockreide's three categories are easy to find in public and commercial life. We have all been "raped" and "seduced" by political or commercial communication at one time or another. You might keep his categories in mind when you are evaluating the ethics of a speaker.

Listening to Your Classmates

When you enrolled in this course, you probably thought that your major job would be preparing and delivering speeches. While that is surely important, you can now see the importance of active, attentive listening. No speaker can do well without listeners. No one can have a significant public speaking experience

Lecture listening is listening for long-term retention and can be facilitated by the use of association and repetition. (© *University Information Services Photo*)

without an audience, and your job as a member of the audience is vital to your classmates.

Clearly, your classmates need a friendly, supportive group that shows interest in the topic and the situation. Boredom, disinterest, and hostility are terrible "turnoffs," even if exhibited by only one audience member. Review all the points in this chapter about "getting into" the speech, and then apply them in class. Your classmates will thank you for it, and when it's your turn to speak, you will be glad you did!

Listening and Life

At the root of good listening is an orientation to life and to other people that is immensely rewarding. One of the nicest comments you can make about a friend is that he or she is a "good listener." When we say that about someone, we mean that the person *cares* about others and shows that caring in active listening behavior. Dr. Ralph Nichols emphasizes the importance of listening in basic human interaction.

The seven facts about listening presented by Nichols state the case eloquently. Good listening behavior is at the root of a full, productive life for all of us.

1. The most basic of all human needs is to understand and to be understood.
2. It is almost impossible to hate a person whom we fully understand.
3. The best way to understand people is to listen to them.
4. We are at the mercy of those who understand us better than we understand them.

Receiving Messages: Listening

5. When people make decisions, it is for their reasons, not ours.
6. We must face with courage the fact that when we succeed in "hearing a person out" our own position may become quite modified.
7. The wise listener is attentive and nonevaluative; asks only unslanted questions and praises those statements by an adversary that can honestly be praised.

(Dr. Ralph G. Nichols, "The Struggle to Be Human," February 17, 1980)

A Listening Checklist

The following checklist will help you remember some of the things you can do—before and after a speech—to improve your listening skills.

1. Do I know how I feel about this topic before the speaker begins?
2. Am I ready to change my mind on this topic?
3. Did I work hard enough at listening? Do I need to expend more effort?
4. Did the details of the message interfere with the main point?
5. Was I able to visualize the percepts presented?
6. Did my notes really help me, or are they just notes?
7. Did I let any aspect of the message irritate me unduly?
8. Did anything in the speaker's appearance or manner unduly affect me?
9. Was I responding just because others in the audience responded the same way?
10. Did this speaker really interest me?

Summary

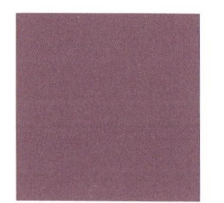

The act of receiving a message is usually called listening, and in many ways the listener's task is more difficult than the speaker's. Listening involves selection, retention, and interpretation. Selection occurs for two reasons: (1) we can assimilate messages faster than most talkers can deliver them to us, and (2) we have predispositions about topics, persons, and institutions that make us more or less willing to accept the information.

There are three types of retention: short-term, short-term with rehearsal, and long-term (lecture). Decoding (using selective elements of the language system) also affects retention. Interpretation comes into play when we utilize existing schemas to analyze and organize the incoming information. These larger schemas tell us what the message *means*. Interpretation also involves evaluating nonverbal signals as part of the message.

Typical listening is not efficient. The listener is as responsible for the success of the speech as the speaker and should work at the art of listening by improving efficiency and by listening constructively and objectively. Good listening not only improves communicative ability but can also have a profound effect on our lives and the way we live them.

On Your Own

1. Try to assess your own reading rate by counting words in a book or article and asking a friend to time you. How fast did you go? How does this compare with your "listening rate?"
2. Examine your lecture notes from another class, such as history. Did they help you remember the salient facts? How did you take the notes?
3. If we only remember 25 percent of what is presented, what part of the message do you think you will remember? Why did you remember that specific part?
4. Can you think of more examples of "rapist communicators" and "seducer communicators?" What could be done to alter the ethical structure of these sources?
5. Take one of the more common listening tests, such as the Watson-Barker or the Kentucky test. How did you compare to others? What can you do about it?

Suggestions For Further Reading

Bostrom, R., and E. Waldhart. 1988. Memory models and the measurement of listening. *Communication Education* 37: 1–13.

Brockreide, W. 1972. Arguers as lovers. *Philosophy and Rhetoric* 5: 1–11.

Weaver, C. 1972. *Listening Behavior*. Indianapolis: Bobbs-Merrill.

Wolvin, A., and C. Coakley. 1985. *Listening*. Dubuque: Wm. C. Brown.

Four

Managing Communication Apprehension

Powdermilk Biscuits! They give shy people the strength to get up and do what has to be done!

Garrison Keillor

Key Terms

communication apprehension
shyness
reticence
state apprehension
trait apprehension
reinforcement
rhetoritherapy

Objectives

After studying this chapter, you should be able to:

1. Differentiate among reticence, shyness and communication apprehension
2. Distinguish between state apprehension and trait apprehension
3. Know how to conduct a simple measure of apprehension
4. List the typical ways in which speakers can control apprehension
5. Accept the fact that some apprehension is inevitable, and even necessary for good communication

In this class you will probably experience an emotion common to almost everyone—the tension produced by standing up and speaking. This tension, sometimes called "stage fright," "speech fright," or "speech anxiety," is more accurately termed *communication apprehension*, and is caused by a variety of factors related to communication.

Communication apprehension is a fact of life for persons with all levels of experience. Beginners often feel that their apprehension is due to their lack of experience or ability, but everyone experiences different amounts of communication apprehension in different circumstances. As we gain experience and knowledge, our apprehension generally diminishes.

Several years ago, the Speech Communication Association reported the results of a survey asking American adults to rank the most tension-producing events in their lives (*Spectra*, 1973). The poll produced the following results:

1. Speaking before a group
2. Height
3. Insects
4. Financial problems
5. Deep water
6. Sickness
7. Death
8. Flying
9. Loneliness
10. Dogs
11. Driving a car
12. Darkness

Odd as it may seem, the majority of respondents found the idea of making a speech before a group more frightening than death!

One of the significant goals of this course is to build confidence and manage communication apprehension. In order to do this, we first need to know what apprehension is, and how to tell if our own apprehension is significant.

The Nature of Communication Apprehension

Most people are apprehensive about many different communicative tasks, not just making a speech. Those who fear making a speech probably also fear an important interview or hesitate to speak up in a discussion. In addition, there is a form of communication apprehension specific to listening—usually called receiver apprehension (Wheelis, 1975). Many people simply say to themselves, "I'm just shy and there's nothing I can do about it." Shyness, however, may or may not be the same as communication apprehension. It is more closely related to "reticence." *Shyness* is a personality trait of persons who avoid social interaction. If you are shy, you avoid most social occasions, not just communication. *Reticence* is the unwillingness to communicate, and is not necessarily the same as communication apprehension (Burgoon, 1976). If you are reticent, it simply means that you don't talk much; it does not necessarily mean that you do so out of fear. *Communication apprehension is the fear-like emotional reaction that accompanies many communicative situations.*

It is extremely important to understand the differences among these three characteristics because the remedies for each are different. Researchers have found that apprehension can be alleviated, if not cured. One of the best ways to reduce apprehension, for example, is to take a basic speech course! So your enrollment in this public speaking course is the first positive step toward alleviation of this problem.

What you may not have realized is that this nervousness is perfectly normal—the heritage of primitive human beings whose very survival depended on their body's ability to prepare for "fight" or "flight." Whenever you encounter an emergency situation, one in which you suddenly become afraid, angry, or perceive the need for great physical effort, the nervous system prepares the body for action. First, the heart begins pumping more blood to the brain, the muscles, and skin. Blood is also diverted away from the stomach and intestines in order to supply those same organs. As a result, the digestive system slows to a crawl, and the central nervous system, heart, and muscles receive extra oxygen and energy necessary for clear thinking, quick reactions, and intense physical exertion. At the same time, the pupils of the eyes dilate to produce sharper vision; the level of blood sugar rises to provide added energy; and the skin perspires in order to flush out excess wastes and to cool the body.

These physiological changes are not only normal, they are often desirable, because they prepare the individual for a higher level of effort. When you feel your palms becoming moist, the butterflies fluttering in your stomach, and your muscles beginning to tremble, you are poised for extraordinary performance. The key lies in interpreting your anxiety as a healthy sign that you are *ready* to cope. The question

John F. Kennedy experienced extraordinary "stage fright" but his speaking style reflected only his youth, energy, wit, and intellectualism. (© UPI/Bettmann Newsphotos)

Managing Communication Apprehension ■ ■ ■ 55

Figure 4.1

Heart rates for high and low communication apprehension during various stages of a five-minute speech. "T" represents the trait anxiety, and "S" the state of anxiety. Source: M. Motley, "Stage Fright Manipulation by (False) Heart Rate Feedback," Central States Speech Journal, pp. 186–191.

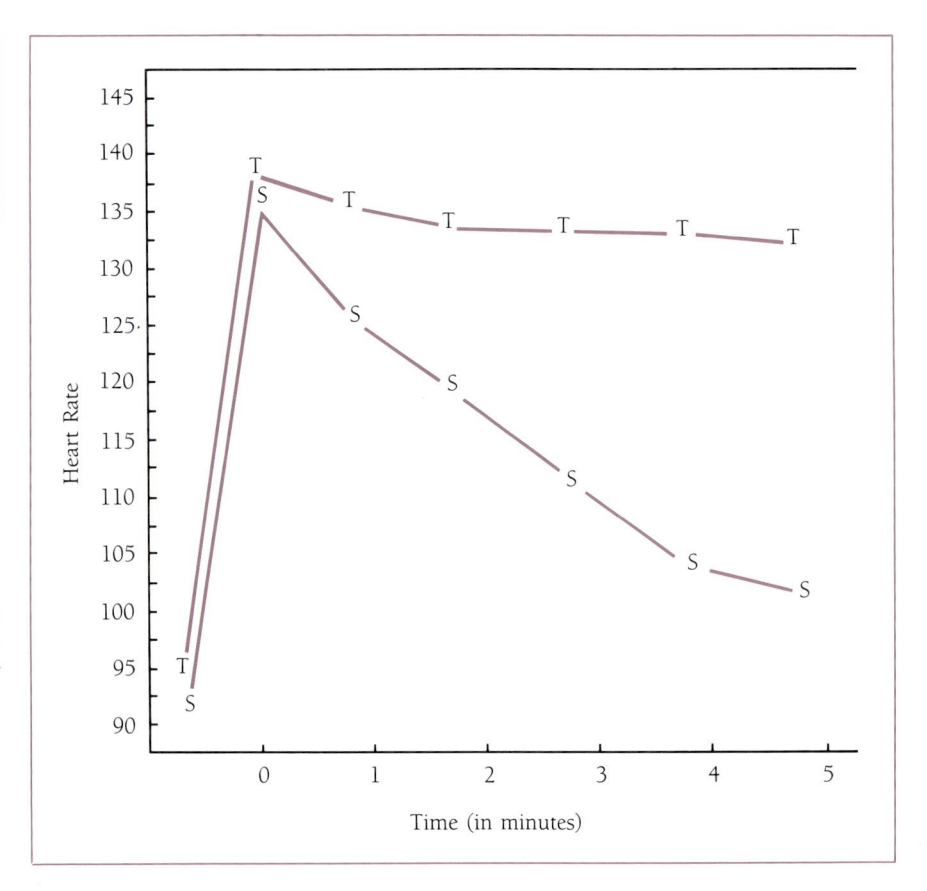

to ask is not "How can I get rid of my nervousness?" but "How can I make this emotional tension work for me, not against me?"

The differences between those with state apprehension and those with trait apprehension are illustrated by the graph in Figure 4-1. The trait anxiety is labelled "T" in this graph and the state anxiety is labelled "S." At the beginning of the speech both groups have about equal heart rates (a good indicator of experienced fright). As the speech progresses, the "state" group (S) begins to manage the apprehension, and by the end of the speech the heart rate has returned to almost normal. These heart rate differences have been observed by Motley (1976) and Booth-Butterfield (1987). The data in Figure 4-1 show that at the onset of a speech *everyone* feels apprehension. Some learn to manage it a little better than others.

Unfortunately many of us never overcome our fear of audiences. One of America's most distinguished actresses recently reported that, despite forty year's experience on the Broadway stage, she still becomes terrified before each performance. President Kennedy was so frightened before some speeches that he became physically ill. Not everyone can completely overcome the adjustment problems that accompany public speaking, but most of us can take some positive steps to alleviate these difficulties.

State or Trait?

Researchers disagree over whether communication apprehension should be called a "state" or a "trait," that is, if it is something that only happens before impending communication situations, or whether it is a more enduring personality characteristic. Some researchers feel that communication apprehension can only be caused by a pending communication task. They base this conclusion on research that shows that prior to communicative activity (such as a speech or an important interview) the apprehension rate rises sharply. Other researchers feel that communication apprehension is an enduring characteristic, based on studies that show that individuals vary in degree of apprehension and that these variations seem permanent. If communication apprehension is a state, we need to treat the circumstances; if it is a trait, we need to treat the individual.

What does this mean to the beginning speaker? Beginning speakers almost always have some apprehension and must learn to cope with it.

Edward R. Murrow, the famed television news reporter, summarized the problem of communication appprehension this way:

> *The best speakers know enough to be scared. Stage fright is the sweat of perfection. The only difference between the pros and the novices is that the pros have trained the butterflies to fly in formation.*

Almost every student experiences apprehension when speaking in front of a class for the first time. As you gain experience in public speaking, you learn to control tension and reduce anxiety. (© *Laimute E. Druskis/Jeroboam, Inc.*)

Managing Communication Apprehension

Dealing With Apprehension

In almost every speech class, students rank as one of their principal goals the alleviation of anxiety. Your enrollment in a public speaking course is the first step toward acquiring the experience and skills that will help you speak with confidence. However, you will probably never overcome all your apprehension toward speaking, nor should you. "Removal of anxiety," says noted educator Gerald Phillips, "produces a person willing to participate unskillfully" (1980). Your apprehension, in other words, helps you perform better.

Building Experience

In general, we participate in activities that we find rewarding. We tend to repeat experiences we find pleasant and avoid those we do not. Psychologists call this *reinforcement*. Our lives are shaped by reinforcement much more than most of us care to admit. When we were children, almost all of our behavior was determined this way. Now that we are adults, we are still manipulated by rewards—money, grades, prestige—and so on.

The implications for communication are obvious: If others reward us for speaking, we tend to speak more. Research shows that students who receive positive comments on their speeches have less communication apprehension than those who do not (Bostrom, 1963).

What this means is that building a series of small successes will condition you to enjoy the experience of public speaking. You can do this by seeking public speaking in a non-threatening atmosphere, such as a fraternity or church group. You should also try to build a variety of experiences, such as telling stories or participating actively in groups because these communicative situations can carry over into public speaking. In addition, you should rely on the support of your instructor and your classmates. If you give them a chance, they can help a great deal in alleviating apprehension.

Controlling Tension

One of the reasons you feel fearful is that your body changes—your heart beats faster, your breathing becomes more rapid, your hands and knees tremble, and your mouth gets dry. You become aware of these physiological changes and your awareness makes you even more frightened. This "vicious cycle" is a real problem.

You will probably not be able to control your heart rate (though those skilled in biofeedback can do this), but you can certainly control your breathing. If you take slow, deep, deliberate breaths, your body gets the oxygen it needs, and the rest of the fright reactions slow down. Placing your hands on the lectern deliberately and holding an index card, which applies a specific motor function to the hand, controls trembling. Moving during the speech (controlled movement, not pacing up and down) tends to dispel the effects of heightened physiological affect.

You need to listen to what your body is telling you: that this situation is important, and that you need to expend some real effort. If you view your symptoms this way, rather than as a handicap, they can be a real help.

Making Thorough Preparation

Substantive evidence shows that learning to speak well produces a significant reduction of communication apprehension (Phillips, 1980). Phillips called this method of treatment *rhetoritherapy*. One real source of anxiety is the nagging feeling that your speech isn't really very good. The best way to cure this is to make it good! If you are sure of your facts, if you care about your topic, and if you feel that what you have to say is really important, you have *increased* the reasons for performing well. On the other hand, if you haven't done a thorough job of preparation, you can expect to be apprehensive.

The more familiar you are with your material, the less likely you are to be fearful. Preparation has many other desirable side effects, so it should be your principal means of fighting apprehension. In Figure 4.2 is an actual example drawn from a recent public speaking class.

Figure 4.2

Complete and accurate preparation and strong feelings about a topic can eliminate apprehension and fright.

After five years with a large corporation, Max decided that his career would be helped if he completed his bachelor's degree. Accordingly, he enrolled in night courses at a nearby state university, and one of his first courses was basic public speaking. Max felt out of place on the campus: He was 24, married, and dressed differently from the other students. Further, they seemed to be at home in this environment, and he was uneasy.

When his first speech assignment came, Max suffered from profound apprehension. His hands trembled, his throat was dry, he couldn't see his notes, and he finished after only two minutes—in a six-minute speech assignment. Max was miserable.

He felt that he wouldn't be able to finish the course in the present circumstances and took action to drop. When he brought the drop slip to his instructor, the topic of apprehension came up. Max confessed his feelings. The instructor encouraged Max to talk about his feelings and asked Max to give the class another chance. In the previous round of speeches, one student had attacked the chemical industry, particularly the industry's use of pesticides. Max had been upset by this attack, since one of his company's products was paper packaging for one of the large chemical companies. Max felt that the role of pesticides in American agriculture was largely misunderstood and that the chemical companies were getting a black eye for something that they didn't deserve.

The instructor encouraged Max to develop his ideas into a speech. Max found statistics showing how agricultural productivity depends on pest control, how important high agricultural production is to the basic economy of the United States, and how much food would cost if some basic pest control wasn't used. The more he prepared, the more interested he became in the topic, and when the time came to deliver the speech, Max launched into it with the fervor of an evangelist. His speech was too long for the assignment, but other than that, it was highly informative.

After class, the instructor asked Max about his apprehension, and Max realized that aside from a bad moment at the beginning, his strong feelings about the topic had eradicated his fright. He continued with the course and even came to enjoy speaking. Next semester, one of his former classmates mentioned his speech on pesticides to a friend, and Max was asked to visit a local service club and repeat the experience. Though apprehensive, Max spoke at the luncheon and received a gratifying round of applause.

In spite of severe communication apprehension, Eleanor Roosevelt became one of the most admired and outspoken women in the history of the United States. Her speeches effectively displayed her passion for the underdog and her incredible love for humanity. (© UPI/Bettmann Newsphotos)

Thinking Positively

Though many problems cannot be solved merely by thinking positively, sometimes a specific change of thought pattern can help. Apprehension is one condition to which we can apply "positive thinking" effectively.

Remember, you are in control. To help enhance this feeling, work for audience response. When you ask a listener a question or elicit some other response, it reinforces your feeling of control. Most speakers find that this is a real confidence builder. Be careful—use only devices that you *know* will work. There is nothing worse than telling a joke or trying for a reaction and having it fail dismally.

Concentrate on your audience—make eye contact, and notice how well they respond to this personal interaction. Remember, they don't know how nervous you are, and you don't have to tell them! Don't expect to be perfect. No one is. You will probably make mistakes just like everyone else. Simply continue and apologize if you feel you must. Most of your listeners will empathize with you.

Tactics to Avoid

Never postpone your speech because you are apprehensive. Many students delay their speeches because of apprehension, hoping it will disappear. It never does. Speak when you are assigned to speak. Better yet, volunteer.

Taking drugs or alcohol to relieve the apprehension is probably the worst thing you can do. Tranquilizers, unless used with a physician's advice, do little good for the transient apprehension (state anxiety) that you might feel prior to speaking.

Drinking mildly relieves apprehension for some persons, but increases apprehension for others. Alcohol impairs speaking ability for most people, and the result is a poor speech and more apprehension.

Summary

The tension produced by an impending speech is often called anxiety, stage fright, or nervousness but is most properly termed communication apprehension. This kind of apprehension, one of the most serious problems that faces beginning speakers, usually involves trembling, dry mouth, increased heartbeat, and the like. These responses are normal but interfere with speaking.

One important question is whether apprehension is a state caused only by an impending speech, or an enduring personality trait. State apprehension is fairly easily alleviated; trait apprehension is more difficult. The first step in coping with apprehension is self-diagnosis.

One deals with apprehension by gradually building up experience, especially rewarding experiences associated with speaking. Learning to control emotional tension is another good method. Probably the best thing any beginning speaker can do is to prepare well. Thinking positively is helpful.

On Your Own

1. Reflect on one day of your communication activities. List them in order of their importance. Did any of these create a particular amount of apprehension? Can you think of any reasons why one might have been more stressful than another?
2. Do you have a friend who is not a "talker?" Interview the friend to determine if the lack of talking is the result of shyness, reticence, or apprehension. Report on the method you used to determine your judgment.
3. Take your pulse before your next speech. Can you detect any difference between this rate and your normal rate?
4. Call a total stranger who has some information you need (such as an airline reservations agent). Does this communication task make you apprehensive? Why or why not?

Suggestions For Further Reading

Booth-Butterfield, S. 1987. Action assembly theory and communication apprehension. *Human Communication Research* 13: 386–398.

Burgoon, J. 1976. The unwillingness to communicate scale. *Communication Monographs* 43: 60–79.

McCroskey, J., and V. Richmond. 1980. *The quiet ones: Shyness and communication apprehension.* Dubuque: Scarisbrick.

Motley, M. 1976. Stage fright manipulation by (false) heart rate feedback. *Central States Speech Journal* 27: 186–191.

Phillips, G. 1968. Reticence: Pathology of the normal speaker. *Speech Monographs* 35: 39.

Part Two

Preparing the Speech

Five

Getting Started: The First Speech

The way to start something is just to start. There's got to be a first time for everything.

Raleigh W. Boswell

Key Terms

research
condense
thesis
expand
sort
body
summarize
conclusion
introduction
manuscript
memorized
extemporaneous
impromptu

Objectives

After studying this chapter, you should be able to:

1. Recognize personal skills and knowledge as having good topic potential
2. Relate to a potential audience's interests and needs
3. Know how to condense, expand, sort, and summarize potential context
4. Define manuscript, memorized, impromptu, and extemporaneous modes of delivery
5. Recognize particular listening tasks involved in the first speech assignment

There are moments in everyone's life when we have to do something that we have never done before. For you, one of these moments is coming soon—you will be making a speech. Anything unfamiliar can be threatening, but you can take several specific steps to prepare and present your first speech. In this chapter we will explore some of the dos and don'ts of making your first speech.

Learning to speak is similar to learning anything else: You start with something simple and then progress to more complex activities. So this chapter begins by showing you how to prepare a very simple speech—a relay containing a minimal amount of new percepts. Creating a speech like the one presented here uses a series of short steps, each of which is relatively simple.

Choosing a Topic

First, before you speak, you must have something to say. For the first speech in this course, you should look for a familiar topic; in other words, choose a subject on which you already have a good store of knowledge. Many students get stuck in this step, wondering what they can possibly say that will interest anyone else. The first step is to *look within* for material that will be worth communicating. The second is to *look without* at the specific characteristics of your audience and determine what might be useful to them. Following this advice gives us two fundamental rules for beginning public speeches:

Choose a topic with which you are familiar and on which you have a comfortable background of experience.

Adapt your topic so that it has some potential utility for the members of your audience.

The rationale for these rules is simple. Your task is to relay percepts from your system to the audience's system. In order to do that, you must possess them in the first place. Without a comfortable background on the topic, you will not be able to select the proper wording and relate the percepts to others. The topic must have some interest for the audience; otherwise their perceptual defenses will tend to exclude the messages you send. Many factors contribute to the construction of an interesting message, but one of the most basic is the general concept of utility.

Looking Within: Yourself As a Resource

Each of us possesses resources of which we aren't always aware. As *individuals,* each of us looks at life, at love, and even at breakfast in a unique way. You may be surprised to discover that your approach to some ordinary aspects of life is interesting, but it is often true. We all need to search for these unique parts of ourselves.

Here's how one student found a speech topic by looking within herself. When this student was in elementary school in a rural district, 4H meetings were an important part of her life. She learned to sew at these meetings and liked the

When Corazon Aquino became president of The Philippines in 1986, this quiet woman found herself at the center of international attention, a position requiring eloquence under fire. (© *Reuters/Bettmann Newsphotos*)

hobby so much she kept it up through high school. When she got to college, she made some of her own clothes and occasionally mended her boyfriend's shirts. When the time came to make her first speech in speech class, she thought sewing might make a good topic. In this fast-paced era, however, she was worried that the subject matter might be a bit old-fashioned, but on reflection, she hit on a natural consequence of the sexual revolution—encouraging men to sew! Accordingly, she chose as her first speech topic "A Sewing Kit for the Busy Man" and demonstrated how a few dollars invested in clothing repair could save many more dollars in replacement clothing.

This student followed the first fundamental rule for beginning speeches—choosing a topic that was very familiar to her. She was not burdened by problems of background preparation and research, and was able to add a personal dimension to the talk that was very helpful in these first stages.

Looking Without: The Audience

Our second rule states that you should adapt your topic to suit the group you are addressing. In the example above, the speaker was halfway through her preparation when she realized that the topic was great for the men in the class (or at least the men who did not know how to sew) but was not very useful for the women (at least the women who knew how to sew). Accordingly, she contemplated what might be useful for the listeners who already could sew and decided to focus on the nature of the sewing kit as a travel aid and as an inexpensive gift. The sewing kit topic had great utility for the audience because it addressed their needs: College students like to dress well and have little money with which to buy clothes. Few male or female students consider clothing repair even though it saves money, or even know how to replace a button on a shirt, let alone fix a tear. Concern with the needs of the audience led to a specific, useful topic for this speech.

Sometimes students forget that their speech class is an audience composed of real persons. Student speakers often begin a speech by saying: "Mr. Mayor, Mr. Speaker, Honored Guests, and Friends..." Obviously, Mr. Mayor is not present; the student is dreaming of the day he does speak before the mayor. Few student speeches are less meaningful than this kind of "practice." Always keep in mind that your class is composed of *real* people, with real lives, attitudes, and backgrounds. Though your main purpose is to learn public speaking, part of this skill is recognizing the needs and wishes of your classmates.

Preparing the First Speech

Once your topic is chosen, you need to get specific about what you are going to communicate and how you will present it. For your first experience in front of a group, it is a good idea to use the following:

1. *Research the speech by* finding out as much as you can about the topic. Read, do field work, interview other persons. Take detailed notes and transcribe them onto note cards. You might start with an article you have read or an interesting item from a textbook from another course. Then go to the library and examine the card catalog under your general topic.

2. *Condense the speech in*to a simple sentence. Think of it this way: If you could only tell your audience one thing about the topic, what would it be? For the above example, the speaker chose: "A simple sewing kit can save you money." Other examples might be: "Cheap houseplants can make your room comfortable and appealing," or "Shopping at a day-old bread store can stretch your budget." This sentence is called the *thesis*.

3. *Expand the thesis by answering the questions* "why?" or "how?" If you are speaking on houseplants, for example, you would want to explain the soothing effects of horticulture in most rooms. You might even mention some of the research in the enhanced productivity associated with plants in a work environment. Write down these ideas.

4. *Sort these ideas into groups.* For this first speech, you should have at least two and no more than four groups—the "main headings" of your speech. This will be the *body* of your speech. Your outline might look like this:

TOPIC: "Saving Money at a Day-Old Bread Store."

THESIS: Shopping at a day-old bread store can stretch your budget.

WHY? Bakeries usually leave baked goods in the supermarket only a few days and then take them to a day-old store.

HOW? These items, slightly stale, are usually half the price of fresh-baked items.

HOW?	When bread is toasted, its flavor is restored. Rolls and doughnuts can be restored in a variety of ways.
WHY?	You can save three to ten dollars a week in bread costs by patronizing these stores.

Each of these points, of course, should be amplified and discussed.

5. *Summarize* the speech by repeating the thesis and the main subheads. This will serve as your *conclusion*.

6. Think of something to say at the outset that will grab the audience's attention and orient them to your topic. Now you have an *introduction*.

The speech might now look like this:

TOPIC:	"Saving Money at a Day-Old Bread Store."
INTRODUCTION:	If your food budget is somewhat less than Michael Jackson's, you might be thinking about saving money, especially if you need your funds for the necessities in life, such as clothes and movies.
THESIS:	Shopping at a day-old bread store can stretch your budget.
WHY?	Bakeries usually leave baked goods in the supermarket only a few days and then take them to a day-old store.
HOW?	These items, slightly stale, are usually half the price of fresh baked items.
HOW?	When bread is toasted, its flavor is restored. Rolls and doughnuts can be restored in a variety of ways.
WHY?	You can save three to ten dollars a week in bread costs by patronizing these stores.
CONCLUSION:	You can get more nutrition for less money if you patronize a day-old bread store. Bread is nutritious and is usually sold for half-price at these stores. Flavor can be restored by toasting. If you use the bread for sandwiches, you won't even notice the difference.

This uncomplicated plan is usually foolproof: any speech structured in this way is going to succeed. Later in this book we look at specific ways in which you can elaborate on this basic plan, but these basic elements will probably be present in most of your subsequent speeches. As you explain each main point, you can fill in essentials of your speech—the information you gathered in the first step, examples, illustrations, and so on.

Now you have a strategy to apply to your topic. You are going to *research, condense, expand, sort, summarize,* and *introduce*. You can think of the overall organization of your speech this way: "Tell 'em what you're going to tell 'em; tell 'em; tell 'em what you told 'em."

Your instructor may want you to submit an outline; once you complete the above steps, you will have an outline that you can use when you deliver the speech, or you may want to jot down the main points on cards to hold in your hand. Whatever method you use, it is vital that you write out the main points in some form because we do occasionally forget. If you forget in the middle of a speech, it can be a disaster unless you have *something* with you to help.

Methods of Spoken Presentation

In giving a speech or presentation, we typically prepare material on paper as a reminder of what we are going to say. On one extreme, we could write the entire speech, but this method is not usually effective unless some important characteristics are added, such as true interaction with the audience. It is typical for political figures to employ speech writers, usually because many modern politicians are simply not able to write. The typical excuse given is that the speaker does not have the time to spend on the manuscript, and writing is a staff function. Delivering a speech that someone else has written is always risky business. Nonetheless, it is not always a bad idea to use a manuscript for a speech, and this represents one of the principal ways in which the written and the oral modes interact. Let's look at the main ways in which these interactions occur.

Manuscript Speeches

A word-by-word preparation for delivery, the *manuscript* is an excellent method to insure that all your ideas are included in the speech, particularly when your words have to be weighed carefully. There are, however, some very severe handicaps in undertaking a manuscript speech.

The first involves written style. It is rare to find someone who can write "orally," that is, compose in written form, sentences that sound appropriate for speaking. Most persons' writing styles are quite different from their spoken styles. Written style, when delivered orally, often sounds wooden and affected.

A second problem is that of delivery—the necessity of keeping your eyes on the manuscript. While reading a manuscript, you cannot expect to see the listeners. This means you will not be able to react to the audience and will lose the impact of good eye contact.

A third problem arises from the difficulty of departing from the prepared manuscript when the situation calls for it. Highly skilled speakers can do this, but most cannot.

In most cases, then, you should not use a manuscript, and beginners should *never* use them.

Memorized Speeches

A *memorized* speech is a manuscript speech without a manuscript! The advantages of the memorized speech are that eye contact is maintained, and delivery is more free because the speaker is not chained to the podium. Memorized speeches

Millions of American schoolchildren have memorized Abraham Lincoln's Gettysburg Address, one of the most celebrated manuscript speeches in our country's history. (© *The Bettmann Archive*)

have the same problems as manuscript speeches, however, and there is an additional one—the vagaries of memory. Few situations are worse than starting a speech and having the mind go blank. Once again, a beginner should *never* try this method.

Extemporaneous Speeches

An *extemporaneous* speech is one in which the outline is carefully prepared, but the specific words are not chosen in advance. The main advantage of the extemporaneous speech is that you can control the content and the direction of the speech and simultaneously retain the freshness and conversational quality of less formal interpersonal interactions. Many speakers use the extemporaneous method with a memorized outline. This is a good technique but must be used carefully. Extemporaneous speaking requires careful preparation and rehearsal.

Impromptu Speeches

Speeches given with no preparation are called *impromptu*. This type of speech is usually a bad idea, but sometimes people are called on unexpectedly to "say a few words." The best strategy for an impromptu speech is to make it short; few speakers want to be remembered for it. Every so often, we see a speaker who has the rare ability to perform well in an impromptu situation, and so we are tempted to try it. This is a lot like a singer from the University Glee Club attempting to sing an aria at the Met. It can be done, but the likelihood for success is small.

Getting Started: The First Speech ■ ■ ■ 71

Practicing Your First Speech

<mark>Practice is absolutely essential.</mark> If you can practice in front of a listener, all the better, but if you can't, do it alone. Stand while you speak, and if possible, watch yourself in a mirror.

Read the introduction word-for-word and decide if it sounds strained or forced. If so, change it. Do the same for the conclusion. Make sure that you can read your notes. Try standing behind a lectern or in a setting similar to your class. If you plan to use a chalkboard, practice using it.

<mark>Time the speech, particularly if your instructor has given you a specific time limit.</mark> You should try to come very close to this time limit. Speakers who do not prepare well think that they speak for only three or four minutes but are really going on for ten or fifteen minutes. (We all love the sound of our own voices!) Speech classes have limited time and cannot extend unlimited time to everyone.

Delivering Your First Speech

Many students find that a mixture of the manuscript and extemporaneous methods is the best way to approach the first speech. Though we recommend the extemporaneous approach for most speeches, you can safely modify the extemporaneous method for the first speech. It may be helpful to write out, word-for-word, your introduction and conclusion. This gets you through two of the most difficult

As a beginning speaker, your method of delivery should be extemporaneous. This type of speech requires careful preparation, but it has a fresh, spontaneous quality to it that will keep audience interest. (© UK Information Services)

Preparing the Speech

parts of your speech, and cushions that first moment when you face the class. It is extremely important that you make a *readable* copy of the introduction to use in the speech.

It is useful to write out the conclusion because it is essentially a summary of your speech; when you itemize these main points in writing, you will have a much better sense of the contents and direction of the speech.

As we learned in Chapter Four, apprehension is sometimes a problem for students in their first public speaking experience. Writing out these important segments substantially reduces fright!

Physical delivery is important, so you should try out the room where you're going to speak. If the room has a lectern, you should see if it suits you: Some lecterns are too high for some students; too low for others. You may want to use note cards if you have no lectern, because they are much easier to handle than a written outline. Step up to the front of the room with confidence, take a deep breath, look directly at the audience, and start!

Listening To Beginning Speeches

For your classmates' first speeches the listener's main job is to be a sympathetic, interested receiver. The last thing a beginning speaker needs is an inattentive audience. There are other reasons for listening well to your classmates' first speeches.

As this course progresses, you will be preparing more complex messages to present to the class. One vital concern in this preparation is audience analysis, which we will explore further in Chapter Six. In order to inform or persuade an audience, it is necessary to know something about them. In this first assignment, you have a unique opportunity to collect information about your class as a future audience. In addition, you may make a new friend or two. As you listen, try to answer the following questions:

- Why did this speaker choose this topic?
- What does this topic tell me about this person?
- If I were to meet this person socially, would I want to discuss this topic, or use it as a conversational springboard?
- Which aspects of this topic are interesting to me? Why?
- Should I accept this point of view without question, or do I need more information?
- What have I learned from this speech?

Your instructor may allow you to ask questions during the speech or immediately after. A good listener tries to have at least one good question, and one that advances understanding of the topic.

Summary

The first speech presents particular problems that other speeches do not. Like so many other activities, it is important to start simply.

For the first speech, a sensible topic choice is something that does not require a great deal of research or extensive background. The speaker and the audience are the best sources for the topic of the beginning speech. The topic search starts when you look within yourself for possible background and look without for information that the audience might find interesting or useful.

The next step is to organize the speech into a simple plan:

INTRODUCTION

THESIS

BODY

    1.   Main point

    2.   Main point

    3.   Main point

CONCLUSION

The thesis and main points evolve from the process of condensing, expanding, sorting, and summarizing. With these tasks accomplished you are ready to practice the speech. Practice with a listener if one is available.

In most speaking situations your delivery should be extemporaneous, but for the first speech, a combination of the extemporaneous and manuscript approaches is recommended. Writing the introduction and conclusion word-for-word will help you adjust to the new experience.

Use the first speech as a springboard for getting to know as much about your prospective audience as you can.

On Your Own

1. After listening to classmates present their first speeches, try to decide what each individual is like. What can you determine about the group in general?
2. Were certain speakers more at ease than others? Try to find out if this was their first speech or if they had previous experience in other groups.
3. Make a list of topics that you think would be interesting for speeches this semester (quarter). From these lists, the instructor will prepare a master list showing class interest.
4. Make a list of the topics that were presented. Classify them by theme or by content. Does this process help you with number 1 above?

Suggestions For Further Reading

Bradley, B. 1984. *Fundamentals of speech communication.* Dubuque: Wm. C. Brown.

Whitman, R., and T. Foster. 1987. *Speaking in public.* New York: Macmillan.

Six

Audience Analysis

Real communication occurs only when we see the expressed idea and attitude from the other person's point of view.

Carl Rogers

Key Terms

audience analysis
receiver orientation
selective listening
empathy
electronic audience
demographic audience analysis
situational audience analysis

Objectives

After studying this chapter, you should be able to:

1. Recognize specific ways in which audiences differ
2. Know how receiver orientation enhances communication success
3. Understand empathy as a basic tool for speech preparation
4. Enumerate specific ways in which group memberships, gender, attitudes, economic status, educational level, ethnic background, and age affect specific message acceptance
5. Balance audience adjustment with specific communicative purposes

In earlier chapters we examined the communication process, specific issues of speaking and listening, and some of the problems in communication apprehension. We are now ready to consider more specific kinds of speech preparation.

Preparation is a detailed process, involving a number of steps that all fit together. The first and most important step is the "diagnosis" of the potential listeners, often called *audience analysis*. Audiences differ a good deal, and these differences affect your preparation and presentation. To illustrate this point, in the following speech made in New York in 1901, a former Confederate general named John Brown Gordon completely disarms his New York audience by appealing to their common interests and sense of humor.

> Let me say before beginning my lecture that although you are to listen tonight to a southern man, a southern soldier, yet I beg you to believe that he is as true as any man to this Republic's flag and to all that it truly represents.
>
> Our last visit was cut short by circumstances over which we did not have entire control, and for which we cannot be held exclusively responsible. [Laughter.]
>
> Twenty months passed before our next visit. The war was over. We had changed our minds and had concluded not to set up a separate government. When we returned to you again, therefore, we came to stay. No more with hostile banners waving in defiance above gray-clad battle lines, but rallying now with all our countrymen around this common flag, whose crimson stripes are made redder and richer by southern as well as northern blood, and whose stars are brighter because they emblem the glory of both northern and southern achievements. We returned not with rifles in our hands, demanding separation as the price of peace; but with hands outstretched to grasp those extended by the North in sincere and endless brotherhood. We returned, too, without lingering bitterness, or puerile repining; but with a patriotism always broad and sincere, now intensified and refined in the fires of adversity, to renew our vows of fidelity to that unrivaled constitutional government bequeathed by our fathers and theirs; and by God's help to make with them the joint guarantee that this Republic, and its people and the states which compose it, shall remain united, coequal, and forever free. [Applause.] (Gordon, 1923).

Notice how General Gordon's successful adaptation is due entirely to his careful analysis of how a post-Civil War New York audience might react to a former southern soldier.

In Chapter Three we learned that listeners do not always receive messages in the exact form in which they are sent. Specifically, they select and interpret incoming data, and this selection and interpretation depends on their inner environment—percepts, language, schemas, and affects—which are both the content and end product of the communication process. A speaker who misjudges the mind state of an audience can be in real trouble.

We can think of these mind states as logical stepping stones to the changing of behavior: As messages are sent from speaker to audience, the content of the message alters the percepts, language, schemas, and affects of each listener. The resulting change in inner environment of the audience members may ultimately lead to a change in their external behavior.

The implication of this communication chain for public speaking is important. Because people differ greatly in percepts, language, and schemas, we can't expect everyone to react to a speech in the same way.

The Importance of Audience Analysis

Audience analysis is the process of compiling data on the characteristics of an audience that may influence their response to the speaker's message. Such characteristics include demographic information on age, sex, ethnic background, educational background, and religious orientation, as well as information on their internal environments—their beliefs, values, expectations, attitudes, knowledge, and experience. Naturally, the general nature of your audience influences the way you approach the preparation of the speech. By understanding the backgrounds of your listeners, you can make appropriate decisions regarding topic choice, method of delivery, language, and visual aids.

If you aren't convinced that audience analysis is important, you should observe a modern criminal trial and note the emphasis lawyers place on jury selection. Lawyers spend a great deal of time on this aspect of a trial because they have found that certain types of jurors vote in certain predictable ways. Women, for example, tend to vote for the defense more often, and men tend to vote for the prosecution (Brändstatter, Davis, and Schuler, 1978). Even though your speech may

As the dynamic pastor of Glide Memorial Church in San Francisco, Cecil Williams' sermons are exuberant and often controversial. (© *Janice Mirikitani/ Glide Memorial United Methodist Church, San Francisco*)

Franklin D. Roosevelt, a skilled and engaging orator, made effective use of radio to reach a wide audience. His plain language and use of metaphors helped listeners understand the complexities of economics and government. (© UPI/Bettmann Newsphotos)

not involve life or death matters, you will find that audience analysis is a vital first step in preparing and delivering a successful speech.

Audience analysis is especially important in the classroom. You might easily find yourself in a class predominantly composed of physical education majors, sorority women, foreign students, or freshmen and sophomores (and, of course, don't forget your instructor!) These differences could have a dramatic effect on the kind of speeches you prepare and what material will be effective.

Adjusting to a specific audience depends on a more general willingness to adjust to any receivers. This is not as easy as most people think. Although we all share many percepts, schemas, and affects, the inner environments of different individuals range from minor to the extreme. Therefore, your first task is to become aware of these differences and determine how they might affect the audience's response to the speech. People who are sensitive to the expectations and needs of their listeners are said to be *receiver-oriented*. In general, in considering the inner environments of our audience, we must explore (1) selective listening, (2) the process of empathy, and (3) the effects that the electronic world has had on receiving behavior in general.

Audiences and Selective Listening

One important fact about listeners is that they *select* things to attend to and to remember. *Selective listening* is an individual's propensity to choose only part of a message to hear and remember. Most listeners retain only about 25 percent of the available message in lecture listening (see Chapter Three); exactly *which* 25 percent is the crucial question! Figure 6.1 shows how different cognitive structures of listeners are likely to affect the ways that they listen to a specific speech.

Many people might think that the example in Figure 6.1 is extreme, but research on listening confirms that different persons can react to the same speech in very different ways (Kelly, 1970). The best way to attack the problem is to try to understand how the other people think. In the next section, we will see how this works.

Figure 6.1

Most listeners selectively listen to only 25 percent of a speech. However, as shown in this example, which 25 percent depends on the cognitive structure of each individual

---

An investment firm decides to use community public speaking as part of its public relations effort. They call the program "Investments and You" and target service clubs and local groups as likely audiences. Irwin Jones, the city editor of the local newspaper, is invited to speak to the account executives who are going to participate in the program. Jones's purpose is to encourage the executives to use the newspaper to extend the range of their messages. Here is a portion of his speech:

If you take a typical audience for a typical club meeting, you will probably have thirty-five to forty in the audience. I've seen the speech material that you folks have prepared—it's really good. It would be a shame to confine this useful information to only thirty-five or forty persons at a crack. So your problem is coverage. You simply aren't getting enough of it for the time you are investing in the talks.

As you might have guessed, I have an idea that I think will help the situation. When you go to speak—say to a PTA—try to say something that is newsworthy. If you're going to buy bonds instead of stocks, think in terms of a headline that might read "Stockbroker Foresees Slump in Stock Prices" or something similar. Then summarize your speech and write a brief news release about the speech, its content, and the situation. We might use it in our paper, in which case it will reach eighty thousand readers. Or a smaller paper might pick it up. Now you've got real coverage.

Now here's how you write a news release...

As the speech continues, two listeners have these thoughts:

Listener A: a new employee, female, with one small child. Speech—good golly, I haven't made a speech since I was in college. Club meetings—I guess I should join some clubs. New in town, need some social contact. He's seen the speech material Mr. Weaver put out—what guck. I hope I can depart from the company line if I get to give some speeches. PTA—Michael (her son) will want me to join the PTA. I want to, I just don't know if I have the time. Eighty thousand readers? You gotta be kidding. Even if their circulation is eighty thousand, he's talking about something on page 42, next to the recipes. But he's right, it extends the audience.

Listener B: Executive vice president, 46, male, ambitious. Club meeting—I must remind Grace (his secretary) to pay my club dues. Thirty-five to forty—don't see what's wrong with that. You bet that material is good! I wrote it. The PTA, for crying out loud! They don't buy stocks! I was thinking of the Kiwanis or the Thoroughbred Club. Market slump? You idiot! Never say "slump!" Well, we could write releases ourselves, in the public relations department. I can edit them before they go out. Eighty-thousand—great! That will look good in the quarterly report. This guy seems to know his stuff. Maybe we could hire him to come in one day a week to write releases. He looks like he needs the money. He'd do better if he got a new suit.

Audience Analysis ■ ■ ■ 79

Empathizing with Audiences

One of the most important characteristics of a good speaker is the ability to empathize. *Empathy* is the ability to see things the way the other person does. Most people feel that they do this adequately, but, in fact, few are skilled empathizers. Wendell Johnson of the University of Iowa was fond of illustrating this tendency by calling it the "ITTYTWIT" fallacy. ITTYTWIT is an acronym for "I Think That You Think What I Think." Most of us have fallen into this trap from time to time.

The "Electronic Audience"

Television has made most audiences more aware, better informed, and more "communication-prone." It also makes most people more easily bored, more restless, and harder to talk to. If you have been to a movie theatre recently, you may have heard members of the audience talking while the movie is being shown—a direct result of family interaction during television watching. Because of new electronic media you might face more of a problem in getting and keeping attention than a student thirty years ago.

The term *electronic audience* is used to describe the differences that technology have created in the behavior of listeners. People are more likely to participate than to simply observe. This is good in a way, because we *want* our listeners to interact with us, but it is more taxing on the speaker and makes much more difficult the processes of selecting interesting topics and supporting them with interesting data.

Demographic Audience Analysis

Each of us listens for different things, depending on the situation and our interests. For some reason, college students tend to listen better to material that pertains to tests and grades than to more general information. These kinds of systematic differences stem from obvious traits, such as ethnic or racial background, religious orientation, or sex. The identification of such traits is called *demographic audience analysis*. With this information, a speaker can better empathize with listeners, adapt the message in order to win their attention, understand their frame of reference, and respond to their needs. Let's look at some specific factors that are important in audience analysis. (See Figure 6.2.)

Gender

Males and females are likely to select different data to pay attention to. Females are more likely to pay heed to a message's specific data (especially "social relational" data), and they tend to focus on how parts relate to each other and the whole, though they also seem more easily distracted by competing details. Males, on the other hand, tend to hear more general ideas and to restructure messages in terms of their own goals, (in the process "blocking out" details that might be

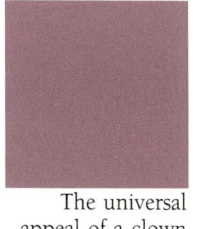

The universal appeal of a clown overcomes all age, gender, and status differences in this mixed audience. (© Michael Markowitz, Photo/Graphic Arts)

contradictory) (Weaver, 1972). Overall female or male "superiority" in listening has not been demonstrated.

Women are typically thought of as being more persuadable than men. Indeed, some studies of persuasion have shown that women are affected more by persuasive messages than men (Bostrom, 1983), though this difference is probably less due to biological factors than to cultural patterns.

Age

Most speakers don't face audiences of children, and they can be thankful for that! Children can be a demanding audience, and the usual preparation and delivery methods don't work too well. Children require more visual material, more opportunity to respond and answer, and have shorter attention spans.

The age factor is not significant in groups extending from the early twenties to middle age, but does play a large role for audiences over sixty. Older persons are definitely different in their interests and knowledge levels. A person who has worked a lifetime is less apt to be patient with a speaker who is not as well prepared as possible. A special effort should be made by the speaker to ensure that the message is relevant, well prepared, and forcefully delivered. Economic and political issues are likely to be viewed as important by older persons. Travel and recreation are also topics of continuing interest.

Educational Level

You may be able to learn in advance the educational level of your audience. If so, some important differences should be noted. If your group is composed entirely of engineers, for example, you know that each listener has completed a bachelor's degree. Other than the obvious differences in intelligence, the audience's educational level affects the speaker's tasks in many ways.

Those who have completed college are more interested in foreign affairs, ecology, and consumer affairs; one reason is this group's increased exposure to newspapers. A college-educated audience is more likely to depend on a newspaper as a main source of information than is a group of less educated individuals. This means, for example, if you were to select an item from the daily paper as an introductory remark, or as an illustration, you would have a better chance of getting a response with a college-educated group. If the group is not as well educated, you should depend more on television or sports for illustrations or examples.

Economic Status

The audience's economic status is an important factor to consider when examining choice of topic. For example, an audience in the economic middle class is probably not going to be interested in the food stamp program, unless to hear of its abuses. Those in a high income bracket might well be interested in the Caribbean as a potential vacation spot, while those in a low income bracket are probably going to be more interested in a camping outing. Americans are fond of minimizing economic class differences, but these distinctions are often quite important and will affect the general interest in, and subject matter of, a speech.

Racial, Ethnic, or Cultural Background

Ethnic affiliations sometimes create particularly sensitive audience-issue relationships. For example, Jewish-Americans tend to take a pro-Israel stand, and black Americans tend to view forced school busing differently than white Americans. Americans of Hispanic, Chinese, and native Indian backgrounds have identifiable political positions, voting habits, and interests. All of these ethnic and cultural groups are important and need to be considered in speech preparation.

Attitudes

If your speech is persuasive in nature, knowledge of the basic position of your audience is vital. Persuasion varies in its effects, depending on the audience's initial position. If you are presenting a speech asking for support on an ecological issue, it is crucial to know whether your potential audience is for this issue, neutral, or against it. If they are for it, you will be *reinforcing* the attitudes they hold, if they are neutral, you will be *shaping* the attitudes they hold, and if they are against it, you will be *changing* the attitudes they hold (Bostrom, 1983). A different persuasive technique is needed in each case.

Group Membership

Almost everyone belongs to at least one group that has special interests and that influences its members' reactions to communications. For example, "man-

Figure 6.2

Demographic audience analysis identifies such traits as ethnic or racial, education and economic level, sex, age, and religious orientation. These traits affect specific message acceptance.

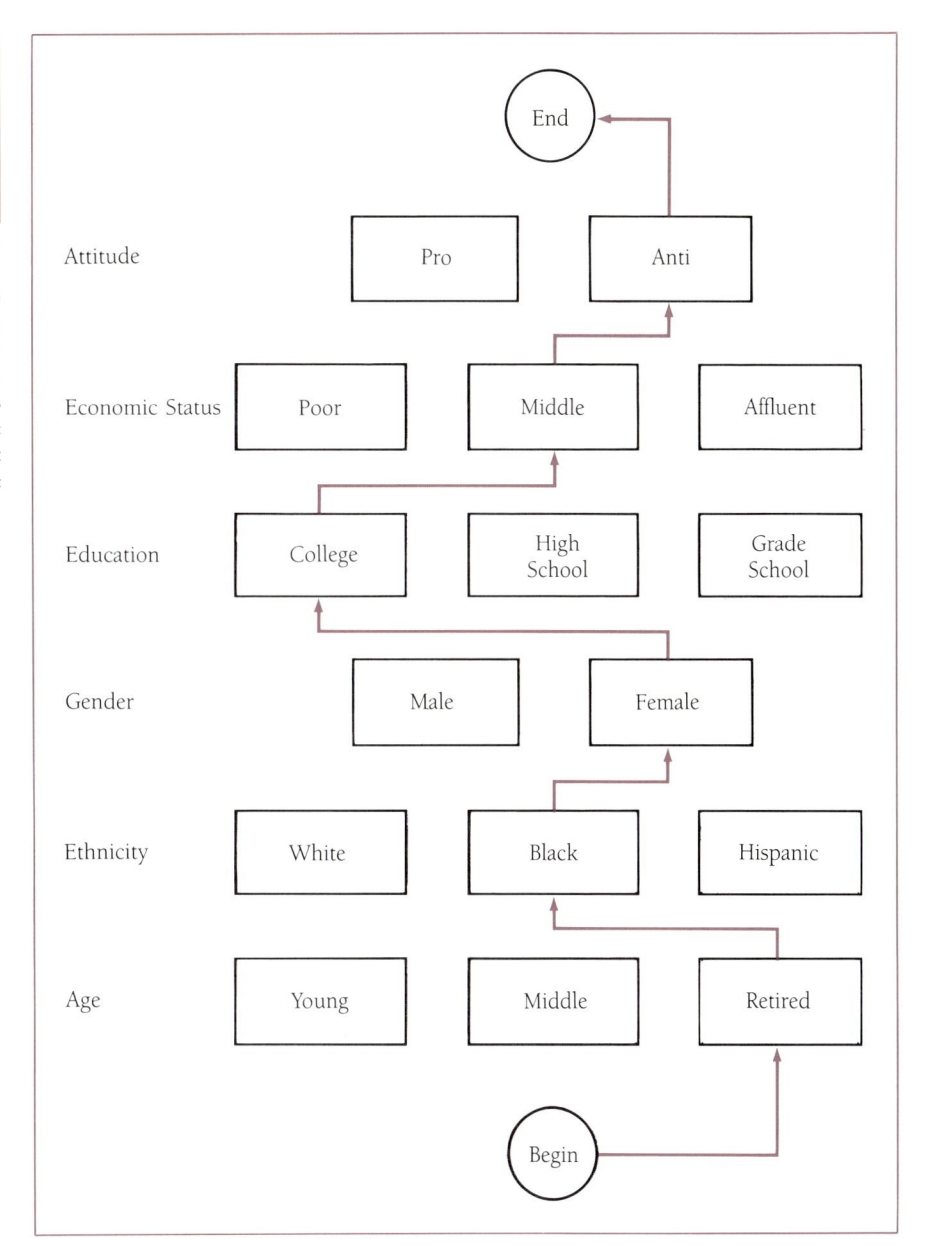

Attitude		Pro	Anti
Economic Status	Poor	Middle	Affluent
Education	College	High School	Grade School
Gender		Male	Female
Ethnicity	White	Black	Hispanic
Age	Young	Middle	Retired

Begin → Retired → Black → Female → College → Middle → Anti → End

agement-oriented" persons tend to reject positive statements about labor groups, and students are frequently suspicious about the motives of faculty. It is certainly not difficult to allow for these special interests; the trick is finding out in advance what these interests are. If you are invited by a Masonic lodge to speak at a banquet, your first step should be to find out as much as you can about this organization, its origins, and how it differs from other groups. Let us look at some specific groups that need specific attention.

Audience Analysis ■ ■ ■ 83

Political Groups

Most Americans consider themselves either Republicans or Democrats, but there are other parties, such as the Libertarian Party, the Socialist Party, and so on. Many speech topics, such as Medicare, welfare, food stamps, and the like, have a distinctly political "slant." Similarly, foreign policy topics often imply a political viewpoint. You need to adopt different methods when you speak to the Young Socialist discussion group, for example, than when you address the Republican Women's alliance.

Your first step is to analyze the party's history and to determine its current positions. If you are as well-informed as your audience, you are well on your way to achieving real rapport. One speaker, addressing a group of Indiana Democrats, mentioned in his speech that Franklin Roosevelt had instituted social security in the 1930s against the strong wishes of the Republicans then in the Senate. He was astonished to discover that his audience did not know this. His credibility with this group took a decided upturn as a result.

Religious Groups

Another significant source of audience differences lies in religious orientation. You must be familiar with the general position of church groups when you are invited to address them. For example, you would not advocate specific methods of birth control to a group of Catholic women without some specific attention to the church's position on this issue. Similarly, if you planned to speak in favor of abortion, you should be extremely careful if you have fundamentalist Protestants in your audience. Political groups and religious groups tend to be associated (fundamentalists tend to be Republicans, for example, and Catholics tend to be Democrats), but this is not a hard-and-fast rule.

Unfortunately, you cannot always know the group membership of your audience. You can, however, determine from general population statistics the incidence of these groups in American culture and assume that the same proportion exists in your group. The same is true about audience attitudes. You might depend on public opinion polls to give you some help here. Common sense should prevail most of the time.

Many speakers are so afraid of offending a specific segment of the audience that they end up saying nothing. The news story in Figure 6.3 illustrates this point in a political setting.

You must strike a delicate balance between tact and the need to advocate your position. A good speech usually offends *someone*, no matter how careful you are.

Situational Audience Analysis

Once you have done a general analysis of your audience, you are ready to analyze the particular time, place, and character of the audience that you will face. The analysis of a particular audience and its situation is called *situational audience analysis,* and is an extremely important step in the construction of a speech.

Figure 6.3

When speakers are overly sensitive to their audience, they may not say anything at all. Such is the case in this news story.

> VALICENTI FILES FOR MAYORAL RACE
> (from the Miami Herald, December 31, 1980)
> Port St. Lucie, Florida.
> Anthony Valicenti said Tuesday he has opened his campaign bank account and picked up filing papers from City Hall.
> Valicenti has lived in Port St. Lucie since 1976, the year he left the police force because of disability.
> Valicenti says that he has no platform yet. "I'll get that as the campaign goes along and hear what the people have to say," he said.
> He declined to describe himself as conservative, moderate, or liberal.
> "Let's just say if the community's conservative, I'll be conservative."
> He said it was too early to criticize specific city policies.

One important factor concerns the purpose of the meeting and the particular circumstances that face the group. If the group is assembling to discuss an important policy change, your speech should relate to this topic.

The nature and purpose of the organization are also important. A speech class is different from a work group in terms of the nature of the group identity. A social or fraternal group is vastly different from a political or religious meeting.

The size of the audience not only determines particular types of delivery but also influences choice of topic. More feedback is available in a smaller group and consequently more complicated topics can be discussed and understood. In a larger group the usual visual aids are not as easily used, and speed of presentation must be slower. Your presentation should proceed just a little faster than your slowest audience member can handle.

Your relationship with the group is also very important. If you are a member of the group (such as in speech class) and if you are familiar to most of the members, you can do many things that you can't do if you are a stranger. One of the immediate tasks facing a stranger is to establish some kind of rapport with the group, and the most usual way is through self-disclosure. One speaker used this method when she said, "My topic today is 'Women in the Workplace.' Now if I were as well paid as Jane Pauley—and I really wish I were—I wouldn't have to worry about babysitters." In this one statement of self-disclosure, an immediate bond was established.

One of the most important factors to consider is the time of day. People are usually most attentive after they have been at work an hour or two; though 8:00 a.m. is a popular hour for meetings, you must consider your audience's state of mind if you face a group at that time. Similarly, if you are presenting a speech to a group after a big dinner, you can expect some sleepy listeners.

Audience Checklist

Now that you've looked at your prospective audience from the point of view of their gender, their age, their membership in specific groups, and their attitudes, you are ready to explore the group from the viewpoint of your particular speech. The following checklist should help in your analysis:

Audience Analysis

As a seasoned political activist and speaker, Bella Abzug clearly demonstrates awareness of her audience's characteristics and circumstances. Here, she delivers a speech with the assistance of a sign-language interpreter. (© Michael Rothstein/ Jeroboam, Inc.)

1. What brought this group together to become this "audience"? Where does this group's identity come from? What do they have in common with each other?

2. What is the occasion that brought about this *particular* meeting? Is this part of their regular routine or a special event? If so, in what way is it special?

3. What specific requests has this group made about this particular speech?

4. Where do you fit in? Are you one of many speakers, or are you the featured speaker?

5. What are the audience's percepts? What particular experiences have created these percepts?

6. What kinds of basic linguistic differences are present in the group? Do they come from a part of the country in which a specific language subgroup is present? Do they share a common set of "inside" terms that mean something to them and no one else? For example, policemen sometimes use the term "civilian" to refer to the rest of us, and they don't always mean it kindly. Be aware of specific usages.

7. What kinds of schemas guide their basic view of the world? How do these schemas relate to your topic? How do they relate to *your* schemas?

8. What emotional connections are likely when these schemas are activated? How do these people "feel" when confronted with specific stimuli? For exam-

ple, Mike Royko, a prominent newspaper columnist from Chicago, created an uproar when he threatened to feed a stray cat to his piranha. Pets have a particular power to arouse listeners.

9. What are their typical patterns of behavior? When are they likely to engage in them? What triggers them? For example, if you are preparing a speech to overweight persons, you can be sure that most of them are afflicted with certain kinds of overeating. You would need to study this behavior pattern and adapt to it in your preparation.

Once you complete the checklist, you will have some specific information about your prospective audience that will help you prepare a speech. Before you can make any specific preparations, however, you have another job—deciding on a general subject or topic for the speech. We will discuss this procedure in Chapter Seven.

Summary

Audience analysis is the process of paying specific attention to the nature of the listeners that will compose your audience. Different types of people perceive things differently, so your analysis of the characteristics of this group is extremely important.

Audience analysis begins with a study of receiver characteristics in general. Most communicators forget that receiving is much more difficult than sending, and good speakers are *receiver-oriented*. Speakers should also attend to selective listening, and be aware of the effects on communication of the electronic audience.

Empathizing with listeners involves an understanding of current modes of information transmission in our culture. Most of us are products of the electronic age, and our listening habits are affected by the electronic media.

Demographic audience analysis concerns such factors as age, sex, educational level, economic status, audience attitudes, and racial or cultural background. In addition, specific group membership is also important.

Situational audience analysis concerns the many factors that are involved in a particular meeting or audience. Time of day, nature of the group, and purpose of the meeting are some of the many things that should be considered in situational analysis.

Before a speech you should complete an audience checklist which will remind you of the specific characteristics that will be important in the construction of the speech.

On Your Own

1. After you listen to some speeches by your classmates, you can begin to formulate some ideas about them. Select a few items from the checklist and fill in the information. Then ask members of your class these specific questions in order to see how well you did.
2. Select a typical group in your community that invites speakers to appear on a regular basis (Kiwanis, Rotary, and so on). Construct an audience checklist for them.

3. What role can public opinion polls play in audience analysis?
4. If you are a regular churchgoer, examine the ways your minister, priest, or rabbi adapts to the audience. Is it realistic?
5. How do popular television programs present images of political figures? Do these actor/politicians lead their audiences, or do they simply adapt to them?
6. Compare these television politicians to real political figures. What differences do you see?
7. Apply demographic characteristics—gender, group membership, and the like—to yourself. How do they affect the way you look at the world?

Suggestions For Further Reading

Bostrom, R. 1983. *Persuasion*. Englewood Cliffs, N.J.: Prentice-Hall.

Bradley, B. 1978. *Fundamentals of speech communication*. Dubuque: Wm. C. Brown.

Clevenger, T. 1966. *Audience analysis*. Indianapolis: Bobbs-Merrill.

Kelly, C. 1970. "Empathic listening." In *Small group communication*, eds. R. Cathcart and L. Samovar. Dubuque: Wm. C. Brown.

Rosenfeld, L., and V. Christie. 1974. "Sex and persuasibility revisited." *Western Speech* 38: 224.

Weaver, C. 1970. *Listening behavior*. Dubuque: Wm. C. Brown.

Seven

Choosing A Topic

> I do not believe that one should speak unless, deep down in his heart, he feels convinced that he has a message to deliver. When one feels, from the bottom of his feet to the top of his head, that he has something to say that is going to help some individual or some cause, then let him say it.
>
> Booker T. Washington

Key Terms

general purpose
inform
convince
beliefs
stimulating
commemoration
persuade
specific purpose
narrowing
appropriateness
hidden agenda
intrinsic credibility
extrinsic credibility

Objectives

After studying this chapter, you should be able to:

1. Distinguish between traditional speech purposes and communicative functions
2. Define the four traditional speech purposes: to inform, to convince, to commemorate and to persuade
3. Understand the functions of the audience checklist
4. Show how to *narrow* a topic
5. Recognize the role of personal background in topic choice
6. Understand the role of hidden agendas and credibility in topic choice

Once you carefully analyze your prospective audience, you are ready to make some basic decisions about selecting a topic for your speech. If you are receiver-oriented, you can make choices that will fulfill the best interests of your listeners. In Chapter Six, you learned how to assess the inner environment (attitudes, beliefs, schemas) of the audience. With this assessment, you can decide which of the communication processes—relaying, externalizing, stimulating, and activating—will alter the inner environment of an audience in the desired way. In order to do that, however, you must make decisions about the topic, the general purpose, and the specific purpose of the speech. In this chapter, we will examine how this is done.

If "you are what you eat," it is equally true that you are what you *talk about*. The way that you present yourself is closely related to the topics about which you talk. We soon tire of the person who speaks constantly about nothing but sports or computers, or who tries to enhance his own importance by addressing momentous topics ("Armageddon is Near!"). The choice of topic tells an audience a great deal about the speaker. In communicative public speaking, audience, task, and topic all interact and should form a coherent whole.

Purpose and topic are very closely related, and it is very difficult to say which choice should come first. In this chapter, we will first discuss choosing a general purpose, and then selecting a specific purpose, and finally choosing a topic. When you prepare your speeches, however, you will probably consider purpose and topic simultaneously.

Methods of Classifying Purpose

Although audiences often ask for a specific topic, they usually allow the speaker wide latitude in selecting a general purpose, that is, how a speaker intends to affect the inner environment of the audience.

The request usually takes a general form, such as "show us where microcomputers are going these days" or "offer some investment tips for the novice investor." Note the use of the words *show* and *offer*. Few people have analyzed communication processes well enough to be familiar with words like *relay* and *externalize*, let alone more complex activities. Here is a list of some of the more common words compiled from representative program requests:

inform	define	enlighten	suggest
persuade	argue	illuminate	impress
convince	discuss	set forth	convey
stimulate	plead	reveal	relate
exemplify	demonstrate	state	present
prove	tell	make aware of	show
point out	teach	express	explain

One way to choose a purpose is to group these words into sensible categories, and then to translate the audience request into a coherent speech purpose that follows principles of effective communication. For example, suppose that during Christmas vacation, you are asked by your church group to "discuss" freshman life at college. The word *discuss* means very little in this context, but you have been given a clue—the group is interested in what happened to you in your first semester. You could say that you will "demonstrate," or "enlighten," or "point out," but basically you are trying to describe a speech in which you relay your experiences. Or you might choose words like *express, reveal, show,* or similar terms more descriptive of externalizations. The real problem is that words like *tell* or *relate* do not clearly discriminate between communicative purposes, whereas words like *inform* or *stimulate* do. So you must first decide what you want to achieve in your talk about the first year of college and clearly categorize your purpose so your audience knows what you plan to do. The first step in this process, of course, is to determine the *general purpose* of your speech.

Determining the General Purpose of the Speech

Today, the purposes of public speaking are generally classified into categories derived from ancient rhetorical forms. The most common categories are *informing, convincing, commemorating,* and *persuading*. In general, "inform" means to pass on information, "convince" means to change someone's point of view, "persuade" means to move someone to action, and "commemorate" means to please the audience or to invoke other emotional responses. Generally when an audience contacts a speaker the persons extending the invitation are not specific about these four traditional purposes, so the speaker needs to translate their program request into one of these traditional purposes.

Setting and Audience

The speaker is not always free to select the general purpose. Sometimes the setting and the expectations of the prospective audience determine the purpose for us. For example, an engineer from an electric utility company was recently invited to address a group of businessmen. The engineer was asked to explain the electric company's future policy concerning nuclear reactors. The engineer was told that if she wanted to speak on another topic the group would seek another speaker. So in this instance, both topic and purpose were predetermined. The engineer was expected to inform—relay information about the company's plans for nuclear power. Any other purpose was not acceptable.

Traditional Speech Purposes

Suppose, on the other hand, that the group had chosen a topic but had not specified a purpose, that is, if the group had simply asked the engineer to speak on nuclear reactors. In this case, the engineer could have chosen how she wanted to affect her audience. The general purpose of the speech could have been to inform,

Leo Buscaglia, author and lecturer, is closely identified with his topic—love. (© C. Steven Short)

to convince, or to persuade her listeners (most speakers in this kind of situation rarely choose to stimulate audiences about nuclear energy). Each purpose would have led to a different path in selecting her topic. Let's look at various purposes and see how they are chosen.

Inform

If the engineer chooses to *inform* her audience, the most appropriate method would be the relay. In fact, the relay is the principal communicative component of informative speaking. If the engineer plans to do this, she might then focus on an objective description of reactor construction and design, trying to create new percepts in the audience. Given today's economic climate, she might discuss materials costs, expected productivity, and typical reactor efficiencies as compared to the price of coal and other alternative fuels. She might also include related issues, such as safety in the coal mines.

Preparing the Speech

Convince

Suppose the particular group already has well-established percepts and detailed information about nuclear power. The engineer might think about going a little further with the audience by convincing them that nuclear reactors are really a good source of energy. We would now say that she plans to *convince* the audience because she plans to change her audience's "beliefs" about this topic. *Beliefs* are commonly thought of as "objects plus attributes" (Fishbein, 1967). A belief about a certain car would include the object, such as Volkswagen, and at least one attribute, like "economical." A belief about engineers might include the engineers themselves and the attribute "smart." Another way of defining beliefs is to say that they are objects plus schemas.

Returning to our engineer, we can see how she might want to change the audience's beliefs. In her case, the object is a nuclear reactor, and the schemas are any of the audience's general orientations toward reactors, such as the danger to the neighborhood, how it might conserve our energy supply, and the like. The engineer might focus on the lessons learned since the Three-Mile Island incident, what new safety procedures have been instituted, and how the cost of nuclear energy relates to the cost of oil. She might also bring up America's vulnerability in the area of world oil supplies. All of these relays are aimed at particular types of audience schemas, specifically those of evaluation of nuclear power.

Commemorate

We still occasionally use speeches to remind us of the importance of a specific event. In this kind of speech, we traditionally refer to the values that a group shares, the importance of the occasion, and the worth of the individuals involved. These values, of course, are *stimulating* in that they describe shared emotions (see Chapter Two). This type of speech has traditionally been called a speech of *commemoration,* and the most typical examples are commencement addresses, dedication speeches, and the like. We will look at some specific examples of these speeches in Chapter Sixteen.

Persuade

If specific action is required of the audience, the engineer may choose to *persuade,* which is what we do when the topic requires some particular action on the part of the receiver. In the case of the engineer, we might envision a situation where a group is protesting against a proposed reactor, or petitioning a public service commission to deny a construction permit for a new reactor. In this case, the engineer may wish to persuade the audience to alter these actions. Persuading obviously uses both stimulation and activation.

Traditional Purposes and Communicative Functions

As you construct your speech, you should build it out of the smaller units of communicative functions. "Informing" a group about plans to build a nuclear

Table 7.1

Comparison of speech purposes, communication functions, and end products.

Traditional Speech Purposes	Communicative Functions	End Product
inform	relay	percepts
	externalization	person, perception, schemas
commemorate	stimulation	affect new schema
persuade	activation	behavior new schema affect
convince	relay, stimulation	concepts percepts arousal new schemas

reactor involves a number of very specific relays, some concerning nuclear power, some concerning the local community, and some concerning money. "Convincing" involves relays, language, and schemas. Table 7.1 lists traditional purposes of speeches and their corresponding communicative functions (see Chapter Two). The last column of the table presents the typical end products of the purposes and functions.

Let's examine a few examples to see how these purposes fit together. A speech with the title "How a Computer Works" would fit in the first category: "Inform." The speaker would gather information on the inner workings of data processing equipment and relay it to the audience. Almost all "How To" speeches fit into this category. Informative speaking is almost always composed of relays.

Some speeches with an informative purpose use externalization. For example, a speech on your interpretation of the word *brotherhood,* would actually be an externalization. The focus is on your *interpretation.*

Speeches that have other purposes are more complex. The simple externalization only calls for the receiver to take in the content of the message and perhaps store it. A speech that aims to stimulate seeks a stronger reaction. The receiver is asked to *feel* as a result of the communication, to be more than just a simple receiver. A speech that asks the audience to consider the plight of Asian-American children left behind in Vietnam also compels the audience to feel, along with the speaker, the sadness inherent in this kind of human tragedy. Other examples include "inspirational" messages, "motivating" instructions ("I know you can do it!"), and most interesting of all, "aesthetic" speeches.

The persuasive speech calls for more than internal response on the part of the receiver—it calls for action, usually some motor response. This type of communication is the hardest of all, since it is difficult to move people to physical action. (Try asking people to get up and march around the room, you'll see how difficult it is!) The difficulty increases as the strangeness of the response increases. When you ask someone to please pass the potatoes at the dinner table, you normally get a quick response. In a speech, however, a request to go to a specific grocery store and get you a potato would probably be met with disappointing results. You may even be disappointed if you ask for signatures on a petition.

Fortunately, not all speakers demand immediate receiver response. As discussed in Chapter Two, the more typical activating communication asks for a *potential response*. For example, when your instructor asks you to read an assignment, you don't go out and do it immediately, you wait until you are ready to study.

As you examine Table 7.1, you will see many similarities between traditional speech purposes and communicative functions. Always remember that interpersonal settings and public speaking settings are considerably different (see Chapter Two).

When you have decided on a general purpose for your speech, you are ready to choose a specific purpose.

Determining Specific Purpose

The general purpose of the speech identifies how you want to affect the inner environment of the audience. The *specific purpose* is a precise statement of what you wish to accomplish. The specific purpose should concentrate on one aspect of a subject. Limiting yourself to one distinct idea will help you select which information to include.

To illustrate how the general purpose, specific purpose and topic are all interrelated, let's look at a specific case. Lewis has been invited by a luncheon club to discuss personal computers. The program chairperson was not very specific about the speech; he only said "you have about thirty minutes, and we wish you would talk about personal computers." Lewis is not sure whether he wants to convince the audience that personal computers are (or are not) a good thing, whether he wants to persuade the audience to buy (or not to buy) a personal computer, or simply to inform them about personal computers generally. He chooses "to convince" as his general purpose, and he is ready to choose his specific purpose. Because the field of personal computing is rather large, he needs to choose a specific aspect. He decides to convince the audience that personal computers are overrated as a home unit and that most of the advertising about personal computers is unsubstantiated. He now has a specific purpose, which is principally aimed at changing the schema system of the audience. In addition, this purpose can be stated simply: "The purpose of this speech is to convince the audience that personal computers are not as useful in the home as current advertising makes them out to be."

Notice that Lewis has included the general purpose in his statement, his topic, and a specific statement about what he wants to achieve with the audience. He can now decide what kinds of material to use in the speech—whether to relay information, to externalize, or to activate. If, for example, he chose to relay information about personal computer design, the subject matter might never touch on his own feelings on the topic. On the other hand, if he chose to externalize these feelings, he might mention how much fun he has with personal computers. However he chooses to present the topic will be influenced by his analysis of the audience's schema system, as we learned in Chapter Six.

You can see how a speaker proceeds from topic to general purpose to specific purpose. For example, if the topic is "tires" and the general purpose is to inform, a specific purpose might be "To inform the audience of some of the long-wear characteristics of modern automobile tires." If the topic is "weather forecasts" and the general purpose is to persuade, the specific purpose might be "To persuade the audience to be more careful in making plans based on television weather forecasts."

Using items 6–9 from the audience checklist in Chapter Six, you can construct a fairly accurate description of the inner environment of an audience. Assume that you are now at point A and that after the speech you wish to be at point B. This checklist should help you determine which communication processes will be most effective in moving the audience from A to B and how to focus your material in order to bring about this desired change.

A careful analysis of these specific characteristics should at least give you an idea of the general direction of a successful speech. Now you need to decide which specific elements of communication—relaying, externalizing, arousing, or activating—will be the most effective in moving this particular audience from point A to point B. In other words, you need to ask what would be the most effective *content* of the speech (see Chapter Eight). Figure 7.1 illustrates how you might proceed from one point to another.

Ethical Issues

Basic ethical considerations should affect your choice of topic and purpose. Even though many communicative functions seem to be inherently manipulative, ethical speakers choose their topics and purposes based on *altruism, that is, a desire to help others.* Altruistic behavior is an important consideration in the way we look at communication generally and public speaking in particular.

The most important aspect of ethical choice is the responsibility to the listener. Let's look at that important problem next.

Figure 7.1

The most effective content of a speech will move an audience from Point A to Point B.

Point A	Point B
1. What percepts does the audience have? How do things look to them?	1. What percepts should they have? How should things look to them?
2. What kinds of schemas organize these percepts? How are they accustomed to categorizing and classifying their experiences? What kinds of language do they now use?	2. What kinds of schemas ought they use in organizing these percepts? How can they reclassify and restructure them? Do they need new ones? Do they need new language for the schemas?
3. What emotional connections are likely when these schemas are activated? How do these persons "feel" when confronted with the percepts and schemas that are presently used?	3. What emotional connections are desirable in these contexts? What would be an appropriate way to "feel" when confronted with these new percepts and schemas?
4. What are their typical patterns of behavior? When are they likely to engage in them? What "triggers" their actions?	4. What would be a more useful pattern of behavior? When should they be engaged? How can they be "triggered?"

Choosing a Topic

The examples in this chapter have covered only situations where the audience requested a particular topic, and the speaker simply responded; a speech does not always evolve this way, however. Often you have to choose your own topic. In speech class, this is almost always the case. Choosing a good topic is probably the most important part of the preparation process.

At the beginning of this chapter, we noted that the choice of topic and of general purpose usually go together. In most situations, the occasion and the audience determine topic choice. For example, you would not discuss corruption in American business in an after-dinner speech when the audience expects to be entertained, nor would you present a lighthearted account of a ski weekend at a seminar meeting called to discuss political issues. Common sense is a valuable tool in fitting the topic to the occasion.

In the classroom, your topic choices are extremely important. You face a *real* audience composed of real people with real needs. Try to choose interesting, meaningful topics that will be appropriate for this group.

Sources of Topics

Where does one find topics? There are a number of good sources.

Personal Knowledge

Your own knowledge and interests are the first place you should look for topics. Each of us has a fund of general interests that have significance for others. Do you enjoy country music? The country music culture abounds in interesting topics:

- The Image of the Trucker in Country Music
- Dolly Parton as a Folk Heroine
- Marriage and Fidelity in Country Music
- The "New" Grand Old Opry
- Religious Attitudes in Country Music
- Nashville Recording: Big Business
- Country Music on Cable Television

Do you collect coins? Most persons have only a superficial knowledge about coins. If you are a collector, you might discuss:

- Coins and Vending Machines
- Inherent Value of Metal and Coin Values
- Should You Save Your Pennies?
- The Susan B. Anthony Dollar

- Coins and Medals
- How to Invest in Coins

Perhaps you are a camper or backpacker. Many topics could come from this hobby:

- Cooking on the Trail
- Avoiding Bears
- America's Wilderness Areas
- Staying Warm in a Tent
- James Watt and the Park System

Perhaps you are a movie buff. Here are some topics that might come from this interest:

- The New Movies from Australia
- Mel Brooks as Comic Genius
- Rating Systems: What Does "R" Mean?
- Monster Movies
- Using the Home Box Office
- Why Woody Allen Makes Me Sad

Your personal knowledge can be a gold mine of prospective topics, but you have to be willing to dig a little to find interesting and significant areas to talk about.

Current Events

In American culture, newspapers and television news reports set the "agenda" of what people think is worth talking about. In other words, people generally think and talk about what the news media thinks and talks about. Palmgreen and Clarke (1977) found that television news was the strongest influence in agenda-setting for national issues, and newspapers were the strongest influence in agenda setting for local issues.

Your job is to keep up with current issues by reading newspapers and magazines and by watching at least one network news show, so that you'll have an idea of what the rest of the world thinks is significant. Here are some topics suggested by the national news:

- Congress and the War Powers Act
- Air Safety and National Boundaries
- The Academy Award System: Time for Reform
- Presidential Primaries
- Miss America: An Ordeal for Everybody
- Computer Security

Here are some topics that might be suggested by reading state and local news:

- Safety and the Highway System
- Is College Football Worth It?
- Basic Skills and Our Schools
- Overcrowding and Prison Systems
- Have We Overdone the Co-ed Dormitories?
- Disposing of Nuclear Waste: Not Here, Please

As you might guess, keeping up with current events has other benefits, such as finding content for speeches, helping you do better in political science and history, and just being an all-around better voter and citizen.

Great Ideas

Certain great ideas have endured for centuries. They usually relate to life and love, birth and death, war and peace, marriage and children, materialism and idealism, and the meaning of happiness. It is no accident that all of the religious leaders in all major religions have addressed these topics, but great ideas need not be limited to religious literature.

You probably reflect often on what it takes to make someone truly happy—material goods, physical health, position in society, power, love, and so on. Well, so have most of the great philosophers of this world, and it is worth our time and

Your hobby or extracurricular interest can provide material for an entertaining and informative classroom presentation. (© Michael Markowitz, Photo/Graphic Arts)

Choosing A Topic 99

effort to read them. A speech topic that relates to one of the great universals of human experience will frequently receive more attention and respect from the audience than a speech about designer jeans and where to buy them. In any communication situation you should be on guard against becoming trivial. Here are some topics based on the great ideas of history:

- The Value of an Education
- Interfaith Marriage
- Free Enterprise
- The Supremacy of Laws or Individuals
- National Symbols and Everyday Life
- Hidden Signs of Prejudice

Narrowing the Topic

Almost every beginning speaker chooses a topic that simply cannot be covered in a five- or ten-minute speech. The general topic needs to be *narrowed* so that it fits the interests and expectations of the audience.

Appropriateness

The student who chooses the topic "Our Interstate Highway System," may well discover a problem of *appropriateness*. Though most people use the highway system, few people really care about the New Jersey Turnpike. Moreover, you may not be the most appropriate source for eulogizing the interstate highway system. On the other hand, the audience might be interested in a more narrow version of the topic, such as: "Defensive Driving on the Interstate Highways," or "Financing Our Highway System." In both examples, the general topic has been significantly narrowed to fit an audience interest or specific avenue of research.

Time Limits

Audiences have strong expectations about time limits and listen poorly when speakers abuse them. If you have a five-minute time limit in your class, you are probably limited to a speech of 750 words in length—less than five typewritten, double-spaced pages. The only way to keep within these boundaries is to limit your topic before you begin.

The following list shows how you can narrow some broad topics:

General Topic	Narrowed Topic
Pope John	Pope John and the Solidarity Union
The Grateful Dead	Evolution of a Rock Group
Pets	Cats and College Students

Jazzercise	Using an Exercise Program to Tone Muscles
El Salvador	Military or Economic Aid to El Salvador?
Interior Decorating	Low-Cost Prints for the Apartment
Scuba Diving	Diving in Lake Michigan
Summer Vacation	Working Vacations in National Parks
Caring for a Car	Tire Maintenance
Las Vegas	Keeping Your Money in Las Vegas
Solar Heat	Solar Devices for the Older House

All of these topics could be narrowed even further. Remember that a shorter, more specific presentation always has greater impact than a longer, rambling speech. Narrowing is one of the most important steps to achieving a well-constructed speech.

Let's review the steps involved in choosing a topic. First, you must relate the various functions of communication to the four traditional speech purposes: to inform, to convince, to commemorate, and to persuade. Second, you construct an audience checklist, based on ethical principles. Third, you look within your own experience and knowledge and analyze the specific audience you plan to address. Finally, you begin the task of choosing the topic. Let's examine how a typical college student might approach the process.

Mary, a college student, studies her audience—a group of freshmen and sophomores in a basic public speaking class. One thing that stands out in Mary's mind is that all these students are undergoing a change in lifestyle, moving from a life of parental supervision to a life on their own. This change almost inevitably leads to experimentation—some students begin smoking, others start drinking, still others start staying out late, and so on. In high school Mary participated in a science project that studied the effects of alcohol; she also had a close friend who narrowly escaped death in an auto crash with a drunken driver.

The behavior of many of Mary's fellow students seems alarming. Alcohol abuse seems to be one of the hallmarks of life as a college student. Mary decides that information about alcohol would be an outstanding topic for a speech, meeting the standards of germaneness, ethicality, and immediacy.

Mary is sure that the general topic of "Alcohol Abuse" is high on everyone's list of important topics, particularly after seeing a barrage of television spots that urge young people to "just say no" to all types of drugs. She decides that her goal is to inform college students of some of the problems inherent in alcohol abuse and relate it to the current "war on drugs."

Notice that Mary has taken some specific knowledge and interest, analyzed the specific characteristics of her potential audience, and related both of these to a topic of contemporary social importance. Mary's next task is to narrow the topic.

"Alcohol Abuse" could include hundreds of different subtopics:

- The Nature of Alcoholism

- The Effects of Alcohol on the Central Nervous System
- Traffic Accidents and Alcohol Usage
- Alcohol and the Workplace
- Why Pilots Don't Drink

The list could go on and on. Mary first decides to narrow the topic to "Frequencies of Alcohol Usage in the United States." This seems *too* narrow, however, so she decides to include some statistical data about the nature of alcohol abuse and its resistance to treatment. Mary's final topic: "The Risks Involved in Using Alcohol."

Speech Purpose, Topic Choice, and Listening

Determining the speaker's purpose is one of the most important listening skills. Many speakers signal their purpose with such statements as, "Today I want to persuade you that...," but many others are less skilled, and the listener must make this judgment during the presentation. Though the speaker's topic is usually clear, the speaker's purpose is sometimes less clear. Research shows that clear understanding of the purpose of the presentation aids in understanding and retention of the material.

Hidden Agendas

Many contemporary speeches contain *hidden agendas—ulterior motives* of the speaker. For example, in 1966 Richard Nixon travelled throughout the country speaking on behalf of Republican candidates for office. Each of his speeches concentrated on a local candidate and general Republican philosophy of government. Yet the principal purpose of his speeches was to prepare the way for a bid for the 1968 presidential nomination, which he subsequently received.

When a representative of a grocery chain says, "I only want to inform you about the reasons why groceries are going up in price," or the president of a labor union says "All I want is to explain some of the background of this strike," the true purpose ought to be obvious to the audience. Frequently, however, speakers are more subtle and the true purpose is hard to discern.

Your first task as a listener is to evaluate the speaker's stated purpose. Most speakers will be very straightforward about the goal of the speech. Read the speech in Figure 7.2, and note how Alan Alda stated his purpose.

Topic Choice and Source Credibility

Listeners should also evaluate the speaker's *right to speak* on a given topic. The subject of credibility is discussed in detail in Chapter Fourteen, but you should be aware at this point of the importance of a basic evaluation of any speaker. If the speaker has chosen heart transplants as the topic, your first question ought to be, "Is this person expert enough to speak on this topic?" If the individual does not

Figure 7.2

Alan Alda's purpose, in his commencement address at Drew University, was to offer advice to the graduating class that would be remembered. (© UPI/Bettmann Newsphotos)

> I was very touched by your very warm welcome and I would like in return to say something to the graduating class that will have some meaning for you. I actually hope I can say something that will set you so on fire that you will never forget it, because I remember twenty-three years ago when I was graduating from college and I was on your side of the academic footlights. I sat there and listened to some very distinguished commencement speakers who gave us encouragement and words of wisdom and guidance, and nobody could remember a damn thing anybody said. Well, I am going to tell you something that you will remember. And I'll even tell you when you'll remember it. You may not believe this as you sit there today...getting ready to go into your careers, but the day will come eventually...when at some point in your lives, maybe...a year from now, or maybe ten or fifteen years from now, when you are going to look up from your work and wonder what the point of it all is. You wonder how much you are getting accomplished and how much it all means (Linkugel, Allen, and Johannesen, 1982).

possess specific knowledge, training, background, or experience, he lacks *intrinsic credibility*. You should then look for cues of *extrinsic credibility*, that is, you should determine if the speaker has thoroughly researched the topic.

Manner of presentation is also important. Student speakers would typically not say, "In my opinion, artificial heart surgery is to be preferred over heart transplants," but rather, "In the opinion of Dr. Lyman Denny, chief of surgery at Toronto General Hospital, artificial heart..."

Evaluations of the right to speak on given topics include assessments of competence, preparation, and responsibility. Schwartzman (1987) has noted how these issues, first articulated by Plato and Cicero, are still important today, especially for technical topics, such as the hearings about the "Three-Mile Island" reactor failure. In today's culture many people assume that since they have a right to a private opinion on almost any topic, they also have a right to speak on almost any topic.

Summary

Your choice of topic is an important clue to the kind of person you are. Careful attention needs to be paid to both topic choice and communicative purpose. General purposes are often determined by the setting and the audience. Traditional speech purposes include: to inform, to convince, to commemorate, and to persuade. Speeches intended to inform typically utilize relays; speeches intended to convince use relays and externalization; speeches intended to commemorate usually produce emotional involvement; and speeches intended to persuade activate audiences and create behavior patterns. Typical speeches in most business and classroom situations are intended to inform, to convince, and to persuade.

Specific purpose can be determined once a topic is chosen. Topics need to be based on audience analysis and the desired "mind state" of the audience before and after the speech. Good topics spring from personal knowledge, current events, significant ideas in history and philosophy. Topics should always be narrowed as much as possible to accommodate time limits and the speaking situations.

On Your Own

1. Using a contemporary dictionary, make a list of verbs that designate one kind of communicative activity. What can you conclude from this list?
2. Keep track of a representative group of television commercials. Do television commercials persuade? Inform? Convince? Defend your answer.
3. Try to remember how you felt the last time someone told you they planned to persuade you? Would they have been more effective if they pretended only to inform?
4. Does a speech have to be funny for you to enjoy it? Explain.
5. Review the lists of suggested topics presented in this chapter. How can they be narrowed further?
6. While at church or synagogue, try to determine the specific purpose of the sermon or homily. What behaviors, if any, are called for?

Suggestions For Further Reading

Goffman, E. 1959. *The presentation of self in everyday life.* Garden City, N.Y.: Doubleday.

McCombs, M. 1976. Agenda-setting research. *Political Communication Review* 1: 1-7.

Palmgreen, P., and P. Clarke. 1977. Agenda-setting with local and national issues. *Communication Research* 4: 435-452.

Reid, L. 1980. *Speaking well.* New York: McGraw-Hill.

Eight

Materials: Finding the Content for the Speech

The need for information—the need to know—is as basic to man as the need for food, clothing, and shelter.

Raleigh Boswell

Key Terms

experience
invention
topoi
definition
relationship
Reader's Guide
card catalog
examples
illustrations
comparison
contrast
repetition
quotation

Objectives

After studying this chapter, you should be able to:

1. Distinguish between firsthand and secondhand information
2. Amplify your experience into interesting content
3. Use the "topics" to generate ideas
4. Gain some basic familiarity with the library
5. Use examples and illustrations to alter percepts
6. Understand the role of definitions in altering language
7. Illustrate the nature of listening for content

Now that you have analyzed your audience, determined your purpose, and chosen your topic, you are ready to select materials that will develop and support the major ideas in your speech and that will alter the inner environment of your audience in ways you choose.

Information can alter the percepts, schemas, language, and affects of audience members. Your listeners, in turn, will be free to accept or reject the message transmitted. Obviously, the success of this method depends on the content and delivery of the information presented. The *quality of the information is crucial* and will be the key to the success or failure of your speech. Selecting the information to use in your speech is the subject of this chapter.

In this chapter, we focus on the sources and forms of supporting materials: where to find them and how to use them in order to clarify and sustain the message you want to transmit.

The information you gather for your speech is of two basic types: *firsthand* (from direct experience) and *secondhand* (from other than direct experience). Whether you decide to use firsthand or secondhand information or both, your goal is to become a credible source. One way to do this is to develop a substantial fund of knowledge on your chosen topic. Certainly, there is little point in speaking to an audience if you do not know more about the subject than they do.

If you are an expert on the Middle East and were physically present in Beirut during the fighting, you will certainly be accepted as credible when you say "While in Beirut, I saw ..." However, most of us do not have this kind of direct experience and so must rely on accounts furnished by others.

Suppose that you hear a speaker say "The U.S. Department of Agriculture reported in 1987 that tobacco acreage was diminished." The speaker probably got this information from a newspaper, which in turn picked it up from a wire service, which got it from a Department of Agriculture report, which was written by a bureaucrat who gathered information from a number of field workers who had surveyed a sample of farmers. In other words, most information of this nature is not secondhand, but third- or fourthhand.

Your first job is to cast your net widely and gather as much material as you can. We will explore the gathering process as it relates to both firsthand and secondhand content.

Firsthand Information: Your Own Resources

Your background and experiences are vital sources of information. Everyone is knowledgeable about some topic: a job in a fast food restaurant or in a bar, a colorful relative or a talented friend, or an event in which you participated, such as a Greenpeace demonstration or the bronc-riding contest at the county rodeo. We are all storehouses for this kind of speech material. The first step in preparing this type of information is to organize it and adapt it to our communicative requirements.

Experience

Beginning speakers often do not believe that their personal experiences are worth sharing. Although some speakers know they have done something unusual, such as working as an intern in a Congressional office or going on a wilderness survival hike, most people undervalue their experiences. You should see your varied experiences for the rich resources they are. You may have to dig deeply in order to discover the hidden significance. You need to see the *implications* of the experiences for preparing the content of your speech. Look at the following experiences and their corresponding implications for speech material.

Activity	Implication
Spent two days camping out to get Bruce Springsteen tickets.	General force of rock groups as opinion leaders in today's culture.
Had a rough time in college math course.	Problems inherent in high school instruction, especially in math and science.
Can't afford a car.	Economic structure of American society.

Even a miserable experience can be an interesting resource for a speech. George was a student who hardly ever drank, but after a party at a friend's house, he was obviously drunk. George elected to drive home anyway and on the way was stopped by a police officer who worked in the local alcohol control program. George was tested, his blood alcohol was found to be over the legal limit, and he was taken to jail. When George was released the next day, he wondered exactly how the "breathalyzer" machine could detect alcohol in the bloodstream. He spoke to some of the police officers who were involved in the program and discovered how the machines work and how alcohol is transferred from stomach to bloodstream and then to air in the lungs. When the time came for him to make a speech in class, he knew a good deal about this process and could use it as supporting material.

Your experiences are played against the rich fabric of your personal background and identity. What events mean to *you,* coming from your own religious, ethnic, or regional background, is important material for a speech because you are unique. See Figure 8.1 for an illustration of one man's unique view of technology.

Ideas

Everyone has ideas. Where do they come from? You may think that you get an idea only if you sit under a tree and wait for an inspiration. It doesn't work that way. Almost all ideas come from applying some kind of analysis to the subject at hand.

The process of "having an idea" was called *invention* by the ancient rhetoricians, and they made a serious study of it. You have an idea, they concluded, only if you are willing to work at it. One of their methods was to apply what they called *topoi,* or "topics," to the subject in order to stimulate the creative juices.

Figure 8.1

Neil Postman, *The Technical Thesis*, Seton Hall University, 1978.

> Everyone must have a favorite and real example of the tyranny of numbers. I have several, the most recent having occurred a couple of months ago. I and several people of reputed intelligence were together in a hotel room, watching a television program called "The Miss Universe Pageant." Now, even in a nontechnicalized culture, a beauty pageant would be, it seems to me, a degrading cultural event. In this one, pure lunacy was added to the degradation by the utilization of computers to measure the measurements, so to speak, of the women involved. Each of the twelve judges was able to assign a precise number to the charm of a woman's smile, the shapeliness of her bosom, the sensuality of her walk, and even to the extent of what was called her "poise." But more than this, as each judge assigned a number, a mother-computer, with legendary speed, calculated the average, which was then dashed on the upper right-hand corner of the TV screen so that the audience could know immediately, that Miss Holland, for example, was a 6.231 on how she looked in a bathing suit, whereas Miss Finland was only a 5.827. Now, as it happened, one of the people with whom I was watching believed, as he put it, that there is no way Miss Finland is a 5.827. He estimated that she is, at a minimum, a 6.3, and maybe as high as a 7.2. Another member of our group took exception to these figures, maintaining strongly that only in a world gone mad is Miss Finland a 5.827, and that she should count herself lucky that she did not get what she deserved, which, as he figured it, was no more than a 3.8.
>
> Now, the point is that here were two people whose minds had passed the point of crisis and were already in a state of rigor mortis, although they apparently didn't know it. As I left the room and headed for the hotel bar, a similar scene from my high school days came drifting back to me. Because I had received an 83 in English, I had missed by a fraction being eligible for Arista, the high school equivalent of making the Dean's List. I therefore approached my English teacher, a gentle and sensitive man by the name of Rosenbaum, and requested that he reassess my performance with a view toward elevating my grade two points. He regarded my request as reasonable and studiously examined his record book. Then he turned toward me with genuine sadness in his face and said, "I'm sorry, Neil. You're an 83. An 84 at most, but not an 85. Not this term, anyway."
>
> Now, you understand, I trust, that both Rosenbaum and I were crazy. He, because he believed I was an 83 or 84 at most, and I, because I believed his belief. He had been fair. He had reviewed the numbers, which were both precise and objective. To him, my performance *was* the numbers. To me, as well. This is reification of technique, from which, several years later, I began to recover almost completely. I often wonder if Rosenbaum got better, too. The disease is not, however, so easy to overcome, because ultimately technicalization is more than a bias of culture. It is a bias of mind. Its assumptions become an interior voice which excludes alternative modes of expression.

Corbett (1965) summarized many of the *topoi* of the classical rhetoricians and constructed "topics" to guide the modern student:

Definitions
1. Genus or Kinds
2. Division

Comparison
- 1. Similarity
- 2. Difference
- 3. Degree

Relationships
- 1. Cause and Effect
- 2. Antecedent and Consequence
- 3. Contraries
- 4. Contradictions

Circumstances
- 1. Possible and Impossible
- 2. Past Fact and Future Fact

Testimony
- 1. Authority
- 2. Testimonial
- 3. Statistics
- 4. Maxims
- 5. Law
- 6. Precedents

The last section, "Testimony," would clearly be labelled "Research" today and would include many other forms of research than Corbett lists. "Genus," "Relationships," "Comparison," and "Circumstances," however, are all highly relevant to the process of idea-making as the communicator approaches it. We might say that these topics represent a *creativity system,* and the application of these topics begins the process of creativity.

How does this process work? In Chapter Seven, you will recall, Mary was considering a speech on the general topic of alcohol and its use among young people. Mary wants to examine some of the problems inherent in using the drug, but has only some isolated statistics and doesn't know where to start. So she first applies the topic *definition* to alcohol. This step stimulates her to think about what alcohol "use" means, what "alcohol" means specifically (does beer count?), and perhaps what the definition of "abuse" might be. She might also consider whether alcohol is indeed a "drug" as we use the term.

To apply the topic *comparison,* Mary would compare alcohol use to other vices, such as smoking, overeating, and the like. To apply the topic *relationship,* she investigates the causes of alcoholism (physical and psychological), its consequences, its opposites, and societal factors that contradict attempts at control (human nature, the Constitution, and so on).

You can apply these topics to almost any subject, and it's a rare subject

Materials: Finding the Content for the Speech

Activist Bobby Seale's fervent and emotional speeches helped focus world attention on the Chicago Seven conspiracy trial. (© *Peeter Vilms/ Jeroboam, Inc.*)

that doesn't yield an idea or two after this kind of analysis. Even if you feel that your original ideas are adequate, it is useful to run through the topics anyway—you may remember an experience in your past or come up with a new idea!

Emotions as Resources

One of your own emotions, such as indignation, can be a marvelous starting point for a speech. Your reasons for being indignant, of course, must be legitimate and worthwhile, but the emotion is worth exploiting. If the subject matter affects you, this reaction is testimony to the force of the material, and it is not wrong to share your emotions with others. However, you need to analyze the emotion, understand why it was generated, how it applies to others, and other significant characteristics before you shoot from the hip. A speech that starts out "I am absolutely FED UP!" is at least going to be interesting, and you should explore this resource.

Personal Background

Your personal background and identity can be a valuable resource. What the arms race means to a Midwesterner, to a Georgia farmer, or to a Maryland fisherman can result in interesting comparisons; what this issue means *to you,*

110 ■ ■ ■ **Preparing the Speech**

coming out of your own unique background, is an important source of materials for a speech. Important background characteristics, such as race, religion, hometown or region, gender, and tradition all are worth exploring.

Secondhand Materials—Research

Now that we've examined some of the ways in which you can use yourself as a source of materials for a speech, let's turn to the more common external sources.

Interviews

If you plan to talk about banking or money, you will want to talk to a banker or two. You might be surprised how many people are willing and eager to talk about their professions. You must be careful, however, not to abuse these sources. Here are some suggestions:

1. Call well in advance for an appointment.
2. Be on time for the appointment and dress carefully.
3. Prepare a series of questions for the interview. Keep any hostile or loaded questions out of the interview.
4. Take a notebook, but try not to spend all of your time writing. You may prefer to use a tape recorder instead.
5. Offer to bring in a copy of the finished speech or notes.

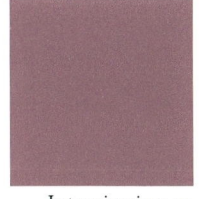

Interviewing an expert can provide not only the information you are looking for, but also may give you such intangible factors as the expert's enthusiasm or feeling for his field that will add a new dimension to your presentation. (© Michael Markowitz, Photo/Graphic Arts)

Materials: Finding the Content for the Speech   111

6. Ask for any available printed matter. Many organizations will give you literature to supplement the interview.

7. Take no longer than a half-hour and thank the source profusely when you leave.

8. When the interview is over, sit down immediately and check over your notes.

Take care to be courteous and polite. After all, someone else may want to interview this person; if you leave a bad impression, you may dry up the source for everyone else at your school.

Libraries

One of the best sources of information is the campus or public library. The biggest problem in using a library is that it contains so much information, you will undoubtedly find more than you need. So you should learn how libraries help you find specific material. Generally, this material is divided into two types—periodicals and books.

Periodicals

Almost all libraries have a collection of periodical literature (magazines and journals) to which they subscribe. Your first task is to find out which periodicals are available, where the library keeps them, and how they are bound. A current list is always available at the reference section of the library, but libraries differ and you may want to check at the circulation or information desk to see where this list is located.

You will notice that libraries keep materials for long periods of time, so it is useless to search through all their issues of *The New Yorker*—you'll never get through them. If the library stores past issues of a periodical for twenty years, this means looking through 200,000 pages!

Fortunately, all libraries have references called *indexes* that will make your search much easier. The most popular is the *Readers' Guide to Periodical Literature,* which indexes a number of publications that are considered "popular," such as *Reader's Digest* and *Popular Science*. Other indexes include the *International Index* the *Art Index.*.

Let's take a look at what you might find in the *Reader's Guide* by returning to the example of Mary, who is still interested in the effects of alcohol on young persons. She has applied the topics but now needs more factual information and would like to find articles on the subject in the library. Her first step is to check the *Reader's Guide* and look up "Alcohol." The *Reader's Guide* appears annually, with monthly volumes for the most up-to-date material. Figure 8.2 shows *The Reader's Guide* entry for "Alcohol." She sees a number of subheadings—"Physiological effects," for example. As she scans the subheadings and entries, some seem more useful than others. For example, under "Alcohol and youth," she sees an article entitled "Campus report: is there a drinker in the house?" (Wellesley's Alcohol Informational Theatre).

Figure 8.2

Partial listing for "Alcohol," *Reader's Guide,* January-March, 1987.

Alcohol
   See also
  Drinking customs
  Physiological effects
  Body heat boosts alcohol's effects. il *Prevention* 39:6 Ja '87
  Hangovers: tips before you toast. D. Webb. *McCalls* 114:105 Ja '87
  Lipid takes a stand against alcohol [phosphatidylinositol; research by Theodore F. Taraschi and others] D. D. Edwards. Sci News 131:38-9 Ja 17 '87
Alcohol and air pilots
  Bottle to throttle. *Sci Am* 256:86 F '87
Alcohol and automobile drivers
  Every 27 minutes ... L. Weltner. il *Read Dig* 130:136-8 F '87
  Michael Spinks wrecks car, faces DUI charge. *Jet* 72:46 Ap 6 '87
Alcohol and employment
  A promise of renewal [film industry worker] D. B. Smith. il *N Y Times Mag* p52 F 15 '87
Alcohol and Indians (American)
  A girl's anger rouses her kinfolk from an alcoholic daze [work of Shuswap Indians A. and P. Chelsea in Alkali Lake, B.C.] M. Green. il pors *People Wkly* 27:83-4 Ja 26 '87
Alcohol and the aged
  Alcohol: how much is too much? W. A. Nolen. il *50 Plus* 27:82+ Mr '87
Alcohol and women
  The day my family saved my life [excerpt from Betty]; ed. by Chris Chase. B. Ford. il pors *Good Housekeep* 204:132-3+ F '87
  Drinking. L. Van Gelder. il *Ms* 15:38 F '87
  Frank as ever, former First Lady Betty Ford describes her harrowing years of addiction. A. Chambers. il pors *People Wkly* 27:88-89+ Mr 9 '87
Alcohol and youth
  See also
  Project 714 (Organization)
  Alcoholism: yes, it can happen to you. D. Hymes. il *Curr Health 2* 13:18-21 F'87
  Campus report: is there a drinker in the house? [Wellesley's Alcohol Informational Theater] K. FitzGerald. il *Ms* 15:30 F '87
  The law and youth substance abuse [American Bar Association report] il *Child Today* 16:4 Ja/F '87
Alcohol as fuel
  Some dare call them ... robber barons [government agricultural subsidies and gasohol program] M. Fumento. il *Natl Rev* 39:32-3+ Mr 13 '87
  Test for alcohol in gasoline? il *Consum Rep* 52:194 Ap '87
Alcohol in chocolate *See* Chocolate
Alcoholic beverages
  See also
  Beer
  Wine
  Wine coolers
  The hot and cold of it. J. F. Mariani. il *Mot Boat Sail* 159:30 F '87
  Party hearty without getting drunk. J. Friedrich. il *Mademoiselle* 93:296 Mr '87
  The thinking woman's drinking guide. il *Glamour* 85:200-3 Ja '87
Alcoholics and alcoholism
  See also
  Alcohol--Physiological effects
  Children of alcoholics
    History
  The geography of drinking. C. J. Smith. il map *Focus* 36:16-23 Wint '86
    Rehabilitation
  See Alcoholics and alcoholism—Therapy
    Therapy
  Sobering facts on rehab. R. Phalon. il *Forbes* 139:140+ Mr 9 '87
    Soviet Union
  War on Soviet alcoholism. N. Morris. il *Macleans* 100:48 Ja 19 '87
Alcoholics' families
  "We have a problem". J. Marks. il *Parents* 62:78+ Mr '87
Alcoholism *See* Alcoholics and alcoholism

Figure 8.3

FitzGerald, K. (1987). Campus Report: Is There a Drinker in the House? [Wellesley's Alchohol Informational Theatre] *Ms,* 15:30 (February).

Recording sources, on an index card provides a simple and accurate method of logging your references.

"K. FitzGerald" is the author, "il" indicates that the article is illustrated, and finally, "Ms" refers to the publication in which the article appeared. The "15.30 F '87" refers to the volume number (15), the page number (30), and the date (February 1987). Mary notes all this information and checks if the library carries *Ms*. If it does, she is in business. The next step is to find the article, make notes, and perhaps use the notes in the speech.

You will undoubtedly find that some periodicals listed in the *Reader's Guide* are not available in your library, but it will probably have enough periodicals to help you gather information. Be sure that you do not confine your search to one month or even one year of the index. You may want to go back several years in search of material.

Record your information carefully. You will want to be able to use the data to construct a bibliography. You might record the entry above on an index card as shown in Figure 8.3. If you are to submit a bibliography with your speech, you can simply alphabetize the cards and type them in a list.

Books: The Card Catalog

Every library has a card catalog that lists many types of entries—by author, title, and subject. The *subject* entries will be of greatest use to you.

Looking through the card catalog, you might find an entry similar to the one in Figure 8.4. This card indicates that the library has a book titled *Computer-mediated Information Systems* and that it covers information networks, computer networks, and electronic mail systems. It was coauthored by Roxanne Starr. The rest of the material on the card tells you where to find the book and how it is cross-listed.

Figure 8.5 shows cards for another book on another topic. Three different cards for the same book means that the book is cataloged in the library under different categories. You can look under the author's name, the title of the book, or the general subject.

Figure 8.4

Kerr, Elaine B.
                Computer-mediated Information Systems
             (Human communication research series)

Includes index.
1. Information Networks. 2. Computer Networks.
3. Electronic Mail Systems. I. Hiltz, Starr Roxanne.
II. Title. III. Series.
TK5105.5k47   1982   001.64'404   8208841
ISBN 0-12-404980-X   AACR2

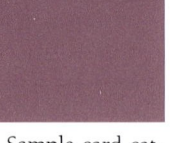

Sample card catalog entry, by author.

Figure 8.5

One book is cataloged under three entries: general category, author's name, and title of the book.

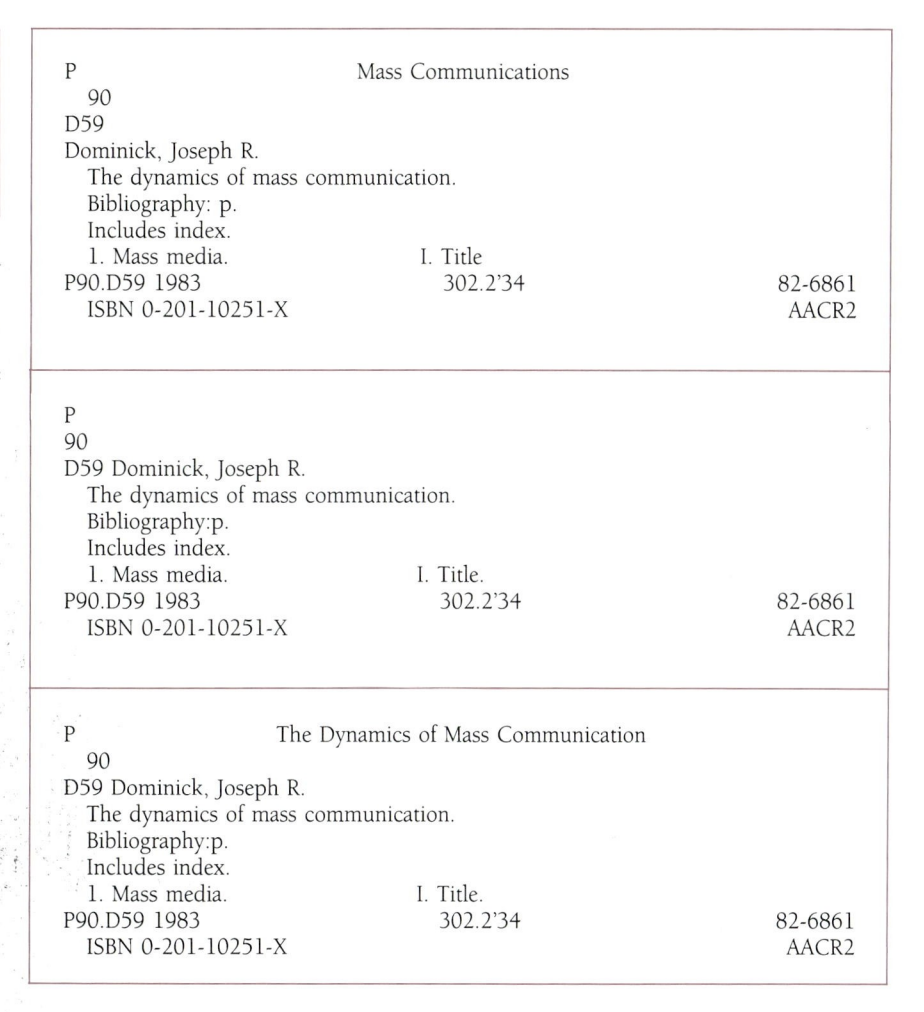

```
P                        Mass Communications
  90
D59
Dominick, Joseph R.
   The dynamics of mass communication.
   Bibliography: p.
   Includes index.
     1. Mass media.         I. Title
P90.D59 1983                  302.2'34            82-6861
   ISBN 0-201-10251-X                             AACR2
```

```
P
  90
D59 Dominick, Joseph R.
   The dynamics of mass communication.
   Bibliography:p.
   Includes index.
     1. Mass media.         I. Title.
P90.D59 1983                  302.2'34            82-6861
   ISBN 0-201-10251-X                             AACR2
```

```
P                  The Dynamics of Mass Communication
  90
D59 Dominick, Joseph R.
   The dynamics of mass communication.
   Bibliography:p.
   Includes index.
     1. Mass media.         I. Title.
P90.D59 1983                  302.2'34            82-6861
   ISBN 0-201-10251-X                             AACR2
```

Current Events

Current events can often be used as sources. Record the event and where you heard about it (radio or TV news, newspapers, or other sources) and enter it in your bibliography in the same manner. For example, if you are working on a speech concerning alcohol and youth, the daily newspaper is a rich source of instances of arrests for drunk driving, accidents, and so on. Events are reported in the newspapers long before they get into the library. And don't forget editorials and letters-to-the-editor. All of these can be extremely helpful.

Computer Databases

One interesting source of information is a computer database. Numerous databases are available to anyone who has access to a personal computer and a modem. Some of these information services are available through major newspapers, others are provided by stockbrokers and similar organizations. News and reference systems are available. Your library probably has a computer search system available for specific topics, but these systems are sometimes expensive.

The computer is becoming more important as an information source in our society, and students of speech should be willing to use this source as readily as they use the library.

Selecting Materials—Speech Composition

Once you have gathered all of your material, your next step is to compose your speech. You have the "raw material"; you now need to figure out what it means, where you're going with it, and why it will have impact on your audience. One task, of course, is the organization of the material (see Chapter Nine), but before you are ready to organize, you need to rethink the purposes of the speech, and determine if your research has changed your mind in any way. Often research does that. Then you need to look at your goals once again.

In Chapter Seven, we discussed the aim of speech content to change the audience's percepts, constructs, and affects—what many psychologists call "cognitive" elements. Let's look at what you can do with your material to try to change these elements.

Adding New Perceptions

How do you use material to affect the audience's perceptual process? Suppose, for example, that you have selected "The Vanishing Prairie" as your topic. Your goal is to get your audience to perceive the prairie as it once was and as it is today. You plan to present information about the prairie, but you know that mere facts will never give your listeners a sense of the way the prairie was when the bison roamed over it, and the way it has been transformed into suburban lawns and kept artificially green with chemicals. So you need to use material that relays these sensations—sights, smells, scope, vista, and so on. Probably the best way to make these sensations vivid is to use examples and illustrations.

Examples

There are generally two kinds of *examples: real* and *hypothetical*. Real examples come from your own experience ("My Uncle Jim once had a problem of this type...") or from one of your sources ("The National Association of Manufacturers, for example, handles alcoholism by ..."). When you use one of your sources, it is useful to cite your source. It's fine to preface your use of examples with the phrase "for example," but don't overdo it.

Hypothetical examples are those that you invent. If you would say "Let's take the typical college student and look at the pressures exerted on him or her to drink. If this typical student is in a fraternity or sorority, for example, this is what will happen to him or her." In composing hypothetical examples, you are usually describing a "typical" item—a typical worker, mother, or widget that serves your purpose. Or you might want to describe a typical dam, highway, or telephone system. This process is limited only by your imagination, but the example should be *functional,* that is, it is needed to change the audience's percept system.

Postman's recollection about numbers, in Figure 8.1, is an extended example, one that is not only personal but particularly striking.

Illustrations

An illustration is a particularly vivid example. It contains more references to sensory impressions than the ordinary example and serves the same purpose that a diagram or a picture does. An illustration, in other words, is a *verbal picture*. The language of the illustration does not have to be flowery or overblown, but it can be loaded with sense impressions that will have the most effect in changing percepts.

Look at this illustration used by a student in a course in basic public speaking:

> *Over one hundred years ago, the famous American writer, Mark Twain, took a trip to Hawaii, on assignment from a newspaper. Twain left from San Francisco on a schooner, a relatively fast sailing vessel. The trip took seventeen days. Twain visited two islands and then came home. His total travel and visiting time was over six months. Last year my mother and father visited Hawaii. They left from Chicago and were in Honolulu in eight hours. They visited four islands and were back home in nine days. Twain's trip was such a curiosity that his lectures on Hawaii were highly popular. Today travel to Hawaii is so common that hardly anyone remarks about it. (Used with permission of Sandra Larson.)*

Changing Concepts and Language

Another important communicative task is altering the audience's concepts by offering new language structures or elements. In the speech about the prairies, for example, you might want your audience to connect the symbol "prairie" with a new set of concepts—a definition.

Definitions

Definitions are an important source of material for a speech, but you must be careful not to overemphasize formal definitions. In the novel *Hard Times,* Charles Dickens satirized a typical schoolmaster, Thomas Gradgrind, who had two pupils: one (Sissy Jupe) had lived among horses all her life, and the other (Bitzer) had never seen a horse.

> *"Girl number twenty unable to define a horse!" said Mr. Gradgrind, for the general behoof of all the little pitchers. "Girl number twenty possessed of no facts in reference to one of the commonest animals! Some boy's definition of a horse! Bitzer, yours!"*
>
> *The square finger moving here and there alighted on Bitzer. "Quadruped, gramnivorous. Forty teeth, namely twenty-four grinders, four eyeteeth, and twelve incisive.*

Sheds coat in the spring; in marshy countries sheds hoofs, too. Hoofs hard, but requiring to be shod with iron. Age known by marks in mouth." Thus (and much more) from Bitzer.

"Now girl number twenty," said Mr. Gradgrind, "You know what a horse is."

Too much emphasis on definitions is not useful, but definitions are important in certain specified instances.

Comparison and Contrast

Concepts can sometimes be changed through *comparison* and *contrast*. By comparing one concept to another, you often bring about change simply because of the nature of the two contrasting concepts. Consider this comparison made by the famous nineteenth-century orator, Wendell Phillips, in his dramatic speech, "Toussaint L'Ouverture."

I would call him Napoleon, but Napoleon made his way to empire over broken oaths and through a sea of blood. This man (L'Ouverture) never broke his word. "No Retaliation" was his great motto, and the rule of his life. I would call him Cromwell, but Cromwell was only a soldier, and the state he founded went down with him into his grave. I would call your attention to Washington, but the great Virginian held slaves.

This speech is usually considered one of the greatest of all time, and you can see how the use of comparison and contrast enhances the effect for which Mr. Phillips strived.

Altering Affects

A third source of material for your speech is aimed at changing the audience's emotional state. Examples and illustrations can be helpful, but several other devices are particularly useful in stimulating affective changes.

Repetition

Repetition is useful because it shows the speaker's emotion and is arousing in and of itself. When William Jennings Bryan spoke to the Democratic National Convention in 1900, repetition of the phrase "Behold a republic" was one of the strongest elements in what everyone agrees may have been his most important speech.

I can conceive of a national destiny surpassing the glories of the present and the past—a destiny which meets the responsibilities of today and measures up to the possibilities of the future. Behold a Republic resting securely upon the foundation stone quarried by revolutionary patriots from the mountain of eternal truth! Behold a Republic in which civil and religious liberty stimulates all to earnest endeavor, and in

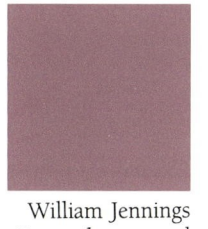

William Jennings Bryan, lawyer and politician, was considered one of America's foremost orators. He gained national recognition as the attorney for the prosecution during the famous Scopes Monkey trial. (© UPI/Bettmann Newsphotos)

which the law restrains every hand uplifted for a neighbor's injury—a Republic in which every citizen is sovereign, but in which no one cares to wear a crown. Behold a Republic standing erect while empires all around are bowed beneath the weight of their own armaments—a Republic whose flag is loved while other flags are only feared. Behold a Republic increasing in population, in wealth, in strength, and in influence, solving the problems of civilization and hastening the coming of a universal brotherhood—a Republic which shakes thrones and dissolves aristocracies by its silent example, and gives light and inspiration to those who sit in darkness. A Republic whose history, like the path of the Just, "is as the shining light that shineth more and more unto the perfect day."

Quotations

Quotations can stimulate affect if they come from a source with whom the audience has a high degree of identification, and of course, if they actually show a high degree of affective involvement. It is difficult to read a quotation as effectively as the original source presented it, and the student should remember that "declamation" of the quotation is not necessary. The rule of thumb is that the quotation is presented word-for-word *only* if the original source's words are so compelling or so interesting that a paraphrase would do it a disservice.

Listening for Content in Speeches

Your largest task in listening to speeches is to decide what is important and what is less important. You will recall from Chapter Three that you can listen as a short-term activity, short-term with rehearsal, or long-term. Moving information from the short-term to the rehearsal mode is not difficult; moving information from the rehearsal mode into long-term memory is much more difficult. It is usually impossible to transfer the entire speech to long-term memory.

Listening for the "Big Picture"

Your first act in listening to any presentation is to try to decide what is truly important, keeping in mind that no more than 30 to 40 percent of the content can be retained. Some focus is therefore necessary. You must make judgments throughout the speech on whether a specific point is worth storing or if the point is only meant to support a larger point or purpose. Though listening for some detail is necessary, you should not clutter up the memory with details at the expense of losing the major point of the speech.

These decisions apply to the *selection* part of listening. The specific act of *retention* involves long-term memory, and requires specific strategies. First, you should rephrase the speaker's illustrations or examples in your own words. Rephrasing statistical data is easy and probably should be done in words that you understand. If a speaker mentions that one out of ten American adults suffers some kind of mental illness, you might think of the size of your high school graduating class and then project the ratio of one-tenth to that group. The image of your class containing twenty-five (say) persons who are in danger of suffering from mental illness is a particularly powerful rephrase.

Second, you should repeat. *Repetition* is a powerful aid to memory.

Third, you should *interpret*. What the content means *to you* may be different from what it means to the speaker. Your conclusions and those of the speaker may or may not be the same. You should keep in mind, however, that your interpretation is (at this point) designed to help you retain the content; more detailed interpretation will follow later.

Note-taking

Research is not clear on whether note-taking is useful because it helps us remember or because we then have a written record of the content. Most research, however, tells us that taking notes should not be done unless the notes can be saved and referred to again. Subsequent reading of the notes then creates a better retention base for information.

Note-taking sometimes creates more problems than it solves. If you are concentrating on writing up notes, you may miss specific nonverbal cues that are vital to interpretation of a speaker's intent. For example, if a speaker intended a statement as a joke, a smile might accompany the content. The listener whose eyes were fixed on the note page would miss the intended irony and record the joke as a serious comment.

Note-taking is helpful in many instructional settings but should be carefully controlled in others. Many skilled speakers prepare handouts that make note-taking unnecessary, and this practice should always be encouraged.

Summary

The process of acquiring material for a speech is a complex one. First you need to become knowledgeable on the topic, primarily to enhance your credibility on the topic, but more importantly to *qualify* as a speaker. No one should speak to an audience who does not have the credentials certifying that one has have the right to speak—and the most important credential is knowledge of the topic.

Materials are of two basic types—firsthand and secondhand. Firsthand materials are those ideas, experiences, feelings, and background that you bring to the situation. Ideas come to us not only through inspiration but also through applying principles, called "topics," to the subject matter. Experience needs to be related to the implications inherent in the experience. Our personal emotions and backgrounds also hold great promise as a source of material for speeches.

Secondhand material, often called "research," is also important. Of the many valid kinds of research, the most accessible to students in beginning speech courses are the personal interview and the library.

After the basic materials are selected, the speaker needs to look at the kinds of changes called for by the speech. Changes in percepts, affects, and language are affected by speech content. Examples and factual data most often affect the percepts; comparison and definition are the best bets for changing concepts and language; and repetition and quotations are the most useful for affective changes.

Effective listening involves decisions about the importance of content and whether particular items are designed to supplement a main point or should be retained for their own worth. Though note-taking is often useful, it should not interfere with other parts of the presentation.

On Your Own

1. Visit the library on your campus and find the card catalog and *Reader's Guide*. Does the library carry any other indexes? What are their names and what do they index?

2. Make a list of persons you know personally who have some particular expertise (golfers, chessplayers, etc.). How could each one of these help you prepare a speech?

3. Compare an article in the *Encyclopaedia Brittannica* to an article on the same subject in any other encyclopaedia. How are they different? How are they the same?

4. Listen to the evening news presented by local reporters and by national television reporters (NBC, CBS, ABC, CNN). What sources do they use? How do they make themselves believable?

Suggestions For Further Reading

Corbett, E. 1965. *Classical rhetoric for the modern student.* New York: Oxford University Press.

Reid, L. 1982. *Speaking well.* New York: McGraw-Hill.

Williams, F. 1985. *The new communications.* Belmont, CA: Wadsworth.

Nine

Organizing the Speech

It is human nature to seek organization in thought, in action, and in deed.

Francis Bacon

Key Terms

formalistic
motivated sequence
retention
code words
structure
chronological
spatial
logical
problem-solving
cause-effect
introduction
conclusions
equivalency
subordination
transitions
outline terms

Objectives

After studying this chapter, you should be able to:

1. Understand the purposes of organization
2. Enumerate the types of organization: chronological, spatial, logical, problem-solving, and cause-effect
3. Assemble an introduction and a conclusion to a speech
4. Understand the basic headings in an outline
5. Use an outline as an aid to delivery
6. Recognize proper organization as an aid to listening

Now that you have analyzed your audience, formulated a purpose, selected a topic, and chosen the material, the next step is to devise an overall structure for the speech. When you begin to organize your material, you will discover relationships among ideas and more importantly, you will arrive at a good overall plan that will make your speech effective.

First, a coherent form will make listening to and retaining your speech easier for your audience. Second, a well-organized presentation will enhance your credibility. Third, careful organization will aid composition and analysis. Often in organizing material you discover a relationship among ideas that you didn't know was present. For these and many other reasons, good organization is a vital part of speech preparation.

Rationales for Organization

Through the years, teachers of public speaking have offered several different rationales for organizing communication. The first, the "formalistic" rationale, stems from our rhetorical tradition and argues that a well-organized speech is "good form." The second, a more utilitarian rationale, contends that audiences think in certain patterns and that speakers should follow these patterns in order to be effective. The third rationale argues that organization is a vital aid to retention of content, and a fourth claims that organization helps the audience understand the speech's content. Each of these arguments is a good reason for organizing speeches. Let's look at each in detail.

Formalistic Patterns

Our rhetorical tradition has given us a number of *formalistic* approaches to the construction of a speech. Classical rhetoricians prescribed a number of steps—a "standard" plan—that all speakers should follow:

1. *Exordium* or introduction
2. *Narratio*, the exposition of the facts of the case
3. *Confirmatio*, the presentation of your case
4. *Confutatio*, the refutation of your opponents
5. *Peroratio*, the conclusion (some rhetorics included a step called *divisio*, in which the speaker outlined what he was going to say right after the *exordium*).

Speeches were organized in this fashion because form was thought to be extremely important and sometimes more important than content. Audiences of that time expected a speaker to follow such a form, and speakers who deviated were considered ignorant of the "truth." We still believe this in many ways. A "formal" affair specifies the kind of dress that the men will wear, black tie (tuxedo) or white tie (tails). Everyone must look the same to satisfy the requirements of form. This is a holdover from earlier traditions, just as the formal approach to communication is still with us in many ways.

Inductive

When you make a number of specific points and then draw a general conclusion from them, you are using inductive organization. Induction is thought to be the basis of empirical thought. For example, if you see thousands of sea gulls and observe that none of them is larger than a pelican, you conclude that "sea gulls are smaller than pelicans." The induction method of reasoning is discussed in detail more specifically in Chapter Thirteen.

In terms of a speech, using inductive order means that you save the conclusion, or the main point, to the end, and hope that the many subordinate points that you make along the way will lead the audience to the same conclusion. Many instructors call this "climactic" order, in that you start slowly and finish "with a bang" with your main point.

Deductive

Deductive logic begins with a general premise and draws specific conclusions from it. For example: "A tight money policy is favorable for wealthy Americans but causes high unemployment. Therefore, a tight money policy can be characterized as a 'help the rich' policy. Any president who consistently advocates such a policy can be characterized as a friend of the wealthy." This is a simple example, and many speakers use more elaborate deductive organization.

In 1953, President Dwight Eisenhower addressed the United Nations with a proposal to set up an International Atomic Energy Agency. He reasoned this way:

Monopolies by great powers of atomic materials tend to lead to confrontation and danger of war.

An international atomic agency would reduce monopolies and diffuse knowledge about atomic materials.

Therefore an international atomic agency would reduce tension and the risk of war between great powers (Public Papers of the Presidents, 1953).

Problem-Solving Organization

When you proceed from the definition of a problem to the proposal of a solution, you are using a *problem-solving* plan. In plans of this type, you often define the problem in terms of the motives that create the problem, the barriers that frustrate the motives, and the goal to which the motives are addressed. Problem-solving plans are particularly useful when your purpose is to persuade the audience.

A speech advocating a nuclear freeze, for example, might begin with a statement of the basic desire to avoid war and live in peace. The speaker might then explore the threat of nuclear destruction in terms of the vast numbers of nuclear armaments available to world powers and the rising probability of their use. This would constitute a statement of the problem and its dimensions. A nuclear "freeze" would then be proposed as a solution to the problem posed.

Chronological Order

"Chronological" means according to time sequence—the Greek word *chronos* means "time." Many times your subject matter will fit a time sequence nicely. When you organize your material this way, you are using *chronological* order. Instructional speeches of any kind usually fit chronological organization rather well. For example, if your topic is "How To Pitch a Tent," you would probably start at the beginning: "First, choose your site," go to the next step, "Clear off the site," and so on until the tent is pitched. You might conceivably follow some other plan, but the time-sequence plan makes good sense for this kind of subject matter.

Spatial Organization

Spatial organization is very useful for describing the appearance of objects, especially in a speech that is aimed at developing percepts. Suppose you have chosen "Football" for your topic. You might begin with the positioning of the linemen and their functions, and then explain the same for linebackers, and lastly, discuss the defensive backs and the safeties. In so doing, you have organized your presentation according to the positioning or spatial order of the players.

Logical Plans

At the beginning of this chapter we mentioned that thought processes and organization are related. When thought processes are paramount, you might want to follow a *logical* pattern in constructing your speech. Of the many ways of approaching logical organization, two of the most popular are inductive and deductive.

One of America's most famous lawyers, Clarence Darrow is best remembered as the attorney for the defense in the Scopes Monkey trial. (© UPI/Bettmann Newsphotos)

Organizing the Speech

- Think
- React
- Analyze
- Speak
- Hear

You could then point out to your listeners that they need only remember the code word "TRASH"—an acronym for the five steps—to recall the steps themselves.

Code words are a handy organizational device but sometimes require a great deal of imagination and planning. They might have unfortunate connotations (like "trash" above), and they risk becoming overly cute.

Increasing the Audience's Understanding

Scott, Osgood, and Peterson (1979) have examined individual differences among people from the point of view of "cognitive structure" and found that each of us seems to use structural schemas to some degree in our storage of beliefs, percepts, language, and affects. These structures are the associative methods we use to organize and integrate these mental events. In other words, we need some internal plan to keep everything straight so that we can use our knowledge. Cognitive "differentiation" is one of the important activities that helps us do this.

Individuals need to be able to differentiate between beliefs about school, for example, and beliefs about trees. This means that if an audience doesn't presently have a schema for concept differentiation, the communicator must supply one.

Another way of considering "understanding" is the alteration of the receivers' schema systems. As discussed in Chapter Two, schemas are the "templates" by which we interpret our experience. One of the principal goals of communicative activity is the alteration of schema systems. Each of us has a set of schemas (personal schemas, political schemas, school schemas, and so on) that help us structure reality. Your "restaurant" schema, for example, strongly affects your behavior and perceptions when you go out to eat. Your behavior and the behavior of the restaurant's employees operate within the strict boundaries of this system; you do not bring your own bread and butter, for example. The essential element in this schema is the nature of the relationships among all of the persons involved—in other words, *structure*. In the same way, the organizational plan you adopt in structuring communication can strongly affect the schemas of both you and your receivers.

The essentials of your subject matter and your purpose will, in the end, determine the nature of your organizational plan. Here are a number of alternatives.

Types of Organization

A message can be organized in several ways, depending on your topic, your audience, and you. Sometimes one topic can be organized several different ways, so you will have to make a decision. Let's look at a few of your options.

Marcus Tullius Cicero (106–43 BC), Roman statesman and author is considered one of the finest classical rhetoricians. (© The Bettmann Archive)

Following the Audience's Thought Sequences

Motivated Seq:
attn
need
satisfact

Another approach is that a speech should follow the logical "thought sequences" that most persons use when they solve problems. Building on this idea, Alan H. Monroe, an influential educator from Purdue University, invented an organizational plan that he called the *motivated sequence*, which was both a model and a plan for organizing messages. His idea was that a speech should follow the way persons think or at least the way they look at a message. The "motivated sequence" begins with an "attention" step, proceeds to a "need" step, a "satisfaction" step, a "visualization" step, and concludes with an "action" step. You can see that this is probably an excellent plan for persuasive messages.

Though the thought sequence approach to organization is useful, it does not fit all topics and communicative tasks. In addition, no two people seem to "reason" in the same fashion (see Chapter Thirteen). It is difficult to force an audience into your interpretation of a "natural" thought sequence if they don't think that way.

Aiding Retention

The third reason for organizing a speech is that individuals organize their own thoughts in order to remember them. A speaker can offer a useful cognitive plan to help the audience keep the elements of the message in order. For example, *code words* make useful mnemonic (memory) aids and useful plans. Suppose you are preparing a speech about the communication process, and you decide that your audience should remember a series of five steps:

Organizing the Speech ■ ■ ■ **125**

Cause-Effect Order

When you proceed by analyzing events and their causes, you are using *cause-effect* organization. Most cause-effect reasoning is indirect. For example, cigarette smoking is commonly considered a cause of lung cancer, but the relationship is far from clear. Cigarette smokers have about one chance in ten of contracting lung cancer and nonsmokers have about one chance in 270. Though the difference between 10 and 270 is persuasive and may lead to the conclusion that cigarettes actually "cause" lung cancer, most of the studies are correlational in nature and strict cause and effect cannot be demonstrated.

Introductions and Conclusions

Even though cause-effect is a useful speech plan, one must be careful not to assume too much. Once the body of the speech is constructed, other organization is still needed. An *introduction* and a *conclusion* are two important organizational elements that will help the audience make sense of the content. The simplest form of speech organization has four parts: introduction, thesis, body, and conclusion. Up to now in this chapter, we have been discussing the body of the speech only. To this body of material you must now add an introduction and a conclusion.

Introductions

An introduction has two purposes: to *capture attention* and to *orient* the audience. Capturing attention is important throughout the speech, but it is crucial in the introduction. Attention is traditionally captured by loud noises, flashing lights, rapid motion, and other strong stimuli. Logically, then, you should be flashy, loud, fast, and noisy. Good taste, however, should always be observed. For example, one student began her speech this way:

"It could kill you! You could die! It's serious! Everyone of us can get it! It's AIDS!"

This introduction seriously oversteps the bounds of good taste. There are more discreet methods of arousing the interest of the audience. Most audiences are ready to turn you off the minute that you begin to bore them, but if you grab their interest early in the speech, you have a better chance of keeping it throughout the speech. Some methods include a startling statement, an interesting story, or a little-known fact. Visual material is sometimes good in the introduction. Formal salutations, such as "Mrs. President! Delegates of the Rose Society! Visitors and Friends!" are poor and do little to advance audience understanding or relationships.

Many speakers feel compelled to introduce their speeches with a joke or humorous anecdote. This is best left strictly to the professionals. It is difficult to tell a funny story and even more difficult to find one that is relevant to your speech. Humor should be pertinent; otherwise, you waste time that you could be using to present your main ideas. In addition, you might tell what you think is a hilarious story and receive no laughs. In other words, you must be extremely cautious in your use of humor, especially in the introduction.

Organizing the Speech

The second purpose of an introduction is to orient the audience to your topic. Many people need time to become accustomed to subject matter, so it is extremely important to allow the listeners to adjust to you and the topic. The introduction is usually a good time for externalization—a personal statement about your interest in the topic and why you wish to speak about it.

Everyone at some point should say "In my presentation (speech, talk) today, I wish to discuss ..." and be very specific in describing your topic. Then you should continue: "In discussing _____, I plan first to treat _____, then _____," and so on. In other words, give an advance "blueprint" of whatever is coming. Only when you become more proficient in public speaking will you want to deviate from this kind of initial statement:

> Whatever you might think, I didn't come here today to discuss the Illinois football team. I do want to talk about a serious problem the football players face today—the increasing burdens involved in big-time athletics and the demands of the classroom.

Conclusions

As mentioned previously, you can't beat this homely advice: "Tell 'em what you're going to tell 'em, tell 'em, tell 'em what you told 'em"; in other words, your conclusion should summarize your main points. Many students have problems summarizing, which means that they have not fully mastered the art of organization. Summarizing entails condensing your speech into a one-minute segment and then repeating it. The summary may consist of the main points or the topic sentences in each of your paragraphs. The art of summarizing is invaluable. President Eisenhower insisted that his aides submit one-page summaries of particular issues, regardless of how complicated they seemed.

Other kinds of conclusions make use of exemplification, narration, repetition, and the like. These kinds of conclusions are usually employed in persuasive speaking. Notice how Marcus Garvey, a pioneer Black separatist, uses repetition in the conclusion to his 1922 defense of the United Negro Improvement Association.

> We shall march out, not forgetting the blessings of America. We shall march out, not forgetting the blessings of civilization. We shall march out with a history of peace before and behind us, and surely that history shall be our breastplate, for how can man fight better than by knowing that the cause for which he fights is righteous? How can man fight more gloriously than by knowing that behind him is a history of slavery, a history of bloody carnage and massacre inflicted upon a race because of its inability to protect itself and fight? Shall we not fight for the glorious opportunity of protecting and forevermore establishing ourselves as a mighty race and nation, nevermore to be disrespected by men. Glorious shall be the battle when the time comes to fight for our people and our race (O'Neill, 1971).

Outlining

The first formal assignment that you will probably have in this class is to construct an outline. Outlines are very useful because they tell you where you are, and where you are going—think of an outline as a road map. First you need to master the mechanics of the system.

Heading System

The foundation of an outline is a heading system. Two principles are involved in constructing the system: *equivalency* and *subordination*. When ideas are equivalent, they get the same level headings. Subordinate ideas are placed under the main heads, as shown below:

> Main divisions—roman numerals
> First subordination—capital letters
> Second subordination—numbers
> Third subordination—lower case letters
> Fourth subordination—numbers in parentheses
> Fifth subordination—lower case letters in parentheses

This procedure results in an outline that looks like the one shown in Figure 9.1.

To understand how outlines work, let's return to Mary who has chosen to speak on alcohol usage. After going to the library, conducting some interviews, and thinking about the issues, Mary ended up with many note cards, three of which are shown in Figure 9.2.

Mary could continue to gather material, but time is short, and the assignment is due soon. Examining the sources, Mary decides that alcohol poses a serious

Figure 9.1

```
I.   ---------------------
     A.  ---------------------
         1.  ---------------------
         2.  ---------------------
             a.  ---------------------
             b.  ---------------------
                 (1)  ---------------------
                 (2)  ---------------------
             c.  ---------------------
         3.  ---------------------
             a.  ---------------------
             b.  ---------------------
                 (1)  ---------------------
                 (2)  ---------------------
                     (a)  ---------------------
                     (b)  ---------------------
             c.  ---------------------
         4.  ---------------------
     B.  ---------------------
         1.  ---------------------
         2.  ---------------------
II.  ---------------------
```

The heading system used in outlines indicates and organizes ideas. Each level is either an equivalent idea, or a subordinate idea.

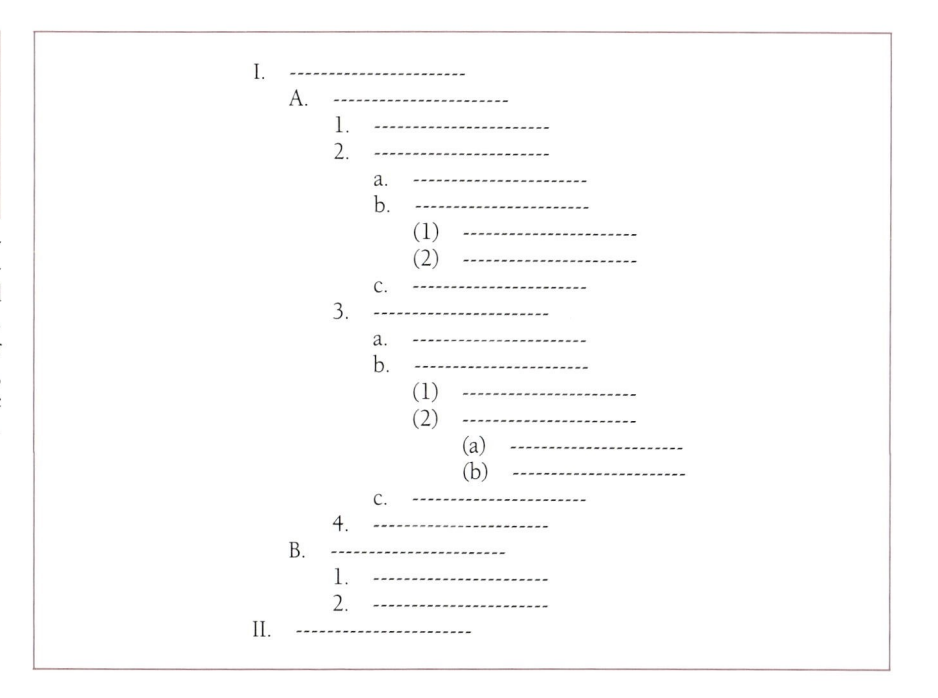

Figure 9.2

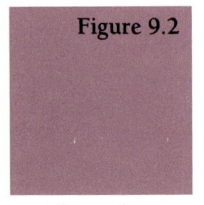

Three of Mary's many notes.

> "About one-fourth of American homes have been afflicted by an alcohol-related family problem, according to a new Gallup survey. That is the highest incidence of problem drinking recorded... twice the level recorded in 1974."
> <u>Los Angeles Times</u>, April, 1986.
> "More Think Drinking is a Problem" George A. Gallup, Sr.

> "In pastoral counselling, the single most serious problem is alcohol abuse."
>
> Father Milton Spring
> Sacred Heart Cathedral
> Interview, August 1, 1987.

> Alcoholism treatment is better than nothing, but much of it is ineffective.
> Constance Holden, "Is Alcoholism Treatment Effective?" <u>Science</u>, v. 236, April 3, 1987, pp. 20-22.

threat, that its use is widespread, and that treatment is difficult. The first rough attempt at an outline might look like this:

> Thesis: Alcohol is one of the most dangerous drugs confronting our society today.
> I. The use of alcohol is far more widespread than most people think.
> II. Alcohol is actually a dangerous drug.
> III. Alcoholism is difficult to treat.

Preparing the Speech

These three main points of the presentation will determine the rest of the structure. (Notice that the material follows a *topical* form, rather than chronological, spatial, or other organizational scheme [a term used when other schemas don't fit].) She is now ready to proceed with further subdivisions.

Let's look at the first main division, "The use of alcohol is actually far more widespread than most people think." Mary sees that there is quite a contrast between what many people (especially college students) think about the effects of alcohol and what it actually does. Therefore, Mary decides to subdivide this part of the outline into two portions: What people generally think about alcohol and what the experts say. The first main point would then look like this:

I. The use of alcohol is far more widespread than most people think.
   A. Many people feel that alcohol is harmless.
   B. Expert opinions say that it is dangerous.

Now Mary is ready to fill in the subdivisions with new material and use her research. The first main point might look like this:

A. Many people feel that alcohol is harmless.
   1. Alcohol forms an important part of our social life.
      a. Fraternal organizations on this campus host social events around beer consumption.
      b. The cocktail party is one of the most common social events in the USA.
      c. Weddings are celebrated with champagne.
   2. In contrast to other drugs, alcohol is legal.
      a. Most laws pertaining to alcohol are limited in scope.
      b. Legislatures have felt that alcohol is not as dangerous as other drugs.

Notice that as Mary proceeds with the organization of this main point, different kinds of supporting material suggest themselves. Many experts call this "amplification." Now Mary is ready to fill in the main headings with references and specific support:

A. Many people believe that alcohol is harmless.
   1. Alcohol forms an important part of our social life.
      a. Fraternal organizations on this campus host social events around beer consumption.
         (1) Last week four fraternity parties were specifically labeled "beer blasts."
         (2) One sorority here has such a reputation for beer

consumption that it is commonly known as "Lager Lou's."

    b. The cocktail party is one of the most widespread social events in the USA.

        (1) Your parents may give cocktail parties.

        (2) The first faculty function this fall was a cocktail party.

    c. Weddings are celebrated with champagne.

        (1) Traditionally, champagne toasts are given at the rehearsal dinner.

        (2) Wedding receptions almost always serve champagne.

        (3) When the bride and groom cut the cake, they typically toast the guests with champagne.

2. In contrast to other drugs, alcohol is legal.

    a. Most laws pertaining to alcohol are limited in scope.

        (1) If you are under eighteen in this state, it is illegal to purchase alcohol.

        (2) Many laws restrict the purchase of alcohol at certain times, i.e., Sunday.

        (3) Many laws restrict alcohol in certain geographic areas, i.e., a county or township.

    b. Legislatures have felt that alcohol is not as dangerous as other drugs.

        (1) Tom Wicker of the *New York Times* points out that cocaine has occupied our national attention, but alcohol is more addictive and dangerous.

        (2) The sale of alcohol generates revenue.

Now Mary is ready to fill out the other main points in the same fashion. You can see that the outlining process accomplished two goals: it organized her thinking on the subject matter of the speech, and it suggested places where she might use new material.

Outlines as Aids to Delivery

An outline also helps the delivery of the speech. Mary chose to write her outline in sentence form—each heading stated as a complete thought. An outline composed of sentences may be viewed as just another form of a manuscript since every sentence in the outline will probably appear in the final draft. This kind of outline is useful for a very formal speech and is very much like reading from a manuscript. On the other hand, an outline composed of topics—that is, one composed of key words and phrases rather than complete thoughts—is probably most helpful on the platform. You can glance at it regularly and know where you are, how you got there, and where you are going, and still focus on the audience. Before Mary actually delivers her speech, she may decide to convert her sentence outline to the more simplified, topic format.

Figure 9.3

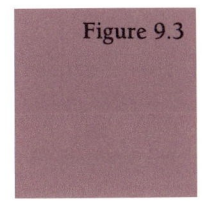

Outlines are the "signposts" that orient the listeners.

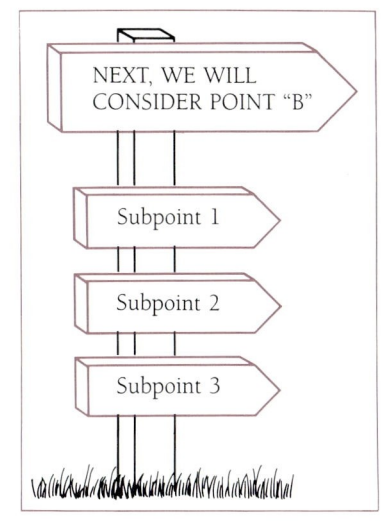

Transitions: Speaking in "Outline" Terms

It isn't enough to *be* well-organized—you should also *sound* organized. One of the ways to do this is by referring directly to your outline as you proceed from point to point. When you do this, we say that you are "speaking in outline terms." Speaking in outline terms not only "says" you are organized, but also serves as a "signpost" to guide the listener(s) through your speech (Figure 9.3).

Let's assume that Mary has finished talking about most of the material under "A.1" and is ready to move to "A.2." Her transition might sound like this:

> *Weddings are a happy time. They are also a formal time in the lives of many persons. But at weddings, we seem to place alcohol in the center of things, too. At weddings, we have champagne toasts. In addition, after the wedding, when the bride and groom are cutting the cake, a champagne toast is almost always used.*
>
> *I think you can see how alcohol is used a great deal in our social lives. Let's turn to the second reason that people believe that alcohol is harmless: the fact that other drugs are illegal and alcohol is not. This is due to two main factors: Legislative opinion is highly inconsistent here; it has only regulated the younger person's consumption, but contends that other drugs are more harmful.*

Notice how the outline *determines* the way these transitions work. Once you get the hang of speaking in outline terms, smooth transitions will come naturally to you.

Listening and Organization

Organization is also a key to good listening. If you want to retain as much of the message as possible, you should try to reconstruct the speaker's message as accurately as you can. Weaver (1972) observed that "a good listener can construct a good speech outline from a rather fuzzy one," which only means that organization can improve your listening even if the speech you're listening to is not well organized.

Organizing the Speech

Reorganizing What You Hear

The speaker's outline may be perfectly clear, but you may have an entirely different purpose in listening. In that case, you will want to fit the material into your basic schema.

You should be able to recognize different patterns of organization when you hear them in a speech. When you hear a chronological order, for example, you should ask, "Is this organization really appropriate for this topic?" If you feel that some other plan might have been better, you might ask yourself why the speaker chose the chronological plan. In this analysis, you might discover something about the speech and the speaker that you might have overlooked otherwise. You can also use your recognition of the speaker's organization to anticipate subsequent points and to remind yourself of previous ones.

Even though most speakers know the value of organization, not all speakers are organized. If this is the case, take brief notes during the speech and later, when you have a chance to reread them, superimpose your own organization on the content to make sense of it. If you have a good idea of the various kinds of organization, you can reconstruct the speaker's material and outline it into a chronological, spatial, logical, cause-effect, or other organizational scheme.

After material has been gathered, you are ready to organize your notes according to one of the organizational schemas discussed in this chapter and develop an outline.
(© Michael Markowitz, Photo/Graphic Arts)

Preparing the Speech

In informal settings, where listeners are permitted questions, it may be helpful to ask the speaker a question that validates your organization. For example, to validate your imposed cause-effect order, you might ask, "Do you think that we might look at A as a cause of B?"

The important thing is to try to make sense of the speaker's organization, and either as you're listening or later, be able to relate it to your own system of percepts, schemas, and language. The interaction between the speaker's organizational system and your own is crucial.

Note-taking

Note-taking can aid in retention, but you must be careful not to spend so much time taking notes that you miss important points. In addition, assiduous note-takers are sometimes disconcerting to a speaker who enjoys some feedback from the audience's facial expressions.

If you must take notes, keep in mind that not everyone is helped by them. Those who are not as skilled in short-term listening with rehearsal are helped by taking notes, while those who are more skillful are not (Waldhart and Bostrom, 1981).

For most people, however, notes form a permanent record, a secondary "communication" that the listener can save. This means that for notes to help you, you must go over them after the speech.

Summary

Organization has several functions, the most important is providing cognitive schemas for the retention of information. There are many rationales for organization, usually classified into formal and functional. Functional rationales propose that organization helps the listeners' retention, follows their thought sequences, or helps their understanding.

Typical organizational schemas include chronological, spatial, logical (inductive and deductive), problem-solving, and cause and effect. The best type of introduction gains the attention of the audience and orients them to the speech topic. The best type of conclusion (especially for beginning speakers) is the summary.

One of the most vital tools in organizing is the outline and the outline system. Outlines can be sentence outlines or topic outlines.

A good listener creates an internal organization plan to use in assimilating and processing speech content but needs to be cautious in taking notes.

On Your Own

1. Think about the meaning of the word "disorganized" when you use it to criticize persons or speeches. What is implied by the criticism?
2. There are many ways to organize communications. Do you feel that one way is inherently best? Why or why not?

3. Show how the consistency model in Chapter Six fits into a theory of organization.
4. When a speaker is highly credible, would you advise this speaker to organize the message anyway? Why or why not?

Suggestions For Further Reading

Becker, S. 1978. Visual stimuli and the construction of meaning. In Randhawa, B., and W. Coffman (eds.) *Visual Learning, Thinking, and Communication.* New York: Academic Press.

Bettinghaus, E. 1980. *Persuasive communication.* New York: Holt, Rinehart, and Winston.

Reardon, K. 1987. *Interpersonal communication: where minds meet.* Belmont, CA: Wadsworth.

Scott, W., D. Osgood, and C. Peterson. 1979. *Cognitive structure: Theory and measurement of individual differences.* New York: John Wiley and Sons.

Schank, R., and R. Abelson. 1977. *Scripts, plans, goals, and understanding.* Hillsdale, NJ: Erlbaum.

Weaver, C. 1972. *Human listening: Processes and behavior.* Indianapolis: Bobbs-Merrill.

Part Three

Presenting the Speech

Ten

Language and the Speech

Man cannot live by bread alone. What profiteth a man if he gain the whole world and lose his own soul? Those who try to trade liberty for security usually wind up by losing both. Eternal vigilance is the price of liberty. Every journey to the forbidden land begins with the first step.

Senator Arthur Vandenberg

Key Terms

social signaling
mediated responses
symbol
abstraction
concreteness
intensity
metaphor
denotative
connotative
verbosity

Objectives

After studying this chapter, you should be able to:

1. Distinguish between social signaling and symbols
2. Understand the process of mediation in language use
3. Recognize degrees of abstraction and concreteness in words
4. Identify the use of metaphors as intensifiers
5. Explain the difference between denotative and connotative meaning
6. Provide more exact words in place of general ones
7. Avoid the use of sexist language
8. Understand the use of language cues in listening

You will recall from Chapter Two that language, schemas, percepts and affects comprise the principal elements in our cognitive system, and are all sources of material for communication as well as end products of the process. Language is of particular interest in communication because it is not only an end product but is also the principal means of transmission.

We don't often think of language as a *result* of communication, but in any message in which definition is the goal, language itself may be viewed as the content of the message. For example, you might set out to explain how the government defines "nuclear disaster." Or you might inform an audience about what meat packers mean by "choice" and "prime" meats. In both of these cases, new language usage is the principal goal of the communicative task.

Communication is defined as human interaction that uses symbol systems, that is, language. Without language, communication as we know it would be impossible.

Language and Communication: Basic Elements

Language is very different from primitive gestures and "social signaling." This may seem like a puzzling distinction at first, but it is a very meaningful one. One way to understand the differences between social signaling and communication is to look at the way animals signal one another and compare it to the way human beings communicate.

Social Signaling

Do animals communicate? They certainly engage in interactive behavior. We say, for example, that the bark of an angry dog "communicates" a warning to others that the dog is ready for action. Sexual displays of many animals also seem to have a "communicative" function.

Many animals seem to transmit information to each other: Bees tell each other the location of good sources of nectar, crows warn each other when hunters are close, and whales sing to each other. At first glance, these seem to be communicative acts. Let's look at each of these communications, and the messages they seem to carry:

Animal	Message
Bee	"If you leave the hive and fly southeast for approximately 200 meters, you will find a neat bunch of flowers that are really juicy."
Crow	"If you guys don't get out of here in ten seconds, you're gonna get blasted."
Whale	"I'm here, lover—where are you?"

These verbal interchanges, of course, never take place. When Dr. Doolittle sang his song about talking to the animals, he asserted that he learned "bear" and other animal languages. These anthropomorphic interpretations, or attributing human traits to objects or animals, are unfortunate.

Human communication, unlike animal signaling, involves the use of symbols. Here, young students are introduced to the alphabet, a set of symbols that make reading and writing possible. (© Michael Markowitz, Photo/Graphic Arts)

What really happens is that the bee enters the hive and does a fairly complex dance in circles and figure eights around the comb. Other bees begin to follow her, and the nature of the dance pattern determines all subsequent behavior. After dancing in line for awhile, the bees break out of the hive and fly at a given angle from the sun and at a given distance. The crow's "language" is really noises of alarm at the intrusion of the hunter, and science has not yet figured out whale sounds, except that they seem to make more of them when other whales are around.

These animal behaviors fall into the category of *social signaling*, a characteristic common to many species. The cat purrs when her kittens are nursing, and the kittens seem to find this comforting. Human beings also do a great deal of social signaling, using facial expressions, positions, unconscious gestures, and the like.

The principal difference between typical animal signaling and human communication is the use of symbolic activity. Most animals are incapable of using symbols. Animal activity that seems to be communicative is mostly instinctive interactive patterns. Some animals, however, do engage in behavior that may be symbolic. For example, a group of researchers at the University of California at Santa Barbara tried to teach language to a chimpanzee. They were able to build a "reading" and "writing" vocabulary of about 130 words for "Sarah," a young chimpanzee whose understanding went beyond the simple meaning of the words to include concepts of class and sentence structure. The teaching process took a long time, but the animal was able to obtain a language level comparable to that of a two-year-old child (Premack and Premack, 1972). Although this study confirmed that the use of symbols is not totally confined to humans, for all practical purposes, animals are not symbol users. In this particular experiment, it should be noted that *humans*, rather than members of the animal's own species, taught language to the chimpanzee.

What is the essential difference between social signaling and symbolic activity? Human beings have learned to "mediate" concepts (see Chapter Two) with verbalizations. At some point we learn to associate concepts with certain sounds. This process is called "mediation."

Mediated Responses

Mediation can be illustrated with examples. If you were to sit on a tack, you'd probably say "Ow!" or something similar. This response is immediate and needs no thought on your part. But if you're playing chess and your opponent says, "Are you ready to resign?" you would probably reflect on the possibilities before you agree or disagree. What you say is *mediated*, or affected by internal processes as opposed to external ones. The "Ow!" sound, then, is not mediated, and the "I resign" sound is mediated. Mediating factors, or the internal factors that influence verbal communication, can be of many types. Typical ones are motivation, degree of learning, and physiological conditions. Percepts, schemas, and affects are also important mediators. Figure 10.1 illustrates the mediated, and therefore different, responses of two individuals to the same information. Their responses are modified by their preexisting attitudes toward the speaker.

Language is one of the most complex mediators having an enormous range of use. Language is usually composed of words and structure (grammar), and words are *spoken and written symbols*.

Use of Symbols

Symbolic behavior is one of the most typically human of all our behaviors. Symbols are fundamentally associated with concepts and concept learning, and the ability to form concepts may well be the distinguishing factor defining the human species. Many organisms have the capability of responding to *classes* of stimuli rather than individual events. A bee, for example, is attracted to individual flowers and other colored objects. In other words, bees "abstract" color as a part of their perceptual system. This very useful abstraction saves the bee the trouble of learning the shape and smell of every nectar-producing flower. The simple ability to respond to color produces seeking behavior in bees that is more effective than a random search would be. In a primitive way, color is a "concept" to the bee.

As we go higher in the evolutionary ladder, animals exhibit more complex abilities to discriminate among stimuli. The higher organisms, including humans, can learn and utilize these abstractions in their behavioral routines. Wolves and coyotes learn faster than wasps and centipedes. Humans are the best learners; they have learned to associate complex sounds, or symbols called "words," with the concepts.

A *symbol*, therefore, is a sound or action that is associated with a concept or class of stimuli. For example, the word *dog* is a large class of stimuli—thousands of animals may be classified as "dog." "Terrier" is a smaller class of stimuli, and "Skye Terrier" is even smaller. Each of these is a concept.

Numbers are also concepts. When you make the sound "three" or when

Figure 10.1

The interpretation of a word is *modified* by positive or negative tendencies in the listener towards the speaker. Here, Sally announces her fiance is a painter. Her mother, who has positive tendencies towards Sally, interprets "painter" to be an artist. While Joline, Sally's envious friend, envisions "painter" as a housepainter.

you write a "3" on paper, everyone knows what you mean—not "four," or "five," or "blue." The "three" can pertain to anything: blades of grass, malted milks, or elephants. "Three" used without a particular context can present certain difficulties, and in learning mathematics, you must learn to think abstractly before you can manipulate the symbol system with facility.

As in other aspects of communication, language skill and efficiency is partly dependent on understanding. In this chapter, we will examine some of the basic principles of language and then look at ways that you can improve your language to become a better speaker.

Language and the Speech

The Study of Language

Whatmough (1956) claimed that language is the principal means by which humanity has acquired preeminence in the world:

> *Language is the means by which man symbolizes and orders his concepts of the universe.... Arrangement and rearrangement in sequence permits endless variety. Meaning in the end is limited only by the universe itself and by man's ability to comprehend it.*

Language is the essence of thinking, reading, speaking, and listening. According to psychologist George A. Miller (1951),

> *Thinking is never more precise than the language it uses. Even if it is, the additional precision is lost as soon as we try to communicate the thought to someone. The importance of a precise language is most clearly demonstrated by the value of mathematical language in science. It is only necessary to compare the Arabic with the Roman system of numbers in order to recognize the tremendous advantage of a good notation over a poor one.*

Precision is one of the most important goals of language. Because language is composed of words, precision depends heavily on agreement among users about the exact usage of words. Typically we measure precision by the degree of abstractness or concreteness in the word.

Abstract and Concrete Words

In his book, *Language In Thought and Action* (1941), S.I. Hayakawa describes an "abstraction ladder," which ranges from the very concrete to the very abstract. He points out that we might use the words *cow* or *farm asset* to describe the same physical entity. *Abstraction* is the process of using words to describe large classes of things. Unfortunately, we sometimes use a word for the larger classification when we should be using the word for the smaller classification. In Figure 10.2 we see an example of specific and abstract terms. At the center is one specific Sequoia tree in the Sierra Nevada, named the "General Sherman." However, each of the terms of each layer *also* refers to this specific tree.

Abstraction is a powerful linguistic tool, as any mathematician will tell you. The abstract phrase "a + b" can stand for 1 plus 2, or for 25 plus 29, or for 3,261 plus 4,119. Obviously, abstraction can be useful, but the individual who habitually uses the term *wheeled conveyance* instead of *1972 Pinto* is in big trouble.

In this speech, William Graham Sumner, a famous conservative advocate, asks his audience to be less abstract and more precise in its use of the word *society*:

> *When you see a drunkard in the gutter, you are disgusted, but you pity him. When a policeman comes and picks him up you are satisfied. You say that "society" has interfered to save the drunkard from perishing. Society is a fine word, and it saves us the trouble of thinking to say that society acts. The truth is that the policeman is paid by somebody, and when we talk about society we forget who it is that pays* (Sumner, 1923).

Figure 10.2

Abstraction layers: from the most specific to the most general.

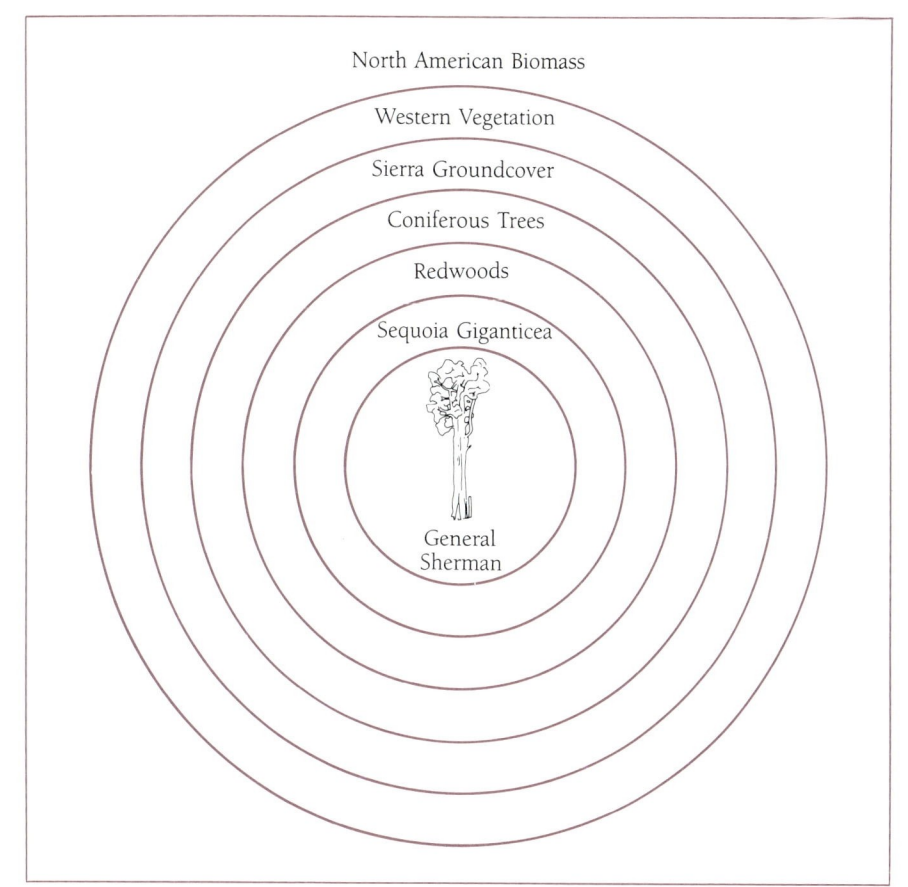

- North American Biomass
- Western Vegetation
- Sierra Groundcover
- Coniferous Trees
- Redwoods
- Sequoia Giganticea
- General Sherman

We do not, of course, recommend that everyone stop using abstract words, but using them can be dangerous in certain situations. President Reagan, for example, stoutly defended U.S. intervention in Nicaragua on the grounds that the U.S. stands for "democracy," and the Nicaraguan government stands for "communism." A few miles away, in South America, another country stands for "democracy" even though the government is repressive, stifles individual liberties, spends millions of dollars on armaments, and tortures political prisoners. When we compare these different types of governments, it would help to be accurate and concrete.

Research shows that *concrete* words are more easily remembered (Winnick and Kressel, 1965) and are generally more meaningful (Paivio and Steeves, 1967), which means that they fit into existing schemas more easily.

Intensity

Another characteristic of language that we need to be aware of is *intensity*. Some words have more intensity than others: *Fascist* is more intense than *bossy*, and *compelling* is more intense than *interesting*. Intensity can be manipulated in a number of ways. Figure 10.3 illustrates, in a very simple way, the varying degrees of intensity

Language and the Speech

Figure 10.3

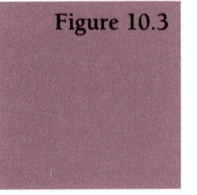

"The intensity gauge."

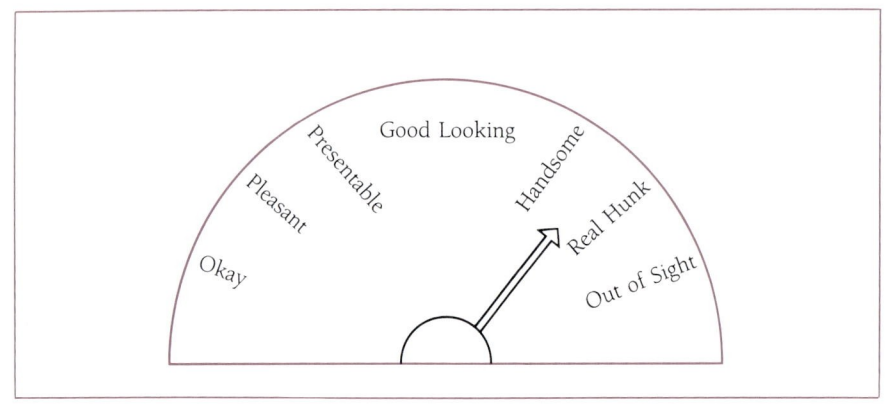

[Figure: semicircular gauge labeled from left to right: Okay, Pleasant, Presentable, Good Looking, Handsome, Real Hunk, Out of Sight]

that are possible in a situation. For example, there is clearly a significant difference in perception between an "okay" acquaintance and one who is "out of sight."

Metaphors

One of the most useful types of intensifiers is the *metaphor*—a figure of speech—that *compares* two items. In this speech Alan Alda uses the metaphor of a butcher shop to describe "midlife":

> *I think it is safe to say that a lot of you, maybe most of you, are going to experience this, since the sentence "What's the purpose of all this?" is written in large letters over the mid-life crisis butcher shop. You can't miss it as you lug the carcass of your worldly success through the door to have it dressed and trimmed and placed in little plastic packages for people to admire (Lunkugel, Allen and Johannson, 1982).*

Bowers and Osborn (1965) conducted an interesting research study on the power of metaphor by comparing literal and metaphorical conclusions in different speeches. Two examples of phrases used in literal conclusions were "Freedom is no longer with us," and "shortsighted lobbyists." The corresponding metaphorical conclusions were "This is the death rattle of liberty" and "those economic seducers." In both cases the metaphorical conclusions were more memorable and effective.

Adjectivals

Adjectives and adjectival phrases can also be used to intensify language in a speech. Notice the way Adlai Stevenson II used adjectivals in this speech describing Sir Winston Churchill:

> *The great aristocrat, the beloved leader, the profound historian, the gifted painter, the superb politician, the lord of language, the orator, the wit—yes, and the didactic bricklayer—behind them all was a man of simple faith.*

Imagine how less effective this passage would have been if he had said only "aristocrat, leader, historian, etc."

Multiple Interpretation of Words

Many words have multiple interpretations or meanings, a factor that complicates the process of using precise language. Meanings are highly individualized, as someone once said, "Meanings are not in dictionaries, but in people." To illustrate this, consider the way many people use the term *drink*. For one person, the phrase "Let's have a drink" denotes having a cocktail; to another it simply means water or a soft drink. Let's look at some of the ways we can make these meanings more intelligible.

Denotative Meaning

Denotative meaning, often called "historical meaning," is a meaning acquired through usage. This kind of meaning is typically recorded in dictionaries. For example, the word *home* is defined by *Webster's New Collegiate Dictionary* as:

1. A family's place of residence. 2. The social unit formed by a family living together. 3. A congenial environment. 4. A place of origin. 5. The objective in various games.

Garrison Keillor, former host of the popular radio show "Prairie Home Companion", is a gifted storyteller. Keillor's exceptional command of the language is evident in his Lake Wobegon stories. (© UPI/Bettmann Newsphotos)

Language and the Speech ■ ■ ■ 151

The word *home,* of course, has a variety of meanings, based on its history. The use of the word in baseball, for example, is fairly recent (in the past 100 years). Words evolve as our use of them evolves, and many interesting changes take place. A *chap* was once a peddler, and a *colonel* was once a commander who led a column (*colonello*). The *Oxford English Dictionary* lists thousands of historical usages. This fact alone ought to cure you of the idea that dictionaries contain "meanings." Actually they contain word histories, some of which are current and some of which are hopelessly out of date. Many dictionaries simply cannot keep up with current usages of many words, such as *network, interface, hardware, bug,* and the like. But this is what makes language interesting!

Connotative Meaning

Many words also have emotional resonance. If you are a college freshman who has just moved into a dormitory, you probably read the above passage on the definition of *home* with a slight emotional pang. Home has, for almost everyone, a profound emotional meaning.

Connotative meaning can be created on the spot. At one commencement ceremony, one speaker told this joke: "I am reminded of the remark the stallion at a horse farm made when they brought him a zebra instead of the expected mare. 'Okay,' he said, 'but you've got to take off your pajamas first.'" The joke got a polite titter. Fifteen minutes later, however, when the featured speaker got up and saluted the audience with "Governor Smith, Chancellor Williams, members of the faculty, distinguished guests, and fellow zebras and stallions," it was several minutes before he could continue. Not only was this speaker quick-witted, but showed understanding of the nature of immediate connotative meaning.

Using Language Effectively

You can use several strategies to make the language of your speech more effective: (1) use words that convey precise meanings; (2) avoid overworked words; (3) adapt your language to the audience and the situation; (4) avoid verbosity; (5) avoid sexist language; and (6) choose vivid, colorful language. Let's look at each of these strategies.

Using Precise Language

You should be extremely careful about your choice of words, particularly if the audience may misunderstand your meaning. If you review the section on abstractions, you will see how easy it is to be abstract when you could be specific. The following list compares some vague or abstract words and more precise equivalents:

Vague Word or Phrase	More Specific Phrase
This year	April 23
Tall	74 inches
Intelligent	Gets A's in mathematics
Slow	11 mph
Heavy	230 pounds
Europeans	Poles and Hungarians
Communists	Members of the American Communist Party
Lots of students	158 students

Audiences frequently interpret the use of vague terminology as an attempt to cover up the true meaning of what the speaker is saying.

Avoiding Overworked Words

Many words and phrases are so overused that they become trite or start to lose their meaning. In the business world, for example, "bottom line" and "welcome aboard" are two current offenders. When you hear these phrases, you can be sure that the user has paid little attention to precision or meaning.

The word *fantastic* is another example. It is used so often that it has lost much of its meaning. We hear of "fantastic" weather, a "fantastic" date, a "fantastic" car, and a "fantastic" relationship. The point should be obvious.

Adapting Your Language to the Audience and Situation

Various demographic elements differentiate one audience from another (see Chapter Six). A group of junior high students, for example, will have difficulty following a speech with elaborate vocabulary. How can you know the level of language to use with a specific audience? The *Thorndike-Barnhart* word list, based on the average vocabulary of most ninth-graders, is available in many libraries and can be a standard against which to measure the difficulty level of your word choice. You might review Chapter Six on "Audience Analysis" to check where your level ought to be.

Many other situational differences call for differences in language. A church service, for example, demands different vocabulary than does a pep rally. A political rally requires different language than does a student-faculty curriculum committee meeting.

Avoiding Verbosity

Some speakers can't seem to use one word when three hundred will do. Verbosity is another sure sign of lack of thought. Many redundancies are so habitual

Harry Truman revealed his integrity and feistiness during his famous "whistle-stop" campaign. His colorful language and earthiness delighted the voting public and ensured his victory in the presidential election. (© UPI/Bettmann Newsphotos)

that we aren't even aware of them. So we speak of a "true fact," a "final conclusion," and so on. All of us need to speak as directly and to the point as possible.

Avoiding Sexist Language

Look again at the quotation that opens this chapter and Whatmough's quotation in the "Study of Language" section. In both instances the word *man* was used when these writers meant humanity. Many males don't realize that they are offending females when they use masculine pronouns to mean persons of both genders. Consider the following phrase: "When a student takes an examination, he should check all his answers carefully." The phrase could be rephrased "When a student takes an examination, he or she should check all his or her answers carefully." A better rephrasing, however, would be "Students should check their answers carefully when taking an examination."

Sexism in language is the unfortunate residue of sexism in our society. Though we have used such words as *chairman* and *workmen's compensation* for years, we should do our best to avoid them. Avoidance of sexist language is not only common sense but shows sensitivity to the audience.

Choosing Vivid and Colorful Words

Sometimes your message needs more than just a specific word or phrase. Eloquence is a delicate matter and requires taste and imagination. Great writers and orators have the ability to use language of grace and power, but most people unfortunately do not have this talent. Just because you are not Shakespeare or Churchill, however, doesn't mean that you can't at least try to use beautiful or powerful language. If you feel that your language lacks color and power, take a course in modern literature or read some great works of poetry or literature on your own. It might give you some ideas!

Presenting the Speech

Listening and Language

One of the listener's most important tasks is to "interpret" the language of the speech. A listener can learn a good deal about the speaker—sometimes things a speaker doesn't want to reveal—from the speaker's choice of words. Suppose a speaker says "right-wing religious program" instead of "The PTL Club." We know immediately that the speaker is probably biased on the topic and that the speech will probably also be biased.

The ultimate judgment that the listener makes involves the nature of the speaker, and language is an especially effective factor in this kind of judgment. Obviously, you should not be too hasty in making these judgments, but at the same time, language tells you about the speaker's background, training, disposition toward the topic, and many more interesting details.

Similarly, assumptions about the world are often cloaked in particular terms. When the Palestine Liberation Organization (PLO) protested that the media was constantly using the word *terrorist* to describe the group, news reporters began to use the word *fighters* instead. Likewise, many people would be upset if the news media used the word *terrorist* instead of *contra* to describe the revolutionaries in Nicaragua. The use of unfair emotional terms is often called "loaded language." A person who complains about the salt content of potato chips might be called either a "consumer activist" or an "interfering busybody," depending on the speaker. You should always be aware of loaded language when listening to a speech.

Listeners can also detect other features from the speaker's use of language. Someone who constantly uses overworked words will be perceived differently than someone who uses fresh, original language. A speaker who uses abstract terms rather than specific ones probably doesn't know the topic thoroughly. Listeners can glean a good deal of information about a speech from the kinds of terminology that a speaker uses.

Occasionally a listener reacts emotionally to a presentation simply because of a word or phrase. You need to ask yourself about your own reaction; if you are simply reacting to terminology, you might reconsider. For example, a speaker who repeats the term *balanced budget* eight times in a speech is not necessarily an outstanding speaker. It might only mean that this speaker thinks that the audience will like hearing this term.

Diagnose Your Language Habits

As a good listener, you should check your own communications for the specific habits of language discussed in this chapter. If, for example, you habitually use sexist language, you might keep that in mind when you hear another speaker who commits this fault. The first question you should ask yourself is whether or not this is due to a lack of knowledge or simply a bad habit.

If ethnic or religious stereotypes are part of your vocabulary, you should ask yourself where they originated. You need to ask the same questions about the origins of this kind of language when listening to others. Other aspects of the message, such as the main purpose and the content, can help you answer these questions.

William F. Buckley, author, TV host, and founder of *The National Review,* is known for his lofty patrician manner and impressive vocabulary. (© Jan Lukan)

Language as Memory Aids

A particularly interesting phrase is easy to remember but a speech composed of dull language is difficult to retain. A good aid to retention is to reword the important points and choose words that you think will help you remember. Suppose you are listening to a presentation on the relative virtues of caliper brakes versus coaster brakes for bicycles. If you translate "calipers" to "squeezers" and "coasters" to "standers," you might remember better.

Summary

Language is one of the most important components of human communication. Language works because of mediated responses that turn into spoken symbols. Symbols are sounds or actions that correspond with concepts; they can be abstract or concrete. Language can be intensified by using metaphors and adjectivals.

Language is sometimes misunderstood because words and phrases can often have several meanings. Denotative and connotative meanings are both important. To use language effectively, you should use exact, vivid, and colorful words; avoid overworked words, verbosity, sexist language; and adapt language to the audience and situation. Listening to language often yields important information about the speaker.

On Your Own

1. Using any consumer magazine for a source, examine the kinds of words used in typical advertisements. How would you evaluate these words in terms of vividness, verbosity, and specificity? Could you use these words in a speech?
2. Do the same for a group of typical television commercials. How do these words differ from the magazine ads?
3. Analyze the language used in a typical press release issued by a political candidate. What political clichés can you find?
4. Take any typical newspaper story and see if you can shorten the words. Translate each long word into a shorter word. Does it help the story?

Suggestions for Further Reading

Bowers, J. 1963. Language intensity, social introversion and attitude change. *Speech Monographs* 30: 350–61.

Bowers, J., and M. Osborn. 1965. Attitudinal effects of selected types of concluding metaphors in persuasive speeches. *Speech Monographs* 33: 147–57.

Charmichael, C., and G. Cronkhite. 1965. Frustration and language intensity. *Speech Monographs* 32: 107–12.

Miller, G. 1951. *Language and communication.* New York: Appleton-Century-Crofts.

Paivio, A., and R. Steeves. 1967. Relations between personal values and imagery and meaningfulness of value words. *Perceptual and MotorSkills* 24: 357–58.

Weaver, C. 1957. Measuring point of view as a barrier to communication. *Journal of Communication* 7: 5–11.

Whatmough, J. 1956. *Language: A modern synthesis.* New York: Harper and Company.

Winnick, W., and K. Kressel. 1965. Tachistoscopic recognition thresholds, paired associate learning, and free recall as a function of abstractness-concreteness and word frequency. *Journal of Experimental Psychology* 70: 163-71.

Eleven

Delivery: Nonverbal Elements

Never make a gesture simply for the sake of making one.
George Frisbie Hoar

Key Terms

nonverbal
relationships
proximity
body lean
eye contact
touch
facial expression
pitch
inflection
variety
interpretive listening
delivery
quality

Objectives

After studying this chapter, you should be able to:

1. Distinguish between verbal and nonverbal communication
2. Enumerate the main nonverbal signals that occur in interpersonal communication
3. Understand how delivery of a speech relates to the general understanding of nonverbal communication
4. List the ways in which the voice can be used to enhance understanding
5. Approach listening from an interpretive point of view

If you have followed our advice up to here, you have probably composed an excellent speech with a good topic and up-to-date materials. You are now ready for the next step—delivery. Even a business with high-quality merchandise and good prices will fail if it has no organized system to get that merchandise to its customers. That is what you must do—deliver the merchandise to your customers.

Nonverbal Communication

Direct, face-to-face communication has a large channel capacity—you can "send" more than you can with a written message (see Chapter Two). This additional message capacity stems from the things that people do while they are speaking: adopt various positions, take different actions, make different movements, and produce subtle variations with their voices.

Nature of Nonverbal Communication

Simply defined, *nonverbal communication* is everything that is communicated beyond what is expressed in words. At one time or another, everyone has heard a speech in which the communicator's words seem to mean one thing but the "actions" something else. For example, examine the following interchange:

Person A: We're going tomorrow, aren't we?

Person B: Tomorrow is all right.

Person A: Is there something the matter?

Person B: No, that's fine.

Person A: Are you sure?

Person B: Sure.

Let's see how accompanying behavior might modify this interchange:

Person A: (with an intense, slightly hostile expression) We're going tomorrow, aren't we?

Person B: (with a look of intimidated disbelief) Tomorrow is all right.

Person A: (with even more hostility and frowning) Is there something the matter?

Person B: (rubbing hands together, avoiding A's gaze) No, that's fine.

Person A: (frown ceasing, sitting up) Are you sure?

Person B: (continuing to look down, putting hands in pocket) Sure.

Now let's look at the same scenario with a different set of actions:

Person A: (querulously, looking anxiously at B) We're going tomorrow, aren't we?

Person B: (looking at watch, drumming fingers on desk) Tomorrow is all right.

Person A: (edging backwards, speaking slowly) Is there something the matter?

Person B: (looking out window, picking up folder on desk) No, that's fine.

Person A: (remaining rooted to spot) Are you sure?

Person B: (placing folder in drawer, picking up another one) Sure.

After reading these scenarios, you can infer which of these persons has more power and many other qualities about them. In the first case, A is probably the boss and in the second case it is probably B. In neither case are A or B being entirely honest.

Occasionally nonverbal messages are quite direct and specific to the overall function of the communication, but more typically they concern *relationships* between two persons. Communication researchers have discovered that most relationships have specific characteristics: (1) emotional arousal; (2) intimacy; (3) immediacy; and (4) dominance and submission (Burgoon and Hale, 1981). "Emotional arousal" refers to the general level of affect that is created by the relationship; some relationships simply don't have much emotional value and others are quite stimulating. "Intimacy" refers to the level of disclosure and the kinds of activities that are part of the relationship. Married couples are typically very intimate, but often members of athletic teams or other kinds of work groups can achieve a great deal of intimacy in their relationships. "Immediacy" usually refers to inclusion (the degree to which one feels "included") or affection and is typically associated with intimates, though not always. "Dominance and submission" seem to be present in almost all relationships, whether or not they are perceived.

Common nonverbal messages that accompany relational communication are physical proximity, body lean, eye contact, touch, and facial expression. Each of these influences relational communication in typical interactions (Burgoon, Buller, Hale, and DeTurck, 1984).

Nonverbal codes vary considerably from culture to culture. Nonverbal communication in North American culture is much different than in Latin American, Middle Eastern, and Asian cultures.

Proximity

Physical *proximity* denotes intimacy in most situations. People in formal relationships usually stand about two or three feet apart. People in closer (but nonintimate) relationships are typically separated by three feet to eighteen inches. A distance of less than eighteen inches usually denotes intimate relationships. Burgoon and her associates found that close proximity also designates dominance in certain situations. Arousal is a result of proximity.

Body Lean

In standing positions, forward lean usually communicates intensity and interest. Dominance is communicated by backward lean. In interactions where both participants are seated, one person often leans far backward in the chair. This is especially easy with modern office furniture that rocks! Almost always, the person who leans back is expressing power in the relationship. If you are involved in a job interview, you would be ill-advised to lean back in this manner, because your interviewer may feel really uncomfortable—your posture would be incongruent with the situation. *Body lean* is often accompanied by infrequent eye contact.

Eye Contact

Breaking or avoiding *eye contact* is almost a sure signal of a relationship that lacks intimacy and intensity. In addition, the dominant member of a relationship feels comfortable breaking eye contact while the submissive member usually feels constrained to maintain eye contact.

Touch

Touch is one of the most obvious nonverbal messages. *Touch* denotes inclusion, affection, and sometimes control. Touching is almost never done in formal situations, at least in American culture. In other parts of the world, touch is much more acceptable, even in formal relationships.

Facial Expression

Probably the single most important element in nonverbal communication is *facial expression*, which has the most impact and the greatest range of expression of all the elements. Dr. Dale Leathers of the University of Georgia has conducted

Table 11.1

Leathers and Emigh's ten facial expression messages, and the accuracy of their perception.

Type of Emotion	Expression Number	Probability of Correct Response
Disgust	I	88%
Bewilderment	II	82%
Happiness	III	98%
Determination	IV	87%
Fear	V	91%
Anger	VI	93%
Surprise	VII	96%
Interest	VIII	87%
Contempt	IX	89%
Sadness	X	97%

Figure 11.1

Ten facial expressions (Leathers and Emigh 1980). Happiness, sadness, surprise, anger, fear, contempt, disgust, interest, determination, and bewilderment—can you tell which one is which?

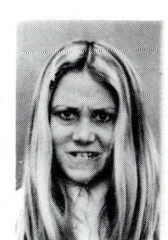

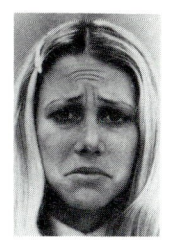

comprehensive research into the kinds of meaning your face can portray (Leathers and Emigh, 1980). Leathers and his associates have classified ten distinct "messages" in facial expressions (Figure 11-1). Table 11-1 shows the names of these emotional messages and how accurate the perception of each of these expressions is likely to be. For example, "surprise" will be identified with 96 percent accuracy, and "interest" with 87 percent accuracy. It should be clear that facial expression is probably the most powerful of all nonverbal elements available to communicators.

Now that we have a general sense of how nonverbal communication works, we can turn our attention to its function in a public speaking situation.

Putting Nonverbal Communication to Work: Delivery

As described in Chapter Three, face-to-face communication differs considerably from written messages. In speaking, delivery carries important messages that can modify and strengthen the words used in the speech.

Using Your Body

Your body can be a powerful communicator by combining nonverbal messages with the specific verbal messages that you have prepared for your speech. Let's look at some of the ways you can blend these messages in your presentation.

Facial Expression

Looking at the photographs presented in Figure 11-1, you can see that you potentially communicate ten different emotions while you speak. Many students, when first confronted with the task of reproducing these ten *facial expressions*, protest that they lack the ability or that "only a skilled actor" can do this! The young woman in these pictures obviously has great communicative sensitivity, but you do not need to be a professional actor or actress to use facial expressions.

Unfortunately, most people believe that if they merely "feel" the emotion, their faces will automatically and accurately reflect this emotion. This is not true. Although there is a direct connection between facial expression and perceived affect (Zajonc, 1985), it is unclear which causes which. In other words, facial expression may influence your emotional state as much as the converse.

Even though some persons misinterpret facial expressions, your face is one of your most powerful message generators. Whether or not you can accurately reproduce all of the expressions presented by Leathers and Emigh, we owe it to ourselves to try. Learning to smile on cue is an excellent beginning. A smile costs nothing and is extremely valuable in the right circumstances. Practice it in the bathroom mirror. Keep it up until you get it right!

Once you learn to present a winning smile (even when you don't feel like it) you are on your way to using your face as an important part of your physical repertoire. Try the ten expressions in front of a mirror at least once a day, and you will be amazed how easy it becomes.

Posture

The way you stand indicates clearly what you think of the audience, the subject, and perhaps most importantly, yourself. A physical slouch can also be a mental slouch in the minds of many audiences. Good posture is extremely important if you wish to take control of the situation.

When you have a podium or a lectern, you might lightly rest your hands on it, especially to keep notes in order. You should stand as erect behind this podium as you can, with your feet spread approximately the width of your shoulders. Many of you have been told to stand with your hands hanging "naturally" at your sides, but the sides are not usually the natural position for hands. Watch people in action in their day-to-day activities. Their hands follow their tasks and thoughts. Yours will, too.

Movement

Movement keeps audiences attentive. The natural attention span of most persons is quite short (less than two minutes), so speakers need to keep working for attention. An easy way to do this is by moving from place to place on the platform. Movements should be short, purposeful, and skillful. Usually, a movement should only consist of two or three steps.

An excellent time for movement is at one of the natural breaks in your speech, when you are going from one major part to another. The movement, together with the transitional phrase (such as "Now let's look at some methods that have been used to accomplish this") is a clear signal to the listener that a new section is coming. Remember, a moving stimulus attracts attention; a stationary one does not. On the other hand, *constant* movement has the same effect as staying still, so don't pace continually during your speech.

Movement can be naturally worked into your speech through the use of visual material, such as a chalkboard or a flip chart. (This subject is covered in detail in Chapter Twelve.) This kind of activity, like so many others, requires *practice*. Don't forget that movement is a natural method of alleviating anxiety. When frightened, your body wants to move. If you plant yourself in front of the lectern, you will not only bore your audience but force your body to assume an unnatural posture.

Avoid movement for its own sake, however. You have undoubtedly seen speakers who paced up and down, fiddled with their keys or their glasses, and shifted their weight from foot to foot. Movement, because of its great potential for attention-getting, must be carefully kept under control. The first rule is "Don't do it if it doesn't have a purpose!" Let the movement be a natural extension of the thought expressed.

Gesture

Few things are more upsetting to beginning speakers than the prospect of learning to gesture. Even the word has an artificial connotation. So don't *plan* to include several gestures; you will probably gesture automatically. If you plan a few good movements on the platform, use one or two visual aids, and have a lectern on which to rest your hands, you will probably be just fine.

You may have seen a particularly skilled speaker, such as Dr. Billy Graham, use gestures in a dynamic and highly communicative way and wish that you could do the same. Dr. Graham would probably not be as effective if he did not use gestures, but Dr. Graham usually speaks to massive audiences and deals with topics that have great emotional impact. Most speakers face much smaller audiences and have purposes that are not as stimulating as "spiritual awakening." In other words, what works at a revival or a political rally may not work for you.

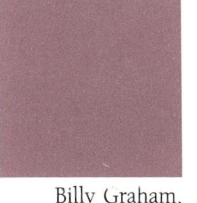

Billy Graham, evangelist, is an effective communicator, whose physical presence contributes to the power of his message. (© *Larry Kielkopf/UK Information Services*)

Delivery: Nonverbal Elements 165

Keep in mind the following points when using gestures:

- Make the gesture appropriate for the occasion. Wide, sweeping hand and arm gestures are inappropriate for a small group.
- Avoid pointing your finger at anyone. Most of us have unpleasant memories associated with pointing fingers.
- Don't count with your fingers, for example, holding up one, two, and three fingers to enumerate your points. Most people know what one, two, and three are without being shown.
- Be interested in your talk and good gestures will follow naturally.

Eye Contact

Do you know someone who avoids looking at you during a conversation? This person is commonly termed "shifty-eyed," and we evaluate him or her accordingly. You want your listeners to feel that you are interested in them, so you should at least look at them. Some speakers gaze at a fixed point at the back of the room; others look everywhere but directly at their audience. It is an excellent practice to look directly at each person at least once in your speech, if your audience consists of less than twenty persons. With a larger audience, you can do the same with the various sections of the group.

Physical Appearance

Although many people would not consider physical appearance an essential delivery element, it is certainly important. You should look your best even in a class presentation. This typically means a coat and tie for men and a dress and heels for women. If you think that physical appearance doesn't matter, consider the shoulder strap that shows, or the open fly. "Disasters" like these hurt the effectiveness of a speech; even small mishaps, like a wrinkled shirt, do the same.

Using Your Voice

Your voice communicates a good deal more than words: Inflection, rate, pitch, and loudness all carry meaning. Your goal should be to make your voice a communicative instrument, so that your message can be presented with maximum efficiency. Let's look at some of the vocal characteristics available to you.

Everyone wants his or her voice to express the person whom they would like to be (which is why most young men experience personal trauma when their voices change). Men typically try to force their voices lower in order to sound more "masculine," and women sometimes try to make their voices lower to sound sexy. Forcing the voice to do something unnatural is always poor procedure. You should strive for your *natural* voice; to do that, you need to find your optimum *pitch*, with which you can achieve more variety and consequently more interest.

Pitch

To find your optimum pitch, you must have a piano. The first step is to start humming notes and match them to notes on the piano. (If you are tone-deaf, you need to have a friend help you.) When you are sure that you can match or closely approximate notes on the piano, you are ready to try to find your optimum pitch.

1. Start by singing your way down the scale. Play lower and lower notes on the piano keys until you can go no lower. For most men this will be somewhere below the "C" below "middle C" and possibly as low as the "F" below that "C." Operatic basses who have extraordinarily low voices can usually sing the "C" that is two octaves below middle "C." For women this low note will be somewhere around middle "C," although many will be able to get a few notes lower.

2. Now reverse the procedure. Try to find where your highest note is. For men this will be within a note or two above middle "C"; for women, close to the "E" above the "C" above middle "C." Then count the number of whole notes between the lowest and the highest notes. For most people this will be ten or eleven notes, though you may have as many as fifteen or sixteen notes (approximately two octaves).

3. Divide the range by three. If your range was eleven notes, one-third of eleven would be 3.667 or four, rounded off.

4. Start at the top of your range and count down this number. The note on which you land will be your optimum pitch. For example, a male with a range of eleven notes with the highest note at the "E" above middle "C" will count down four notes from "E" and land on "A." *This is the pitch at which your voice is the most comfortable,* the strongest, and will show the least fatigue. You might wish to consult a professional voice coach for help in this procedure.

Determining optimum pitch is extremely important because many people artificially raise or lower their voices. Fatigue and strain, and in some cases, serious harm to the voice, can result. In terms of speech delivery, the main benefit of optimum pitch is that *variety* in pitch is possible, and it is variety in pitch that makes different kinds of inflection possible. Inflectional differences are one of the most important tools that you have in delivery.

Inflection

Inflection can be infinitely varied but is usually categorized into two basic patterns—rising or falling (Figure 11-2). In the diagram, the rising inflection of "Where?", denotes that it is a question, and the falling inflection of "Here", indicates it is an answer. Try them in reverse! You will see how different inflections imply different meaning.

With compound inflection, a basic falling or rising inflection is interrupted by another inflection (see Figure 11-2b). Circumflex inflection is basically a gliding pattern, usually used to denote ambiguity of meaning.

Figure 11.2

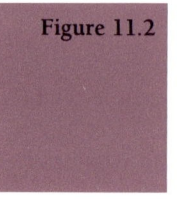

Inflectional patterns.

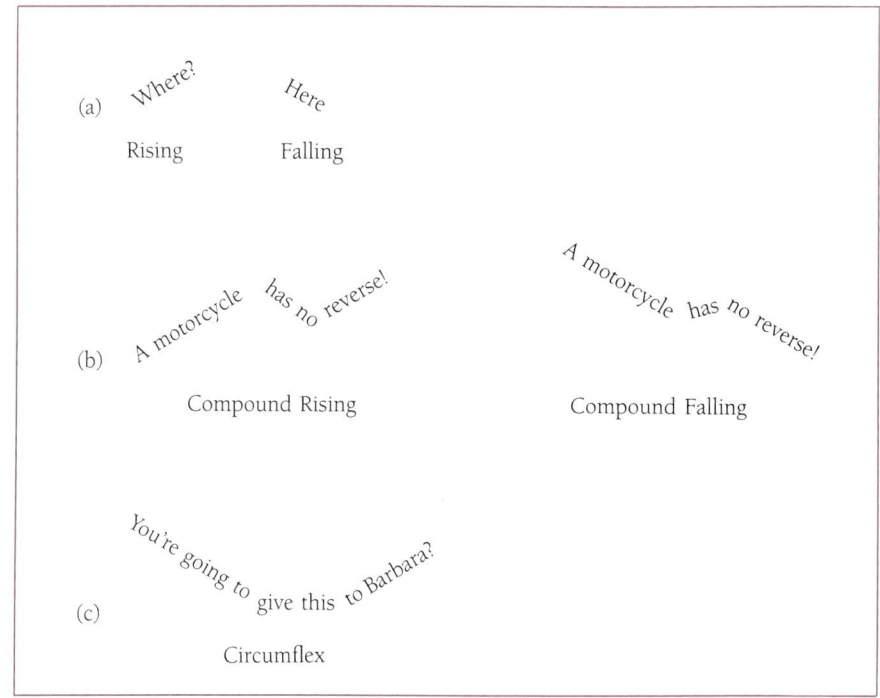

(a) Where?   Here
    Rising   Falling

(b) A motorcycle has no reverse!   A motorcycle has no reverse!
    Compound Rising   Compound Falling

(c) You're going to give this to Barbara?
    Circumflex

Pearson (1985) notes that rising inflection is a characteristic of "typical" feminine speech. If this is true, women need to be especially careful with vocal cues, because rising inflections typically indicate powerlessness and questioning.

Loudness

Your goal is to be loud enough to be heard but not so loud that you irritate your audience. Loudness typically denotes emphasis. If you want to emphasize a point, you can do it by changing intensity—and *not* necessarily by being louder. Intensity simply refers to the audience's perception of the speaker's emotional state. An important point can sometimes be better made with a whisper than it can with a shout.

Quality

Most voices range from "throaty" to nasal, with a great deal of variation between these extremes. You can do little about your natural voice timbre, but you should remember not to force your voice into an unnatural or unpleasant timbre. The range of interpretation of various voice qualities is truly amazing. Though few people can change their voice quality, they can at least be aware of interpretative tendencies and try to adapt to them. For example, if you have a naturally breathy voice, you will have to get used to people thinking that you are sexy. The tape recorder is an excellent tool for analyzing timbre.

Rate

You will remember from Chapter Three that most people can listen much faster than they can speak. As a speaker, your solution is not to speak faster because you simply cannot articulate fast enough to keep pace. "Top Forty" disc jockeys speak at the rate of about 150 words per minute, but few people can go that fast. A rate of about 120 words per minute is ideal for most people.

Varying rate is an important device for emphasis: By slowing down at certain strategic points, you can call your audience's attention to a sentence or a phrase.

Variety

As discussed above, *variety* in pitch, rate, inflection, and loudness is the best tool for vocal emphasis. Most audiences are easily bored and have a short attention span; you can overcome this by using vocal variety throughout your speech, especially for emphasizing important points in your speech. A repetitive, monotonous inflectional pattern, on the other hand, is guaranteed to put your audience to sleep.

The rich, melodious voice of actor Orson Welles is easily recognized by several generations of Americans. He started his career in radio, later moving to stage and screen to become one of America's most versatile and talented actors. (© Frank Siteman/ Jeroboam, Inc.)

Delivery: Nonverbal Elements

Vocal Cues and "Personality"

Like it or not, people stereotype you when they hear your voice. Table 11-2 lists some typical voices and stereotypes that you are likely to encounter. Someone with a particularly nasal voice, for example, is likely to be judged as socially undesirable, even though there is absolutely no evidence that persons with nasal voices are actually unpleasant persons. You should know about these stereotypes and try to change them if possible.

Listening and Delivery: Decoding Nonverbal Messages

As mentioned in Chapter Three, *interpretive listening* is usually associated with the decoding of nonverbal messages. Many persons are skilled at decoding and you should try to improve your ability in this area.

You may have taken a standardized listening test, such as the Kentucky Comprehensive Listening Test (Bostrom and Waldhart, 1987) or the Watson-Barker test, in which interpretive listening is measured primarily through vocal elements. The Watson-Barker test is probably the best measure of interpretive listening (as defined in Chapter Three). If you took one of these tests, your instructor probably informed you of your general standing with regard to this kind of listening. If you record below the median, you need to become more sensitive to what is communicated in the voice.

Unfortunately, most listening tests do not use videotapes of the speaker, so that we cannot measure the other elements of nonverbal communication, such as posture, distance, and facial expression. If you see a speaker ignoring most of these simple communicative devices, you must conclude that the speaker either is simply unaware of them or truly wishes to communicate inappropriate messages.

Becoming fully familiar with the ten expressions of the Leathers and Emigh taxonomy will raise your listening skill level significantly. You also need to take into account vocal delivery. When you hear a speaker with a nasal, unpleasant voice, for example, you should allow for the possible effects, which means *listening past* the vocal elements and focusing on the ideas in the speech.

When you hear a falling inflection in a phrase that seems to call for a rising one (such as a question), you should be able to recognize the inappropriate inflection and go beyond it to glean the meaning from the sentence.

Summary

Nonverbal communication is a powerful tool in your speaking arsenal. This kind of communication typically sends messages about relationships—dominance, intimacy, immediacy, and intensity. The most typical nonverbal messages studied are those of eye contact, body lean, proximity, touch, and facial expression. Facial expression is probably the most important and the most manipulable of these elements, but speakers should practice all of them.

The voice needs particular attention. Speakers should make sure they are

Table 11.2

Vocal types and personality perceptions. (Adapted from Addington, D. 1968. The relationships of selected vocal characteristics to personality perception. *Speech Monographs* 35: 492–503).

Vocal Types	Speakers	Perceptions
Breathiness	Males	Younger, more artistic
	Females	More feminine, prettier, more petite, more effervescent, more highly strung, and shallower
Thinnes	Males	Did not alter listener's image of the speaker, no significant correlations
	Females	Increased social, physical, emotional, and mental immaturity, increased sense of humor and sensitivity
Flatness	Males	More masculine, more sluggish, colder, more withdrawn
	Females	More masculine, more sluggish, colder, more withdrawn
Nasality	Males	A wide array of socially undesirable characteristics
	Females	A wide array of socially undesirable characteristics
Tenseness	Male	Older, more unyielding, cantankerous
	Females	Younger, more emotional, feminine, high strung, less intelligent
Throatiness	Males	Older, more realistic, mature
	Females	Less intelligent, more masculine, lazier, more boorish, unemotional, ugly, sickly, careless, inartistic, naive, humble, neurotic, quiet, uninteresting, apathetic
Orotundity	Males	More energetic, healthy, artistic, sophisticated, proud, interesting, enthusiastic
	Females	Increased liveliness, gregariousness, aesthetic sensitivity
Increased Rate	Males	More animated and extroverted
	Females	More animated and extroverted
Increased Pitch Variety	Males	More dynamic, feminine aethethically inclined
	Females	More dynamic and extroverted

using their voices at the optimum pitch and developing variety in pitch, rate, loudness, and timbre.

Listening for nonverbal cues is usually called "interpretive" listening. Just as elements of speaking need practice, this form of listening also requires constant work.

On Your Own

1. Go back to the beginning of the chapter and reread the dialogues between persons A and B. Then answer the following questions.
   a. Which of these persons do you think is a male and which a female? Why?
   b. Are they really "going tomorrow" (in both examples)?
   c. What events have preceded these two interactions?
   d. Could the same two people be involved in both scenarios? What events would have had to transpire to make it so?

2. Try the Leathers and Emigh expressions in a mirror. Can you do them? Does the expression create the specific emotion?
3. Smile at the next ten persons you see, regardless of the situation. Describe your results.
4. Try the piano exercise described in this chapter. Are you using your optimum pitch? What can you do to change it?
5. Look at the inflection patterns shown in Figure 11.3. Try to use each of these patterns on the same sentence.

Suggestions for Further Reading

Burgoon, J., D. Buller, J. Hale, and M. deTurck. 1984. Relational messages associated with nonverbal behaviors. *Human Communication Research* 10: 351–78.

Dittman, A. 1972. *Interpersonal messages of emotion.* New York:Springer.

Ekman, P., W. Friesen, and P. Ellsworth. 1972. *Emotion in the human face: Guidelines for research and an integration of findings.* New York: Pergamon.

Leathers, D., and T. Emigh. 1980. Decoding facial expressions: A new test with decoding norms. *Quarterly Journal of Speech* 66: 418–36.

Rubin, R., and C. Roberts. 1987. A comparative analysis of three listening tests. *Communication Education* 36: 142–53.

Twelve

Audio and Visual Elements

> There's nothing like a picture. Sometimes it's the only way to get a point across.
>
> Bud Schulberg

Key Terms

attention
selective perception
psychophysical
intensity
extensity
repetition
duration
focal length

Objectives

After studying this chapter, you should be able to:

1. Understand the process of attention and how visual cues affect it
2. Choose among chalkboards, flip charts, prepared visuals, and other speaking aids
3. Be able to draw a simple yet effective diagram to assist the understanding of speech text
4. Understand the strengths and weaknesses of various kinds of audiovisual equipment

Now that you have the basics of your speech well in hand, you may want to consider enhancing the speech's impact with audiovisual aids. Although you can probably get by without them, most speeches are improved by audio or visual materials. These materials have been shown to increase listeners' attention and subsequent retention.

Complex messages in particular are enhanced by visuals. A great deal of research supports this point. For example, two studies done in the 1960s (Anderson, 1966, 1968) showed that a combination of spoken/pictorial presentations could achieve more impact on complex topics than spoken messages alone. In addition, listeners remembered the content of the presentations far longer when pictorial presentations were used.

Audiovisual aids can be as elaborate or as simple as the resources of each speaker. Many beginning speakers say "I'm just not artistic" and feel they cannot create visual aids without professional help. However, anyone who can print block letters and has a little ingenuity and imagination can make an effective, interesting visual aid. In this chapter we explore several kinds of visual aids and suggest ways that your speech can be made more compelling with them. Because the purpose of audiovisual assistance is to stimulate and maintain attention, let's first examine how the attention process works.

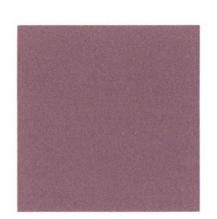

Attention

Your goal as a speaker is to get your listener's attention without having to ask for it. In other words, you would like their attention to be involuntary. Communicators can use involuntary attention factors in a number of ways to enhance their presentation. In this section, the word *attention* refers to the involuntary ways that humans attend to certain stimuli.

Selective Perception and Attention

According to research studies, humans process only one ten-thousandth of the information available to them. We focus on particular stimuli and ignore others. This process is called *selective perception* and is an important psychological process to study for public speaking (see Chapter Three). When you read a newspaper, for example, you only read the stories that interest you. At a party, you may hear two conversations at once, at exactly the same sound level, but you focus on one and ignore the other.

This selecting process usually happens automatically and is heavily influenced by language, attitudes, schemas, and social background. Thus, if you present material outside of your audience's experience and expectation, they will probably attend to it poorly. If, for example, you are discussing "Black English" before a conservative white audience, you may have trouble convincing them that "He be happy" is a legitimate part of an alternative grammar system. You will simply have to overcome this selective attention and perception somehow. The usual way is to use psychophysical methods to maintain attention.

Psychophysical Attention Factors

The term *psychophysical* refers to the interaction between psychological processes and physical stimuli. The discipline of psychophysics deals with physical characteristics of stimuli, such as loudness, brightness, and duration. A sound, for example, is not loud or soft, but can be measured precisely in sound pressure level, or "decibels." Prior to 1940, precise measurement of stimuli and response was the subject of a good deal of psychological research that focused on a number of psychophysical factors: intensity, extensity; duration and repetition; motion; color; and change and contrast. All of these factors are still important in visual presentations and can be used to help a speaker and the audience.

Intensity

Intense stimuli—loud sounds, bright lights, vivid colors—have more attention value than less intense stimuli. Every speaker should speak loudly enough to be heard by the entire audience, and sometimes speakers need to be able to shout. Though shouting is not recommended practice, an occasional "Hey!" to an unruly audience sometimes helps settle them down. When using a sound system with tapes or records, you should make sure that the level is loud enough to gain attention. If you use slides or projectors, you need to make sure that your projector has enough wattage for your room (more about this later). Your charts or diagrams ought to be in vivid colors.

Extensity

Extensity refers to size. A large stimulus has greater attention value than a smaller one. (This means that big speakers have inherent advantages; small ones need to compensate.) You should consider extensity in your preparation of visual aids. A small visual aid is worthless in most speaking situations. "Poster board," which most persons use for visual aids, comes in one standard size— 22 × 28 inches. You should be extremely careful about using anything smaller than that.

Repetition and Duration

Just as a steadily dripping water faucet can get our attention with its incessant drip, drip, drip, repeating words and phrases can be an extremely effective rhetorical device. However, don't be so repetitive that the overall effect is negative.

Duration refers to the length of time that a stimulus lasts. Long stimuli claim our attention. If you live in a city, you are probably used to hearing car horns, so you ignore them. When a horn gets stuck or is blasted for as long as a minute, however, you attend sharply. Similarly, a word that is drawn out slightly in a speech claims attention.

Color

Color is attention-getting. Some colors are better than others: Red, for example, is probably the best for pure attention-getting purposes. In general, bright colors are better than pastels, and contrast is the important feature: An entire visual lettered in bright red and yellow loses its impact, while red/black or yellow/black, for example, are strong attention-getting combinations.

Motion

A moving stimulus is attention-getting. We naturally focus on things that move. (This is why wild animals, on being startled, often freeze into position; an absolutely motionless Arctic hare against a snow-white background is practically invisible, but the moment the hare jumps, it can be seen.) Any good speaker moves around with positive, dynamic gestures. A visual aid that has some motion might be effective in certain situations. However, a demonstration with blinking lights and moving parts may distract the audience from you and your message.

Change and Contrast

This factor is closely related to the factor above: *Motion, duration, repetition,* and *intensity* are all changes from static or ordinary patterns. Audio or visual material can add other kinds of change and contrast to build attention. This implies that several visuals are better than one, and one visual is better than none.

Creating Effective Visual Aids

Probably the most effective visual aids are the ones that *you* prepare. It is easy to borrow a "slick" chart or diagram from another source and adapt your speech

Visual information, such as charts or graphs, can be prepared ahead of time on large sheets of paper. The flip chart enables the speaker to turn the pages quickly and easily. (© Michael Markowitz, Photo/ Graphic Arts)

176 ■ ■ ■ **Presenting the Speech**

Figure 12.1

Preparation is the key to success! Determine the types of visual aids which will communicate the content of your speech, and allow yourself enough time to prepare them.

to it—but then it isn't *your* speech anymore. To make your point, you will probably have to make your own visuals. This is a lot easier than you might think. (See Figure 12.1)

As with every element of speaking, *preparation* is vital. Speakers should start with the speech purpose, proceed to the materials necessary to accomplish the purpose, get a clear idea of the audience's needs, and then add audiovisuals. Particular items in the audiovisual presentation are usually planned in advance. If you plan to illustrate a particular point with a slide or a drawing, you need to assemble the material, bring it to the speech setting, and look at it from the back of the room. If, and only if, it advances your purposes should you use it. Speakers who plan to say "I've got some great slides I took at our meeting in Buffalo" should first decide if the audience cares more about Buffalo or the meeting. Similarly, if you plan to use a chalkboard or flip chart, you should plan *exactly* what you are going to write on these surfaces. In your speech outline, you need to make careful notes about the placement and use of audiovisual aids.

Demonstrations

The simplest visual aid is an object or device that demonstrates a process or use (Figure 12.2). You can also demonstrate *elements* of a larger process. Suppose that you have decided to explain the differences between cross-country and downhill skiing. Though it would be nice to take the listeners out to a snowy hill and show them how these two activities differ, this is not practical in most cases. However, you can bring cross-country skis to your audience and show how they differ from downhill skis; you can bring the different ski poles as well and demonstrate their use, and so on. These items are large enough to be meaningful to an average audience. Be careful about using objects that are so small that they can't be seen by an audience. If you are talking about how to "gap" spark plugs, for example, most of your audience is going to have difficulty seeing the spark gap on the plug or perhaps even the plug itself.

Figure 12.2

One of the simplest and most effective means of illustration is to have objects present in order to demonstrate their purpose and use.

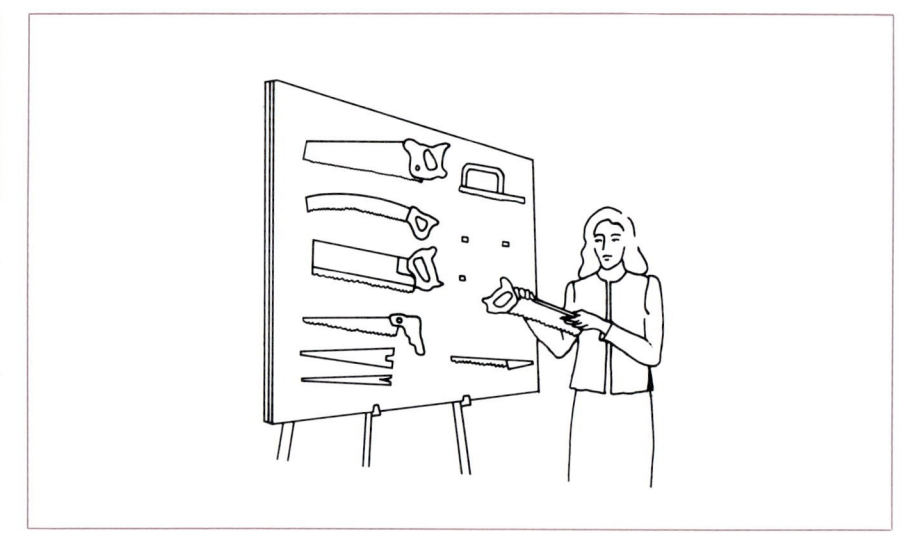

Chalkboard

The chalkboard and the flip chart are probably the most commonly used visual aids; they are inexpensive, reusable, and effective. They are probably the most abused devices as well. If you are planning to talk about the gap in spark plugs, you might decide to draw a large picture of a plug on your chalkboard and illustrate how to adjust the gap. Unless you are an extremely skilled illustrator, however, your spark plug may look like the leaning tower of Pisa. As a general rule, don't draw unless the picture is *extremely* simple or you can draw extremely well.

Another typical abuse of the chalkboard is simply to write something without thinking about its impact. Often speakers see chalk and an empty board and are seized with the impulse to use these implements. A speaker discussing "Reagonomics" might offhandedly write "Interest Rates" on the board but then go on talking about the defense budget. But that term remains on the chalkboard throughout the speech, calling attention to itself despite its relative unimportance. If you plan to write only one word or phrase on the chalkboard it should relate to the thesis of your speech, and you should write it close to the end of the discussion. Otherwise, skip it.

You should not use the chalkboard or a flip chart unless you can print legibly. Sadly, this advice is not always heeded. Don't depend on your own judgment to decide if your printing is legible (never write longhand on the chalkboard!); instead, ask a friend to be the judge of its legibility, and be guided by his or her comments. Your printing should also be large (1/16-of-an-inch high for each foot to your most distant viewer; if your room is 20 feet long, for example, your lettering should be at least 20/16 or 1-1/4 inch).

Never interrupt your speech by chalking a long or involved outline or series of steps. Prepare in advance! If you can't print or draw while you are talking, then don't do it. (See Figure 12.3)

As a reminder, it is useful to write your chalkboard material on a separate sheet of paper or a note card in advance. Colored chalk is inexpensive and very

Figure 12.3

The chalkboard is one of the most common and widely used visual aids. Careful planning and the use of simple techniques are important considerations.

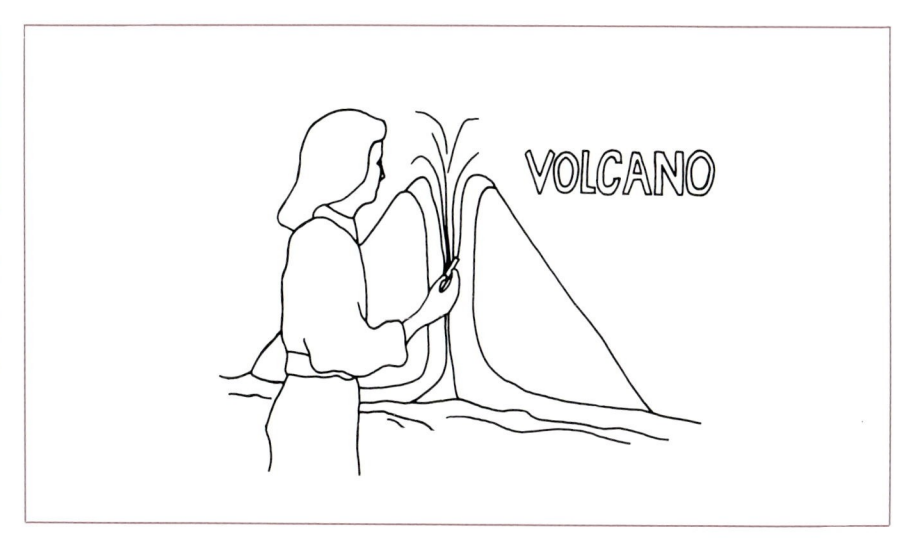

useful. Speakers who assume that chalk and erasers will be available, and who don't arrive in time to make sure they are, deserve the poor consequences. If you are speaking at a new site, bring your own eraser and chalk.

Diagrams

Some illustrative material simply cannot be drawn on a chalkboard or be demonstrated with a hand-held object. When this is the case, you need a diagram to accomplish your purpose.

You do not necessarily need a professional artist, but you do need advance planning and preparation. If you have some artwork available, this is all to the good. Many large organizations have so much demand for particular content that they have prepared charts in advance. (Utility companies, for example, typically spend a lot of time explaining rate structure. As a result, they prepare charts in advance that are available to employees who speak on the topic of rate structure.) If you are interested in this kind of topic, it might pay to ask one of these corporations for permission to borrow visual material.

Most persons will want to construct their own diagrams. This is not as difficult as it sounds. Large pieces of good quality cardboard or posterboard can be purchased at most bookstores or art supply stores. A rough sketch on a small piece of paper is the first step; then you can copy it with pencil onto the large paper. Finally, you can fill in the diagram with "magic markers," acrylic paints, or other devices.

Suppose you wish to explain the workings of an automobile carburetor. If you simply brought a carburetor to your group, they couldn't see enough to make it worthwhile. A diagram, however, can show the interior of the carburetor, as well as the exterior; the various parts in different positions; the parts separate from one another; and the different stages of the carburetion process.

Figure 12.4

The style and type of lettering is crucial to a well presented visual. Use block lettering, paying attention to correct size, and space the letters so they do not appear to blend together, or drift apart.

> # HOLD LID FIRMLY. RAISE ARM.
> Too close
>
> # HOLD LID FIRMLY. RAISE ARM.
> Too far
>
> # HOLD LID FIRMLY. RAISE ARM.
> Good.

Diagrams need not be expensive. White wrapping paper can often be obtained at stores and "magic markers" can be purchased for under a dollar.

Lettering is a vital part of a chart or diagram. You should use:

1. Block lettering (print with all capital letters).
2. Large letters (see Figure 12.4).
3. Proportionate letters (1/7th as wide as they are tall).
4. Plenty of white space.

Whenever you use charts or diagrams, you *must* arrive early at the speech setting and make sure that the facilities in the room are suitable. A diagram that falls or gradually slips down in the middle of your speech is hilarious to everyone but you. Check the fastenings or board clips; see if you need tape; be certain that your tape sticks. And extremely important: Check the lighting in the room and make sure that your visuals can be seen.

Using Audiovisual Equipment

Most beginning speakers are terrified by audiovisual equipment, but this equipment is easier to use than you might think. The important point is that you aren't born with the ability to use audiovisual equipment—you need to learn about it. Practice will truly make perfect; sometimes only five minutes of it! Let's look at some of the most common items in the audiovisual equipment room.

Audio Equipment

Public Address Systems

There are many different kinds of public address systems, but regardless of which type you use, the sound system speakers should be placed *in front of, and away from,* the microphone and directed toward the audience. If the microphone is placed in front of the speakers, the result is ear-splitting feedback.

Audiotape

The biggest problem in using audiotape is cueing the tape so that you can find your exact "cut." The best way to do this is to splice the tape with inexpensive "leader" so that you can see exactly where you are in the tape reel. This takes a little time but ensures that you will be able to start the tape recorder and get your effect exactly on cue. The other way of cueing is to use the numerical foot counter on the tape recorder. The numbers are sometimes hard to see but are better than nothing. Most of the time you should avoid cassette tapes unless you are prepared to re-record your cut exactly.

A second problem with a tape recorder is that most inexpensive models simply do not have enough sound power to carry in a large room. Sometimes you can feed your tape recorder through an existing sound system by using a short extension cord called a "jack" but it is usually easier to borrow a player with more power. For most rooms seating 50 to 100 persons, a 40 to 50 watt amplifier will be more than adequate.

Record Players

The same problem occurs with record players as with tape players—finding the right cut when you want it. Even if the record is divided into cuts, you need some method of spotting the right cut quickly. In radio stations, technicians cue up records prior to starting them; in an ordinary public speaking situation, this isn't possible, so you might want to transfer your material to tape or ask someone to help you with the record. If not, it is doubtful the record player will help you enough to offset the potential problems it offers.

The use of visuals can enhance messages and contribute to the communication process. The equipment pictured here is both reliable and easy to operate. *(Photo courtesey of 3M Audio Visual Division, St. Paul, MN, 1987)*

Audio and Visual Elements

Visual Equipment

Sometimes you find yourself in a large room where an ordinary chart won't work. And sometimes you need a picture. These two situations call for the use of *visual* equipment.

Overhead Projectors

The overhead projector is probably the simplest visual device to use, but you need to make transparencies in order to use it. You can copy almost any line drawing or diagram onto these transparencies. Another advantage is that you can draw on them with a china-marking pencil while you are speaking. This takes practice but is well worth the effort. You need to check letter size and type as projected to make sure that your letters are large enough and easy to read (see section on "Chalkboard" above).

When you make your overhead transparency, use the principles above to check letter size and letter type. After all, the overhead is only a projected chart or diagram. So for a room that is forty feet long, the *projected letter* should measure forty-sixteenths in size, or two and one-half inches. The same principle holds true for the slide projector.

Slide Projectors

For a truly classy presentation, you might try using slides. However, it does require elaborate preparation: taking slides using a 35 mm camera, planning lettering and color, and posing pictures. At one time or another, you have probably sat through a long and boring evening looking at slides of a vacation trip or family barbecue. If you have had this experience, you don't have to be told that slides should have a specific purpose and should not simply show pretty views. For example, a ten-minute speech should never use more than ten or fifteen slides.

You probably didn't know that you can photograph lettering by using extension rings on the lens of your 35 mm camera. These rings are relatively inexpensive and can be obtained at most camera shops. Ask for "close-up" rings. You can print your own lettering, or type legends on a small card. For an even more dramatic presentation, use colored cards and colored inks or a felt-tip pen. You can also buy (or borrow) theatrical gels in a wide variety of colors, mount them in slide holders (also available at low cost at many camera shops), and then write on them.

Slide projectors come in all sizes and shapes. Obviously, you should use one fitted to your room and your needs. The main dimension to consider with slide projectors is *focal length*. This refers to the way in which the projector's lens focuses the image and how far the image can reach; the farther the image is projected, the larger it is, but this depends on the particular projector and a particular lens. So don't try out your slides at home and expect the slide to look the same in the room where you are to give your speech. The general rule is to *always test your visuals in the speech setting in advance so that you can tell if they work*. Follow the guidelines in the "Chalkboard" section to make sure that the projected letters are large enough.

The overhead projector is a popular tool for many types of presentations. It is simple to operate and projects clear images even in a fully lighted room. *(Photo courtesy of 3M Audio Visual Division, St. Paul, MN, 1987)*

Film Projectors

Our advice is: Don't use film projectors. Use videotape instead. Most film projectors are cranky, unreliable, and give an image of poor quality. Unless your institution provides you with a projectionist, it's easier to copy the material on videotape and use a VCR.

Videotape

An inexpensive VCR will save you all kinds of grief. You can use the numerical counter on the machine to cue up your presentation, and have it ready for the right place in your speech. Be careful about audience size, however. If you have more than twenty people, you will probably need an additional monitor. The advantage of videotape is the universal acceptance given the medium of television. The greatest disadvantage is a tendency many speakers have to let the video "tail" wag the "dog" (the speech and the real purpose of the message). You must be extremely careful not to sidetrack your purpose simply because you have interesting video available.

Listening and Visual Aids

Inappropriate or distracting visuals can ruin a speaker's presentation, and if a listener isn't careful to "listen through" the distractions, the substance of the speech can be lost. First, the listener needs to evaluate the *appropriateness* of the audio or visual material. The central idea of the speech needs to be kept firmly in

Audio and Visual Elements

mind, as well as the speaker's basic supporting material. The listener can then use the audiovisual material as reinforcing devices.

Experience shows that many speakers use audio and visual aids inappropriately. When these aids are well planned, however, the listener can relax: The listener's job has been made easier.

Summary

Almost all speeches can be improved by audio or visual aids. Visual aids help speakers in two ways: by capturing and holding the audience's attention, and by reinforcing the message. Attention is a function of psychophysical factors: intensity, duration, repetition, color, motion, change, and contrast. Effective visual aids may be simple, as with diagrams or a chalkboard, or they may be quite involved. Audiovisual equipment is always helpful, and speakers should rehearse before the presentation. Any use of audiovisual equipment provides opportunities for breakdowns, so the speaker needs to take special care.

On Your Own

1. If you have access to a VCR, record some television commercials. When you replay them, note the incidence of motion, color, loudness, intensity, and other psychophysical factors. Estimate the impact of each of these factors.
2. While watching the evening news, note when the directors cut away to show film footage. Assess whether they do it just to have "video," or whether it really enhances the story.
3. Collect editorial cartoons on the same topic. Analyze the way in which cartoonists slant their perceptions of political figures.
4. Examine visual representations of numerical data from a well-known publication like the *Wall Street Journal*. Do they help? Why or why not?

Suggestions for Further Reading

Brigance, W. 1952. *Speech: Its techniques and discipline in a free society.* New York: Appleton-Century-Crofts.

Dominick, J. 1983. *The dynamics of mass communication.* Reading, MA: Addison-Wesley.

Kemp, J.E., and D.K. Dayton. 1985. *Planning and producing instructional media.* 5th ed. New York: Harper & Row.

Tufte, E. 1983. *The visual display of quantitative information.* Cheshire, CT: Graphics Press.

Part Four

Specific Speaking Tasks

Thirteen

Information and Informative Speaking

I never saw a moor
I never saw the sea
And yet I know how heather looks
And what a wave must be.

Emily Dickinson

Key Terms

relay
informative communication
information
development
demonstration
explanation
briefing
self-disclosure
statistics

Objectives

After studying this chapter, you should be able to:

1. Understand the basic nature of information
2. Explain how redundancy and information relate to each other
3. Distinguish between informative speeches that relay and those that self-disclose
4. Understand how new information is developed
5. Understand the strengths and weaknesses of statistics
6. Recognize the principal strategies involved in listening for retention

Emily Dickinson "knew" how heather looks because someone informed her about it; that is, someone who had actually seen a moor relayed the sight and sound in such a way that Dickinson could invoke a percept associated with the word heather. This is one of your purposes in informative speaking: to be a surrogate or "stand in" for listeners who have not experienced the topics of your speech.

It is often difficult to substitute for firsthand experience, so recreating experience is an extremely important problem in communication. Consider the event described in the newspaper story in Figure 13.1. Prior to the time of this article, a case had been made linking the accused to the murder of the victim. In other words, witnesses had testified that the man was guilty. They had relayed events to the jury.

When the juror stated that she could not convict the accused "unless she personally saw him shoot" the victim, the judge and other jurors logically took exception to this position. No criminal proceedings would be possible if this condition were imposed on the prosecution. We must often take action about events *we do not directly perceive* and must proceed sometimes on information that is not firsthand. This process is the basis of *informative* communication.

You will recall from Chapter Two that even though the *relay* form of communication is basically secondhand, third- or fourthhand, this style may serve us well in ordinary communication. The television weather reporter is one example of a long chain of persons who relay information to us; whereas, in courts of law, direct testimony is the only admissible evidence for an event—everything else is "hearsay."

The process of combining relays for the purpose of recreating experience is termed *informative communication,* and in some ways it can be the most important com-

Figure 13.1

Informative communication often allows us to take action about events we have not directly perceived. (*Lexington Herald Leader*)

JUROR SAYS SHE DID NOT VIOLATE OATH

A contempt of court charge against Mrs. Shirley Duer was purged by Judge George Barker after she explained that the wording of a statement she made during the James Herndon trial did not violate her oath as a juror.

Mrs. Duer, wife of Castleton Farm manager Carter Duer, was charged after she apparently said she could not convict James Herndon of murder unless she personally saw him shoot Mrs. Mary Burrell.

The statement came to the judge's attention when jury foreman Wilds W. Olive sent a note from the jury room explaining that one reason the jurors were unable to agree was Mrs. Durer's statement.

"The statement caused some consternation among the jurors," he said Thursday. "Some of them told her, 'You shouldn't be on a jury. You took an oath that you could convict him on circumstantial evidence.'"

"When I made the statement it was an emotionally tense situation," she said Thursday. "We were tired and we were worn out and we were getting nowhere. What I meant was that with the evidence I'd heard I couldn't vote guilty."

municative activity in your personal or professional life. A recent study showed that college alumni with work experience felt that informative speaking was their most important task (Johnson and Szczupakiewicz, 1987). In this chapter we first examine some of the basic principles relating to informative communication and then look at some specific instances of how this communicative form works.

What is Information?

Briefly, information is the absence of *redundancy*. Redundant messages are those that we already know or don't need. For example, if you see an automobile sitting in a lane marked "Left Turn Only" you know that the probability of the car turning left is quite high. The car's blinking directional signal becomes *redundant*. On the other hand, if the automobile is sitting in an ordinary lane, the blinking turn signal carries *information* because you didn't know what the driver was planning to do. In other words, the key to information is the predictability of the message—if you can predict the content of the message before it is delivered, the message is redundant and contains little information.

Most messages are not clearly redundant or informative but lie somewhere between these extremes. When an acquaintance asks, "How are you?" the typical response is, "Good! How are you?" Because this response is so predictable, it carries little information. However, if you respond, "My temperature is 98.6, my pulse is 75, and my blood pressure 120 over 80," the acquaintance might be somewhat taken back but will certainly have much more information. A great deal of our social interaction is redundant, but some of it is informative.

In many circumstances, it is useful to know *how much* information is present in a message. Although most of us are not used to thinking of information in terms of numercial values, it is a useful way to assess the informative character of any given topic for a given audience. In order to do this, we need to know how to measure information.

The Measurement of Information

We measure information in a variety of ways, but the best measure is the one used by the computer—the bit. A bit is one unit of information which stems from "yes-no" choice. For example, if you go to a soft drink machine, you might see a light on the front indicating "EMPTY." This light signals us not to put our money in the machine. The light can only be in one of two states at any given time—on or off. This signal represents one bit of information. If the machine has more than one variety of soft drink, it will have a separate light for each. With two lights, the machine can transmit four bits of information (information represents the number of states that the machine can be in) or the following:

Drink "A" present, Drink "B" present
Drink "A" present, Drink "B" not present
Drink "A" not present, Drink "B" present
Drink "A" not present, Drink "B" not present

With three lights, the machine can signal eight messages:

Drink "A" present, Drink "B" present, Drink "C" present
Drink "A" present, Drink "B" not present, Drink "C" present
Drink "A" not present, Drink "B" present, Drink "C" present
Drink "A" not present, Drink "B" not present, Drink "C" present
Drink "A" present, Drink "B" present, Drink "C" not present
Drink "A" present, Drink "B" not present, Drink "C" not present
Drink "A" not present, Drink "B" present, Drink "C" not present
Drink "A" not present, Drink "B" not present, Drink "C" not present

The progression goes like this:

One signal—two states
Two signals—four states
Three signals—eight states
Four signals—sixteen states
Five signals—thirty-two states

If you are mathematically minded, you may have already discerned a regular relationship: the states rise *exponentially* as the number of signals (bits) increase.

One signal–two states	(2^1)
Two signals–four states	(2^2)
Three signals–eight states	(2^3)
Four signals–sixteen states	(2^4)
Five signals–thirty-two states	(2^5)

But what can this possibly have to do with ordinary communication between and among persons? The answer is that we signal each other in similar but much more complex ways. Ordinary English, unlike the on/off lights of the soft drink machine, follows patterns and has a higher degree of predictability. This affects the amount of information that it can transmit. For example, some letters occur more often than others; "E" appears in English about 13 percent of the time. Here is a string of letters whose frequencies are those occuring in everyday English:

OCRO HLI RGWR NMIELWIS EU LL NBNESEBYA TH EEI ALHENHTTPA OOBTTVA

There are other regularities in English, as well. When "Q" appears, the next letter is always "U." When "T" appears, "H" is much more probable. When "TH" appears, "E" follows over 50 percent of the time. Here is a string with the frequencies of English built into it:

IN NO IST LAT WHEY CRACTIT FOURER BIRS GROCID PONDENOME OF DEMOST

Some of these actually look like words. But perhaps you might be more comfortable using words as the basic unit of analysis rather than letters. Here is a sample of words listed with their frequencies as they occur in English:

THE HEAD AND IN FRONTAL ATTACK ON AN ENGLISH WRITER THAT
THE CHARACTER OF THIS POINT IS THEREFORE ANOTHER METHOD FOR
THE LETTERS THAT THE TIME EVER TOLD OF WHO THE PROBLEM

This gives us a better idea of how we can get *information* from English. The probabilities in the above sample run about .5 for each word on the average. This means that in actuality we only convey about one bit per word in English prose, and probably much less than that in spoken discourse.

An easy way to test the "informativeness" of your speech (after it is prepared) is to compose a manuscript containing every word that you plan to use. Then enlist a friend to be your test subject and read the speech one word at a time. Before each word, ask your friend to guess what the next word is. You will find that some words are totally guessable, and others are totally unpredictable. Keeping track of this "information score" will tell you two things—first, what is truly important and needs emphasis, and second, whether the overall impact of the speech is better than the random probabilities above. An overall score of less than .5 would indicate that the speech has truly new and different data in it. (That is, the listener guesses or "predicts" less than half the words.)

Informative Communication

You will recall from Chapter Two, that the oral channel had two distinct advantages: immediate feedback and broader channel capacity. We need to exploit both of these advantages to make the most of informative speaking opportunities.

Many messages are *predictable*. If you are going to be a successful informative speaker, you should not only be nonredundant in your word choice, you need to be informative in the *material* of your speech: schemas, language, and percepts. A predictable speech is a boring speech, and you need to examine *all* aspects of content for their information value. Finding interesting and worthwhile new percepts and schemas is called *developing* content. Let's look at this task in the next section.

New Percepts

The importance of percepts lies in the sense impressions that you can recreate for your listeners. Therefore, you should carefully examine the kind of percept that your listeners can retain. If the percept is not useful or interesting, your audience will resist retaining it. Obviously, the selection of an interesting topic for your speech will help. If you will review the section in Chapter Six (on Audience Analysis), you will remember that an important part of analysis is the assessment of what percepts the audience already has, together with a specific list of the percepts that you *wish* they had. You cannot do this exactly, but only in terms of the *probable*.

Suppose that your topic is "Shopping for Fruits and Vegetables," and you have many good ideas about choosing fresh produce. Though you might list a number of points to consider in determining whether a head of lettuce is fresh, you should ultimately focus on sense experience—the color of the lettuce, the way it feels when you pick it up, its smell (or lack of smell), and so on. In fact, you may want to bring a few heads of lettuce to your speech. At the very least, you will want to have some kind of visual assistance that will make the percepts clear to your listeners. We will examine this problem in greater depth when we discuss the demonstration speech.

New Language

Quite often new language is the purpose of an informative communication, in that a new linguistic frame of reference is timely and useful. For example, learning that the Latin American term *machismo* refers not just to masculinity, but to a whole way of life for the Latin male, centers around knowing just what *machismo* means. Similarly, a talk that tries to explain the provisions of the First Amendment is basically linguistic in nature, exemplifying the points of law affected. For example, the Federal Communications Commission recently repealed the "Fairness" Doctrine, which required TV stations to give "equal time" to opposing points of view. The Commission reasoned that modern media systems, because of their increased diversity, are inherently more "fair" and no longer need legislation. The term *fair* is at the core of this kind of speech. You hope to change the way listeners use the word. Any time that you use definitions, exemplifications, or formulas you are affecting the language system of your receivers.

Repetition and restatement are useful tools in creating new language. Repetition helps in two ways: first by insuring better retention, and second, by focusing on the word itself, and not its content. Putting the new definition to work is another useful technique. For example, if you are explaining the word *brotherhood* from the point of view of a fraternity or sorority member, you might want to show how the word applies to specific acts by group members.

New Schemas

Presenting a new schema is even more difficult than presenting a new percept or new language because it frequently involves both language and percepts as bases for the schema. Instilling new schemas may also be part of persuasive speeches (see Chapter Fourteen), but the line between information and persuasion is not altogether clear. For example, if you "know" that the speed limit is 65 mph on the interstate, this knowledge affects what you do. You will probably not drive faster than 65 because to do so would be unsafe and illegal.

Consider a county extension agent who wishes to "inform" a group of tobacco farmers that the burley should be baled rather than hand-stripped. The apparent goal of the agent is to inform the farmers concerning the advantages of baling, but the *ultimate* goal may well be to persuade the farmers to adopt the procedure. In this case informing and persuading become congruent. One important way in which this extension agent's purposes could be realized is to recast tobacco

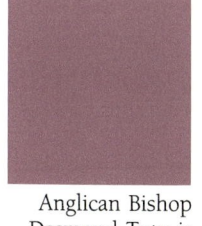

Anglican Bishop Desmond Tutu is an outspoken critic of his government's apartheid policy. He travels extensively to inform the world of conditions in South Africa and to rally support for the Black majority. (© UK Information Services)

farming as a strictly "business" proposition rather than a family activity. This involves drastic changes of schema and may be successfully done by using examples and social comparisons.

Development of new schemas is an important part of the speaker's task. The *topoi* of classical rhetoric (see Chapter Six) offer good guidelines for development, but the specific audience and the topic are probably the most important aspects of development. In the appendix, read Antonio Navarro's speech and note how he develops information about the role of Hispanics in American business by using *definition* (of the word *Hispanic*), *cause and effect* (reasons for Hispanic emigration to the United States), and *refutation* (numbers of Hispanics in managerial positions in American business). This is an excellent example of development.

Informative speaking seems to have a number of specific forms that are used repeatedly. In the next section, we examine some of these forms and then look at ways in which we can make these methods more effective.

Successful Informative Speaking

You can adopt several specific strategies to make your informative speaking more successful. These depend, of course, on the type of informative speech that is demanded. Let's look at a few of these.

The Demonstration

Probably the most commonly used form of informative public speaking is the *demonstration*, usually defined as the presentation of an act or a process without intermediate steps. For example, a nurse may choose to demonstrate a specific injection procedure to a diabetic patient, rather than elaborately explaining all of the background information.

Settings for Demonstrations

An example of a simple demonstration is one in which a speaker performs a cooking technique to inform the audience about a recipe. (You are probably familiar with cooks who whip up fancy recipes on television.) It is certainly possible to present an informative speech about how Bordelaise sauce is made, by simply listing recipe ingredients and procedures. But the *demonstration* carries more impact when audiences can actually see what is done. In many businesses, new personnel are trained on plant and office equipment using the demonstration.

Preparing Successful Demonstrations

You should first decide whether a demonstration is practical. For example, if your topic is "Changing a Tire on a New Car," you might hold the talk in the parking lot and actually change the tire, but this kind of demonstration is not always possible, and you may be much better off using a visual aid and other kinds of materials. In an industrial setting you cannot always obtain the equipment that you need for a demonstration, so you may have to use other methods. In classroom speaking, a good rule of thumb is to use a demonstration only if you can carry the demonstration material with you.

Second, you should rehearse the demonstration at least once before your speech. Even if you have worked with this particular process a number of times and are utterly familiar with it, you can't always tell if the equipment is going to work. If, for example, you are planning to demonstrate *origami* (the Japanese art of paper folding) or macrame, you would be well advised to choose a simple pattern and practice it several times. If your demonstration fails in the middle of the speech, it will be a disaster.

Third, you should highlight your demonstration with visual aids, usually a chart or a handout. Most demonstrations have a number of critical elements that can be highlighted this way, and your audience will appreciate your preparation. In demonstrating how to make a Bordelaise sauce, for example, you might distribute the recipe after the speech.

Explanations or Briefings

This form of informative speaking provides information that supplements other information already known. Political figures use this form a good deal: When the Secretary of State signs an agreement with another country, for example, he might *brief* the Congress and the press on the background for the agreement, the expected benefits, and the administration's rationale for the agreement.

Appropriate Uses for Explanatory Speaking

Business organizations frequently use this form of speaking as a part of community relations programs. Utility companies, for example, constantly explain to customers why gas, electricity, or telephone service is going to cost more next year.

The explanation should never turn into a promotional event. If, as an oil company representative, you are asked to brief a group about oil prices, you had better give a complete explanation. Your credibility will suffer terribly if you merely stick to the "party line."

Explaining Efficiently

As discussed in Chapter Six, audience analysis is the key to effective choice of material. If you are speaking to a local Kiwanis club, you can bet that this group is sophisticated about economic problems. Talking down to a knowledgeable audience is a sure way to lose them. To employees in your organization "cost-effectiveness" might seem to be the most important point, but to consumers "quality" or "durability" might be much more vital. Figure out which aspects of your explanation will be most relevant.

Imagine an admissions counselor from a university trying to explain a new restrictive admissions policy to a group of prospective students. From the university's point of view, admitting only high-quality students and a lack of dormitory rooms may be two very important factors that changed the school's admission policy. The prospective students, however, may be more interested in the specific courses and high school grades required for admissions.

Answering Questions

You are undoubtedly familiar with presidential press conferences, since they usually receive wide publicity. You may not know, however, that the President's press organization frequently "orchestrates" these conferences with planted questions and answers. (You may feel that your speeches should also be followed by "friendly" questions, but don't count on it!) An important part of most explanations is the question period; if you refuse to answer questions or cannot answer them, you should not speak in the first place.

Frankness and openness are important qualities for a question period. If you disagree with your company's policy, for example, you had better admit it (though you might also mention that your company is right more often than it is wrong, and that you are attempting to make changes). Or if you are defending college athletics, you would be well advised to admit that occasionally there are abuses. Blindly defending a stupid action will strip your presentation of effectiveness. Practically speaking, you might want to discuss your speech with your boss beforehand. If you do have a problem, you are better off canceling the speech than trying to lie your way through a difficult situation.

During a press conference, politicians are asked to define, clarify, and explain policies and issues. Here, former mayor of San Francisco, Diane Feinstein, answers questions in a characteristically forthright and open manner. (© *Tom Gibbons*)

Self-Disclosure

One special form of informative speaking focuses on the speaker—the revealing of attitudes, background, and experiences that create a person's character. In previous chapters, we have called this process *externalization*, but some researchers refer to it as *self-disclosure*, and it occurs in a variety of settings.

Self-Disclosure in Public Speaking

Self-disclosure is necessary when the focus of the speech is on the source rather than the message. For example, if you introduce yourself to a new group, you disclose significant facts about yourself so that the group will know you better. Legitimate occasions for self-disclosure in a public speaking situation are rare. The person who simply talks about himself is usually boring. However, self-disclosure is important in certain situations. If you have done something that a certain group finds difficult to accept, you may need to explain your behavior by stating the factors in your background that led to this act. Consider the problem faced by a juror whose peers on the jury disagree with her. Vote after vote is taken and this juror finds she is the one dissenting vote in an 11 to 1 decision. This kind of situation is not as rare as you might think. The pressures created by such a situation may call for a significant degree of self-disclosure on the part of the dissenting juror. Note that self-disclosure only seeks *understanding* on the part of the listeners, not agreement. It is easy for the self-discloser to move past explanation into justification, which has a strong persuasive flavor.

Another legitimate use of self-disclosure arises when distinguished speakers outline their beliefs in an inspirational way. In this situation self-disclosure *involves* listeners in a way that no other method can. When President Carter wanted to explain his feelings about racial integration in the South, he chose self-disclosure as a method. He described an incident that occurred on his father's farm in the 1930s when Joe Louis, the heavyweight boxing champion of that era, was fighting Max Schmeling, an avowed racist. The only radio on the farm was in the family house, and the black tenant farmers and neighbors gathered under the window to hear the broadcast of the fight. After Louis knocked out Schmeling in the second round, the group of blacks walked quietly across the road and then broke into cheers, apparently thinking it would have been wrong for blacks to cheer the defeat of a white while that close to the Carter house. President Carter's disclosure of this touching incident illustrated his personal experience of racial injustice and highlighted his determination to continue to work for civil rights.

Look at the way Gary Hart used self-disclosure in this speech announcing his withdrawal from the 1988 presidential race:

I say to my children and other frustrated and angry young people, I'm angry, too. I've made some mistakes; I've said so. I said I would, because I'm human. And I did. Maybe big mistakes, but not bad mistakes.

But I'm an idealist and I love this country deeply, and I want to serve this country. The events of this week should not deter any of you who are idealistic young people from moving on and moving up. I would say to the young people of this country the torch of idealism burns bright in your hearts. It should lead you into public service and national service. It should lead you to want to make this country better.

Hart's use of self-disclosure was intended to make a statement about the process of news gathering and also cement his relationships with his campaign workers.

Effects of Self-Disclosure

Self-disclosure is most commonly used as a distinct part of a speech that has another purpose, that of "warming up" the audience and establishing a relationship. Research shows that self-disclosure and liking are highly correlated (Jourard, 1959), that is, when a speaker discloses something personal, audience members like the speaker better. In addition, people are more likely to self-disclose to persons that they like. A speaker might well use this as a device to indicate liking to an audience.

Self-disclosers are usually perceived as more attractive to listeners than those who do not self-disclose (Worthy, Garay and Kahn, 1969). Therefore, many speakers use a significant act of self-disclosure as an ingratiating device. This technique is typically used in introductions to speeches because it serves to orient the material as well as ingratiate and involve the listeners.

Statistical Presentations

Few aspects of American culture are more pervasive than statistics. Numbers are the magic wand of modern communication, and communicators must be familiar with statistics and statistical reasoning in order to be effective. Let's look at this important form of informative speaking.

Statistical Reasoning

The basic assumption behind statistical reasoning is that observations can be classified into similar categories and counted. This is not a problem when we are counting the same item, such as the numbers of manufactured widgets, the number of cars on the road at any given time, or even the number of persons attending baseball games in cities of given sizes. When we begin to group certain kinds of human behaviors into numerical categories, however, we automatically run into problems.

Statistical reasoning assumes that the events counted or compared are similar and can be classified in a reasonable way. A second assumption is that adding these numbers makes sense in a numerical way. Recently a right-wing mem-

C. Everett Koop, Surgeon General of the U.S., informs and educates Americans on major health issues. This often involves explaining complicated medical matters in a manner that the general public can understand. (© UPI/Bettmann Newsphotos)

200 ■ ■ ■ Specific Speaking Tasks

ber of a vigilante group in the Midwest appeared on the Phil Donohue talk show and asserted that the world was being dominated by the "Jewish communication industry," and cited as evidence the "vastly overrating of the Nazi holocaust by Jewish publishers." He felt that the figure of six million Jews sent to the ovens was grossly in error and that the true figure was probably three million at the most. If you think about this for a moment, you will see the absolute irrelevance of his argument: Executing six million persons is, of course, twice as bad as executing three million, but anyone who executes three million persons is still monstrously criminal, as is any society that condones it. Not only is this statistical argument meaningless, it really has very little to do with the hypothetical existence of a "Jewish communication industry."

This kind of misuse of statistics is also illustrated by advocates of the nuclear arms race who give "parity" with the Russians as a national goal. "Parity" means that if the Russians can kill fifty million Americans, then we need to be able to kill at least that many Russians, not forty-five million. This is an excellent example of the misuse of numbers.

In short, numbers aren't meaningful in certain contexts, and any attempt to use them in these contexts exposes inherent problems in reasoning. Statistics, more than any other kind of information, must be subordinate to the basic purpose of the communication and not the other way around. Then, too, statistics are sometimes vital to your presentation. If you contend that Castro has wrecked the Cuban economy, you had better have production figures to back up your claim.

Reporting Methods

Another difficulty with statistics is in the method of gathering and reporting them. For example, the FBI compiles an annual "crime" report in which various kinds of criminal incidents are totaled. If you think about this for a moment, you will see that the definition of "crime" is enormously variable, depending on the interpretation of the victim and the local police: An "assault" to one victim or policeman might be "a little roughhouse among the boys" to another, and systematic perceptions of this kind may vary widely among regions. Statistics of this type are further complicated by the system used in reporting. If you are presenting information about the incidence of rape, you should be guided by the fact that many rapes go unreported due to the personal reasons of the victim or victim's family, the nature of rape trials, and so on.

In short, when reporting statistics concerning human behavior, the speaker should constantly be aware of potential problems in the reporting systems and take them into account.

Polls

One of the most common forms of statistical reporting is the poll. Polls are part of television ratings, product information, and election predictions. The national television networks live and die by their ratings, even though they know that the error factor is sometimes enormous. Before the 1980 election the polls

Figure 13.2

When reporting the results of a poll, the communicator must remember that the potential for error, in a poll, can be very large.

> Every poll has a built-in error factor. You can calculate this very simply by taking the proportion yielded by the poll, subtract it from 1, multiplying these two numbers together, dividing this by the number of persons sampled and then taking the square root of all of this. This is the "standard error" of the proportion, and the formula looks like this:
>
> $$\text{Standard error} = \sqrt{\frac{\text{Proportion} \times (1 - \text{Proportion})}{\text{Number in Sample}}}$$
>
> Thus, if CBS says it has 46% of the audience, we can evaluate this statistic by calculating the standard error of the proportion .46. First we multiply .46 times .54 (1 − .46) and get .2484. Then we divide this by the sample size (which they never tell us—but usually is around 1000). This gives us .0002484. Following that, we get the square root of .0002484 which is .01576, or approximately .016 or 1.6%—voila! the standard error. A 95% confidence interval will be approximately two standard errors in either direction, so we would be 95% confident that CBS actually had between 43% and 49% of the audience (46% + or − 3%). This is pretty rough, but gives you an idea how these figures are arrived at. You can see, for example, how little adding more respondents to the sample increases the standard error.

unanimously predicted a close election between Jimmy Carter and Ronald Reagan, but Reagan won in a landslide.

In general, presentations can be improved by including statistical information, but the presenter must be careful not to overvalue this kind of content simply because it is numerical. Numbers often have a way of obscuring the truth. (See Figure 13.2).

A Sample Informative Speech

In Chapters Seven through Nine, we followed the exploits of Mary, a typical college student who is preparing a speech "to inform students about the nature of alcohol in the United States." Here is Mary's completed speech.

Comparisons and contrast

When you think about the use of alcohol, what kind of image comes to your mind? Do you think of a glamorous couple, clothed in evening dress, sipping cocktails at a luxurious night spot—or do you think of a hopeless, homeless derelict, clutching a bottle of muscatel and lying in a heap of rags in an alley? Most of us can picture both kinds of alcohol users, and unfortunately the two are not as far apart as we might think.

Purpose statement	It is the purpose of my speech today to inform you of some of the facts about alcohol usage in the United States.
Division and purpose statement	There are many interesting facts about alcohol and its use. In this speech, I would like to concentrate on three main points: the use of alcohol is far more widespread than most of us think; alcohol is actually a highly dangerous drug; and alcoholism is more difficult to cure than is widely believed.
	How many social occasions do you attend every year? If you are like me, you go to a good many parties, receptions, open houses, and other less formal social gatherings. In our country, many of these occasions are accompanied by the use of alcohol in some form or another.
Specific instance	On this campus, for example, fraternal organizations host social events around the consumption of beer.
Relay	Last week there were four fraternity parties specifically labeled "beer blasts," and one sorority here has such a reputation for consumption of alcohol, they are popularly known as the "Lager Lou's."
	But alcohol consumption is not confined to sororities and fraternities. The "cocktail party" is one of the most widely practiced social events in the United States.
Relay	I would imagine that most of you in this class have parents who occasionally give a cocktail party—I know mine do. This fall on this campus, the first formal faculty function was a cocktail party.
Invokes well-known schema—"weddings"	Not only do we use alcohol casually, we integrate it into the most important events of our lives. Few weddings take place without champagne—not in church, of course, but at the receptions and the rehearsal dinners. The "stag party" the night before is traditionally celebrated with a good deal of strong drink. At ballgames, we eat hot dogs and beer, and at Christmas, we celebrate with punch. Professor Robert Strauss of the University of Kentucky, in the book *Contemporary Social Problems,* established that over 100 million Americans use alcohol in one form or another.
	In addition to the social uses of alcohol, we are all aware that many persons are solitary drinkers.

Specific relays	Alcohol is largely unregulated in our society. When regulation occurs, it is usually confined to specific groups, such as the young, or specific times, such as Sunday. Many states (such as Mississippi) have separate prohibition laws on a county-by-county basis, but these are the exception rather than the rule. Other states, such as California, permit alcohol sales in grocery stores and on any day of the week. Apparently most state legislatures feel that alcohol is essentially harmless. In addition, its sales brings in significant amounts of revenue for the states.
	You can see that alcohol is probably our most widely used drug. Now let me turn to the threat posed by alcohol. Rather than an innocuous social lubricant, alcohol is actually a highly dangerous drug.
	Tom Wicker of the *New York Times* has written on the vast amounts of media attention recently given to cocaine usage. Even the President's office has been involved in the "War on Cocaine." Wicker points out, however, that alcohol is not only more widespread but may be just as dangerous.
Relays–Gallup Poll	According to a recent Gallup Poll, over one-fourth of all American homes have been afflicted by an alcohol-related family problem.
Analysis	Even if we look at the possible error in this polling estimate, we can be *sure* that *at least* twenty percent of our homes have been affected, and perhaps as many as thirty percent. This is a staggering number. AIDS has been called an "epidemic," but its frequency of occurrence is nothing like alcohol-related problems.
Relay	When I began work on this speech, I interviewed Father Milton Spring of the Sacred Heart Cathedral in my home town. Father Spring told me that the single most important problem he faces in pastoral counseling is the use of alcohol. Nothing causes more problems to his parishioners—not unemployment, nor other drugs.
	According to Dr. Lawrence Wallack of the University of California at Berkeley, alcohol is the *direct* cause of 80,000 to 100,000 deaths each year in the United States. In addition to the direct deaths, alcohol is implicated in some way in another 100,000 deaths. He goes on to add that drinking is the leading cause of death for teens in alcohol-related car crashes. Anything that affects one-fourth of American homes

and kills over 100,000 of us each year is obviously "dangerous."

The last point I want to make today is that alcohol problems are more difficult to treat than most of us think. When I talk with other college students about alcohol they usually tell me that they can "handle it." This certainly may be true. But there are many things about alcohol that most of us don't know.

The first is that alcohol treatment is usually only effective for persons with stable relationships, minimal psychological problems, no history of past treatment failures, and minimal involvement with other drugs.

Definitional classification—new language

I am sure that some problem drinkers do indeed fit this profile. But think about some of the persons you know who have experienced personal difficulties because of alcohol usage. Isn't it true that a great many of them have lost their jobs and have suffered serious relational problems because of drinking? In other words, the milieu and effects of problem drinking almost inevitably make treatment difficult, if not impossible.

In addition, your genes may be working against you if you are a problem drinker. There is strong evidence to indicate that a tendency toward alcoholism is passed on from one generation to the next.

Specific relay

We may be able to diet and lose weight, to change our hair style, and to dress differently, but we can't change our genetic heritage. In other words, many problem drinkers have inherited tendencies that make the treatment of the problem much more difficult.

Summarizes

Today I have presented a few facts about alcohol usage, and I hope that they have been informative ones. The research I did for this speech shows that alcohol is our most widely used drug, and that it is actually far more dangerous than most persons think. In addition, alcohol problems are more difficult to treat than most persons think. Most of us in this room use alcohol in one way or another, and we will be faced with many situations in which alcohol is served. I hope these facts that I have presented today can help us all make intelligent choices.

Listening to Informative Speaking

In Chapter Three we discussed the fact that "lecture listening" results in only 25 percent efficiency. This means that only one-fourth of the material in a speech is retained. Key words, definitions, facts, or plans presented in the speech are likely to be lost. To overcome this attenuation, you need to make an extra effort, involving decisions on significance, efforts for retention, and note-taking.

Significance

Not everything that a speaker says, of course, is of vital significance, and you will immediately be able to reject a good deal of any speech as trivial—the jokes in the introduction, the personal references, and even many of the illustrations and examples. However, you cannot make a judgment unless you have a good idea of the speaker's purpose. So your first task is to assess that purpose and evaluate it against your own value system and needs.

Once you know the purpose, you can evaluate the remainder of the material to determine whether it is advancing the purpose or whether it can be forgotten. After all, we can't expect to remember everything, so we should exercise control. Even if a major portion of the speech is connected to the purpose, you may still be able to discard it. Trying to remember too much is a good way to remember nothing.

Retention

Once you have decided that a part of the speech is important, your next task is to attempt to retain it, that is, move it from your short-term memory to your long-term memory. The most common way of achieving this goal is to hold it in a "rehearsal" mode (repeating the item to yourself a number of times) until it can be transferred.

Association is another good method of retention. If you are listening to a speech explaining the differences in computing language, and you want to remember the names of two important languages, BASIC and FORTRAN, you might visualize a personal computer sitting on a baseball field on top of first base to help you recall "BASIC." Similarly, you might visualize a computer on the walls of a fort, to call up the word FORTRAN. These associational methods may sound outlandish, but they can sometimes work. You need to practice them, however, because they can often lead to false associations with disastrous results.

Note-taking

If the situation permits, you may wish to take notes in order to have a permanent record of important parts of the message. Research on note-taking shows that simply taking notes, in and of itself, does not help us to remember facts about the message (Searle, 1984). When notes are used subsequently for review, however, they do contribute to memory and, of course, can also be used as a permanent reference.

Summary

The basic form of informative communication is the relay, in which the communicator acts as a surrogate for an actual sense experience or other incoming data. Recreating experience is quite difficult, and some kinds of experiences are probably unsuitable for this kind of communication. Nonetheless, many facets of our social structure depend on the relay, particularly the legal process.

Information is defined as the lack of redundancy in, or predictability of, a message. A predictable message carries little or no information; an unpredictable one carries more information. Most ordinary communication is predictable to one extent or another because the structure of language and society determines a great deal of our behavior. The basic unit of information is the "bit," which is defined as the amount of information carried in a message system with two equiprobable outcomes.

Informative communication usually aims at the creating of new percepts and language, though new schemas may also be included.

Specific forms of informative speaking are the demonstration and the explanation. Self-disclosure is an important form of exposition but is more often used as a means rather than an end in most speeches. Statistical presentations are difficult, especially because of our tendency to overvalue statistical evidence.

Listening to informative presentations involves judgments about the importance of various parts of the speech and attempts to retain them. Note-taking is a useful aid to memory but is not always as valuable as we might think.

On Your Own

1. Ask three friends if they would rather be "intelligent" or "well-informed." Ask them why. Compare these reactions to your own feelings.
2. Count the factual statements in the sample speech in this chapter. How many of these would you expect an average audience to retain (see Chapter Three for retention notes)?
3. Numbers bore some people. Do you know why? What gender differences do you observe here? If you do observe any, can you explain them?
4. List some reasons why speakers might assert that they "only wish to inform" when they actually intend to persuade?
5. During the next speech assignment, make a list of questions that you would like to ask the speaker. Try to predict the speaker's answers. Then, ask the questions and compare your predictions with the actual answers. How do you explain the differences?

Suggestions for Further Reading

Barker, L. 1971. *Listening behavior.* Englewood Cliffs, NJ: Prentice Hall.

Cherry, C. 1961. *On human communication.* New York: Harper & Row.

Howard, D. 1983. *Cognitive psychology.* New York: Macmillan.

Jourard, S. 1959. Self-disclosure and other-cathexis. *Journal of Abnormal and Social Psychology* 59: 428–31.

Pierce, J. R. 1961. *Symbols, signals, and noise.* New York: Harper & Row.

Williams, F. 1984. *The new communication.* Belmont, CA: Wadsworth.

Worthy, M., A. Garay, and G. Kahn. 1969. Self-disclosure as an exchange process. *Journal of Personality and Social Psychology* 13: 59–63.

Fourteen

Persuasive Communication

> For mankind makes far more determinations through hatred, or love, or desire, or anger, or grief, or joy, or hope, or fear, or error, or some other affection of mind, than from regard of truth, or any settled maxim, or principle of right, or judicial form, or adherence to laws.
>
> Cicero, DE ORATORE, Book II, cxli.

Key Terms

affect
reinforcing
shaping
implicit responses
behavioral intentions
coercion
incongruity
imbalance
dissonance
credibility
safety-trustworthiness
qualification-expertness
normative-identificatory
compliance-dynamism
motivated sequence

Objectives

After studying this chapter, you should be able to:

1. Identify the differences between informative and persuasive speaking, based on whether the speaker emphasizes relaying, externalizing, stimulating, or activating

2. Differentiate among speeches that change, reinforce, and shape responses

3. Illustrate the ways that attitudes are actually potential behavior

4. Show how persuasion is often actually coercion

5. Illustrate how cognitive consistency operates in typical persuasive speeches

6. Define the four principal forms of credibility

7. Recognize the affective elements involved in speeches of stimulation

8. Understand some of the difficulties in listening to persuasion

Cicero's words show us that speakers have always puzzled over the problems inherent in getting people to *believe in* an issue. There is satisfaction, of course, in informing persons; there is also satisfaction in stimulating them. When it comes to an issue about which you really care, you want your listeners to agree with you and *behave* accordingly.

In Chapter Thirteen we examined informative speeches—speeches designed to create new percepts, language, or schemas—but many situations demand more from the audience. If you are speaking about health foods, you may not be content to be informative about good nutrition; you might also want your listeners to practice good dietary habits as a result of your speech. A police officer conducting a safety seminar for student drivers wants the audience to *understand* principles of safety on the road, but also wants the group to *drive safely* as a result of this understanding. A minister might want his or her congregation to *know* the principles of ethical conduct, but would be much more satisfied if they *practiced* these principles in their dealings with others.

"Affect" or emotion, you will recall from Chapter Two, is an important element in our inner lives. Persuasive communication typically emphasizes affect as an important outcome, more so than other forms of communication, because persuasion seeks to *change behavior* and so needs to invoke the kinds of affect that we usually call "motives." As Cicero observed, emotional appeals are one of the surest ways to accomplish this goal. As a consequence, writers on communication have associated persuasion with the creation or recreation of affect, though affect alone is not the best test of persuasion—the main goal is *action*.

Informative speaking mainly uses relaying and externalization as the basic forms of communication. To achieve action, persuasive speaking uses *stimulation* and *activation*.

Persuasive communication occurs in a great many settings. Persuasion occurs in the arts, in politics, in education, and in our personal and social lives. Persuasion can also be part of public speaking. In this chapter, we will look at the general process of persuasion and then discuss how you can successfully adapt this form to speaking.

Definitions of Persuasion

The word *persuasion*, like *communication* and *information*, is badly misused by many persons. Therefore, a good definition is a necessary prerequisite to our understanding of the concept.

Persuasion and Action

Any good definition of persuasion must include action as an end product of the communicative interaction. Action is a good word when we are describing simple communicative aids. But there are many more complex kinds of action, such as starting a diet or disparaging your professor after a tough exam. Although we could classify either of these actions as possible outcomes of persuasive communication, persuasion more typically produces a "response." Miller (1980) has examined responses to persuasion and has classified them as changing, reinforcing, and shaping responses.

Changing Responses

Miller describes change of response this way: "Smokers are persuaded to become nonsmokers, automobile drivers are persuaded to walk or to use public transportation, Christians are persuaded to become Moslems, and so on." These are relatively drastic changes, yet sometimes these "conversions" do occur, and persuasion is the main element that stimulates them.

Reinforcing Responses

This type of response occurs when the speaker modifies an existing attitude or behavior. For example, when addressing a group of sales representatives, a sales director tries to reinforce the staff's existing drive for more sales and subsequent personal and financial rewards. At a political party rally before an election, a candidate urges campaign workers to get out the vote and to work harder, attempting to strengthen their existing commitment to the party.

Shaping Responses

Shaping occurs when the audience has no previous experience with, or knowledge about, the topic. For example, a message urging an audience to support an underground newspaper would be an example of shaping response if this particular audience had never been exposed to an underground newspaper.

Using Miller's three end products of persuasion supplies the elements for a comprehensive definition:

> **Persuasion is communicative behavior that aims to reinforce, shape, or change response.**

This working definition still has some problems, however. If you recall the discussion of communication processes in Chapter Two, you remember that it is unusual for communicators to get an *immediate* response. Sometimes the response is delayed or never performed. If you persuade someone to diet, for example, the responses are performed slowly over a long period of time. Yet communication changes *something*, if not the immediate response. More commonly, we say that communication changes *attitudes* and *behavioral intentions* rather than immediate responses. So we first need to understand the nature of attitudes and behavioral intentions and how they are affected by our messages.

Attitudes and Behavioral Intentions

Few concepts have been of greater importance in the field of social science than "attitude." Social attitudes are extremely important to almost every major theory of social psychology. The word *attitude* derives from the Latin word *aptus,* meaning position or orientation. When astronauts steer a space shuttle, they use "attitude controls," which position the craft in space. Similarly, our attitudes define our positions concerning a number of social issues. Most people have an attitude about college, about communication, and about public speaking. We possess attitudes about Republicans, about books, about the Rolling Stones, and about marriage. What exactly do we mean when we say we "have" an attitude?

First, attitudes are usually *implicit responses,* or private ideas and feelings of which other people are not aware. At the same time, these ideas and feelings have an external, observable component. For example, if you are happy about buying a new Madonna record, you might have an internal feeling of excitement and might also exhibit other observable behavior—smiles, laughter, and statements such as "awesome" and "rad!" However, *you do not necessarily have to display your attitude to have one.* Some of our most important inner feelings and attitudes are intensely private and are not overtly expressed.

Exactly how these inner and outer elements of attitudes are related is not known. Figure 14.1 shows one interpretation of how attitude might be illustrated

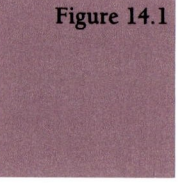

Figure 14.1

The "inner" components of an attitude are the private (unseen) ideas and feelings of an individual; while the "outer" components are the observable results of an attitude.

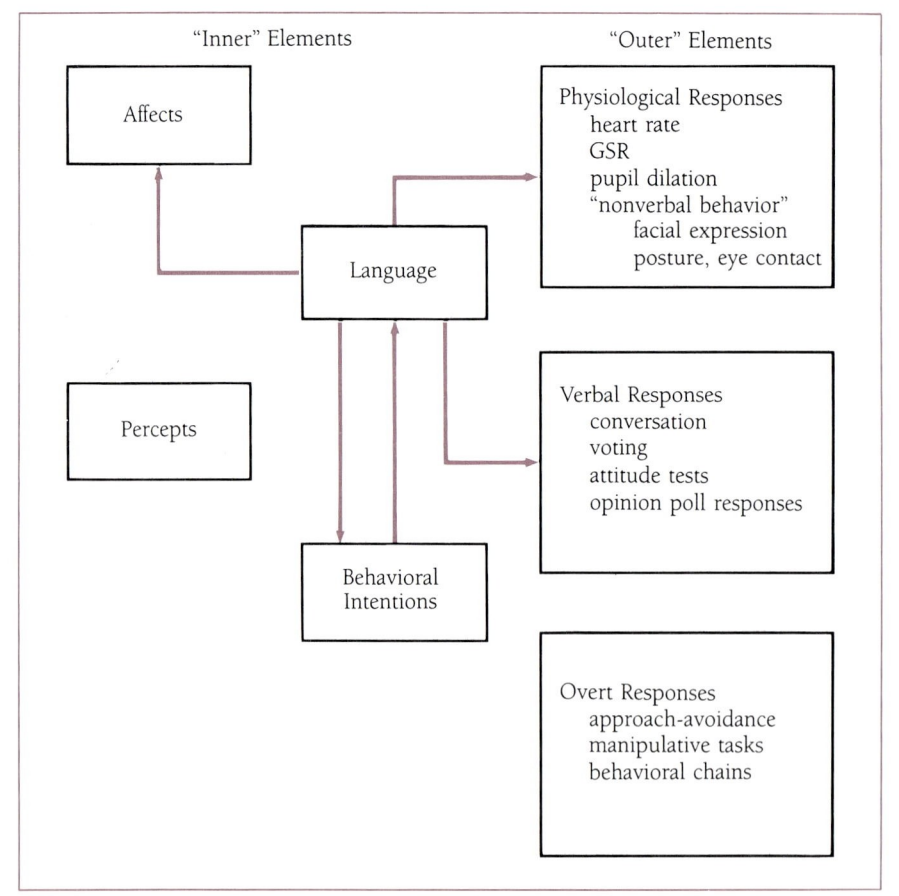

"Inner" Elements | "Outer" Elements

- Affects
- Language
- Percepts
- Behavioral Intentions

Physiological Responses
  heart rate
  GSR
  pupil dilation
  "nonverbal behavior"
  facial expression
  posture, eye contact

Verbal Responses
  conversation
  voting
  attitude tests
  opinion poll responses

Overt Responses
  approach-avoidance
  manipulative tasks
  behavioral chains

in a diagram. The inner components of an attitude include some of our "old friends" —affects, schemas, percepts, and language—and a new one, "behavioral intention." A *behavioral intention* is a special kind of schema in which *potential* behavior governs the structure of the response.

The outer components of an attitude are its observable aspects, nonverbal behavior, actions, statements, and other behavior. For example, you might have an extremely negative attitude about a company that is a habitual polluter. You also plan to boycott that company's products and urge your friends to do the same. Many persons have attitudes without behavioral intentions, but hardly anyone has behavioral intentions without attitudes.

All of these elements need not be totally consistent, and often they are not; that is, our attitudes and our actions are often not the same.

If a speaker has the choice between changing attitudes and changing behavior, which should he choose? Unfortunately, we don't have that choice. In a political speech a week before an election, for example, a speaker would probably say: "Vote for Sabina Letftwinkle because..." The speaker certainly could not expect the audience to rush out and vote for Sabina because the election isn't until the following Tuesday. The best the speaker could hope for is that the speech will instill in listeners a positive attitude about Sabina that would carry over to election day. This does not mean that speakers are not interested in behavior or ultimate actions; in fact, the ultimate meaning of attitudes is probably to be found in the behaviors that they influence. However, most persuasive communication is aimed at influencing the internal components of attitudes or behavioral intentions of the listeners.

Persuasion or Coercion?

Sadly, many persons still believe that physical force is a legitimate means to bring about behavioral change. Physical coercion rarely, if ever, changes attitudes and might even reinforce them; unfortunately, it does appeal to a certain kind of person in our society. As a consequence, many people confuse persuasion with coercion, even though they have important differences. They both aim at influencing behavior, but the effects are drastically different. Coercion is usually effective only under conditions of surveillance (Kelman, 1961), while persuasion is more permanent. Coercion creates attitudes of hostility and resentment toward the source, while persuasion is essentially neutral. Given these characteristics, why would anyone choose coercive means?

At the root of the problem is the fact that coercion is sometimes easier than persuasion, at least in the short run. Many persons simply won't be persuaded unless they are coerced. The following news story, entitled "Mugged Judge Getting Tough," is an example of an individual who changed his attitude only after circumstances changed it for him.

> *Michigan Supreme Court Justice G. Mennen (Soapy) Williams, known for his liberal stand on crime, proclaimed through bruised and stitched lips Thursday that it's time city dwellers were granted "freedom from fear."*
>
> *The six-term governor and former ambassador was mugged by three men Wednesday*

Figure 14.2

This simple diagram shows how persuasion and coercion overlap.

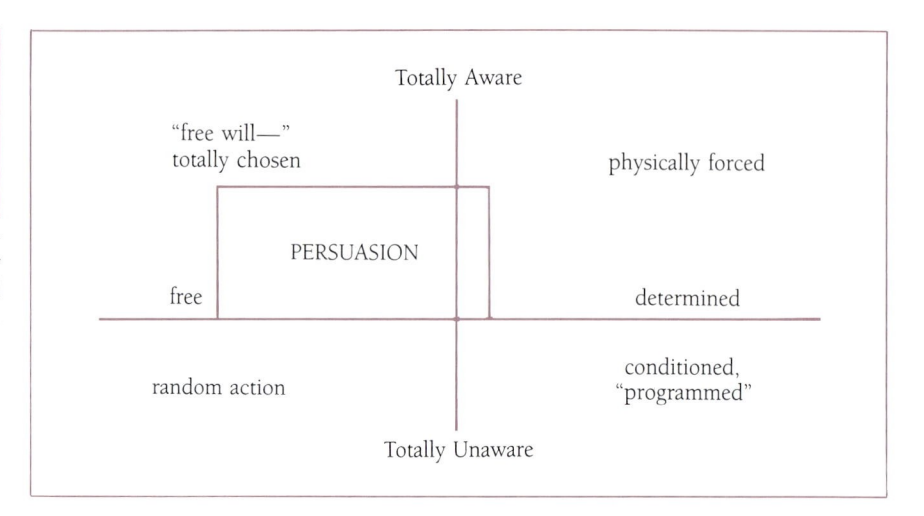

(Diagram: A coordinate plane with vertical axis from "Totally Unaware" (bottom) to "Totally Aware" (top), and horizontal axis from "free" (left) to "determined" (right). Four quadrants are labeled: upper-left "'free will—' totally chosen"; upper-right "physically forced"; lower-left "random action"; lower-right "conditioned, 'programmed'". A box labeled "PERSUASION" straddles the center, mostly in the upper-left quadrant but extending slightly into the upper-right.)

> *night at the townhouse of his vacationing secretary where he had gone to pick up the mail and water the plants.*
>
> *"I was sort of surprised a thing of this kind could happen on a main street," the 6-foot-3, 215-pound justice told reporters outside Supreme Court chambers in Lansing after completing a full morning's workload Thursday.*
>
> Lexington Leader, June 4, 1976.

Judge Williams had been convinced that criminals should be treated liberally until he was mugged, and then he decided to get tough. In other words, he needed coercion by an external event to change his belief. The efficiency of such change makes many persuaders want to simplify matters by resorting to coercion.

Another common shortcut to persuasion is simple deception. Deception and coercion are inherent in interesting ways. Unfortunately, many common persuasive acts contain a little of each. Figure 14.2 illustrates the way the two interact.

Persuasive speakers rarely tell the audience *everything* so in a sense a little deception is always present. In addition, persuasion sometimes contains some elements of implied force, such as speeches that warn an audience with implied reward or punishment. For example, a speaker who says "Brush your teeth or they will fall out" is utilizing a threat of punishment and is straying on the border of coercion. However, there is a big difference between this type of warning and the threat "Brush your teeth or I will hit you." In short, persuasion occurs when there is an absence of physical forcing; coercion is the use of force to induce behavior.

How Does Persuasion Work?

The basic mechanism of persuasion operates through the interaction of a credible source presenting an attitude-discrepant message that creates internal tension. In other words, when the input is contradictory to your present condition, you feel tension. Psychologists have described this tension in various ways, calling it incongruity, imbalance, or dissonance. This tension, if effective, results in attitude change. The name of the process that operates in the juxtaposition of a credible source with a novel or attitude-discrepant idea is called variously imbalance, incongruity, or dissonance.

To illustrate how persuasion works, suppose that you are the marketing director of a major airline, and you learn that a noted novelist, (call him "John Smith"), hates air travel. You decide that it would be grand for Delta if you could persuade Smith to start flying Delta, to respond to his many invitations to speak and attend conferences. So at the beginning of the persuasive interaction, the situation looks something like the diagram in Figure 14.3. You are the "source" and Smith is the "receiver." The arrow and minus sign drawn from Smith to the airplane expresses his negative attitude about air travel. The arrow and plus sign drawn from you to the airplane represents your positive attitude about air travel.

You construct what you think is an excellent message, reminding Mr. Smith that air travel is safe, that many persons have learned to enjoy it, and that it will save him time. Before you do that, however, you need to make sure that he sees you as a *credible* person who really knows about air travel, has years of experience with Delta, and has his best interests in mind. If your credibility is sufficient, then the situation would change to the one shown in Figure 14.4. This situation, known variously as *imbalance, incongruity,* or *dissonance,* will be termed *inconsistency* in this chapter. The receiver's perceptions don't "add up," and therefore create discomfort. As a result, the receiver, consciously or unconsciously, wants to change them.

To return to our example, we will assume that Mr. Smith's conflicting cognitions—his negative attitude about air travel and his positive attitude about you—produce psychological discomfort, and you hope that he will change his cognitions so that your persuasive interaction appears like the one shown in Figure 14.5. As shown in this diagram, the receiver has become more positive about the communication object. Your message has been successful, and Mr. Smith is now more positive about flying. In other words, you have changed his attitude and persuasion has taken place.

Unfortunately, Mr. Smith's attitudes can change in more than one way. An equally likely outcome is pictured in Figure 14.6. In this case, Mr. Smith changes

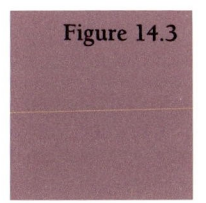

Figure 14.3

A simple form of persuasion where the source relays a "positive" attitude to the receiver who has a "negative" attitude.

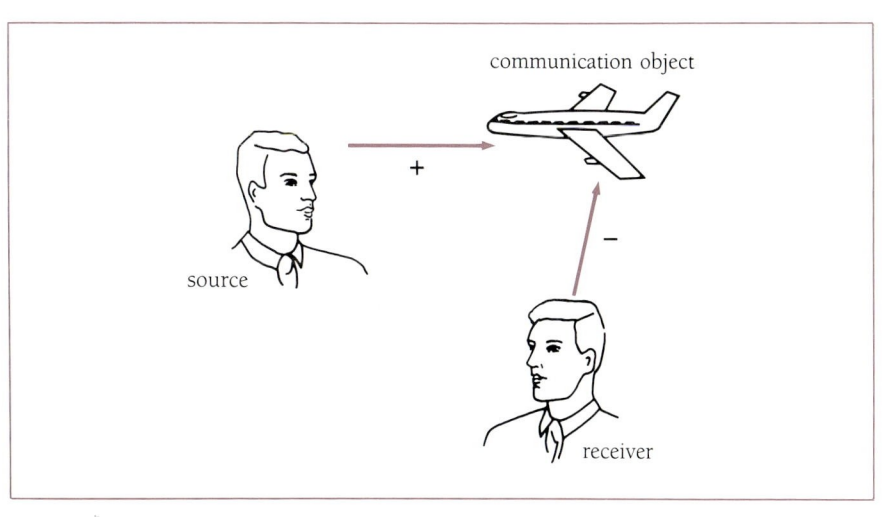

Persuasive Communication ■ ■ ■ 215

Figure 14.4

Inconsistencies occur when the receiver believes the source is "credible" while still having a negative attitude towards air travel. This creates a situation where the receiver may consciously or unconsciously want to change his perceptions.

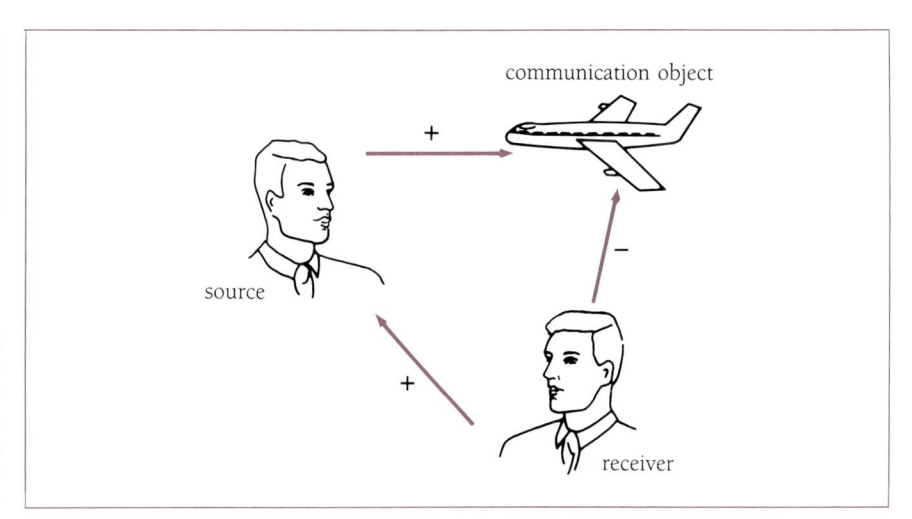

Figure 14.5

When the receiver has become more positive about air travel, the source has "persuaded" the receiver to change an attitude.

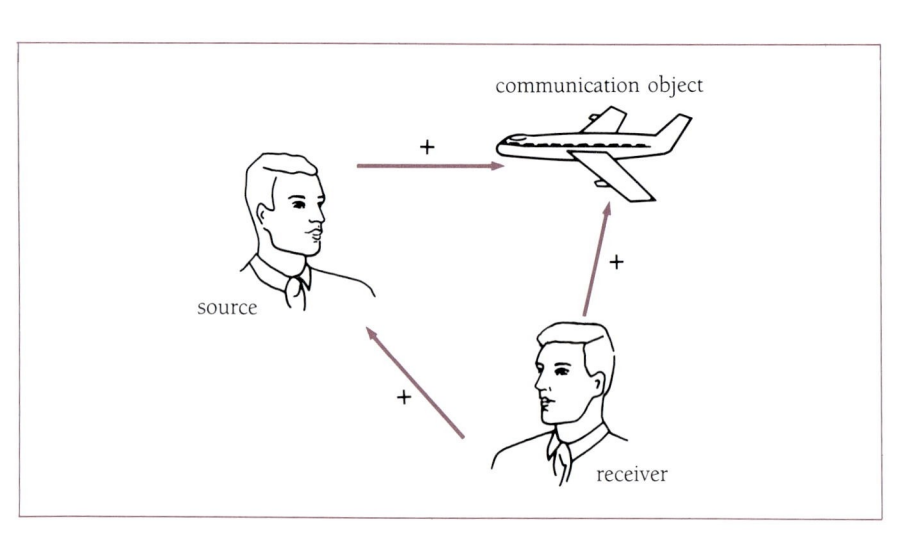

Figure 14.6

Attitudes can be changed in different ways. The receiver may well change an attitude about the source rather than air travel.

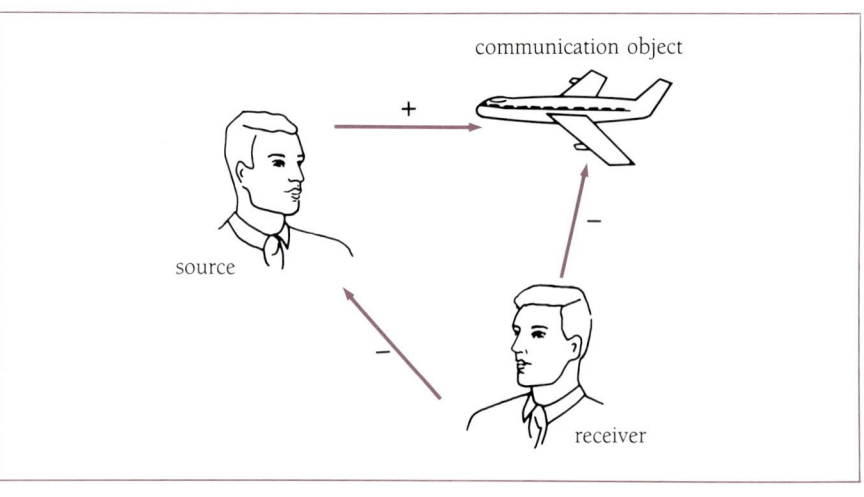

Figure 14.7

The source can be more successful when credibility outweighs the receiver's negative attitude. Thus increasing the chances of persuasion.

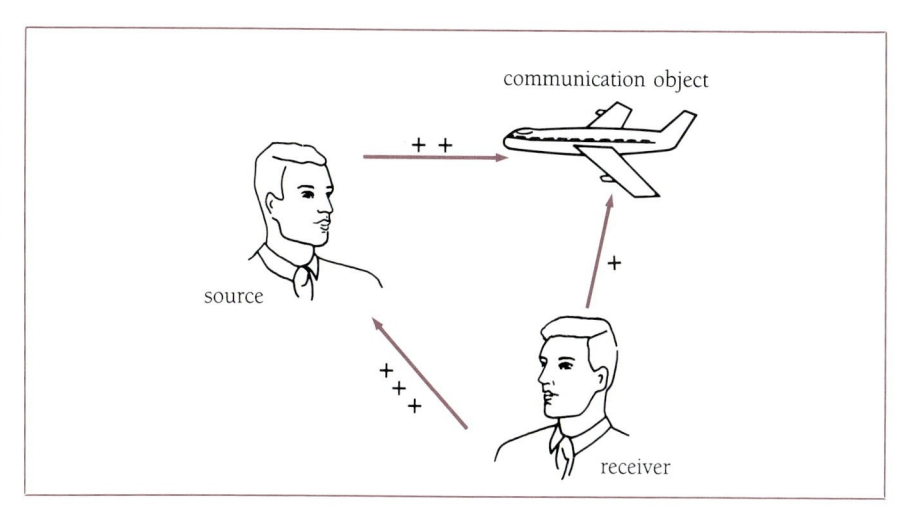

his attitude about you rather than about flying. His cognitive system is consistent once again, but not in the way you wanted.

In other words, you cannot guarantee that your message will produce the desired result. This prospect often upsets people when they realize that even with their best intentions their persuasive communication may result in only a negative shift about their own credibility—and more often than they might think (Bostrom, 1983).

Does this mean that persuasion is impossible, or risky at best? No—because you have many ways of improving your chances. One way is to change the receiver's evaluation of the source (perception of *credibility*) so that it is stronger than the evaluation of the communication object. Figure 14.7 illustrates this situation.

As shown in this diagram, when the source's credibility and evaluation of the object are both strong, the receiver's evaluation of the object has a good chance of moving from negative to positive.

Realistically, however, few persons can attain this much credibility in most circumstances. And if credibility is really low, listeners have a problem in saving "face" if they adopt the persuader's ideas. Changing attitudes as a result of a persuasive message presented by a low-credible source might well make the changer look foolish. Saving "face" is one of the most important ways in which people keep equilibrium in social interactions (Applegate, 1985) and surely operates in the persuasion situation. Clark (1984) suggests that persuaders can meet this problem head-on with face-saving strategies, such as mentioning that times change, that everyone changes attitudes once in a while, that information has come to light that justifies change, and so on.

In general, however, one of the best ways to persuade a receiver to change a position and still allow the receiver to save "face" is to accrue as much credibility as is possible. Let's look at ways that credibility is developed and maintained.

Credibility

Originally, when people used the word *credibility* they meant "honesty." In 1987, the Reagan Administration suffered a serious "credibility loss" when it was discovered that two high-ranking members of the national security staff had secretly channeled money to rebels in Nicaragua. Credibility, however, is not one simple factor but is composed of several characteristics.

Safety-Trustworthiness

Whom do you trust? Some persons more than others! Trustworthiness is the characteristic of credibility that relates to the basic truthfulness of individuals. Since truthful persons are "safe," most researchers use "safety" together with trustworthiness when discussing this factor. Some persons tell the truth; others are inclined to stretch the truth. Receivers are usually very sensitive to issues of self-interest as it relates to trustworthiness. For example, a building materials salesperson might tell you that a new patio added to your house would increase the value of the house by much more than the cost of the materials. When receiving such a message you might realize that the salesperson is right, but that the salesperson has a vested interest in selling you the building materials. Whenever salespeople receive a commission, the issue of credibility becomes particularly germane. This is why many corporations pay salespersons a straight salary rather than a commission.

A speaker who is perceived as highly qualified on a particular topic, such as Ralph Nader on consumer issues, will be very persuasive with audiences. (© Peeter Vilms/Jeroboam, Inc.)

218 ■ ■ ■ Specific Speaking Tasks

Qualification-Expertness

This basic credibility factor concerns whether the source is able to speak with authority on a particular issue. If you are concerned with the possible danger of nuclear power plants, for example, you would definitely want to listen to someone who had extensive training in nuclear physics. Many executives of nuclear power companies lack this training and also lack trustworthiness because of vested self-interest.

Just who is qualified to speak on a particular issue is always in doubt. Ralph Nader is clearly an important "voice" for the consumer on many issues, yet he lacks formal training in highway safety or nuclear engineering. He has been able to train himself on these issues so that his credibility has been consistently high.

Qualification-expertness seems fairly straightforward but is not always as easy to analyze as it seems. It depends heavily on the approach to the topic and the treatment that you give it.

Normative-Identificatory

This characteristic of credibility is often exploited in advertising. Commercials for a national brand of pudding, for example, do not discuss the quality of the ingredients used in the pudding but rather show Bill Cosby and a group of smiling children eating the dessert. These commercials are enormously effective because families *identify* with Bill Cosby, star of a popular, family-type television show. As a beginning speaker you probably do not have this kind of normative-identificatory credibility so you can do little to get an audience to identify with you. However, you can deal with the problem in a constructive way in certain situations. President Reagan, when speaking to a group of broadcasters, reminds the audience that he began his career as a sports announcer. Every presidential candidate, when speaking to the American Legion, ostentatiously wears the Legion cap. If you can find areas of identification with your audience, you would be foolish not to take advantage of them.

Compliance-Dynamism

This credibility factor, involving the audience's perception of the speaker's power, is more subtle than the factors above; in fact, it is usually not thought of as a characteristic of credibility at all. People are more easily persuaded by persons with power than persons without power. Powerful persons can ask and receive compliance, and often adopt mannerisms we call "dynamic."

Power is often exhibited in nonverbal cues, such as eye contact and posture, so your delivery of a persuasive speech is an important factor in determining your credibility. Hesitant speech is perceived by most persons as a lack of confidence. A dynamic, assertive delivery, on the other hand, is usually interpreted as an indicator of confidence and thus power.

Practically speaking, you will probably not have all these characteristics, but you still need to present a persuasive speech. In order to do so, you can also create credibility through the construction of the speech.

Constructing the Persuasive Speech

The first step in constructing a persuasive speech is to analyze your audience (see Chapter Six) and decide if you have intrinsic credibility based on your own experience and background. If not, you will need to base your persuasive appeal on extrinsic credibility, which will be the case for most college students. Two main factors contribute to external credibility: evidence and organization.

Evidence

"Evidence" is the citation of both fact and opinion. Usually evidence is defined as statements that logically lead to belief, but many experts contend that anything that leads to belief is evidence. McCroskey (1969) points out that:

> *Evidence may significantly increase immediate audience attitude change or source credibility when the source is initially perceived to be moderate-to-low credible, when the message is well-delivered, and when the audience has little or no prior familiarity with the evidence included or similar evidence.*

Research also shows that evidence has little effect if the message is delivered poorly, if the audience is already familiar with the evidence, or if the source is already perceived as being highly credible. It is obvious that you need to find fresh, interesting sources for your speech, and you also need to be careful with your delivery. Perhaps most importantly, you need to be quite careful about the kinds of evidence you include. Specifically, you need to make sure that you differentiate between factual statements and opinion statements.

Factual Statements

Although most people associate "facts" with "truth," a factual statement *must be able to be validated through sense data*. In other words, a factual statement must contain within it a means of verification. For example, if you say, "The Washington Monument is 169 meters high," we can verify the statement by visiting the monument and performing some kind of measurement, perhaps with a long measuring tape (Bostrom, 1983). This fact is not easily verifiable now, of course, but presumably reliable sources have verified the measurement in the past. The important idea is that the statement is *capable* of empirical verification.

A factual statement does not have to be long or involved. Notice how Dr. Roy Wilkins used a simple factual statement in this address to the NAACP (O'Neill, 1971):

> *In the Watts district of Los Angeles last year the unemployment rate was more than 30 percent, a rate higher than that during the great, nationwide Depression of the 1930s. The Negro teenage rate is nearly 25 percent, as against 13 percent for white teenagers.*

When you, as a student, include factual statements in your speech, your first step is to *cite your sources,* so that listeners can find out for themselves if they so desire. For example, if you were to use the above statement from Dr. Wilkins, you might say: "According to Dr. Roy Wilkins in his past address to the NAACP, in the Watts district ..."

Opinion

If you examined topics that are most often chosen for persuasive communication, you would be struck by how many of them have no real factual basis. It almost seems that when data is scarce, opinions are the strongest. Consider the legality of abortion, for example. The basic factual issues surrounding the abortion dispute focus on when "life" begins. One group feels that life begins in the third trimester; another group believes that it actually begins at conception. Note that the fetus is the same, regardless of how people define it. One group feels that it is advocating a "pro-choice" position; the other group feels that it is adopting a "pro-life" position. Obviously these values are in conflict, and if you hope to persuade someone on this topic, you will need to depend heavily on highly credible sources who agree with your position so as to give yourself and your position credibility.

Audience analysis should be at the core of your search for credible opinions. You need to look for sources that not only are deemed credible by your audience but have earned the right to speak on your particular topic.

Once you have gathered sufficient factual material and opinions, your next step is to organize them into a persuasive plan.

Organization

You can approach the organization of persuasive speeches in several ways. Your first task, of course, is to review the main types of organization presented in Chapter Nine: chronological, logical, spatial, cause-effect, and problem-solving. Of these, logical, cause-effect, and problem-solving are particularly apt for organizing a persuasive speech.

Motivated Sequence

One of the most interesting speech plans, the "motivated sequence," was devised by the distinguished educator Alan H. Monroe and appears in many modern texts on public speaking (Ehninger, Monroe, and Gronbeck, 1978). Monroe's design of a good persuasive speech looks like this:

1. *Attention Step.* Alert the audience to what is planned; make sure that all are paying attention.
2. *Need Step.* Demonstrate to the audience that there is a significant need.
3. *Satisfaction Step.* Show that what you propose will bring about the satisfaction of the need.

4. *Visualization Step.* Demonstrate what things will look like if your proposal is adopted.

5. *Action step.* Call for specific action.

Many times all five steps are not absolutely necessary; in other circumstances, one might choose the simpler problem-solving plan.

Problem-Solution

A simpler version of the motivated sequence is the problem-solution plan, which divides the speech into two main parts. For many audiences, creating a belief that there is a problem is quite enough. Look at the way that Jenkin Lloyd Jones, a well-known publisher, approached the problem of the "generation gap" in this speech excerpt:

> *Who raised the most lopsided generation in human history? We did. Who collapsed when little Phyllis went into a tantrum because Mary's mother was going to let her go steady at thirteen? And who hurled little Phyllis into a premature monogamy for which she was not physically or psychologically prepared? And who is reaping the whirlwind? We are.*
>
> *Who has retained our children, in one measure, in their swaddling clothes long after they should have been given responsibility and, in another measure, has put them under artificial and deleterious pseudosophistication which would assume that they were more adult than they are? In the state of New York, on the eve of one's twenty-first birthday, one is still supposed to be such a child that one isn't supposed to know enough not to shoot a cop. But we have decided that three years before reaching age twenty-one one knows enough to pick a president of the United States. Who created this dichotomy? We did. (Linkugel, Allen and Johannson, 1982.)*

Only at the end of this speech did Mr. Jones propose a solution—returning to family structure with stronger interactions and stronger traditions. This is typical of problem-solving speeches, because once the existence of the problem is accepted, the solution is often obvious. When it is not, of course, more attention is needed. For example, solving the problem of AIDS in our society could take many forms—education, discipline, hygiene, and the like.

Stimulation—Arousing Audiences

In our examination of persuasive speaking we have focused on *activation*, which is primarily aimed at attitude change. The stimulation of affect is also a part of persuasion and in many circumstances is a legitimate persuasive end in and of itself.

Most people have heard "inspirational" or "motivational" speeches that tried to create a state of excitement or other appropriate feelings. For example, the half-time locker room speeches in which Knute Rockne fired up his Notre Dame football team are legendary in the sports world. This kind of persuasive speech is a difficult

Shirley Chisholm was the first black woman to enter Congress and was an effective spokesperson for minority rights and urban needs. Here, with a Martin Luther King photo for a backdrop, she delivers an "arousing" speech. (© Hap Stewart/Jeroboam, Inc.)

task and requires a good deal of preparation, but it is not totally beyond the ability of beginners and you may wish to attempt it.

The first necessary ingredient of the arousing speech is the presence of arousal in the speaker. William Jennings Bryan once said that eloquence was "thought on fire," meaning that the speaker had to be fired up before an audience could be the same. The speaker needs to communicate this enthusiasm in a meaningful way to everyone present.

The second component is *arousing content*—material that stimulates an emotional response. In the following excerpt from a speech by Eldridge Cleaver on the death of Dr. Martin Luther King, look how Cleaver's bitterness and disappointment are brought out (O'Neill, 1971):

> *Is the death of Dr. King a sad day for America? No. It is a day consistent with what America demands by its actions. The death of Dr. King was not a tragedy for America. America should be happy that Dr. King is dead, because America worked so hard to bring it about. And now all the hypocritical, vicious madmen who pollute the government of this country and who befoul the police agencies of this country, all of the hypocritical public announcements following the death of Dr. King are being repudiated and held in contempt, not only by black people but by millions of white people who know that had these same treacherous political gangsters made the moves that clearly lay within their power to make, Dr. King would not be dead, nonviolence would prevail and the terror would not be upon us. These people, the police departments, the legislatures, the government, the Democratic Party, the Republican Party, those commonly referred to as the Establishment or the power structure, they can be looked upon as immediate targets and symbols of blame.*

Persuasive Communication

In preparing speeches that have the goal of arousal, it is important to keep in mind the audience's basic schema structure that ties the emotions together. Robert Plutchik (1980) concludes that emotions are a combination of a general "arousal" state (a general activation) and specific schematic identifiers that enable us to classify the nature of the emotions that we are feeling. For example, when you are elated, you have coupled basic arousal with the specific schemas that you have associated with elation. When you feel grief, you have invoked a schema associated with loss, grieving, and the like. Plutchik contends that the basic arousal of different emotions is the same, but the schemas involved are different. For example, if one experiences an emotional "high" while watching a sunset at the seashore, the attribution would produce feelings of appreciation of "natural beauty." But when exactly the same emotion is experienced in church, the attribution is to goodness, reverence, or the like. This means that the speaker must be sure that these schematic elements are clear in the speech or very familiar to the audience.

Now that we've explored the process of persuasive speaking, let's turn our attention to how best to listen to persuasive attempts. As with listening to other kinds of communication, listening to persuasion is probably as important as constructing and delivering a persuasive speech.

Listening to Persuasion

Before listening to a persuasive speech, you should review the general process of persuasion and identify the elements as they affect you. You can use the inconsistency model presented in this chapter when you listen to a persuasive message that is opposed to your own position. Instead of denigrating the source, you might reconsider your position on the communication object.

A clear example of a receiver changing attitudes about the source rather than the communication object occurred in 1985, when the *Lexington Herald-Leader* published a series of stories about illegal gifts to University of Kentucky basketball players by local businessmen and wealthy sports fans. Instead of changing their attitudes about the way the basketball program is administered, many readers chose to attack the *Herald-Leader,* canceling their subscriptions and accusing the newspaper of distortions, bad faith, and other hidden motives.

Another crucial factor in listening to persuasion is a thorough knowledge of credibility. Many persuaders manipulate their credibility through normative and compliant means. For example, a widely shown commercial promoting batteries featured Mary Lou Retton, a U.S. gymnast and Olympic gold medalist. Miss Retton is clearly an expert on gymnastics, but her knowledge of flashlight batteries is probably minimal.

Propaganda Techniques

You should also learn to recognize certain traps that persuaders use. In 1937, the Institute for Propaganda Analysis published a list of propaganda devices in common use at the time. Some have changed over the years, but they are still worth our attention.

The Bandwagon Effect

"Jumping on the bandwagon" simply means falling for the argument that "everyone is doing this; you will be out of touch if you don't"—a popular device used by television commercials. Persuasive speaking that relies exclusively on opinion often utilizes this effect. You need to ask yourself if the opinions and individuals cited are credible. Public opinion—a large bandwagon—is interesting but often wrong.

Half-Truth

The half-truth is another device used by unscrupulous persuaders to fortify their case. Suppose, for example, that you hear a speaker say: "Natural fluoridation of drinking water produces discoloration and mottling of the enamel on teeth." Although this statement is true, natural fluoridation also prevents cavities. What the speaker didn't say is that artificial fluoridation is never done in the same high concentrations of natural fluoridation, so that discoloration of the teeth is hardly a worry. This person has told you a "half-truth." It was true, but it was only part of the truth.

Hasty Generalization

Hasty generalizations are another familiar device. Recently a number of fundamentalists have declared that AIDS is "God's punishment for homosexuals,"

Propaganda devices include the spreading of ideas and information as a form of public action, as the girl in this picture demonstrates. (© Kent Reno/Jeroboam, Inc.)

Persuasive Communication

implying that all homosexual men have AIDS or will contract it eventually. Not only is this silly, but untrue. Simply because some homosexual men have AIDS certainly doesn't mean that they all do. The statement also ignores the fact that many women and heterosexual men have AIDS. This is a typical hasty generalization.

Name-Calling

Have you ever heard someone characterized as a "punk"? The name carries pejorative connotations, and to characterize a young person with bizarre dress habits as a "punk" is not only inaccurate but unfair. Whenever you hear name-calling, you can be sure that the persuader has little real evidence and is resorting to propaganda.

Plain Folks

Persuaders, especially those in positions of power, often attempt to masquerade as "ordinary folks." Political candidates go to homely picnics, labor leaders pretend that they are plumbers, and presidents of large corporations hang out at the factory gate, talking with workers. The spectacle of a governor of a large state sitting in a fifth grade classroom seems ridiculous, but the device deceives many gullible people.

Transfer

Transfer is the device of associating with already credible institutions, such as religious and educational institutions. Advocates of the "Star Wars" defense system have been careful to associate their research with NASA, hoping that the prestige of the organization (despite the Challenger disaster) will make a doubtful program more acceptable.

Summary

Persuasion is usually defined as communication that tries to stimulate *action,* or the shaping, reinforcing, or changing of responses. Usually we say that persuasion aims at changing attitudes, which are schemas that involve affect and behavioral intention. Persuasion and coercion are closely related in function but are far apart ethically.

The most important basic process in bringing about persuasion is the desire to resolve inconsistencies among source evaluations and communication objects. These inconsistencies are usually termed imbalance, dissonance, and incongruity. Also, to be a successful persuader, you must be credible. Most student speakers need to work on extrinsic rather than intrinsic credibility.

One excellent organizational plan for persuasive speeches is the motivated sequence of Alan Monroe, which proceeds logically from need to action. Another is the problem–solution plan.

Listeners to persuasive speeches should be aware of propaganda devices, such as the bandwagon effect, name-calling, half-truth, hasty generalization, transfer, and "plain folks."

On Your Own

1. Analyze some of the speeches of the Reagan administration on behalf of the "Star Wars" weapons system. How have they utilized credibility?
2. Do you know anyone who uses too much evidence in persuasion? Why do you think so? How much is too much?
3. Popular speakers tend to "follow the crowd" more often than unpopular ones. Try to explain why, using the consistency theory.
4. Identify the most credible person you know. Why did you choose this person?
5. Analyze an instance in which someone attempted to persuade you but instead produced the opposite effect? Did "balance" or "dissonance" have anything to do with it?

Suggestions for Further Reading

Bostrom, R. 1983. *Persuasion.* Englewood Cliffs, NJ: Prentice-Hall.

Clark, R. 1984. *Persuasive messages.* New York: Harper & Row.

Institute for Propaganda Analysis. 1937. *Propaganda analysis.* Detroit: Institute for Propaganda Analysis.

Miller, G. 1980. On being persuaded: some basic distinctions. In *Persuasion: New directions in theory and research,* eds. M. Roloff and G. Miller. Beverly Hills: Sage.

Miller, G., and M. Burgoon. 1973. *New techniques of persuasion.* New York: Harper & Row.

Reardon, K. 1981. *Persuasion: theory and context.* Beverly Hills: Sage.

Fifteen

Logic and Reasoning

Berenger: Life is an abnormal business.
Jean: On the contrary. Nothing could be more natural. And the proof is that people go on living.
Berenger: There are more dead people than living. And their numbers are increasing.
Jean: The dead don't exist, there's no getting away from that.
Berenger: I sometimes wonder if I exist myself.
Jean: You don't exist, my dear Berenger, because you don't think. Start thinking, then you will.
Logician: Another syllogism: All cats die. Socrates is dead. Therefore Socrates is a cat.

Eugene Ionesco

Key Terms

proposition
fact
value
induction
deduction
syllogism
premise
enthymeme
Toulmin Model
evidence
warrant
claim
support
reservation
qualifier

Objectives

After studying this chapter, you should be able to:

1. Appreciate the value of logic in constructing a speech
2. Understand why audiences react well to presentations that they perceive to be "logical"
3. Distinguish between inductive and deductive logical patterns
4. Distinguish between "syllogism" and "enthymeme"
5. Identify the principal elements in the Toulmin model: evidence, warrants, claims, qualifiers, support, and reservations.
6. Construct a logical argument according to the Toulmin model

Everyone wants to be perceived as logical: If you point out to a friend that his statements are illogical, it is usually taken as an insult. On the other hand, few people take the time to reason out the strict logical relationships in their statements. Consider the following dialogue:

George: Did you register for the draft on your eighteenth birthday? I did.

Kelly: Certainly not. Why support the administration's war policies in Central America?

George: But the law says that you *must* register. If you don't, you're a lawbreaker.

Kelly: Some laws are immoral and therefore one should ignore them. No one is required to obey an immoral law.

George: How do you know if a law is immoral or not? Some people don't think that the draft is immoral.

Kelly: It's obvious. If a policy supports war, it's immoral.

George: What would you do if the generals who run the army decided that the law was immoral, and they attacked Mexico because they thought Mexico was immoral?

Kelly: My goodness, they wouldn't do that.

George: If they can decide what is or isn't immoral, just as you think you can, I don't see why they shouldn't.

Kelly: Listen, that's different. The country couldn't run if everyone acted that way.

George: Well, doesn't that apply to the draft as well?

Kelly: I don't see why you are trying to trap me into saying something I don't want to say.

You can see how an obvious illogicality can pollute a personal dialogue. The inconsistency of Kelly's position not only reduces his ideas but affects George's evaluation of him as a person.

Speakers who talk to groups of people have an even greater responsibility to be logical, reasonable, and accurate. In this chapter, we examine some characteristics of good logic and logical messages. In order to deliver coherent messages, you should understand what logic is and how it works—both from a formal point of view and from a more practical perspective.

The Logic Schema

As we discussed in Chapter Two, communication involves percepts, affects, language, and schemas. One of the most important schemas involves logic or "logicality." Unfortunately, people do not always agree on what logic is or should be. We need to be aware of what people *think* logic is and what it ought to be. First, let's explore how audiences typically handle logic.

Audiences and Logic

Audiences, of course, are not always logical. You might be espousing a reasonable, carefully studied position, but if your audience feels that you are not logical, the effect will be that the audience will not believe you. If you will remember how schemas worked in basic communication processing, you will have a clue to how logic works. Logic is a schema, which includes elements of believability.

> Most audiences utilize "logic" schemas in processing new information.

When you are preparing your message, you need to understand some of the basic ways that these schemas are employed by typical audiences.

Atmosphere Effect

Audiences usually react to the logical "atmosphere" of a speech. In one interesting experiment (Bettinghaus, 1980), communication researchers prepared a message in which the words *logic* and *logical* appeared with great frequency. For example, the speech contained such phrases as: "So, logically, you can see from the

Senator Paul Simon is perceived by the public as a "logical" rather than an "emotional" person. This perception can be an asset in a political career. (© Gary Sigman)

Logic and Reasoning ■ ■ ■ 231

previous points that ..." In another version of the same speech, they eliminated these words: "So you can see from the previous points that ..." The speech that used the word *logic* (and derivatives) was judged to be more logical and also produced greater opinion change than the version without these words. It made little difference to the listeners whether the logical structure of the speech was sound; the important thing was that the speech *sounded right*. This "atmosphere effect," well known to communication researchers for a long time, may upset speech purists, but it is an important factor that must be considered. It is essential not only to *be* logical, but also to *sound* logical.

Natural Logic

Certain thought processes are apparently used by everyone regardless of their formal logical validity. Consider the following two statements:

1. Cigarettes are much worse for your lungs than cigars
2. Cigars are much better for your lungs than cigarettes

The principles of formal logic would hold that these two statements are exactly equivalent. However, after hearing the first statement, people would tend to judge both cigarettes and cigars negatively; after hearing the second statement, they would tend to judge both cigars and cigarettes more positively. Even though both statements make the same comparison between cigars and cigarettes, those listeners evaluating the statements would make different judgments, depending on whether they hear the word *better* or *worse*. Similar comparisons—taller and shorter, richer and poorer, and the like—work the same way. Certain kinds of thought processes occur "naturally," independent of formal logic.

Information Process and Reasoning

Most people confuse information and logic. The average audience feels that a speech is logical if it contains a lot of data. Apparently the schema associated with a great deal of new information is associated with the schema labeled "logical"; when one is activated, apparently the other is also. As a result, when a speaker presents a large amount of data, the audience tends to think "logical" rather than "emotional."

Working with Logic in Speaking

We have two goals in this section—to *be* logical and to *appear* logical. In order to achieve the first goal, we need to know something about the process of reasoning.

Process of Reasoning

Basically, logic is the science of combining statements in an acceptable way. Some statements cannot go together; others can. So your first task is to begin with very clear statements or "propositions."

Propositions

Propositions, the "building blocks" of logic, are single statements of a characteristic, such as "Reading ability produces good grades." A speaker starts with a proposition that is acceptable to everyone and then proceeds to develop it logically. The proposition ought to be different from the conclusion of the argument for the logical structure to make sense. Sometimes speakers simply assert propositions, one not necessarily deriving from another, and think that they have proceeded logically. The conclusion must be the result of the logical development of the proposition.

Two very important kinds of propositions are *factual* propositions and *value* propositions. Just as you should distinguish facts from opinions in persuasive speaking, you should distinguish between factual statements and opinion or "value" statements. Suppose you have an "opinion" about whether corporate employees should be subjected to mandatory tests for drug use. Your opinion would mainly depend on at least two strong values, one about the place of drugs in our society and another about the civil rights of the average employee.

Many persons would assert that values are much more permanent and of greater significance than opinions. Whether one calls these statements evidence of "deeply held, central attitudes," "strong personal opinions," or "values" is largely a matter of personal preference. What is important is that they are different from statements of fact; and are especially different from another form of proposition, that of policy.

Policy propositions refer to future action. When the government proposes that we should build the "Star Wars" weapons system or that we should stop dumping nuclear waste in the ocean, it is proposing future action. In the U. S. Congress, policy propositions take the form of bills. In your speech class, if you deliver a speech advocating a proposition of policy, you hope for change in behavior on the part of your audience.

You will remember that the main purposes of communication (Chapter Two) included communication to "activate." Another way of describing communication that uses propositions of policy is to note that they are primarily *activating* in nature.

Whether you choose a proposition that is a statement of value or one of policy will depend upon your purpose. When you want someone to simply agree with you, you use statements of value. When you want to activate or change an audience, you use propositions of policy.

Traditional Forms of Reasoning

Once propositions are identified, you must fit them together. You do this two ways—through inductive reasoning and deductive reasoning.

Inductive Reasoning

You will recall from Chapter Fourteen that evidence is one key to enhancing your credibility and being a successful persuasive speaker. Moreover, you have an obligation to make sure that your evidence fits your proposition. Suppose you wish to prove the proposition "Drinking causes automobile accidents." You could not ethically use the traditional scientific method, that is, select sixty persons at random, give thirty of them a substantial amount of alcohol and the other thirty a placebo, and then keep score to see who arrived home safely and who didn't. For one thing, the drinkers might run into some innocent persons along the way.

So all you can do to build your case is depend on your evidence and the inductive process. *Induction*, you will recall, is the generation of a broad statement based on a number of specific statements. For example, you might obtain a sheaf of accident reports from police departments all over the country, and count how many accidents were linked to alcohol. You might also try to acquire insurance company records on problem drinkers.

You can see that when you induce in this manner, you can never be quite sure of your results. Induction never gives you perfect proof, no matter how much new evidence you obtain. Induction, however, is usually sufficient for most people to take action. Consider the relationship between cigarette smoking and the incidence of lung cancer in our population. One out of ten heavy cigarette smokers dies of lung cancer, and one out of 270 nonsmokers dies of lung cancer. You might agree with the cigarette companies that it has not been proved beyond a shadow of a doubt that cigarettes cause lung cancer, but a great many people have accepted the statistical evidence and stopped smoking.

Deductive Reasoning

A second form of reasoning is *deductive*, where we derive statements from one another. Usually when we put a general statement and a specific statement together, we can produce a third specific statement. These statements may look like this:

> *East Coast writers of fiction are effete intellectual snobs.*
>
> *John Smith lives in Cape Cod, Massachusetts, and has written over twenty works of fiction.*
>
> *Therefore, Mr. Smith is an effete intellectual snob.*

This form of deductive reasoning is called a *syllogism*. The first two statements are called *premises*, and the third statement, which follows from the premises, is called the *conclusion*. Speakers, however, are rarely this explicit in their reasoning. Usually, communicators use a form of reasoning called the *enthymeme*, in which one of the premises is implied. For example: "Eric is a policeman. I could never stand people who enjoy violence." This enthymeme could be more formally stated:

> *All policemen enjoy violence.*
> *Eric is a policeman.*
> *Therefore, Eric enjoys violence.*

When the premises of the syllogism are apparent, it is easy to see the structure of the argument, but it is also easier to invent counter-arguments for them. Part of the power of the enthymeme lies in the assumption that the audience agrees with one of the premises; and it is definitely one of the more persuasive forms of reasoning (Bitzer, 1959). Notice how Walter Cronkite uses the enthymeme, in his following speech on the freedom of the press.

> When the Supreme Court handed down its Boston bank ruling, it also was considering a case in California where reporters had tried to exercise what they felt should be a right or privilege—access to jails and prisons for the purpose of reporting on conditions there. The case involved the Alameda County Jail, where in 1972, a federal judge had found conditions so "shocking and debasing" that they amounted to cruel and unusual punishment. When an inmate committed suicide under questionable circumstances, a San Francisco television station asked permission to visit the jail and film conditions there. The sheriff said "no," prison policy excluded the press.
>
> The TV station sued, and a lower federal court ruled that the sheriff could not bar reporters altogether, and ordered him to permit limited access. The Supreme Court, however, overruled the lower court, finding that the press had no greater right of access to government facilities than the general public.
>
> Explaining the majority's position ... the Chief Justice drew a distinction between *gathering* news and *distributing* it.
>
> Now, on several occasions, the Court had emphasized the importance of informed public opinion and a free press. But *those* cases, he explained were concerned only with communicating information once it is *obtained*. They did not—and I quote—"remotely imply a constitutional right guaranteeing anyone access to government information beyond that open to the public generally."
>
> Now that, to me, is high grade hogwash! Obviously, the general public cannot parade at will through the jails and prisons. That simply would be unmanageable. But then, the same can be said with respect to the White House and the State Department and the Capitol Building, can't it? In ruling that the press has no more right of access than the ordinary citizen, the Supreme Court has decided that the *public* has no particular right to know what goes on in public institutions, beyond that which the government chooses to reveal.

The enthymeme appears in this progression of points:

- Although the public cannot "parade" through public institutions to inspect them, the public has a right to know what goes on in them.
- *The press represents the public.*
- Therefore, the press has the right of access to public institutions.

The second premise—"The press represents the public"—is *assumed* by Mr. Cronkite. He feels that all of his listeners agree with him on this point, and if they do, his argument has much greater force.

Former newsanchor, Walter Cronkite, in his speech on freedom of the press, bases his argument on the premise that "the press represents the public." This is an example of a ethymeme because Cronkite *assumes* that the audience agrees with him. (© UPI/Bettman Newsphotos)

You can use the enthymeme only after careful audience analysis to discover the kinds of statements that your audience will accept without question. You can see that ethical problems can arise from this kind of structure; for example, the "bolstering" of a questionable proposition by using it as the assumed premise in the enthymeme.

Toulmin's Model of Reasoning

An interesting model of logical relationships was proposed by Toulmin (1958). The basic idea behind Toulmin's model is that a logical argument begins with evidence, and then proceeds to "claims" by means of a "warrant." The basic structure of Toulmin's model is shown in Figure 15.1.

Let's see how Toulmin's model works in a real example. Suppose that you are speaking on the influence of television on students' patterns of reading behavior. Surprisingly, you have discovered (through research) that grade school students who watch television a great deal are better readers than students who do not watch so much. You want to conclude that television is a desirable part of our society. Your logical structure would look similar to the one shown in Figure 15.2.

At first glance, you might think that this structure is not at all different from typical syllogisms. Douglas Ehninger and Wayne Brockreide (1963), however, have pointed out four major differences:

Specific Speaking Tasks

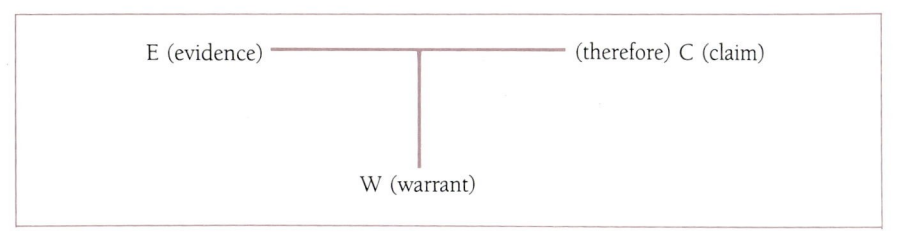

Figure 15.1

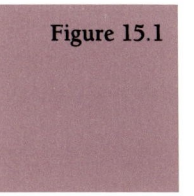

Basic elements of Toulmin's Model of Reasoning.

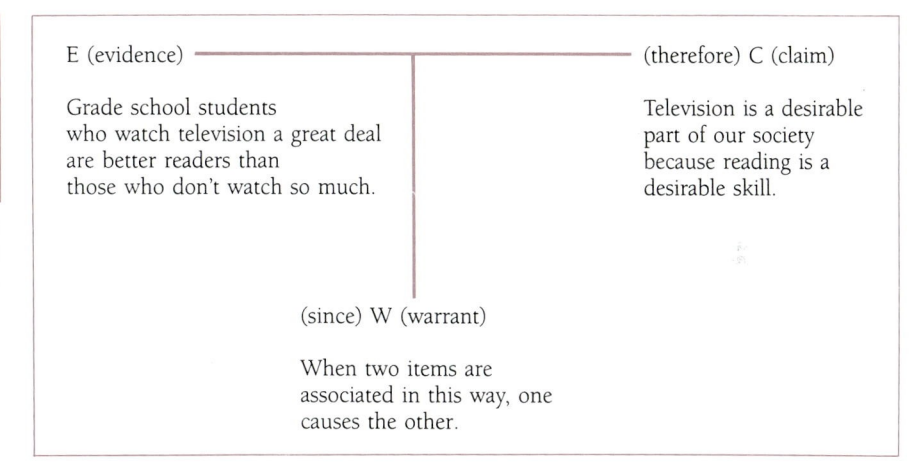

E (evidence) ─────────────── (therefore) C (claim)

W (warrant)

Figure 15.2

Specific statements inserted in the Toulmin model.

E (evidence) ─────────────── (therefore) C (claim)

Grade school students who watch television a great deal are better readers than those who don't watch so much.

Television is a desirable part of our society because reading is a desirable skill.

(since) W (warrant)

When two items are associated in this way, one causes the other.

1. In the Toulmin model, proofs are displayed in a spatial pattern to help communicators see the dynamic relationship between the elements. Syllogisms are primarily static in nature.
2. The Toulmin model provides for the explicit support of warrants, emphasizing the importance of the warrant in the overall structure of the argument.
3. The Toulmin model emphasizes the relationship between the evidence and external events; evidence has a factual cast in the model that it might not have in syllogistic reasoning.
4. The Toulmin model provides explicit limitation on the force of the claim. The qualification of the claim is extremely important in this kind of communication and does not necessarily take place in the syllogistic form.

The Toulmin model includes three elements that we have not yet discussed—*support, reservations,* and *qualifiers.* Let's see how these three elements fit in our example.

As presently worded, the warrant in the example is not well supported, that is, there is not much support for the causal relationship between television-watching and better reading. After all, a child might be a better reader because of family factors, higher intelligence, or a host of other determinants. To find support for the warrant (that is, specific support for a cause-effect relationship), imagine that you find research studies that altered children's television viewing in some

Logic and Reasoning

Figure 15.3

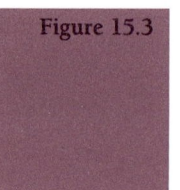

"Warrant" and "Support" added to the basic Toulmin model.

E (evidence) ──────────────────── (therefore) C (claim)

Grade school students who watch television a great deal are better readers than those who don't watch so much.

Television is a desirable part of our society because reading is a desirable skill.

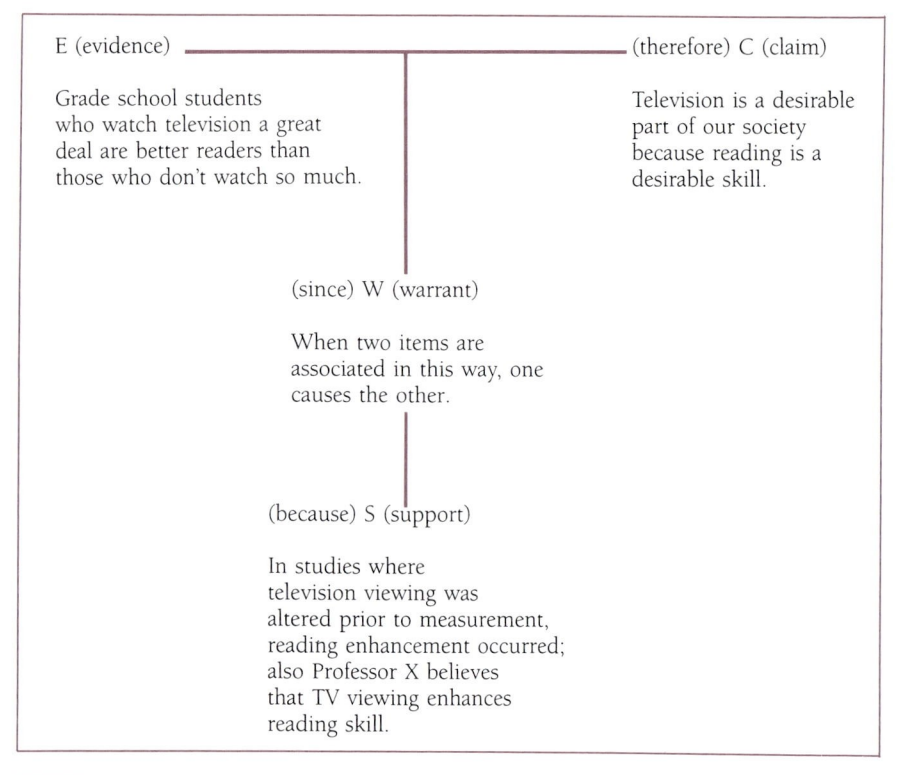

(since) W (warrant)

When two items are associated in this way, one causes the other.

(because) S (support)

In studies where television viewing was altered prior to measurement, reading enhancement occurred; also Professor X believes that TV viewing enhances reading skill.

Figure 15.4

Extended Toulmin model, including qualifiers and reservations.

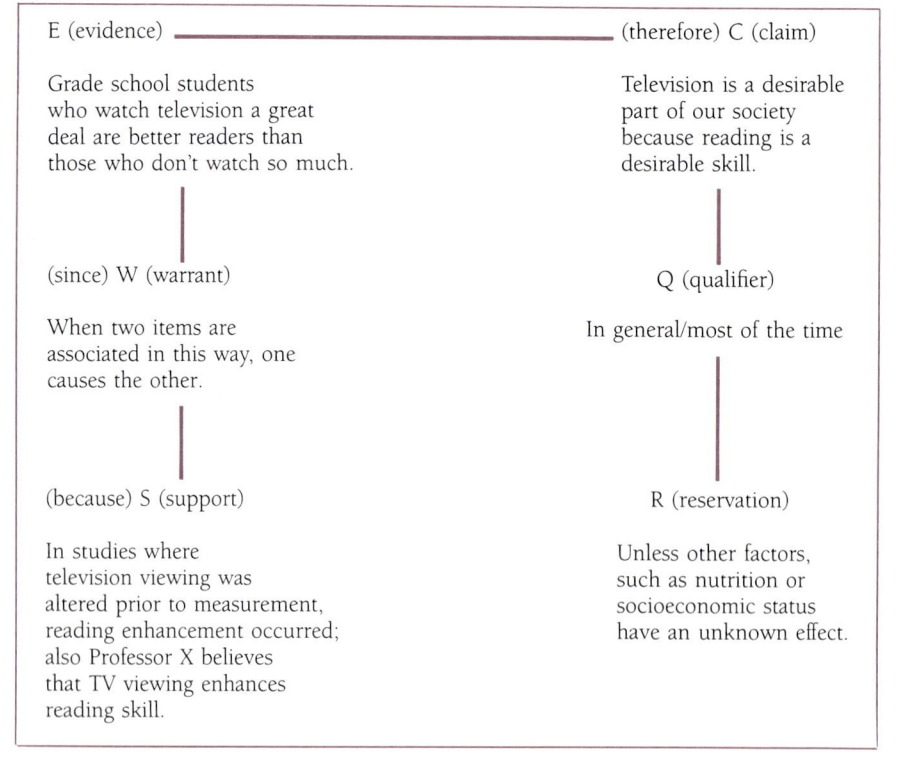

E (evidence) ──────────────────── (therefore) C (claim)

Grade school students who watch television a great deal are better readers than those who don't watch so much.

Television is a desirable part of our society because reading is a desirable skill.

(since) W (warrant)

When two items are associated in this way, one causes the other.

Q (qualifier)

In general/most of the time

(because) S (support)

In studies where television viewing was altered prior to measurement, reading enhancement occurred; also Professor X believes that TV viewing enhances reading skill.

R (reservation)

Unless other factors, such as nutrition or socioeconomic status have an unknown effect.

Specific Speaking Tasks

Figure 15.5

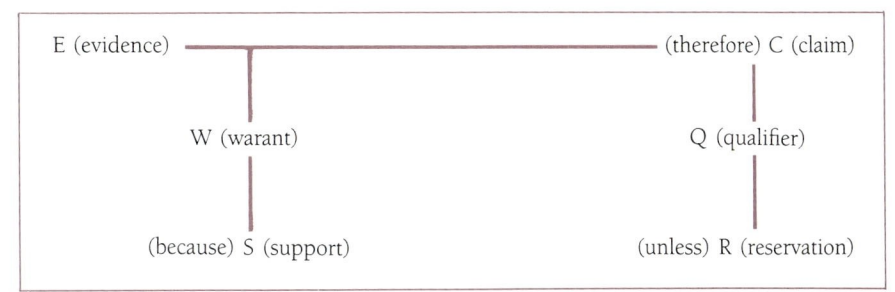

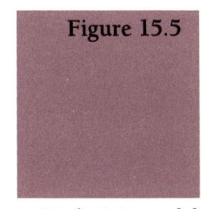

Toulmin's model without statements.

```
E (evidence) ——————————————————— (therefore) C (claim)
             |                                |
         W (warant)                       Q (qualifier)
             |                                |
(because) S (support)              (unless) R (reservation)
```

way, with the result that their reading skills were enhanced. You also find an article by a distinguished expert, who believes in this specific cause-effect relationship. You now have support for the warrant, as shown in Figure 15.3.

Even though the warrant is now supported, you need to admit that the claim is only partially true because reading is not an absolute value on which everyone agrees. So you might add the qualifier "in general" or "most of the time" to your claim. Further, reasonable people would concede that even the best research might not reveal some unknown factor that might cause the association or a factor that intrudes in the relationship, such as socioeconomic status or nutrition. These factors, or reservations, may now be added to the model (see Figure 15.4).

When you rename the specific arguments, Toulmin's model looks like the one shown in Figure 15.5.

The process of adding qualifiers and reservations could continue indefinitely, so you need to structure your argument according to the situation and the specific limitations of the communication task. It is important to recognize, however, that these elements are vital in constructing a logical argument in a speech.

The Toulmin model also serves as an excellent method for organizing your arguments. After analyzing the warrants, support, qualifiers, and reservations, you can see how each of these factors fits into the claim and the overall presentation. In fact, you might even use these terms in your speech. However, the Toulmin model is a pattern of argument, not a full-blown speech outline. Its strength lies in the establishment of true claims based on evidence. It certainly is no substitute for the primary patterns of speech organization, such as problem-solution.

Whatever structure you use, it is most important that you analyze your own logical processes. It is easy to assume an argument is logical just because you believe in it and to fall into silly logical traps as a result.

Summary

Everyone wants to be logical, but logic must be practiced. Some of the most logical-sounding arguments are, in fact, illogical, and you must understand logical processes to make your communication valid.

Logic is the relationship between propositions. Beginning with sensible, supportable propositions will help assure that your structure is sound.

The traditional forms of logic are induction and deduction. More than likely, we would want to use the Toulmin model, which uses support, warrants, evidence, claims, qualifiers, and reservations to compose a logical argument.

On Your Own

1. Read the "Letters to the Editor" column of your local newspaper. Are these letters making specific claims in the Toulmin sense, or do you have to infer them?
2. After your analysis in question 1, supply the claim statement that you think the letters need. Why did you choose these statements?
3. For your next persuasive speech, construct your argument according to the Toulmin model. Then use parts of the structure as your outline.
4. Here are three different claims that we hear often. Construct a full Toulmin model (see Figure 15.4) for each of these:
    a. "Star Wars" technology will make the world a safer place.
    b. Abortion should be made available for all women on demand.
    c. Buy American!

Suggestions for Further Reading

Andersch, E., L. Staats, and R. Bostrom. 1969. *Communication in everyday use.* New York: Holt, Rinehart, & Winston.

Bettinghaus, E. 1980. *Persuasive communication.* New York: Holt, Rinehart, & Winston.

Bettinghaus, E., G. Miller, and T. Steinfatt. 1970. Source evaluations, syllogistic content, and judgment of logical validity by high- and low dogmatic persons. *Journal of Personality and Social Psychology* 16: 238–44.

Bostrom, R. 1983. *Persuasion.* Englewood Cliffs, NJ: Prentice-Hall.

Ellis, A., and G. Beattie. 1986. *The psychology of language and communication.* New York: Guilford Press.

Howard, D. 1983. *Cognitive psychology.* New York: Macmillan.

Reynolds, R., and M. Burgoon. 1983. Belief processing. In *Communication Yearbook VII,* ed. R. Bostrom, 83–104. Beverly Hills: Sage.

Sixteen

Speaking in Specialized Settings

Not every end is a goal, the end of a melody is not its goal; however, if the melody has not reached its end, it would also not have reached its goal.

A Parable
Friedrich Nietzsche

Key Terms

group purpose
group dynamics
cohesiveness
structure
identity
network
positional relationships
welcome
dedication
introduction
nomination
thanks
apology

Objectives

After studying this chapter, you should be able to:

1. Understand how presentations are adapted for small groups
2. Distinguish among different kinds of group purposes
3. Identify three important elements in group dynamics: cohesiveness, structure, and identity
4. Describe a hypothetical communication network in a large organization
5. Understand how positional relationships affect presentations in a large organization
6. Recognize the distinguishing characteristics of speeches of welcome, dedication, introduction, nomination, thanks, and apology

Our study of public speaking thus far has concentrated on general principles and guidelines that apply in most speaking situations. Some special circumstances, however, call for specific adaptation of these guidelines. In this chapter, we examine some of the most common of these circumstances and discuss how you adapt to each of these tasks.

The special settings include the small group, the large organizational meeting, and special speaking occasions. In small groups you need to adapt your speech to suit the purpose of the group and the group dynamics. In large organizations you must be concerned with informational networks and positional issues. For special occasions speakers should remember that the principles of good speaking and good communication are still paramount.

Speaking in Small Groups

Working with groups is an extremely important part of day-to-day life. You work in groups for decision-making, for support, and even for entertainment. A common group experience is the "committee"—a small, formal work group given a specific task. Of course, you belong to a great many informal groups that are often more important than the formal ones.

In small groups, you probably won't "make speeches," but you do communicate in ways that are quite similar to more formal presentations and that use many principles of public speaking. For example, you will be more effective in a small group when you work hard on material, organization, language, and topic choice before the meeting. Good delivery is as important in a group of five as it is in a group of fifty. Nonverbal communication may be even more important in a small group than in the public speaking situation. In short, good speech is important in a small group, and the informality of the situation should not tempt you to get "sloppy." For example, you may not always use a formal outline in a group discussion, but you should always prepare as specifically as you would for a speech (see Chapter Eight for discussion on general process of gathering materials). Good ideas, good evidence, and clear thinking are always important.

How then, does speaking in a group differ from speaking before an audience? Some elements of public speaking principles require adaptation, depending on the group's *purpose* and *dynamics*.

Group Purpose

Although some groups might not have a specific purpose, most groups do. It is quite important to have a firm grasp of the group's purpose prior to participation because the form of your speaking will depend on this purpose. Communication, you will recall, relays, stimulates, activates, and externalizes. In public speaking, you inform, convince, persuade, and commemorate. In group discussion, all of these activities take place, but the group purpose is usually quite different. Groups typically exist to solve problems or to reach consensus.

When the group's purpose is to solve problems, *creativity* is an important

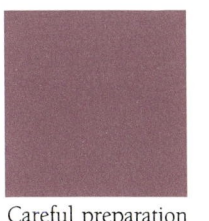

Careful preparation and good delivery is as important in a small group as it is in a formal public-speaking situation. (© Eileen Christelow/ Jeroboam, Inc.)

asset. Groups solve problems by proposing and testing ideas, and sometimes the quality of the group's solution is determined by the number of ideas offered. Every member should be as well prepared as possible.

Consider this example: In a typical junior high school, absences are approaching crisis levels, and the faculty of the school feels that some action has to be taken. The school principal appoints a committee of parents, teachers, and students to propose solutions. She feels that the perspectives of all three groups should be represented. More importantly, each of these groups needs to understand the other groups' point of view. Before the committee convenes, the parents must prepare by learning the faculty's needs and concerns, the teachers need to get some idea from the students why truancy is high, and the students need to do preliminary research on why the principal considers the whole situation a problem. In other words, preparation needs to be both general and specific. After the preparation, the committee needs to propose solutions and to suspend evaluation until they analyze each solution. Then, and only then, should they "test" the various solutions offered, with the goal of proposing one to the principal. The group tests solutions by discussing them carefully and examining them for defects.

When the group's purpose is to reach consensus, *persuasion* is the most important process, and the group's activities become subtly different. In a consensus group, it is vital that everyone agree, and the nature of the discussion centers on adopting a solution to suit the group, not the other way around. In other words, in a consensus group, it is not the quality of the solution that is at stake, it is the degree to which group members agree. In a problem-solving discussion, however, the group can adopt what they think is the best solution, even if one or two members do not agree with the final solution.

In our example, the principal may feel that it is more important for the group to agree than to arrive at the best solution possible because the solution may be restricted by exigencies of school board rules, physical restrictions, budget problems, and the like. When consensus is vital, communication should emphasize externalization, rather than on relays of facts or other kinds of evidence. "Open-mindedness," or the ability to see the other person's viewpoint, is one of the best tools a participant can bring to this kind of group activity.

Group Dynamics

Every group is different, and participants need to be aware of group differences so they know how to conduct themselves during group discussion. The unique internal characteristics of a group are usually described as the "group dynamics." Group dynamics involve three important characteristics: *cohesiveness, structure,* and *identity*. All groups differ in these characteristics, and paying attention to each of these will help you adapt your communication to your particular group.

Cohesiveness

Cohesiveness refers to the quality of the group that makes it "cling" together. Cohesiveness can be created by a number of factors: common goals, common background, liking for one another, external forces or pressures, and so on. Many groups are formed because members have a common interest. One recent example is "Mothers Against Drunk Driving," a group that was formed because of a common interest in lobbying for legislation to get drunks off the road.

A speaker can take a great many more risks in a highly cohesive group than in one less cohesive. In a highly cohesive group, a speaker's normative-identificatory credibility (see Chapter Fourteen) is ordinarily much higher, which means that speakers can succumb to the temptation to skimp on preparation, knowing that the group will be more accepting. Obviously, this is a poor idea; your responsibility is simply that much greater in this kind of a group.

Structure

Structure is another important aspect of group life. Not all groups are formally organized, but some have instituted specific roles, such as "chairperson" and "recorder." Even when structure is not formally designated, many groups have structure because of the members' personalities, differences in background and expertise, and other factors. Leadership in many groups is simply a matter of structure. Leaders often are those persons in positions of influence, even though they may not have inherent leadership qualities. Another problem lies in the definition of leadership. A leader may simply handle group maintenance tasks—as a facilitator—while other members have the real influence. Nonetheless, leadership is one of the most interesting factors in the study of small groups simply because of the influence potential that leaders have.

When a group is highly centralized, all of its communication needs to be "cleared" by the leader, who typically utilizes power this way. For example, Bradley (1978) demonstrated that power is the single most important influence in upwardly-directed communications. Many of us wish power were not so important in group life, but without it, participation becomes chaotic and unproductive.

Not everyone can talk at once in any size group, so a formal procedure, commonly called "parliamentary procedure," has evolved. With this procedure, the chairperson assigns the "floor" and action is taken in the form of "motions." Gouran and Geonetta (1977) have shown that some formality helps small groups focus on the topic at hand, which indicates that formal structure might help small groups as well as large.

Recently researchers have begun to study the role of the female leader in mixed and male groups. Yerby (1975), for example, studied the success of female leaders in small groups. She found that when the group was balanced (two males and two females), group members were more satisfied with the leader and with their own performance. In addition, more positive attitudes about gender roles predict greater satisfaction with group activity when the group has a female leader. Wood (1979) also showed that the group purpose was an important factor in the evaluation of leaders, and that the gender of group members would interact with the group's purpose in influencing these evaluations. In other words, the acceptance of female leaders may depend on the type of group that it is.

Identity

Identity is another important group characteristic that is often the result of a formal designation, such as "work team" or "accounting department." Sometimes, however, identity is a bit less formal and more colorful. A group of student nurses at a major Midwestern medical center, who decided to put in extra time at the hospital on Saturdays, were soon called the "Saturday Nightingales." But even prosaic terms such as "the fourteenth floor" or the "guys in the tool room" are often applied when the individuals involved recognize themselves this way.

In a group with a high degree of identification, a speaker needs to be aware of the particular identificatory factors present. Just as the persuasive speaker with normative-identificatory credibility is more effective, so is the group member. Problem-solving in this kind of group may be more difficult, but consensus is typically more easily accomplished.

Participation and Group Influence

The total amount of a member's participation strongly affects that member's influence in the group. Bavelas (1953) showed that "central persons" have more influence and are more satisfied with group performance than "peripheral persons." Many other research studies have shown that this is true of almost all groups, even when centrality is not formally constituted. These studies indicate that participation is one of the principal indices of group influence.

Not all group members participate equally, of course. What factors lead one person to be influential and another to hang back? Persons with communication apprehension (see Chapter Four) are also inhibited in group situations. Jablin, Siebold, and Sorenson (1977) showed that communication apprehensiveness significantly limited the participation in brainstorming groups.

Other factors limit a member's participation in groups. In the groups studied by Burgoon (1977), reticent group members had received little reinforcement from group activity and this lack of reward had established a pattern of avoiding communication.

Participation is not only beneficial for individuals in the group but also for the group in general. Hirokawa (1980) showed that highly interactive groups were more effective decision-makers than less interactive groups.

Speaking in Organizational Settings

Levinson (1973) estimated that over 90 percent of the U. S. working population is employed by large organizations. We should, therefore, be concerned with how communication works in a large organization and how public speaking is used in this setting. In this section, we examine two major functions of organizational communication—networking and relationships—and explore how they relate to the public speaking task.

Communication Networks

One of the most interesting characteristics of an organization is the way that "networks" of communication are constituted. For organizational speaking, your first task in audience analysis is to assess the organization's network structure.

A *network* is the general communication pattern in a large organization. Small groups have structure; before an aggregation of persons can be called a group, some sort of structure is necessary. In large organizations, however, structure takes on a different meaning.

In modern organizations, networks are extremely complex and sometimes very frustrating. For example, in a typical hospital two different networks operate to keep the hospital running. One of these is "administrative," consisting of office and secretarial staff, food service personnel, and the like. This well-defined network is usually headed by a "hospital administrator." At the same time, another network, headed by a "chief of medicine," deals with medical matters: treatment procedures, purchase of medical equipment, scheduling of operating rooms, and so on. Some of the problems in modern hospitals (and part of the reason that hospital costs are so high) are inherent in this dual network system.

The organization's formal and informal networks typically prescribe how communication flows in the organization. Formal networks follow organizational charts—people in one section are supposed to communicate through their managers. Informal networks arise through friendships and extraneous group membership, such as churches, and have little relation to organizational charts. Even though the organization might base its communication on the formal network, you should be aware of the existence of informal channels and their effectiveness in transmitting information throughout the organization.

Consider, for example, the Universal Widget Company, whose organizational chart is pictured in Figure 16.1. The assembly department wishes to pass the message to the billing department that the price of widgets is going up. Following formal channels, the message goes to the production manager, then to the assistant unit manager, then to the accounting manager, and finally to the billing department. At the same time, however, that the message was started through official channels, the transportation manager, Elizabeth, ate lunch with John who works in the assembly department. John passed the news to Elizabeth who, in turn, called her friend Pete in the billing department and told him. As a result, the billing department was already aware of the price change long before receiving "official" notification.

Networks of authority involve power relationships. Some supervisors in a formal network try to persuade their subordinates to perform certain tasks; others simply give orders. In more progressive organizations, supervisors attempt to "sell" employees on certain tasks.

Networks function to a large extent according to the organization's philosophy or culture. Within each philosophy formal networks will vary.

Positional Relationships

Another essential element in organizational communication concerns the communicator's and listeners' positions in the organization's hierarchy. Whether the communication is "upward" or "downward" significantly affects how the communication is received. When analyzing the audience (see Chapter Six), you should be quite specific about the position of your listeners within the organization. If your audience is composed of subordinates, your task is quite different than if it is composed of supervisors.

Daniel Ellsberg, who was responsible for "leaking" the Pentagon Papers to the press—the most extraordinary leak of classified documents in the history of the United States—is shown here participating in a panel at UC Berkeley. (© *Jane Scherr/Jeroboam, Inc.*)

Speaking in Specialized Settings ■ ■ ■ 247

Figure 16.1

The Universal Widget Company's organizational chart showing formal and informal channels.

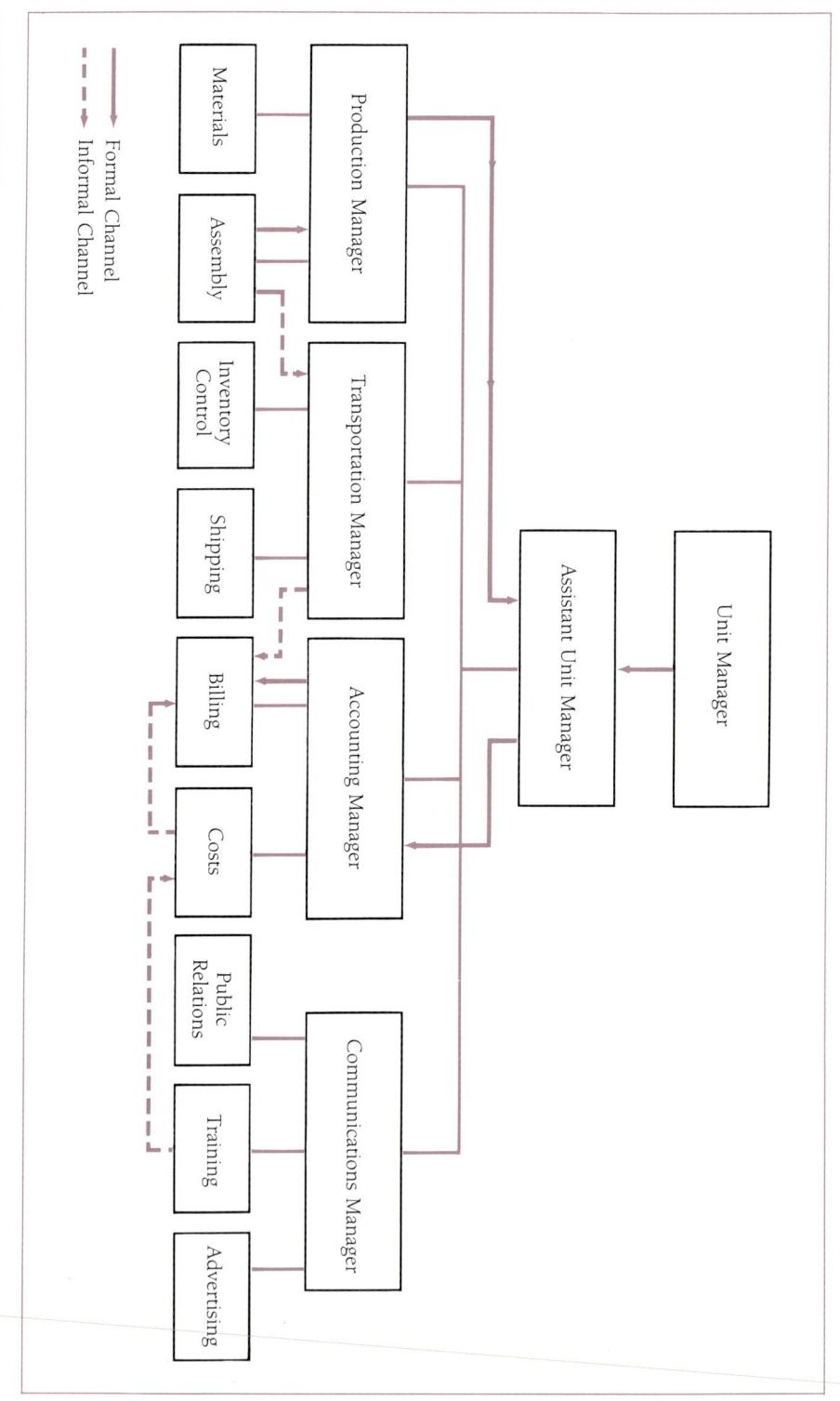

248 ■ ■ ■ Specific Speaking Tasks

The position of the speaker and of the prospective audience is one of the most important factors in the preparation of any oral presentation. A superior talking to a group of subordinates usually adopts one style, and a subordinate speaking to a group of superiors usually adopts another. Jablin (1979) has examined several characteristics of this kind of organizational communication. Let's examine some of his conclusions in greater detail.

Upward Influence

Interestingly, the "upward influence" of a superior has a strong effect on subordinates. Employees are more satisfied with their superior when a great deal of influence is exercised with his or her superiors. In addition, subordinates seem to interact more with the superior who has upward influence. Though Jablin urges that this conclusion be accepted only tentatively and proposes no explanation for this phenomenon, it seems reasonable to conclude that those persons who excel in upward persuasive communication also excel in downward persuasive communication. A credibility effect may also be responsible: An individual judged to have influence within the organization may be viewed as being high in qualification-expertness (see Chapter Fourteen).

Personal Characteristics

The personal characteristics of both the superior and the subordinate also influence communication between them. One interesting characteristic is the "internal" versus "external" perception of locus of control. "Internal" persons feel that their behavior is inner-directed and that they are "in charge" of their lives. "Externals," on the other hand, feel that other persons, circumstances, and the organization have more effect on outcomes than they do. In terms of communication, internal supervisors tend to use persuasion more than external supervisors. In other words, a supervisor who is confident in her or his ability and position in an organization tends to use persuasive rather than coercive influence on others. On the other hand, internals are more susceptible to persuasive messages aimed at higher-level needs, such as long-term goals and actualization, and externals are more susceptible to persuasive messages aimed at lower-level needs, i.e. daily schedules, monetary rewards, and physical appearance.

In addition, subordinates are more satisfied with a superior who is highly credible, not apprehensive, and nonauthoritarian. Whether these "satisfaction" indices can be translated into successful persuasive ability has not been demonstrated, though it seems reasonable to conclude that a supervisor who is perceived as more satisfying by employees would be more persuasive than one who is less so.

Semantic-Information Distance

The "semantic-information distance" between superiors and subordinates, usually defined as the disparity in the language used by each group to describe their perceptions of themselves and their structure, is another important factor in organizational communication.

When this distance is high, subordinates' morale is low. Probably the most significant aspect of the semantic-information distance is that managers tend to misperceive the attitudes held by their subordinates. This means that managers are often confronted with significant problems in persuasive communication without recognizing them as such.

All of these organizational characteristics affect specific speaking situations in organizational settings. Individuals who are preparing presentations for meetings or conferences, need to have some elementary notion of how these factors apply to them. Obviously everyone cannot conduct a research study to determine semantic-information distance in the specific organization. But some assessment can be made through thoughtful attention to organizational practices, typical habits and patterns of internal communications, and even through the stories that employees tell one another (Brown, 1985).

Speaking in organizations is much like speaking in other circumstances, in that the speaker must consider audience analysis, specific function, topic choice, research, language, delivery, and visual materials. What is different is the "corporate climate," speakers' and listeners' positions, and semantic-information distances. Good preparation will involve some attention to all of these.

Speaking For Special Occasions

From time to time, commemorative speeches are used to solemnize special occasions. The most common special occasions summarized in Table 16.1.

Many of the principles involved in the composition of the five types (or *genres*) shown in the table can be used in any specialized speech.

Generally, commemorative speaking invokes statements of value (see Chapter Fifteen). Although values are sometimes defined as statements of "core" attitudes (Rokeach, 1973), every culture has shared positions that are more significant than the term *attitude* indicates. Some of these values are truthfulness, fidelity, fairness, loyalty, patriotism, and the like. Specific subcultures may also subscribe to specific values, such as "profitability" in the business community and "faith" in the religious community.

These values are used as the basic mechanism for *stimulating* (see Chapter Two). It is important to distinguish between the speech that stimulates through

Table 16.1

Types of special occasions.

Occasion	Type of Speech	Function
Welcome	Commemorative	Externalize
Dedication	Commemorative	Externalize, relay, stimulate
Introduction	Informative	Externalize, relay
Nomination	Persuasive	Relay, actuate
Thanks	Commemorative	Externalize
Apology	Persuasive	Externalize

shared values and the speech that stimulates by invoking relays with high affective value. The commemorative speech utilizes the shared values approach and highlights, contrasts, and defines these value statements. With these principles in mind, let's turn to the specific use of short commemorative speeches for special occasions.

Speeches of Welcome

One of the most common of the special tasks is the speech of welcome. If you were in charge of the National Association of Broadcasters meeting in Pittsburgh last year, you would have "welcomed" all the participating broadcasters with a short speech. On a more prosaic level, speeches of welcome are presented at meetings and conventions and whenever one group (or individual) visits another.

Speeches of welcome should always be short. Specific mention is made of the individuals who brought the groups together. In general, this type of speech takes the form of an externalization, where the welcomer externalizes feelings of pleasure at the prospect of being together with the new arrivals.

Notice how the following short speech of welcome utilizes the externalization as well as enduring value structures:

I can't tell you how happy we are to host this third annual conference on women's concerns in an industrial society. When this group was formed, we never dreamed that the State meeting of the group would be here, and we are delighted to have you. The growth of this organization not only shows how important the role of women has become in our industrial society, but also how effective all of us have been in carrying this message to the rest of the world. As we work together in this conference, let us remember that we speak for thousands of women everywhere whose plight we share, and who need our support. Once again, we welcome you, and wish you a profitable and useful conference.

Dedication Speeches

A *dedication* typically refers to the initiatory ceremony of a new facility. New schools, new roads, new shopping centers, and even new ships are usually "launched" with a dedicatory speech. The word dedicate implies that the new facility is "given" to a group that formerly did not have it, but the dedicatory ceremony almost always marks the date when a facility begins operation.

Most speeches of this kind dedicate the facility to an abstraction—a community value, such as service, economic development, good government, or the like. It may seem incongruous to dedicate a shopping mall to economic development, but often builders do just that, as shown by the following dedication.

Thanks for coming here today and thanks for your interest in the Woodford Day Care Facility. As we dedicate this new enterprise, I hope we all remember the many hundreds of people who made this facility possible with the generous donations, long hours of hard work, and their support, especially when times were tough. We need to be especially grateful to the Farmers and Merchant's State Bank, the Moore's Corpo-

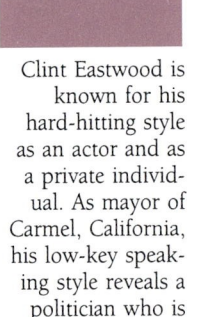

Clint Eastwood is known for his hard-hitting style as an actor and as a private individual. As mayor of Carmel, California, his low-key speaking style reveals a politician who is friendly and approachable. (© Holly McFarland)

ration, Rogers' Food Stores, and the faculty of Simpson State College. These groups helped in an especially generous way and without any of them, we would not have our new building. Let us always remember that there is nothing more important than a child, and that child care is the world's highest calling. It is no cliche that a culture is known by the way that it treats its children. We intend that our children have the best of everything, and we intend to make the Woodford Day Care center a model of what every facility like this should be.

Introductions

A very common special occasion is the introduction of a speaker, visitor, or dignitary. Speakers must be careful not to be repetitive or redundant with this simple speech. Usually a short personal anecdote suffices in the speech of introduction. If the audience knows absolutely nothing about the person being introduced, of course, biographical material can be relevant.

If you are introducing a speaker, your task is to enhance the speaker's credibility—and a review of the various types of credibility discussed in Chapter Fourteen will be useful.

Nominating Speeches

In terms of content, a nominating speech is quite similar to a speech of introduction. A nominating speech, however, is a persuasive presentation that aims to enhance the attitude of the audience. A nominating speech should have two basic parts: a description of the qualities needed in the office, and a listing of the candidate's characteristics that fit these qualities. During the 1956 Democratic National Convention, Senator John F. Kennedy nominated Adlai Stevenson for the Presidency. Notice how Kennedy used these two elements in his eloquent speech:

> *Consider, too, the four years that face us here at home. For here too, the absence of ideas, the lack of new leadership, the failure to keep pace with new developments, have all contributed to the growth of gigantic social and economic problems, problems that can't be postponed or explained away, but problems that in the next four years will burst upon us with new velocity. Problems of distressed farmers, the problems of our declining small business, the problem of our maldistribution of economic gains, the problems of our hopelessly inadequate schools, and the problems of our nation's health. These are the problems that cry for solution. They cry for leadership, and they cry for a man equal to our time.*
>
> *And the Democratic Party can say to the nation today: we have such a man.*
>
> *We can offer to the nation today a man uniquely qualified by inheritance, by training, and conviction to lead us out of this crisis of complacency and into a new era of fulfillment and a new light.*
>
> *During the past four years, his wise and perceptive analysis of the world crisis has carried through the vacillations and contradictions of official Washington to give understanding and hope to the people at home and abroad. And his eloquent, experienced, and courageous outlook on problems here at home have stood in shining contrast to the collection of broken promises, neglected problems, and disastrous blunders that pave the road from Gettysburg to the White House.*

Apology

The "apology" is actually a speech of "self-defense." When individuals feel that they have been misunderstood, misrepresented, or attacked, they often use defensive communication (Gibb, 1961).

The usual strategy is simply to explain the circumstances and deny wrongdoing. However, in Gary Hart's Spring 1987 withdrawal from the 1988 presidential campaign, he focuses on the tactics of the press rather than his own behavior:

> *In that spirit, I hope you'll ask yourselves some searching questions: about what is right and what is truthful; about the propriety of a newspaper conducting a questionable and inadequate surveillance of one presidential candidate; about whether the urgency of meeting a deadline is subordinate to hearing the truth, and about whether it's right or good journalism to draw an extraordinary conclusion before hearing some rather ordinary facts.*

Notice that Hart does not confirm or deny; instead, he attacks the media. This strategy shifts the emphasis of the dispute to a more favorable ground (to the speaker), i.e., attacking the press. In the long run, a better tactic is to explain your position, and how you have been misunderstood and to reemphasize the values that led to your actions. Most importantly, if you are wrong, admit it! Nothing is to be gained by defending an indefensible position.

Summary

In this chapter we examined several specialized settings of public speaking—the small group, the organization, and specific commemorative occasions. When speaking to a small group, you should be aware of how the group's purpose affects communication in general as well as your specific presentation. It is also important to understand how the dynamics of a particular group influence communicative behavior in the group.

In organizational settings, you should understand specific communication networks and how they are constituted. Your position in relation to others in the organizational hierarchy is also fundamental.

When preparing speeches of welcome and dedication, beginning speakers need to be extremely careful for two reasons. First, these types of speeches generally focus on values, both of the speaker and of the audience. Beginning speakers should exercise care in selecting value structures that will be in agreement with those of their audience. Secondly, speeches like these require elevated language that can prove difficult for the inexperienced or unskilled speaker.

On Your Own

1. Identify the groups to which you belong. List the characteristics of some of them, especially structural and identity characteristics.
2. Interview members of a formally designated group, such as a cheerleading squad, the university orchestra, a sorority, the ROTC, or other groups. Do each of these "designated" groups represent a "real" group? What are your reasons for saying so?
3. Do you have a part-time job? Observe "organizational" behavior in your job. Can you discern positional relationships from these observations?
4. Contrast some formal ceremonies (such as weddings, funerals, and the like) with the commemorative occasions described in this chapter. How are they alike? How are they different?
5. Assume that you have been asked to chair a meeting. What general introductory remarks might you make to begin the meeting, aside from introducing the topic and the task?
6. If you were asked to introduce Lee Iaccoca to your speech class, what would you say? On what elements would you focus?

Suggestions for Further Reading

Fairhurst, G., E. Rogers, and R. Sarr. 1987. Manager-subordinate control patterns and judgment about the relationship. In *Communication Yearbook X,* ed. M. McLaughlin, 395–414. Beverly Hills: Sage.

Kellermann, K., and S. Jarboe. 1987. Conservatism in judgment. In *Communication Yearbook X,* ed. M. McLaughlin, 259–281. Beverly Hills: Sage.

Gibb, J. 1961. Defensive communications. *Journal of Communication* 11: 141–48.

Yerby, J. 1975. Attitude, task, and sex composition as variables affecting female leadership in small problem-solving facilitation in problem-solving groups. *Speech Monographs* 42: 160–68.

Appendix

Sample Speeches

Antonio Navarro

Hispanics and Corporate America

The following speech was delivered by Antonio Navarro (formerly with W. R. Grace and Company), at the Southeast Bank Conference, Miami, Florida, on October 1, 1986. In this speech, Mr. Navarro, a successful Hispanic executive, primarily intended to *inform* his audience. Notice how his use of facts and statistics underlies the major contentions that he makes. Mr. Navarro's audience consisted principally of other Hispanics.

Reference to common experience of "Lotto" television advertisement	Last week when I was pondering how to start this talk I was riding the New York subway and I saw an ad for the New York Lottery that I must have seen thousands of times before, but never focused on. It showed a group of happy-looking millionaires, winners of Lotto, as they call the lottery in New York, and the caption read: "Lotto made our American Dream come true." I thought to myself, that is wrong. It is discouraging. It's downright immoral. Luck and chance don't make the American Dream come true. Hard work, against whatever odds, makes the American Dream come true. We, here in this room, we *are* the American Dream.
Transition	Addressing a group of your peers is a difficult task at best. That's why Congress never gets anything done. But addressing a group of fellow "Hispanics" is really asking for trouble. I am sure each one of you knows as much about this subject as I do—and would probably like to tell us about it. You may get that opportunity when we reach the questions and answers.
	I'd like to first clear the air of some well-established misapprehensions as I frankly see them. After all, we have not come here to hear platitudes. I will do my best to contribute something to what we know about ourselves.
Definition and Analogy	To begin with, I take issue with the term "Hispanic" itself. Though a useful term for political purposes (in fact, invented for that purpose, to show our collective clout), it is not very helpful otherwise. While Hispanics presumably share a language and culture inherited from Spain—and all of us who have lived in South America know that even *that* concept is not 100 percent valid—there is at least as much difference between some countries in Hispanic America, say, for instance, between Guatemala and Argentina, as there is between France and Belgium or, for that matter, between England and the United States. To call us all Hispanics is approximately equivalent to calling the French and Germans Europeans and dealing with them as one. Geographically

accurate, but unrealistic. And certainly unproductive, if you want to win us over individually.

I daresay that, by the same token, some residents of South Florida don't particularly relish being called "Anglos." Labels are no fun.

But let's accept the term Hispanic for lack of a better solution right now, and let's examine the Hispanic issue or, more honestly, the Hispanic problem. I have some pertinent statistics.

Statistics

According to the the National Council of La Raza and the U.S. Bureau of Census, Hispanics are the second largest minority group and one of the fastest-growing U.S. sub-populations. The Hispanic population in 1985 in the mainland U.S. stood at nearly 17 million. It increased by 16 percent since 1980, while the U.S. population as a whole increased by only 3.3 percent. Hispanics account for 40 percent of *legal* immigration.

Hispanics are a heterogeneous group, to say the least. The census shows 61 percent of *mainland* Hispanics were of Mexican origin, 15 percent Puerto Rican, 10 percent Central and South American, 6 percent Cuban and 8 percent other.

Repetition of the term "Hispanics" and parrallel constructions throughout

Hispanics remain the least educated major U.S. subgroup. As of 1984, the median number of school years completed by Hispanics 25 years old and over was 11.3 years—less than a high school education—compared with 12.2 years for blacks and 12.6 for "white" Americans. (And don't blame me for the "white American" characterization either; that's the term used by the U.S. Census which, however, officially recognizes that Hispanics can be of any race. So don't be offended.) Hispanics, also, have the highest school dropout rate as well among these subpopulations.

Hispanics are more than twice as likely as white Americans to be poor. In 1985, Hispanics accounted for 7.2 percent of U.S. population, but constituted 12 percent of those living at poverty levels.

Hispanics are less likely to own their own homes than either blacks or whites.

And, most depressing of all: Hispanics are less likely either to register to vote or actually vote than black or white Americans.

Reference to authority

By contrast, the situation for the Cuban-American subgroup is far more encouraging. According to a study by Professor Modesto Maidique, of whom more will be said in due course,

21.4 percent of Cuban-Americans in the work force in 1980 held professional and managerial jobs in this country, which is essentially the subject of this talk. That's 21.4 percent for Cuban-Americans versus 15.1 percent for all Hispanics combined. That was in 1980, before the Mariel influx, but things haven't changed much. A more recent U.S. Census report, covering 1985, shows 19.1 percent of Cuban-Americans in managerial and professional jobs against 8.6 percent for Mexican-Americans, 12.5 percent for Puerto Ricans, 11.6 percent for the total population of Spanish origin, and 25.2 percent for the U.S. population overall. To cite Maidique, in 1980 the unemployment rate for Cuban-Americans was 5.6 percent, not only below the all-Hispanic unemployment rate of 8.9 percent, but even below the overall non-Hispanic rate of 6.5 percent. I have procured copies of the most recent report from the U.S. Census, issued December 1985, and they are available to you somewhere in this room, courtesy of Dr. Keane, Director of the Census.

Disclaimer

Let me say right here that I don't mean to offend any particular component of the Hispanic community. This talk reflects the facts as they have been provided to me and the conclusions derived from those facts are my own personally. The disparity between the progress of the Cuban-American immigrants and that of the Mexican-Americans and Puerto Ricans is amenable to analysis and explanation; it is the result of some very logical factors.

To begin with, both Mexico and Puerto Rico export primarily manual labor. The reasons they do so are many and quite obvious. For one thing, Mexico has a 2000-mile border with the United States which, despite recent efforts at control, is still quite permeable to legal and illegal passage. The Puerto Ricans, as well, have virtually unimpeded access to the job market in the United States since they are U.S. citizens by right of birth. I don't have to elaborate to this audience on the difficulties Cubans have encountered and continue to encounter in attempting to come to this country.

Analysis

While Puerto Rico and certainly Mexico both have well qualified, highly skilled members of their work force who could, and do, make a contribution in the U.S., the fact is that, mostly, they do not have to emigrate, because they have opportunities for employment and for making a contribution in their own countries. Both nations have a good degree of industrialization where capable people are needed and are welcome. Mexico has had a revolution, though it's an old one and it may be wearing a bit thin, but while it has a predominant political party, it is not a totalitarian government, and never was. So, it is a country where enterprise can still flourish and where talented people can realize their potential. Therefore, the ratio of manual labor to managerial labor that leaves Mexico and Puerto Rico is high and this affects the statistics.

Because of our history and earlier dependence on the United States, Cuban industrial managers and other leaders were generally well attuned to American ways and indeed practiced them in their industries and businesses in Cuba. The English language, and its use in business, was probably not as foreign in Havana as in Mexico City or even San Juan. The transition, therefore, was not as difficult as it might be for other Latin countries.

Specific example

But the most important reason perhaps is a sad one. The Cubans cannot go back. They have nothing to go back to. Therefore, the intensity of their commitment to this country and to their work in this country has to be greater, and it shows. Mexican-Americans and Puerto Ricans—and here I would include the South Americans and Central Americans who come here–have very much in mind the prospect, the intention, to return to their countries. How many times have you or your corporations been approached by a friend in South America who has a son, who will eventually run the family business, but who would like to spend a little time in this country to learn the ways of American corporations so that he may practice them back home? That is not the case for the Cubans and in my view is an additional explanation of the Cuban success story.

Attributes credibility to his source

As an aside, the Central and South American immigrants come out reasonably well in the statistics, probably because, generally, they are too far away to export much manual labor and tend to send us the more qualified or the more daring. They are not included in this discussion simply for lack of time. Also, my friend Arturo Villar, publisher of *Visa Magazine,* an astute observer of the Hispanic scene, has a theory about the top levels of *all* Hispanics which I hope he will share with us during the Q&A: Essentially that at the top differences vanish.

Note the speaker's use of "presumably"

Let's, then, examine what the Hispanic success has been. Is it in fact a success? Professor Maidique makes a compelling statement in his study that success is indeed a reality for the Cubans in South Florida. And I guess no one questions what the entrepreneurial class has managed to achieve in this city, a city which has so graciously and so unselfishly, though not always ungrudgingly, accepted the Cubans, and which, in return, for this enlightened policy, has seen the Cubans improve the economic standing of South Florida. However, there is still much to be done, and there are some intelligent and presumably well-informed people who believe that the Hispanics are not doing all that well. There is, for instance, a recent article by a distinguished Cuban journalist living in Spain (but being published frequently in the newspapers of this city), Carlos Alberto Montaner, an old friend of mine from the early days of the revolution. In an article in the *Miami Herald* last August, he had the following to say:

> "Latins number some 15 million, or maybe 20 million (the exact figure, in fact, is 16,940,000 as of March, 1985). By the turn of the century, they will probably number 30 million. If the economic and political crisis in Mexico and Central America blows up, a hair-raisingly reasonable prospect, that figure might double. This of course makes a lot of Americans nervous. The white (and even black) American stereotypes of Hispanics is extraordinarily negative. They are thought to be lazy, untidy, noisy, dirty, quarrelsome, dangerous and ill-mannered."

Refutation by analysis and introduction of new schema

Out of that litany of goodies, I will accept only noisy. (On the tennis courts they call me The Voice, and when my Cuban partners don't show up other players ask "where are your friends, we don't *hear* them.") As to dirty, I have never seen an ethnic group that uses more Johnson's baby powder than we do. After saying all that, Carlos Alberto says what we need is reverse discrimination: "More scholarships for Hispanics, more opportunities in government and private industry, more Hispanic names in show business, more, much more, tolerance and acceptance of them. "For instance," Montaner says, "what explanation can there be for the fact that the legendary list of the CEO's of the 500 biggest American corporations contains the name of only one Hispanic, Goizueta, a Cuban who heads Coca-Cola?"

I think Montaner got carried away and he's looking at things from Spain, which tends to have a certain remoteness and, I am afraid, a certain bias. The facts are different. If you consider that there are, let's say, a million Cuban-Amercicans in the United States today, and you further consider that the total population of the U.S. is 239 million people (to be exact 238,740,000 as of July, 1986), you would conclude that the percentage of Cuban-Americans in the total U.S.

population is less than one percent. In fact, it is half of one percent. When you then reflect that in the *Fortune 100* we already have one Cuban by the name of Goizueta, when we really should have only half a Cuban, you can see that we could get away with just having the "Goi" and saving the "zueta" for the *next* one hundred companies.

Personalizes by use of story

I was on a television talk show recently in New York on the subject of immigration. At one point the hostess, Ponchita Pierce, baiting me about this same subject, asked, "Don't you find it significant that, in 1986, there is only one Cuban you can say is at the pinnacle of corporate America?" "Well, Ponchita," I answered, "when you get right down to it, there aren't that many pinnacles."

And she was wrong anyway. In my own limited knowledge there are executives like Enrique Falla, George Arellano, Arturo Sterling, Joaquin Blaya, Luis Echarte, Alfonso Fanjul and countless others that, if not at the corporate pinnacle, are damn near it. In my very own company, the President is Carl N. Graf; but his full name is Carlos Nogueira Graf, and he comes from Uruguay.

Actually, while it is true that of the *Fortune 100* Chief Executive Officers there is only one Hispanic (Goizueta again), there were only 9 Irish-Americans, 4 Jewish-Americans and 3 Italian-Americans although their respective percentages of the U.S. population are surely higher than that. Pretty Waspish group, that list.

The fact is that the Cubans at least, in an immigration period only 20 years old, less than one generation, have accomplished a great deal. Much older immigrations, we forget, had a lot of trouble. It took the Irish many generations to produce a Kennedy or a Reagan, the Italians to produce an Iacocca or, I hate to say it, a Cuomo, and the Jews a Kissinger or Lehrman.

Political bias used as humor

Our friend Montaner goes on to say, "How is it that there is hardly anybody of Hispanic origins in the upper echelons of the *New York Times,* the great liberal paper, or the *Wall Street Journal,* a magnificent conservative organ?" Well, he doesn't mention the nationally recognized *Miami Herald,* which I will not attempt to characterize as either liberal or conservative. But, whatever it be, we have a member of its editorial board here with us, Guillermo Martinez, the son of another great journalist, and a man who coins phrases like "ethnic dissonance." Not only is he representing the Hispanics on that newspaper, but he has just been promoted to a specially created position, which recognizes the unique skills and background he brings to the newspaper.

Finally, Montaner says, perhaps prophetically, "Why does not one Hispanic head up any leading university in the country, even in the city of Miami, where Latins form a powerful educated minority?" We know, and Montaner knows, that that particular objection, happily, is no longer valid. Our friend Modesto Maidique has been named to the presidency of the Florida International University and, in fact, there were several other Hispanics considered for that position. Modesto deserves our congratulations.

In all this there is the suggestion of discrimination, and of course there is some. There is always some tension between the established and the newcomers. A Filipino lady on that talk show I mentioned claimed there was a lot of discrimination, especially in the present time.

Relay—personalizes the problem by example; humor used to soften impact of prejudice

I don't think discrimination is an insurmountable problem, and I don't think it is worse now than in the past. In fact, I think there is less. When I attended Georgia Tech a thousand years ago (actually, 1940) I was chosen to join a leading social fraternity, until they found out I was Cuban. It was Atlanta in 1940, xenophobia was a fact of those days, and my fraternity didn't accept Cubans. They wanted me and I wanted them, and we all agreed to lie and say I was from Miami. Humiliating, of course, but I allowed it to happen. Two years later I was elected president of that fraternity and the first thing I did was to change the by-laws to accept Cubans and anyone else—almost (it was still Atlanta and it was still the 1940's). That's working from inside the system. Evolution rather than revolution. This country doesn't need revolutions. And it's indeed a sign of the times that in Atlanta today their flagship corporation, the Coca-Cola Company, is headed by a Cuban.

After this overly long introduction maybe we can devote the last five minutes to the subject of the speech, at least as Charlie Zwick saw it: a personal success story and advice to young Hispanics on how to succeed in the corporate environment.

There are at least 200 success stories in this room that you should hear—and maybe will. I am not going to bore you with mine. Besides it would make you cry: three revolutions, the one against Machado in 1933, Castro in 1959 and Velasco Alvarado in Peru in 1968 is more than anyone deserves. To have worked for *both* Julio Lobo and Peter Grace . . . never mind, I need the job.

Antonio Navarro   ■ ■ ■   **265**

I would rather talk about success generally, how to get there and how to stay there.

Divides question into two different parts

First, we have of course to distinguish between the entrepreneurs and the corporate types. Miami, if full of successful entrepreneurs, it is not exactly jam-packed with executives of large corporations, though it is moving in that direction. Cuban-born Americans have certainly made their mark as self-made proprietors of retail establishments, owners and chief executives of manufacturing concerns, scions of real-estate. We are proud of that. In these independent roles, it is important to remember that *performance always outweighs conformity*. Cubans by nature, by truly Hispanic heritage, were not and are not conformers. I believe that Cuban-Americans often harness that nonconformity and make it a valuable asset in doing or creating something new that translates to profit and success. This is the great privilege of successful independent entrepreneurs. Performance outweighs everything. Serve your customers, and you will succeed. Hard work is the key. *You* are the only one who needs to "accept" you in your own company. The corporate world is different. So what is my advice to those who choose corporate America?

Well, if I have not already confused you, let me try to do it now. My advice is *different* for different generations of Hispanics. The advice to today's Cuban-born generation, *our* generation, as opposed to our children's generation, tomorrow's generation, *has* to be different. In fact it may very well be *opposite* to tomorrow's in some sense.

The advice to my contemporaries is to rely *less* on your Hispanic heritage, Hispanic culture, your Hispanic language. That is not asking you to deny your ancestry; no one likes an ethnic hypocrite. That is not to say to abandon these special qualities you have, but simply to tone them down in order to facilitate your assimilating, and being assimilated by, the corporate culture.

There is in the corporation a premium on conforming, as opposed to the entrepreneur who by and large can do his own thing as long as the bottom line is favorable. In the corporate world, because of the nature of the beast, there is a need for a degree of conformity to certain standards of behavior which form what has been called the culture of any one corporation. Again, that is not to give up entirely the very definite edge that we may have because we have an understanding of more than one culture, and speak more than one language. What I am trying to say is that there is a fine line between, on the one hand, using these extra assets we have as an advantage within the corporation and, on the other, allowing them to become a disadvantage and interfere with your progress.

Let me say rather bluntly that if you don't have the ability to distinguish between what helps you and what hurts you, and cannot ride the fine line between those two, then perhaps you don't have that indispensable sensitivity and, frankly, corporate life may not be for you. Most Cuban-Americans and other Hispanics I know do have this capability.

On the subject of language, no one is suggesting that we give up Spanish. But we *are* saying that plain common sense and elementary courtesy dictate that in business, when there are other workers who speak Spanish, we should be careful to speak in the language which is understood by all who work with us or have a reason to be involved in the same project, and to make an effort to speak English as well as we can. That may seem obvious, but somehow it isn't. We all know how much easier it is to curse in Spanish or shout "tuya" on the tennis court. Arturo Sterling, our sugar tycoon and one of the panelists, may have something to say about that.

Just as the preceding would be advice to the older generation, advice to the coming generation, the younger generation, might read something like this: Rely *more* on your Hispanic heritage and culture, and even language, which you should never, never, allow yourself to forget. The reason you can do this is that, unlike your parents or your grandparents, you are already accepted as a member of the community by virtue of the fact that you grew up within it, and that your early efforts to "belong" have been successful. Therefore, you are just one of the boys except that you have this extra edge, this differential advantage, which should be used judiciously to help you in your progress and in your career.

Take a young person who otherwise meets all qualifications for a promotion to a post abroad, but who also has that extra language and an extra awareness of another culture and its idiosyncracies, and therefore also has a certain flexibility in simply accepting that there are people who "think different and do different and speak different." That person is going to get the promotion over others.

Some further advice, mostly to the young. There is no substitute for dedication, discipline, hard work, proper respect for superiors whether you like them or not, and, above all, reliability, that whatever you are asked to do will get done or your superior will know why it cannot be done or why it cannot be done on time. Other qualities to strive for are respect for the corporation's ethics and for your own ethics. The courage to express and support your point of view. And, perhaps controversial, a certain degree of diplomacy (something called in Spanish "mano izquierda"), which in fact your Hispanic heritage should develop into a healthy command of what is derisively known as "internal politics," a useful art many people pretend to disdain simply because they will not or cannot master it.

There is one other ingredient: honesty. When you are asked a question by a superior, *never, never* lie or equivocate. Always give a direct and accurate response. Too many people today think they can get ahead by lying or covering up or guessing what the boss wants to hear. Not so. You'll be exposed at some point, and that will be the end of that.

I am of course taking for granted that you already have the God-given intelligence which no one else can give you, and the academic preparation or experience that you and your parents have provided for you.

Concludes with quotation

Finally, the generation which follows us—actually it follows *me* at a *greater* distance—should have no problems. They will fit well in the American community, but they will continue to have that differential advantage which a second language and a second culture invariably provide.

The magazine *Nation's Business* provides a fitting quote to end this talk: "Quietly, steadily, Hispanic-Americans have been on the move, building businesses, making jobs, creating wealth. They have proved themselves people with talent and drive, and a taste for success."

All that bodes well for the future of the Hispanic community and the Cuban community in this country. I think that for bringing that into focus, and for getting us together for the first time in my memory at least, we should all be grateful to Southeast Bank and in particular to its Chairman and forward thinking leader Charles Zwick and to *Hispanic Business* magazine.

As for you, friends who put up with me, let's keep dreaming the American Dream. And making it happen.

Thank you.

Thomas C. Collins

Why Shouldn't Our Schools Compete?

Thomas C. Collins (Proctor and Gamble) delivered the following speech before the Council for Academic Excellence, in Columbus, Ohio, November 9, 1986. Mr. Collins' audience is partially made up of members of a special Symposium on Statewide Testing in Ohio Schools. Mr. Collins' principle purpose is to *persuade*. Notice how he uses enthymatic constructions at several places to make his case appear logical. The underlying assumption of this speech is that the same kinds of assessment and evaluations that are appropriate for the business community are also appropriate for education. Notice also his skilled use of statistics and quotations from experts. Most of the persons in Mr. Collins' audience were members of the Council for Academic Excellence in the State of Ohio, a group that had already taken a stand in favor of Mr. Collins' proposals. However, several other interesting proposals are also advanced.

Previews structure of speech

I speak as a businessman who has done some volunteer work for the public schools in Cincinnati and in Ohio. Those credentials make me an expert on nothing—but they at least provide some basis for the three convictions I would like to share with you tonight.

The first conviction is that, if you're trying to do something as well as it can be done, you'd better know how your results compare with other people's results. Feedback on this is virtually automatic in private enterprise. But in the monopoly situation which our schools face, there is a measurement vacuum which needs filling. Meaningful statewide measurement of school results would fill that vacuum.

The second conviction is that the most meaningful measurement of school results is pupil achievement related to aptitude—aptitude being mental maturity, or the ability to learn in school.

The third conviction is that adoption of this measurement by Ohio's schools will, in time, lead to improved student outcomes—and such improvement will surely lead to better public support.

Let me now put some meat on the bones of these convictions.

First, the importance of knowing how your results compare with other people's results. A private enterprise competing head-to-head gets continual feedback from the marketplace. The market doesn't vote every two or four years. It votes every day—with millions of individual consumer decisions.

This unrelenting pressure on quality and cost keeps competitive enterprises on their toes. Our schools lack this impetus. They have no direct competition.

Further, the customers of our schools—both the taxpayers who pay the bills, and the fraction with children in school—are generally not in a position to assess school performance well because they have such little school contact. Thus, informed feedback on the quality of school results is low.

So what happens? Well, school people make judgments on what is needed—and they are generally heeded.

Uses comparision and contrast

Then what happens? Well, we keep spending more and more money. In the last 25 years—from 1960 to 1985—the cost per pupil for public primary and secondary education in Ohio went from $1,264 to $3,288–in 1985 dollars adjusted for inflation.

So in 1985, Ohio spent two and a half times as much per pupil in real dollars as it did in 1960—*two and a half times as much!* Per pupil spending grew at over twice the rate of increase in per capita gross national product.

What has this money gone for? Well, it went for a number of things—to the growth of vocational education and special education of all kinds, to federal programs, to reduced class sizes, to increased transportation, and to the addition of teacher aides. There has been an approximate doubling of staff to pupil ratio in the last twenty-five years.

Rhetorical question

And what results have we gotten for this increase in spending? Well, we don't know—because there are no measures that any of us can have confidence in.

Amplification

We don't know how Ohio's pupils are achieving compared to the past. We don't know how Ohio's pupils are achieving right now in each of the state's 614 school districts. Thus, there is no basis for analysis which could provide state policy makers with insight on which program factors are associated with high pupil achievement.

Ohio is not unique in this. Other states are similarly ignorant. Public elementary and secondary education in Ohio is now more than a $6 billion enterprise. It is the fifth largest item of government expense in the state.

Hidden syllogism—an enthymeme

Surely we must have the best information we can generate on what we are getting for what we are spending if policy makers and the public are to make good decisions on Ohio's schools in the future. And we need *comparative* information—information which can help us to begin to understand how to improve the productivity of our school investments. We simply must fill the present measurement vacuum.

That brings me to my second conviction—that the most meaningful measurement of school results is pupil achievement related to aptitude. There can be no doubt that the bottom line for our schools is pupil achievement. The question is how best to measure that.

Most schools measure achievement versus national norms—obtaining information on how their pupils perform on standardized tests. Those schools making the information public often express results in terms of the percentage of their students performing at or above the mean of all the pupils tested in the nation.

Refutation of present practice

That's fine—as far as it goes. But this information is of quite limited usefulness.

This is simply because achievement has been shown to correlate with aptitude—and the distribution of aptitudes in any given school differs from the country as a whole. No school is a true microcosm of the nation.

Since pupil aptitude correlates highly with socio-economic factors, relative achievement comparisons between districts are generally predictable. Those districts above the U.S. average socioeconomically will be above average in achievement and vice versa. I would submit that a testing program that simply reaffirms this well known fact will not provide meaningful information. On the other hand, if you relate pupil achievement to pupil aptitude, you begin to generate some very useful information.

Outline of terms

In the first place, by comparing achievement of your pupils with achievement of pupils of similar aptitude broadly, you get an "apples to apples" measure.

Secondly, if you can add to that knowledge the ability to single out schools doing a *better* job, then you gain the opportunity to learn what others are doing that you might be able to productively apply yourself. This, of course, is what the schools which are members of the Ohio Council for Academic Excellence are able to do. More about this in a moment.

I have discussed achievement testing with enough educators to be well aware of the common concerns—concerns about reliability, meaningfulness, teachers teaching to the test, etcetera. Each of the concerns has some validity if there is abuse in the way tests are conducted or interpreted.

Minimize problems

There is no doubt, however, that standardized tests—properly conducted and interpreted—can be invaluable in improving school management. Bill Mehrens, Professor of Measurement at Michigan State and immediate past president of the National Council on Measurement in Education, is with us. He can answer questions you might have in the morning session.

Note specific refutation

There is one concern I do want to briefly address though—the concern that aptitude testing might lower teacher expectations. Certainly, if school people were to look at aptitude test results as infallible predictors of what children will achieve regardless of teacher effort and skill, that would be a clear abuse of the purpose of the test.

Teachers must bear in mind that aptitudes are subject to improvement—that the more a child learns, the more likely it is that the child's aptitude will improve.

Outline term used as a transition

This brings me surely and naturally to my third conviction—that adoption of the achievement-to-aptitude measurement by Ohio's schools will, in time, lead to improved student outcomes. This conviction is based squarely on faith in human nature. There is, in our nature, a desire to excel—to do things better than others have done them before and better than others are doing them now.

"Humanity" would have done better!

This is evident in man's progress through all of recorded history.

This desire to do things better is at the root of competitive sports. It motivates those who participate and those who cheer them on alike. And it is at the root of successful organizations—because successful organizations provide a framework for their members to do things better individually and together.

An indispensable part of such a framework is meaningful measurement of accomplishment—a way to set goals and a way to keep score. Such measurement provides focus for energy and initiative—and it reconciles differences in judgment by letting results decide the worth of ideas.

Once teachers and principals see clearly the results being accomplished by other schools with children of abilities similar to their own, isn't there an opportunity to stimulate one of the most productive aspects of human nature? I mean that part of us that asks, "Can't I—can't we—get better than average results?"

Defines competition as "healthy"

In essence, meaningful measurement provides the basis for healthy competition. And why shouldn't our schools compete? Can you imagine the force for good that would come from Ohio's teachers and principles setting out to prove they can get *better results* than average schools?

Not all will succeed, but even those who don't will sharpen their skills in the attempt. And as time goes on, much will be learned—both about what works and what doesn't work. Generally, more of what works will be done—and more of what doesn't work won't be done. And as this happens, over time, our schools will get better and public support will grow.

As a businessman, I have developed deep respect for the public's ability to recognize value in a product or service. As a volunteer who has worked on six school tax levy campaigns, I am well aware of the widespread desire for better value from the school dollar. As value improves, there is no doubt in my mind that public support will improve as well.

At the state level, information on what works and what doesn't work will surely be useful in guiding policy. It will become clear to policymakers that how *well* money is spent is far more important than how *much* money is spent.

Surely, the value of getting meaningful information on results being achieved by Ohio's schools will be clear enough to state policymakers so that some action—whether by legislation or regulation—will be taken to stimulate it.

With respect to the action which the state will eventually take, I would offer only two suggestions.

Specifies proposals

First, the state should make the information it seeks meaningful and simple. The percentage of students achieving at or above national norms relative to aptitude by grade, meets that test. A breakdown of overall results by groups of high, average, and low aptitude students would also be useful for analytical purposes.

The second suggestion is simply that, if the state puts any incentives into its legislation or regulations, it should not put in incentives which reward poor school performance—more money if a school gets below-average results for example.

Promise of reward

If our schools see that they will get more money from the state by doing a poor job than by doing a good job, you can bet that the state will get what it pays for.

For far too long, there has been an emphasis at both state and national levels on minimum rather than maximum achievement. I would suggest that Ohio take the lead in placing the emphasis where it belongs—on maximum achievement for pupils of all aptitude levels.

In the end, however, the most effective leadership on this subject in Ohio—or in any other state—will come, not from the top down, but from the bottom up.

Ohio should take a lesson from soundly run businesses in recognizing that the commitment and ingenuity of individuals cannot be mandated from above.

Accordingly, if I were a state legislator or school board member, I would do what I could to encourage the efforts of the Council for Academic Excellence in Ohio Schools.

This is true bottoms-up effort. It started, interestingly enough, two months before publication of the "Nation at Risk" report. So, while the nation was reading about a "rising tide of mediocrity," there was rising in Ohio an effort to stimulate a "tide of excellence."

Specific mechanism suggested

Members of the Council measure achievement of their pupils in relation to aptitude. Through a program developed by the Educational Testing Service in Princeton, the member districts are able to determine which schools are producing the highest achievement by levels of aptitude for each subject.

Visits to exemplary schools can be arranged so that members can get ideas for improving their own schools. Some principals have sent delegations of teachers to visit exemplary schools in search of ideas to bring back to their own classrooms. Thus, through measurement of results and sharing of "what works," the member schools have valuable tools to help them strive for improvement.

There are currently 60 Ohio school districts in the Council for Academic Excellence. About half of these are above the state average in property valuation per pupil, and half are below. About two thirds spend more per pupil than the state average, and about one third spend less—though there is no direct correlation between achievement levels and spending.

Specific persuasive goal

I hope each of you here this evening representing a school district which is not a member of the Council will strongly consider joining. I think you would find it a helpful step in improving your district.

Equally important, broadening of the base of districts participating will hasten improvement in Ohio's schools generally. As an Ohio patriot, I would like to see that. This

276 ■ ■ ■ Sample Speeches

bottoms-up effort of results measurement and school improvement is unique. There is not another group like this in the whole country.

Thus, Ohio has an unusual opportunity to demonstrate leadership in an area vital not just to the state, but to the nation.

I hope you will help Ohio show this leadership.

Geraldine A. Ferraro

Accepting the Nomination

This was the formal acceptance speech made by Representative Geraldine A. Ferraro to the National Democratic Convention in San Francisco, July 19, 1984. Notice how Representative Ferraro uses externalization as a principal method. As with so many political speeches, here the principal purpose is to *stimulate*.

My name is Geraldine Ferraro, and I stand before you to proclaim tonight: America is a land where dreams can come true for all our citizens.

Externalization

As I stand before the American people and think of the honor this great convention has bestowed upon me, I recall the words of Dr. Martin Luther King, Jr., who made America stronger by making America more free. He said: "Occasionally in life there are moments which cannot be completely explained by words. Their meaning can only be articulated by the inaudible language of the heart."

Tonight is such a moment for me. My heart is filled with pride. My fellow citizens, I proudly accept your nomination for Vice President of the United States.

Extended externalization

And I am proud to run with a man who will be one of the great Presidents of this century, Walter F. Mondale.

Tonight, the daughter of a woman whose highest goal was a future for her children talks to our nation's oldest party about a future for us all.

Tonight, the daughter of working Americans tells all Americans that the future is within our reach—if we're willing to reach for it.

Tonight, the daughter of an immigrant from Italy has been chosen to run for Vice President in the new land my father came to love.

Our faith that we can shape a better future is what the American dream is all about. The promise of our country is that the rules are fair. And if you work hard and play by the rules, you can earn your share of America's blessings.

Introduces "rules"

Those are the beliefs I learned from my parents. And those are the values I taught my students as a teacher in the public schools of New York.

At night, I went to law school. I became an assistant district attorney, and I put my share of criminals behind bars. Because I believe: If you obey the law, you should be protected. But if you break the law, you should pay for your crime.

Geraldine A. Ferraro

When I first ran for Congress, all the political experts said a woman could not win in my home district of Queens. But I put my faith in the people and the values that we shared. And together, we proved the political experts wrong.

In this campaign, Fritz Mondale and I have put our faith in the people. And we are going to prove the experts wrong again.

Comparison and contrast

We are going to win, because Americans across this country believe in the same basic dream.

Last week, I visited Elmore, Minn., the small town where Fritz Mondale was raised. And soon Fritz and Joan will visit our family in Queens. Nine hundred people live in Elmore. In Queens there are 2,000 people on one block. You would think we would be different, but we're not.

Children walk to school in Elmore past grain elevators; in Queens, they pass by subway stops. But, no matter where they live, their future depends on education—and their parents are willing to do their part to make those schools as good as they can be. In Elmore, there are family farms; in Queens, small businesses. But the men and women who run them all take pride in supporting their families through hard work and initiative.

Exemplification

On the Fourth of July in Elmore, they hang the flags out on Main Street; in Queens, they fly them over Grand Avenue. But all of us love our country, and stand ready to defend the freedom that it represents.

Repeats rules analogy

Americans everywhere want to live by the same set of rules. But under this Administration, the rules are rigged against too many of our people. It isn't right that every year, the share of taxes paid by individual citizens is going up, while the share paid by large corporations is getting smaller and smaller. The rules say: Everyone in our society should contribute their fair share.

Reiteration of phrase "It isn't right"

It isn't right that this year Ronald Reagan will hand the American people a bill for interest on the national debt that is larger than the entire cost of the Federal Government under John F. Kennedy.

Our parents left us a growing economy. The rules say: We must not leave our kids a mountain of debt.

It isn't right that a woman should get paid 59 cents on the dollar for the same work as a man. Because if you play by the rules, you deserve a fair day's pay for a fair day's work.

It isn't right that if trends continue by the year 2000 nearly all of the poor people in America will be women and children. The rules of a decent society say, when you distribute sacrifice in time of austerity, you don't put women and children first.

It isn't right that young people today fear that they won't get the Social Security they paid for, and that older Americans fear that they will lose what they have already earned. Social Security is a contract between the last generation and the next, and the rules say: You don't break contracts. We're going to keep faith with older Americans.

We hammered out a fair compromise in the Congress to save Social Security. Every group's had to sacrifice to keep the system sound. It is time Ronald Reagan stopped scaring our senior citizens.

It isn't right that young couples question whether to bring children into a world of 50,000 nuclear warheads.

That isn't the vision for which Americans have struggled for more than two centuries. And our future doesn't have to be that way. For change is in the air, just as surely as when John Kennedy beckoned America to a New Frontier; when Sally Ride rocketed into space; and when the descendant of slaves, Reverend Jesse Jackson, ran for the high office of President of the United States.

By choosing an American woman to run for our nation's second highest office, you send a powerful signal to all Americans. There are no doors we cannot unlock. We will place no limits on achievement. If we can do this, we can do anything.

Tonight, we reclaim our dream. We're going to make the rules of American life work fairly for all Americans again.

To an Administration that would have us debate all over again whether the Voting Rights Act should be renewed and whether segregated schools should be tax exempt, we say, Mr. President: Those debates are over. On the issue of civil and voting rights and affirmative action for minorities, we must not go backwards. We must and we will move forward to open the doors of opportunity.

Uses constuction from Kennedy's "Ask not what America can do for you, but ask instead what you can do for America"

To those who understand that our country cannot prosper unless we draw on the talents of all Americans, we say: We will pass the Equal Rights Amendment. The issue is not what America can do for women, but what women can do for America.

To the Americans who will lead our country into the 21st

century, we say: We will not have a Supreme Court that turns the clock back to the 19th century.

To those working Americans who fear that banks, and utilities, and large special interests have a lock on the White House today, we say: Join us; let's elect a people's President; and let's have government by the people.

To an Administration that would savage student loans of education at the dawn of a new technological age, we say: You fit the classic definition of a cynic: You know the price of everything, but the value of nothing.

To our students and their parents, we say: We will insist on the highest standards of education because the jobs of the future require skilled minds as well as hands.

To young Americans who may be called to our country's service, we say: We know your generation of Americans will proudly answer our country's call, as each generation before you.

This past year we remembered the bravery and sacrifice of Americans at Normandy. And we finally paid tribute, as we should have done years ago, to that unknown soldier who represents all the brave young Americans who died in Vietnam.

Let no one doubt that we will defend America's security and the cause of freedom around the world. But we want a President who tells us what America is fighting for, not just what we are fighting against. We want a President who will defend human rights—not just where it is convenient—but wherever freedom is at risk—from Afghanistan to Chile, from Poland to South Africa.

We want a President who will keep America strong, but use that strength to keep America, and the world, at peace. A nuclear freeze is not a slogan: it is a tool for survival in the nuclear age. If we leave our children nothing else, let us leave this earth as we found it—whole and green and full of life.

I know in my heart Walter Mondale will be that President.

A wise man once said, "Every one of us is given the gift of life, and what a strange gift it is. It is preserved jealously and selfishly, it impoverishes and saddens. But if it is spent for others, it enriches and beautifies.

My fellow Americans: We can debate programs and policies. But in the end what separates the two parties in this election campaign is whether we use the gift of life—for others or only ourselves.

Tonight, my husband, John, and our three children are in this hall with me. To my daughters, Donna and Laura, and my son, John Jr., I say: My mother did not break faith with me and I will not break faith with you. To all the children of America, I say: The generation before ours kept faith with us, and like them, we will pass on to you a stronger, more just America.

Thank you very much.

Lech Walesa

Accepting the Nobel Prize

In 1983 the Nobel Peace Prize was awarded to Lech Walesa (Polish "Solidarity" Group). The following speech was delivered at the Nobel Peace Prize Ceremony in Oslo on December 11, 1983. Mr. Walesa did not actually deliver the speech—he was not allowed to leave Poland at the time. An associate, Bogdan Cywinski (an exiled leader of the Solidarity Union) actually delivered the speech. The text below has been translated from Polish into Norwegian and then into English.

Ladies and Gentlemen:

Identifies himself and group

Addressing you, as the winner of the 1983 Nobel Peace Prize, is a Polish worker from the Gdansk shipyard, one of the founders of the independent trade union movement in Poland.

It would be the simplest thing for me to say that I am not worthy of the great distinction. Yet, when I recall the hour when the news of the prize spread throughout my country, the hour of rising emotions and universal joy of the people who felt that they have a moral and spiritual share in the award, I am obligated to say that I regard it as a sign of recognition that the movement to which I gave all my strength had served well the community of men.

I accept the award with my deepest respect for its meaning and significance, and at the same time, I am conscious that the honor is bestowed not on me personally, but upon Solidarity, upon the people and the ideas for which we have fought and shall continue to do so in the spirit of peace and justice. And there is nothing I desire more than that the granting of the award should help the cause of peace and justice in my country and the world over.

My first words which I address to you, and through you to all people, are those which I have known since my childhood days: peace to men of goodwill—all and everywhere, in the north and south, east and west.

I belong to a nation which over the past centuries has experienced many hardships and reverses. The world reacted with silence or with mere sympathy when Polish frontiers were crossed by invading armies and the sovereign state had to succumb to brutal forces. Our national history has often filled us with bitterness and the feeling of helplessness. But this was, above all, a great lesson in hope.

Expresses gratitude

Thanking you for the award I would like, first of all, to express my gratitude and my belief that it serves to enhance the Polish hope. The hope of the nation which throughout the 19th century had not for a moment reconciled itself with the loss of independence, and fighting for its own freedom, fought at the same time for the freedom of other nations. The hope whose elations and downfalls during the past 40 years, i.e., the span of my own life, have been marked by the memorable and dramatic dates: 1944, 1956, 1976, 1980.

And if I permit myself at this juncture and on this occasion to mention my own life, it is because I believe that the prize had been granted to me as to one of many.

My youth passed at the time of the country's reconstruction from the ruins and ashes of the war in which my nation never bowed to the enemy, paying the highest price in the struggle.

I belong to the generation of workers who, born in the villages and hamlets of rural Poland, had the opportunity to acquire education and find employment in industry, becoming in the course conscious of their rights and importance in society. Those were the years of awakening aspirations of workers and peasants, but also years of many wrongs, degradations and lost illusions.

I was barely 13 years old when, in June 1956, the desperate struggle of the workers of Poznan for bread and freedom was suppressed in blood. Thirteen also was the boy—Romek Strzalkowski—who was killed in the struggle.

It was the Solidarity Union which 25 years later demanded that tribute be paid to his memory. In December 1970, when workers' protest demonstrations engulfed the towns of the Baltic coast, I was a worker in Gdansk shipyard and one of the organizers of the strike. The memory of my fellow workers who then lost their lives, the bitter memory of violence and despair, has become for me a lesson never to be forgotten.

A few years later, in June 1976, the strike of the workers at Ursus and Radom was a new experience which not only strengthened my belief in the justness of the working people's demands and aspirations but also has indicated the urgent need for their solidarity. This conviction brought me, in the summer of 1978, to the free trade union—formed by a group of courageous and dedicated people who came out in the defense of the workers' rights and dignity.

In July and August of 1980 a wave of strikes swept through Poland. The issue at stake was then something much bigger than only material conditions of existence. My road of life had, at the time of the struggle, brought me back to that shipyard in Gdansk. The whole country joined forces with the workers of Gdansk and Szczecin. The agreements of Gdansk, Szczecin and Jastrzebie eventually were signed and the Solidarity Union thus came into being.

The great Polish strikes of which I have just spoken were events of a special nature. Their character was determined on the one hand by the menacing circumstances in which they were held and, on the other, by their objectives. The Polish workers who participated in the strike actions in fact represented the nation.

When I recall my own path of life I cannot but speak of the violence, hatred and lies. A lesson drawn from such experiences, however, was that we can effectively oppose violence only if we ourselves do not resort to it.

In the brief history of those eventful years, the Gdansk agreement stands out as a great charter of the rights of the working people which nothing can ever destroy.

Lying at the root of the social agreements of 1980 are the courage, sense of responsibility and solidarity of the working people. Both sides then recognized that an accord must be reached if bloodshed was to be prevented. The agreement then signed has been and shall remain the model and the only method to follow, the only one that gives a chance of finding a middle course between the use of force and a hopeless struggle.

Our firm conviction that ours is a just cause and that we must find a peaceful way to attain our goals gave us the strength and the awareness of the limits beyond which we must not go. What until then seemed impossible to achieve has become a fact of life. We have won the right to organize in trade unions independent from the authorities, founded and shaped by the working people themselves.

Our union—the Solidarity—has grown into a powerful movement for social and moral liberation. The people, freed from the bondage of fear and apathy, called for reforms and improvements. We fought a difficult struggle for our existence. That was and still is a great opportunity for the whole country. I think that it marked also the road to be taken by the authorities, if they thought of a state governed in cooperation and participation of all citizens.

Solidarity, as a trade union movement, did not reach for power, nor did it turn against the established constitutional order. During the 15 months of Solidarity's legal existence, nobody was killed or wounded as a result of its activities.

Our movement expanded by leaps and bounds. But we were propelled to conduct an uninterrupted struggle for our rights and freedom of activity while at the same time imposing upon ourselves unavoidable self-limitations.

Argues from moral principle

The program of our movement stems from the fundamental moral laws and order. The sole and basic source of our strength is the solidarity of workers, peasants and intelligentsia, the solidarity of the nation, the solidarity of people who seek to live in dignity, truth and in harmony with their consciences.

Let the veil of silence fall presently over what happened afterwards. Silence, too, can speak out.

One thing, however, must be said here and now on this solemn occasion: The Polish people have not been subjugated, nor have they chosen the road of violence and fratricidal bloodshed.

We shall not yield to violence. We shall not be deprived of union freedoms. We shall never agree to sending people to prison for their convictions. The gates of prisons must be thrown open and persons sentenced for defending union and civil rights must be set free.

The announced trials of 11 leading members of our movement must never be held. All those already sentenced or still awaiting trials for their union activities or their convictions should return to their homes and be allowed to live and work in their country.

Uses "identificatory" credibility

The defense of our right and our dignity, as well as efforts never to let ourselves be overcome by the feeling of hatred—this is the road we have chosen.

The Polish experience, which the Nobel Peace Prize has put into the limelight, has been a difficult, a dramatic one. Yet I believe that it looks to the future. The things that have taken place in human conscience and reshaped human attitude cannot be obliterated or destroyed. They exist and will remain.

We are the heirs of those national aspirations, thanks to which our people could never be made into an inert mass with no will of their own. We want to live with the belief that law means law and justice means justice, that our toil has a meaning and is not wasted, that our culture grows and develops freedom.

As a nation we have the right to decide our own affairs, to mold our own future. This does not pose any danger to anybody. Our nation is fully aware of the responsibility for its own fate in the complicated situation of the contemporary world.

Despite everything that has been going on in my country during the past two years, I remain convinced that we have no alternative but to come to an agreement, and that the difficult problems which Poland is now facing can be resolved only through a real dialogue between state authorities and the people.

During his last visit to the land of his fathers, Pope John Paul II had this to say on this point:

> Citations from Pope John Paul II designed as much for Polish listeners as for international listeners

"Why do the working people of Poland, and everywhere else for that matter, have the right to such a dialogue? It is because the working man is not a mere tool of production, but he is the subject which throughout the process of production takes precedence over the capital. By the fact of his labor, the man becomes the true master of his workshop, of the process of labor, of the fruits of his toil and of their distribution. He is also ready for sacrifices if he feels that he is a real partner and has a say in the just division of what has been produced by common effort."

It is, however, precisely this feeling that we lack. It is hardly possible to build anything if frustration, bitterness and the mood of helplessness prevail.

He who once became aware of the power of Solidarity and who breathed the air of freedom will not be crushed. The dialogue is possible, and we have the right to it. The wall raised by the course of events must not become an insurmountable obstacle. My most ardent desire is that my country will recapture its historic opportunity for a peaceful evolution, and that Poland will prove to the world that even the most complex situations can be solved by a dialogue and not by force.

We are ready for the dialogue. We are also prepared at any time, to put our reasons and demands to the judgement of the people. We have no doubts as to what verdict would be returned.

I think that all nations of the world have the right to live in dignity. I believe that, sooner or later, the rights of individuals, of families and of entire communities will be respected in every corner of the world.

Respect for civil and human rights in Poland and for our national identity is in the best interests of all Europe. For in the interest of Europe is a peaceful Poland, and the Polish aspirations to freedom will never be stifled. The dialogue in Poland is the only way to achieving internal peace, and that is why it is also an indispensable element of peace in Europe.

I realize that the strivings of the Polish people gave rise, and still do so, to feelings of understanding and solidarity all over the world. Allow me from this place to express my most profound thanks to all those who help Poland and the Poles. May I also voice my desire that our wish for dialogue and for respect of human rights in Poland should be strengthened by a positive thought.

My country is in the grips of a major economic crisis. This is causing dramatic consequences for the very existence of Polish families. A permanent economic crisis in Poland also may have serious repercussions for Europe. Thus, Poland ought to be helped and deserves help.

I am looking at the present-day world with the eyes of a worker—a worker who belongs to a nation so tragically experienced by the war. I most sincerely wish that the world in which we live be free from the threat of a nuclear holocaust and from the ruinous arms race. It is my cherished desire that peace be not separated from freedom, which is the right of every nation. This I desire, and for this I pray.

Calls for understanding and dialogue

May I repeat that the fundamental necessity in Poland is now understanding and dialogue. I think that the same applies to the whole world; we should go on talking, we must not close any doors or do anything that would block the road to an understanding. And we must remember that only a peace built on the foundations of justice and moral order can be a lasting one.

In many parts of the world the people are searching for a solution which would link the two basic values: peace and justice. The two are like bread and salt for mankind. Every nation and every community have the inalienable right to these values. No conflicts can be resolved without doing everything possible to follow that road. Our times require that these aspirations which exist the world over must be recognized.

Our efforts and harsh experiences have revealed to the world the value of human solidarity. Accepting this honorable distinction, I am thinking of those with whom I am linked by the spirit of solidarity.

First of all, of those who in the struggle for the workers' and civil rights in my country paid the highest price—the price of life . . .

Of my friends who paid for the defense of Solidarity with the loss of freedom, who were sentenced to prison terms or are awaiting trial . . .

Calls for more "Solidarity" in other Socialist countries

Of my countrymen who saw in the Solidarity movement the fulfillment of their aspirations as workers and citizens, who are subjected to humiliations and ready for sacrifice, who have learned to link courage with wisdom and who persist in loyalty to the cause we have embarked upon . . .

Of all those who are struggling throughout the world for workers' and union rights, for the dignity of the working man, for human rights.

Inscribed on the monument erected at the entrance to the Gdansk shipyard, in the memory of those who died in December 1970, are the words of the psalm: "The Lord will give power to his people, the Lord will give his people the blessings of peace."

Let these words be our message of brotherhood and hope.

Dwight D. Eisenhower

Atoms for Peace

Dwight D. Eisenhower, President of the United States, delivered the following speech before the General Assembly of the United Nations on December 8, 1953. President Eisenhower ostensibly addresses this proposal to the United Nations, but actually seeks an international hearing for his proposal that Russia and the United States share atomic technology with other countries. Eisenhower's method is *deductive,* in that he establishes principles first and then proceeds to his proposal.

Introduction

Never before in history has so much hope for so many people been gathered together in a single organization. Your deliberation and decisions during these somber years have already realized part of those hopes.

But the great tests and the great accomplishments still lie ahead. And in the confident expectation of those accomplishments, I would use the office which, for the time being, I hold, to assure you that the Government of the United States will remain steadfast in its support of this body. This we shall do in the conviction that you will provide a great share of the wisdom, the courage, and the faith which can bring to this world lasting peace for all nations, and happiness and well-being for all men.

Clearly, it would not be fitting for me to take this occasion to present to you a unilateral American report on Bermuda. Nevertheless, I assure you that in our deliberations on that lovely island we sought to invoke those same great concepts of universal peace and human dignity which are so clearly etched in your Charter. Neither would it be a measure of this great opportunity merely to recite, however hopefully, pious platitudes.

I therefore decided that this occasion warranted my saying to you some of the things that have been on the minds and hearts of my legislative and executive associates and on mine for a great many months—thoughts I had originally planned to say primarily to the American people.

I know that the American people share my deep belief that if a danger exists in the world, it is a danger shared by all—and equally, that if hope exists in the mind of one nation, that hope should be shared by all.

Finally, if there is to be advanced any proposal designed to ease even by the smallest measure the tensions of today's world, what more appropriate audience could there be than the members of the General Assembly of the United Nations?

I feel impelled to speak today in a language that in a sense is new—one which I, who have spent so much of my life in the military profession, would have preferred never to use.

That new language is the language of atomic warfare.

Narrative

The atomic age has moved forward at such a pace that every citizen of the world should have some comprehension, at least in comparative terms, of the extent of this development of the utmost significance to every one of us. Clearly, if the peoples of the world are to conduct an intelligent search for peace, they must be armed with the significant facts of today's existence.

My recital of atomic danger and power is necessarily stated in United States terms, for these are the only incontrovertible facts that I know. I need hardly point out to this Assembly, however, that this subject is global, not merely national in character.

On July 16, 1945, the United States set off the world's first atomic explosion. Since that date in 1945, the United States of America has conducted 42 test explosions.

Numerical proof

Atomic bombs today are more than 25 times as powerful as the weapons with which the atomic age dawned, while hydrogen weapons are in the ranges of millions of tons of TNT equivalent.

Today, the United States' stockpile of atomic weapons, which, of course, increases daily, exceeds by many times the explosive equivalent of the total of all bombs and all shells that came from every plane and every gun in every theatre of war in all of the years of World War II.

A single air group, whether afloat or land-based, can now deliver to any reachable target a destructive cargo exceeding in power all the bombs that fell on Britain in all of World War II.

In size and variety, the development of atomic weapons has been no less remarkable. The development has been such that atomic weapons have virtually achieved conventional status within our armed services. In the United States, the Army, the Navy, the Air Force, and the Marine Corps are all capable of putting this weapon to military use.

But the dread secret, and the fearful engines of atomic might, are not ours alone.

In the first place, the secret is possessed by our friends and allies, Great Britain and Canada, whose scientific genius made a tremendous contribution to our original discoveries, and the designs of atomic bombs.

The secret is also known by the Soviet Union.

The Soviet Union has informed us that, over recent years, it has devoted extensive resources to atomic weapons. During this period, the Soviet Union has exploded a series of atomic devices, including at least one involving thermo-nuclear reactions.

If at one time the United States possessed what might have been called a monopoly of atomic power, that monopoly ceased to exist several years ago. Therefore, although our earlier start has permitted us to accumulate what is today a great quantitative advantage, the atomic realities of today comprehend two facts of even greater significance.

First, the knowledge now possessed by several nations will eventually be shared by others—possibly all others.

Second, even a vast superiority in numbers of weapons, and a consequent capability of devastating retaliation, is no preventive, of itself, against the fearful material damage and toll of human lives that would be inflicted by surprise aggression.

The free world, at least dimly aware of these facts, has naturally embarked on a large program of warning and defense systems. That program will be accelerated and expanded.

But let no one think that the expenditure of vast sums for weapons and systems of defense can guarantee absolute safety for the cities and citizens of any nation. The awful arithmetic of the atomic bomb does not permit of any such easy solution. Even against the most powerful defense, an aggressor in possession of the effective minimum number of atomic bombs for a surprise attack could probably place a sufficient number of his bombs on the chosen target to cause hideous damage.

Speaks directly to Soviet Union

Should such an atomic attack be launched against the United States, our reactions would be swift and resolute. But for me to say that the defense capabilities of the United States are such that they could inflict terrible losses upon an aggressor—for me to say that the retaliation capabilities of the United States are so great that such an aggressor's land would be laid waste—all this, while fact, is not the true expression of the purpose and the hope of the United States.

States problem; note language usage

To pause there would be to confirm the hopeless finality of a belief that two atomic colossi are doomed malevolently to eye each other indefinitely across a trembling world. To stop there would be to accept helplessly the probability of civilization destroyed—the annihilation of the irreplaceable heritage of mankind handed down to us generation from generation—and the condemnation of mankind to begin all over again the age-old struggle upward from savagery toward decency, and right, and justice.

Surely no sane member of the human race could discover victory in such desolation. Could anyone wish his name to be coupled by history with such human degradation and destruction.

Occasional pages of history do record the faces of the "Great Destroyers" but the whole book of history reveals mankind's never-ending quest for peace, and mankind's God-given capacity to build.

It is with the book of history, and not with isolated pages, that the United States will ever wish to be identified. My country wants to be constructive, not destructive. It wants agreements, not wars, among nations. It wants itself to live in freedom, and in the confidence that the people of every nation enjoy equally the right of choosing their own way of life.

So my country's purpose is to help us move out of the dark chamber of horrors into the light, to find a way by which the minds of men, the hopes of men, the souls of men everywhere, can move forward toward peace and happiness and well-being.

In this quest, I know that we must not lack patience.

I know that in a world divided, such as ours today, salvation cannot be attained by one dramatic act.

I know that many steps will have to be taken over many months before the world can look at itself one day and truly realize that a new climate of mutually peaceful confidence is abroad in the world.

But I know, above all else, that we must start to take these steps—*now*.

The United States and its allies, Great Britain and France, have over the past months tried to take some of these steps. Let no one say that we shun the conference table.

On the record has long stood the request of the United States, Great Britain, and France to negotiate with the Soviet Union the problems of a divided Germany.

Repetition of "on the record"

On that record has long stood the request of the same three nations to negotiate an Austrian Peace Treaty.

On the same record still stands the request of the United Nations to negotiate the problems of Korea.

Most recently, we have received from the Soviet Union what is in effect an expression of willingness to hold a Four Power Meeting. Along with our allies, Great Britain and France, we were pleased to see that this note did not contain the unacceptable preconditions previously put forward.

As you already know from our joint Bermuda communique, the United States, Great Britain, and France have agreed promptly to meet with the Soviet Union.

The Government of the United States approaches this conference with hopeful sincerity. We will bend every effort of our minds to the single purpose of emerging from that conference with tangible results toward peace—the only true way of lessening international tension.

We never have, we never will, propose or suggest that the Soviet Union surrender what is rightfully theirs.

We will never say that the peoples of Russia are an enemy with whom we have no desire ever to deal or mingle in friendly and fruitful relationship.

On the contrary, we hope that this coming Conference may initiate a relationship with the Soviet Union which will eventually bring about a free intermingling of the peoples of the East and of the West—the one sure, human way of developing the understanding required for confident and peaceful relations.

Instead of the discontent which is now settling upon Eastern Germany, occupied Austria, and the countries of Eastern Europe, we seek a harmonious family of free European nations, with none a threat to the other, and least of all a threat to the peoples of Russia.

Beyond the turmoil and strife and misery of Asia, we seek peaceful opportunity for these peoples to develop their natural resources and to elevate their lives.

These are not idle words of shallow visions. Behind them lies a story of nations lately come to independence, not as a result of war, but through free grant of peaceful negotiation. There is a record, already written, of assistance gladly given by nations of the West to needy peoples, and to those suffering the temporary effects of famine, drought, and natural disaster.

These are deeds of peace. They speak more loudly than promises or protestations of peaceful intent.

But I do not wish to rest either upon the reiteration of past proposals or the restatement of past deeds. The gravity of the time is such that every new avenue of peace, no matter how dimly discernible, should be explored.

There is at least one new avenue of peace which has not yet been well explored—an avenue now laid out by the General Assembly of the United Nations.

Legitimizes

In its resolution of November 18th, 1953, this General Assembly suggested—and I quote—"that the Disarmament Commission study the desirability of establishing a subcommittee consisting of representatives of the Powers principally involved, which should seek in private an acceptable solution . . . and report on such a solution to the General Assembly and to the Security Council not later than 1 September 1954."

The United States, heeding the suggestion of the General Assembly of the United Nations, is instantly prepared to meet privately with such other countries as may be "principally involved," to seek "an acceptable solution" to the atomic armaments race which overshadows not only the peace, but the very life, of the world.

We shall carry into these private or diplomatic talks a new conception.

The United States would seek more than the mere reduction or elimination of atomic materials for military purposes.

It is not enough to take this weapon out of the hands of the soldiers. It must be put into the hands of those who will know how to strip its military casing and adapt it to the arts of peace.

The United States knows that if the fearful trend of atomic military buildup can be reversed, this greatest of destructive forces can be developed into a great boon, for the benefit of all mankind.

The United States knows that peaceful power from atomic energy is no dream of the future. That capability, already proved, is here—now—today. Who can doubt it, if the entire body of the world's scientists and engineers had adequate amounts of fissionable materials with which to test and develop their ideas, that this capability would rapidly be transformed into universal, efficient, and economic usage.

To hasten the day when fear of the atom will begin to disappear from the minds of people, and the governments of the East and West, there are certain steps that can be taken now.

I therefore make the following proposals:

Specific proposals

The Governments principally involved, to the extent permitted by elementary prudence, to begin now and continue to make joint contributions from their stockpiles of normal uranium and fissionable materials to an International Atomic Energy Agency. We would expect that such an agency would be set up under the aegis of the United Nations.

The ratios of contributions, the procedures and other details would properly be within the scope of the "private conversations" I have referred to earlier.

The United States is prepared to undertake these explorations in good faith. Any partner of the United States acting in the same good faith will find the United States a not unreasonable or ungenerous associate.

Undoubtedly initial and early contributions to this plan would be small in quantity. However, the proposal has the great virtue that it can be undertaken without the irritations and mutual suspicions incident to any attempt to set up a completely acceptable system of world-wide inspection and control.

The Atomic Energy Agency could be made responsible for the impounding, storage, and protection of the contributed fissionable and other materials. The ingenuity of our scientists will provide special safe conditions under which such a bank of fissionable material can be made essentially immune to surprise seizure.

The more important responsibility of this Atomic Energy Agency would be to devise methods whereby this fissionable material would be allocated to serve the peaceful pursuits of mankind. Experts would be mobilized to apply atomic energy to the needs of agriculture, medicine, and other peaceful activities. A special purpose would be to provide abundant electrical energy in the power-starved areas of the world. Thus the contributing powers would be dedicating some of their strength to serve the needs rather than the fears of mankind.

The United States would be more than willing—it would be proud to take up with others "principally involved" the development of plans whereby such peaceful use of atomic energy would be expedited.

Of those "principally involved" the Soviet Union must, of course, be one.

I would be prepared to submit to the Congress of the United States, and with every expectation of approval, any such plan that would:

First—encourage world-wide investigation into the most effective peacetime uses of fissionable material, and with the certainty that they had all the material needed for the conduct of all experiments that were appropriate;

Second—begin to diminish the potential destructive power of the world's atomic stockpiles;

Concludes with possible outcomes

Third—allow all peoples of all nations to see that, in this enlightened age, the great powers of the earth, both of the East and of the West, are interested in human aspirations first, rather than in building up the armaments of war;

Fourth—open up a new channel for peaceful discussion, and initiate at least a new approach to the many difficult problems that must be solved in both private and public conversations, if the world is to shake off the inertia imposed by fear, and is to make positive progress toward peace.

Against the dark background of the atomic bomb, the United States does not wish merely to present strength, but also the desire and the hope for peace.

The coming months will be fraught with fateful decisions. In the Assembly; in the capitals and military headquarters of the world; in the hearts of men everywhere, be they governors or governed, may they be the decisions which will lead this world out of fear and into peace.

To the making of these fateful decisions, the United States pledges before you—and therefore before the world—to devote its entire heart and mind to find the way by which the miraculous inventiveness of man shall not be dedicated to his death, but consecrated to his life.

I again thank the delegates for the great honor they have done me, in inviting me to appear before them, and in listening to me so courteously. Thank you.

Nicholas Johnson

Scurvy Is A Social Disease

Nicholas Johnson was Commissioner of the Federal Communications Commission from 1970 to 1976. He is an outspoken critic of advertising in general and television in particular. In this speech he urges the graduates of American University to be more aware of the consequences of their actions, of consumerism, and generally to consider a simpler lifestyle. This is an unusual commencement speech, in that a specific persuasive purpose is proposed.

If you had been a European sailor anytime from, oh, 1400 to 1700, say, the likelihood of your dying from scurvy would have been relatively high.

As we now know, scurvy is caused by a vitamin C deficiency. It produces general weakness, hemorrhaging, and ultimately death. It is a relatively rare disease today. A diet that contains almost any quantity of fresh fruits and vegetables will provide enough vitamin C to prevent the disease.

Cures for scurvy were discovered as early as the 1500s. The French explorer Jacques Cartier, who discovered the St. Lawrence River, was taught a cure for scurvy by the Indians in 1536. An English admiral, Sir John Hawkins, used citrus juice to prevent scurvy in 1593.

But citrus juice is expensive. Accordingly, in the words of the *Encyclopaedia Britannica,* "Skippers and owners for a couple centuries found it expedient to be skeptical." In short, in the absence of legal liability for the death of sailors, orange juice cost more than human life. And business then, as now, chose the cheapest path. For two hundred years, sailors went on dying needlessly.

Uses striking anecdote as an introduction

In 1747, a British naval doctor, James Lind, proved the relationship of citrus juice to the cure of scurvy and published his results. Still no response from the medical establishment, or the governmental, naval, or merchant shipping establishments.

Finally, in 1795, the British Admiralty got around to requiring its now-famous daily ration of lime juice.

This story has been put together for us by Dr. Linus Pauling, in his revealing little book, *Vitamin C and the Common Cold.* But perhaps the most striking tidbit of Dr. Pauling's historical voyage is his report that the business community, represented by the British Board of Trade, didn't impose a similar regulation on itself—the merchant shipping companies—until 70 years after the Navy, in 1865!

Note elaborate transition

Lest you think the answer obvious, let me ask you: What would you have done had you been living then? Would you follow your doctor's advice, the advice of the equivalents of our American Medical Association or Food and Drug Administration? Would you have done independent research or reading on your own? If you had been a sailing captain, a young civil servant in the British navy, the head of a merchant shipping company, or a sailor during the 1600s and 1700s, would you have encouraged the availability of sources of vitamin C to sailors or not?

Statement of principal topic

The point is that you as a human being, as an individual living out your life a few moments at a time, must make hundreds of comparable decisions every day—with very little more certainty in the available information. Nutrition is not your only problem but it is not bad for an illustrative beginning.

Diet is important to virtually every facet of your life. It is not a matter of getting enough calories to avoid death—although hunger is still a very real problem for many Americans. It is not just a matter of getting enough vitamins to avoid scurvy and other diseases of malnutrition—although protein, vitamin and mineral deficiencies are common among the affluent and poor alike today. It is not just a matter of avoiding obesity, or a high cholesterol diet—although deaths from coronary disease, to some degree diet related, have gone up 14 percent since 1950 among twenty and thirty-year-olds, and now constitute the leading cause of death for men over 45 in America.

No, good nutrition is more than just avoiding bad health and disease. It is probably one of the most fundamental ways of enabling you to reach more of the full potential you possess to be aware and awake and alive—in short, to be fully human. Diet affects your physical appearance, your energy levels, your intellectual and creative abilities, your mental health and general feeling of well being, even your ability to enjoy love and sexuality.

As with most areas of our lives, however, the principal information that we get about nutrition is given to us by big business, advertising, and the mass media. In fact, it takes considerably more than a conventional college education to be able to fend for one's self in a supermarket, restaurant or drive-in.

The meat we have been eating has brought the level of DDT in our own bodies—which cumulates—to amounts that ought to be a matter of concern. The use of chemical additives is so widespread that many packaged things to eat contain virtually no conventional food products whatsoever. My own rule of thumb is, if I can't pronounce it I don't eat it. Many of us are getting far too much refined sugar and starch every day—including starch fried in hydrogenated, and sometimes rancid, oils. And the more we skimp on meals, or just reach for the most conveniently packaged corporate snack, the greater the likelihood we are missing out on wholesome nutrition.

The reasons are much the same today as they were two hundred years ago: the food business finds it "expedient to be skeptical" about today's nutritional knowledge. The drug industry—which sells hundreds of millions of dollars worth of over-the-counter remedies for colds—finds it "expedient to be skeptical" about Dr. Pauling's very unprofitable, but highly effective, natural cold remedy called vitamin C.

> Narration as transition from nutrition to indictment of food business

Recently I was privileged to attend a luncheon in Washington for Adelle Davis. Mrs. Davis is the author of *Let's Eat Right to Keep Fit* and other books which have now sold over three and one-half million copies. Mrs. Davis is not a "food faddist." She is a nutritionist, a compassionate and charming human being, and a very articulate and persuasive writer, lecturer and television guest. She has probably done as much to make Americans aware of what they are eating as any person in the country today.

Confronted as we are with a maze of non-foods and conflicting corporate claims, I welcome any guidance I can get. And if someone like Adelle Davis is willing to try to help I'm going to do all I can to encourage her. I'm not necessarily going to swallow everything she tells me to—but at least I have the feeling she's on my side.

And so it was that I showed up at this luncheon for Mrs. Davis on April 28th. Seated around the table was the nutrition establishment of Washington—government and industry—and reporters. They were those food page reporters, whose impossible professional responsibility it is to write impartially about food for newspapers dependent for their very survival on supermarket advertising.

I couldn't believe what I was hearing. It was just like a meeting of the FCC. Except that instead of capitulating to an industry that puts garbage in our heads, I was watching government officials capitulate to an industry that puts garbage in our stomachs.

It reminded me of a cabinet officer's reaction to his first exposure to the maritime industry. I was Maritime Administrator under President Johnson at the time. A meeting was to be held with spokesmen for maritime management and labor. Both benefit, almost equally, from the government's maritime subsidy program. After the meeting I asked the cabinet officer his reaction. He turned to me and whispered, "You know, Nick, when I'd close my eyes I couldn't tell who was talking."

Indictment of the Food and Drug Administration

That's how I felt about the Adelle Davis luncheon. The Food and Drug Administration members present were, if anything, even more hostile to Mrs. Davis than the industry representatives. Mrs. Davis is gracious, and not bristling with self-defensiveness as they tend to be. So she was quite willing to acknowledge that she, as all other human beings, may have made some errors. But it was not really so much their inquiring criticism as their attitude that shocked. Instead of viewing Mrs. Davis as one of the nutrition community's most effective spokeswomen, she was viewed as the enemy. Instead of treating her with respect, and trying to learn from her, the luncheon was treated as their opportunity to "get" her.

The reporters picked up the criticism—with glee—and you may have seen their stories. Not a line that could have troubled an advertising executive for Safeway or A & P.

Suddenly I began to get a sense of how Dr. James Lind must have felt two hundred years ago when he was trying to sell the British Navy on the merits of lime juice.

Meanwhile, what do *you* eat? If you are going to act and live *as if* you had a college degree, you are going to have to make a lot of nutritional decisions for yourself. How many grams of protein do you need everyday for optimum health and energy levels? Do you know? Do you know the best sources of protein? Do you try to limit the amount of cholestrol in your diet? Adelle Davis says I don't have to if I eat properly; my doctor tells me I do. Are you going to take vitamin supplements tomorrow morning? Why or why not? If so, which ones, in what amounts, how many times during the day? Are you going to drink coffee this afternoon? Coke? Alcohol? Do you really have enough information to make that decision intelligently?

Two Canadian doctors, the brothers E.V. and W.E. Shute, believe that vitamin E, on the order of 800 mg a day, may help prevent your dying of a heart attack. Do they constitute a modern day version of Dr. James Lind, or are they a couple of quacks? What if your own doctor says, so far as he's concerned, there's "no evidence" vitamin E will do you any good. Does that end the matter for you?

Unfortunately, what is true of nutrition is true of virtually every other aspect of life. You cannot rely on the United States Government, Inc. or the networks' programs—both "brought to you by" ITT—to serve your interests. And you can't really assume that a college education has given you the information and skills you need to cope with daily living either.

But let's take a short quiz to see.

For starters, do you know how to breathe properly and why it's important? Or are you trying to get by with "normal" breathing that provides you with one-seventh of the oxygen your body needs? That's kind of fundamental.

Can you find the North Star at night?

Do you know the difference between the feelings of love and lust and loneliness?

What are the four advantages of using mulch on a garden?

Can you sew a button?

How much heavy exercise do you need in your daily routine?

What is the philosophical or religious doctrine that is yours alone that constitutes that essential beacon—that different drummer—to which you march?

There was a time when "education" was provided children by their parents and wasn't separated from daily living. Some Georgia high school students have been going back to their grandparents to learn basic skills, and writing up what they're finding out. *The Foxfire Book* collects the best of their writing.

Second major point

One of the points I am trying to make is that our educational institutions, like the other institutions in our society, have tended to isolate and detach themselves—and us—from the basic questions of living.

Each of us represents, within ourselves, a microcosm of the universe and of the history of human civilization.

The atoms and molecules from which we began are similar to those that make up the earth's crust, atmosphere and plant and animal life. Our first months were spent as a fish, "breathing" through gills. We later assumed amphibian status. And our first few months after birth we spent as awkward mammals.

Our brains were originally as blank as an unprogrammed computer. We even had to learn how to move our arms and legs, and build up a catalog of sights and sounds and other impressions that would program us with the ability to use our senses. Learning our first language was one of the most complex tasks we would ever undertake.

If you ever plant a seed and watch it grow, you cannot help but be impressed with the "knowledge," the potential, it contains. It knows how to develop roots and leaves, the roots know how to find food and what to do when they run into a rock, and the stems and leaves know how to go about finding the sunshine. It is an altogether stunning performance.

It is in the same sense that there are latent skills, power and sensitivities within you. Some may lie dormant throughout your entire life and never be exercised. It is, admittedly, little more than a poetic way of expressing the fact, but many in the human potential movement argue that few of us are functioning at more than five percent of our potential.

You may never have occasion to develop your potential for musical creativity, just as a root may never encounter a rock. But neither you nor that seed ever totally lose those potentialities. Nor do you lose your potential to be artistically creative, to use your powers of recall and intellectual analysis, the sensitivity of your sight and hearing and other senses, or your potential to feel love and the full range of human emotions.

The Institute for the Achievement of Human Potential in Philadelphia have built a theory of therapy upon these two ideas: that there is a natural progression of human development, and that each of us is utilizing a small percentage of our capabilities. Those who work at the Institute believe that a child literally must go through the proper progression of animal movements, such as crawling, in order to develop the lower base of the brain. They believe that until that part of the brain is programmed the child cannot learn how to see—an obviously necessary prerequisite to learning how to read. They believe that much of what we think of as "brain damage"—hyperactivity, dyslexia, cerebral palsy, or reading difficulties can be most effectively treated by "reprogramming" the child in the proper sequence.

I offer no brief for the Institutes' theory. I claim no expertise as a nutritionist. I claim even less as a neurologist. I urge no more than that the general concept of a natural progression in learning is poetically and philosophically pleasing and useful.

So far we have addressed the process by which you and I evolved from molecular matter into the simplest form of life, and on up the animal ladder to a point in human evolution roughly equivalent to the time when man came down out of the trees and started to wander about on the surface of the earth.

It has never been obvious to me why our schools skip over the millions of years that follow and immediately start educating our children as members of a highly industrialized and urbanized 20th Century.

It might be useful for a child first to learn about natural phenomena while living out of doors: to discover the movement of the stars, the changes in the weather and seasons, which plants are edible, and so forth.

He—or she—might next learn something of life on an integrated family farm: care of livestock; planting and harvesting; simple machinery; road, fence and building construction; and so forth. He might next learn about life in a small village: something of its sociology, the role of simple shops and police protection. Ultimately he could learn about life in larger cities: banking and public utilities, state and federal government, economics and income distribution, and so forth.

Throughout this entire progression students could maintain ties to the prior stages, and weave in an exposure to more conventional academic subjects—such as reading skills and mathematics—as they were naturally needed and desired. They would always be involved in living an integrated whole life in which creativity, religion, productive "work," "study," and emotional and social development would be perceived and lived as an integrated, mutually interdependent whole.

But the point of this suggestion is not to offer a proposal for an additional dialogue about theories of education. You have already completed your college education and so have I. We are not about to go back and do it over again. And there is little more prospect for reforming the educational establishment in this country than there is for reforming the broadcasting establishment.

What I am obviously talking about is designed to be relevant to what you do today and tomorrow and the other days that make up the rest of your life.

When I was a college student I once went to hear a lecture by Dr. Robert Hutchins. He was dean of the Yale Law School at the age of 29, president of the University of Chicago when he was 30, and has spent many of the 21 years since Chicago suggesting proposals for educational reform. The evening I heard him he was especially entertaining—and critical. After the lecture I had an opportunity to visit with him briefly. I asked, "Dr. Hutchins, given the state of conventional college education, just what do you think a college student should do?"

He turned to me with a twinkle in his eye, and replied, "Get your degree as fast as you can, and then get out of school and start getting an education."

Third major point

Books are important to that education, indeed essential. NBC's John Chancellor believes that "we've tended to lose sight of the importance of teaching people to read." As well he might. What television is telling us—and, more importantly, failing to tell us—is literally killing us. The more I study television the more convinced I become of the importance of books, not only as a communications media, or a path of education, but as a survival kit. Probably no more than one to five percent of the American people regularly purchase and read a half dozen to a dozen serious books a year. You now have the skills to put yourself in that elite percentage. But I believe the minimum you ought to read—or at least expose yourself to—is about ten times that quantity. Suppose you were to buy five or ten paperbacks a month. The cost would be minimal: less than a pack or two of cigarettes a day. And the time it would take to read them is substantially less than the time the average American now spends watching television. You don't have to simply absorb what other people want you to know: newspapers, magazines, radio and television. You can take control of your own information, the "programming" of your mind. And once you do find there is plenty of time every day to do your survival reading, I have prepared a little bibliography for you as a "graduation gift" that is attached to this speech, and may offer you some interesting suggestions.

A couple weeks ago a very talented composer, singer and guitar player, John Prine, appeared here in Constitution Hall. One of John's songs sums up my message much better than I can. He sings:

> *Blow up your TV*
> *Throw away your paper*
> *Go to the country*
> *Build you a home*
>
> *Plant a little garden*
> *Eat a lot of peaches*
> *Try and find Jesus*
> *On your own*

I don't know whether John means it literally or not, but I don't.

I don't think you have to blow up your television receiver; I think you can just shut it off, give it away, or cover it with a large tablecloth.

You don't have to throw away your newspaper, you don't even have to stop reading it altogether; you just want to increase the percentage of your reading time that you spend on books, that's all.

You don't have to go to the country. But I do think you need to get a fuller sense of your relationship to the earth from which you came and to which you will return. You need to notice the sun and the moon and the stars, the plant and animal life around you, the wind and the rain, and the other reminders that—in spite of our genocidal governmental policies and our environment polluting corporate policies—we are still mere guests on this small planet.

I think taking care of a garden is a helpful way to do that, but maybe you can get comparable satisfactions from lavishing care on an indoor philodendron.

As for the peaches, that has always been a favorite food of mine. In fact, I did plant a peach tree in the country this spring. But peaches are really a matter of taste. Whether or not you eat organically grown peaches, you really should try to become more alert and aware to what it is you are putting in your stomach.

Whether you want to find Jesus is also a matter of personal choice. You may prefer Buddha, or Swami Satchidananda.

But I'll hold to that part about finding Him on your own. I just never could figure out any other way to do it.

If you are truly educated, and aware, you cannot help but think about the implications of your daily acts. Buying and operating an automobile, for example, is a very significant personal, social, political, economic, and philosophical act.

About sixty percent of all automobile usage is for trips of less than five miles, distances that can be traveled more economically, safely, healthily—and often faster—on bicycle or foot. Not only do automobile accidents needlessly claim the lives of nearly 60,000 people every year, cause over five million injuries, and constitute by all odds the single largest source of air pollution by tonnage while consuming 90 billion gallons of gasoline. Dr. Paul Dudley White, the noted heart specialist, used to contend that the principal hazard of automobiles is that they keep us from getting the essential exercise we need to maintain basic health.

Not only will you think about the kind of transportation systems you use, and the food you eat, but also about the kind of place you live and what you furnish it with, the clothing you wear, the ways you spend your time, and the contribution you make—or choose not to make—to the running of the political community and nation of which you are a part.

One of the heaviest burdens—and blessings—of education turns out to be awareness. Once you are aware you are no longer able to drive a *car* to a meeting of environmentalists. You are unable to eat so much beef once you realize that if the United States were to reduce its livestock production by fifty percent the grain saved thereby would be enough to feed the millions of starving people in the developing countries four times over. You may be able to rationalize away your failure to live a life of service. You may be able to rationalize away your refusal to participate in political action. But there is no way you can apathetically fail to take responsibility for the political, economic and social consequences of your day-to-day purchasing and living decisions.

Many of the ideas I have been talking about are familiar to you in one form or another. What you may not know is the extent to which such thinking is now permeating all educational levels, ages, and geographical regions of this country. Individual choices are beginning to mount in sufficient numbers to affect large corporations in the market place.

During the past ten years the sale of men's suits has actually declined, while the sale of overalls has doubled. Levi's sales continue to double every five years.

Attendance at state parks has increased sixfold in the last twenty years.

Bicycle sales hit 8.8 million last year, and 1972 may be the first year in which Americans buy more bicycles than automobiles.

There are more Americans now tending their own gardens than at any other time in recent history, including the extensive "Victory Gardens" during the time of World War II. Expenditures on seeds and plants have doubled in the last ten years.

Sales of General Electric's electric toothbrushes are half of what they were a mere five years ago, but *The Last Whole Earth Catalog* has sold 850,000 copies.

Cites moral philosophy as support

The teachings of every great religion in the world have warned against the dangers of a life devoted to materialism and conspicuous consumption. Whatever their differences may have been, that is the one thing on which Jesus and Buddha agreed. The Book of Tao tells us that "pride of wealth . . . brings about its own destruction"; "let us . . . return to simplicity and naturalness." The Bhagavad Gita teaches, "the man who . . . abandons all pride of possession . . . reaches the goal of peace supreme." And the Biblical rendition of Jesus' Sermon on the Mount reports His advising, "Do not store up for yourselves treasure on earth, where it grows rusty and moth-eaten, and thieves break in to steal it."

None of these religious leaders was making a plea for the perpetuation of poverty. Nor am I. Quite the opposite. We have the economic resources to eliminate poverty in this country and it is morally indefensible that we have not done so.

What is the most appropriate ratio between the income of the richest and the poorest Americans? Two-to-one? Ten-to-one? Fifty-to-one? Let's be generous. Can't we at least assume that a hundred-to-one ratio between the richest and the poorest in America should be adequate incentive to enterprise? And yet, at the recent ITT shareholders meeting, ITT President Harold Geneen refused a shareholders' plea that he cut his salary from $802,000 to $350,000 a year. Even this salary would presumably still leave him his $795,000 a year in stock options. How do you explain such behavior to that fifty percent of the American work force that is trying to live on $4,000 or less a year?

Principal recommendation

No, I am not urging the blessings of genuine poverty. All I am trying to say is that more and more Americans of economic privilege are discovering that the life style that has been sold us by the large corporations, mass media and advertisers is not all it's cracked up to be. Love is not at all like ginger ale. "Things" (life in general and food in particular) really go better with milk and fruit juice than with Coca Cola. Pepsi does not help you come alive. To own an automobile does not increase freedom—let alone enhance sexuality and social status. Driving a car is just a crummy part time job working for the auto companies, wearing out and repairing their cars for them, and paying them for the privilege. Suburban homes often turn into wall-to-wall, labor intensive prisons. The soil is too poor to grow anything but crab grass, and the homes are located too far from the city for the occupants to participate conveniently in urban life. Aerosol cans put chemical particles in your lungs, are a safety hazard for incinerators, bring you a product that is over-priced, probably unnecessary, and possibly hazardous to your health. Americans are still spending seventy-five percent of their personal consumption dollars on such stuff: food, clothing, shelter and local transportation. As Mason Williams says, "We're like a race horse shot full of speed to make us run harder than is good for us, to win for the owners and lose for ourselves, to win the race for only the price of the chance to run." If there are no other arguments for simplicity in life style on the part of the college-educated affluent, it can at least free up an awful lot of money to spend on other things. The Census Bureau's categories of recreation, education and foreign travel, together, total less than ten percent.

But it is more than just our own lives that are at stake. We have taken our eyes off the goal of the American dream. The pursuit of plenty was not to be an end in itself. Poverty was to be eliminated to make possible a fuller life. And whatever "living" may be, it is not, as Jesus warned us, the mere storing up of treasure on earth. Government in the land of milk and honey was to be devoted to—remember?—"life, liberty and the pursuit of happiness." How sad that so many citizens today see their government as devoted to "death, repression and the pursuit of campaign contributions."

You are part of a select and potentially powerful group of people in America. Only eleven percent of the population over the age of 25 has a college degree. Only fifteen percent of the population earns over $10,000 a year. You are now headed into both elites. I believe, as President Kennedy used to say, that with great power goes great responsibility. You not only have the responsibility to set a good example in the way you live your daily life. You also have a responsibility to use the disproportionate education and income that will soon be yours to help bring America back to its dream.

You *can* "get it together." You have the intellectual tools, the information, and the insights that can enable you to work it out for yourself, to perceive, and live a whole life. Whether you do is up to you. But today *can* be not only the end of your formal education, but also the commencement of your life.

Barbara Jordan

Who Then Will Speak for the Common Good?

In New York City, on July 12, 1976, Barbara Jordan (then Congresswoman from Texas) delivered the Keynote Address to the Nation at the Democratic National Convention. Keynote addresses are similar to speeches of dedication in that principle is more important than specific factual statements. Note how Congresswoman Jordan invokes value statements throughout to set the "note" for the Democrats.

One hundred and forty-four years ago, members of the Democratic Party first met in convention to select a Presidential candidate. Since that time, Democrats have continued to convene once every four years and draft a party platform and nominate a Presidential candidate. And our meeting this week is a continuation of that tradition.

But there is something different about tonight. There is something special about tonight. What is different? What is special? I, Barbara Jordan, am a keynote speaker.

A lot of years passed since 1832, and during that time it would have been most unusual for any national political party to ask that a Barbara Jordan deliver a keynote address ... but tonight here I am. And I feel that notwithstanding the past that my presence here is one additional bit of evidence that the American Dream need not forever be deferred.

Note effective question and answer

Now that I have this grand distinction what in the world am I supposed to say?

I could easily spend this time praising the accomplishments of this party and attacking the Republicans but I don't choose to do that.

I could list the many problems which Americans have. I could list the problems which cause people to feel cynical, angry, frustrated: problems which include lack of integrity in government; the feeling that the individual no longer counts; the reality of material and spiritual poverty; the feeling that the grand American experiment is falling or has failed. I could recite these problems and then I could sit down and offer no solutions. But I don't choose to do that either.

The citizens of America expect more. They deserve and they want more than a recital of problems.

We are a people in a quandry about the present. We are a people in search of our future. We are a people in search of a national community.

We are a people trying not only to solve the problems of the present: unemployment, inflation ... but we are attempting on a larger scale to fulfill the promise of America. We are attempting to fulfill our national purpose; to create and sustain a society in which all of us are equal.

Throughout our history, when people have looked for new ways to solve their problems, and to uphold the principles of this nation, many times they have turned to political parties. They have often turned to the Democratic Party.

Continues question and answer format

What is it, what is it about the Democratic Party that makes it the instrument that people use when they search for ways to shape their future? Well I believe the answer to that question lies in our concept of governing. Our concept of governing is derived from our view of people. It is a concept deeply rooted in a set of beliefs firmly etched in the national conscience, of all of us.

Now what are these beliefs?

First, we believe in equality for all and privileges for none. This is a belief that each American regardless of background has equal standing in the public forum, all of us. Because we believe this idea so firmly, we are an inclusive rather than an exclusive party. Let everybody come.

I think it no accident that most of those emigrating to America in the 19th century identified with the Democratic Party. We are a heterogeneous party made up of Americans of diverse backgrounds.

Effective repetition of "we believe . . . we believe . . . " and "we are . . . " and "we have . . . "

We believe that the people are the source of all governmental power; that the authority of the people is to be extended, not restricted. This can be accomplished only by providing each citizen with every opportunity to participate in the management of the government. They must have that.

We believe that the government which represents the authority of all the people, not just one interest group, but all the people, has an obligation to actively underscore, actively seek to remove those obstacles which would block individual achievement . . . obstacles emanating from race, sex, economic condition. The government must seek to remove them.

We are a party of innovation. We do not reject our traditions, but we are willing to adapt to changing circumstances, when change we must. We are willing to suffer the discomfort of change in order to achieve a better future.

We have a positive vision of the future founded on the belief that the gap between the promise and reality of America can one day be finally closed. We believe that.

This my friends, is the bedrock of our concept of governing. This is a part of the reason why Americans have turned to the Democratic Party. These are the foundations upon which a national community can be built.

Let's all understand that these guiding principles cannot be discarded for short-term political gains. They represent what this country is all about. They are indigenous to the American idea. And these are principles which are not negotiable.

In other times, I could stand here and give this kind of exposition the on beliefs of the Democratic Party and that would be enough. But today that is not enough. People want more. That is not sufficient reason for the majority of the people of this country to vote Democratic. We have made mistakes. In our haste to do all things for all people, we did not foresee the full consequences of our actions. And when the people raised their voices, we didn't hear. But our deafness was only a temporary condition, and not an irreversible condition.

Even as I stand here and admit that we have made mistakes I still believe that as the people of America sit in judgment on each party, they will recognize that our mistakes were mistakes of the heart. They'll recognize that.

And now we must look to the future. Let us heed the voice of the people and recognize their common sense. If we do not, we not only blaspheme our political heritage, we ignore the common ties that bind all Americans.

Many fear the future. Many are distrustful of their leaders, and believe that their voices are never heard. Many seek only to satisfy their private work wants. To satisfy private interests.

But this is the great danger America faces. That we will cease to be one nation and become instead a collection of interest groups: city against suburb, region against region, individual against individual. Each seeking to satisfy private wants.

If that happens, who then will speak for America?

The "common good" idea is drawn from 18th century British liberalism

Who then will speak for the common good?

This is the question which must be answered in 1976.

Are we to be one people bound together by common spirit sharing in a common endeavor or will we become a divided nation?

For all of its uncertainty, we cannot flee the future. We must not become the new puritans and reject our society. We must address and master the future together. It can be done if we restore the belief that we share a sense of national community, that we share a common national endeavor. It can be done.

There is no executive order; there is no law that can require the American people to form a national community. This we must do as individuals and if we do it as individuals, there is no President of the United States who can veto that decision.

As a first step, we must restore our belief in ourselves. We are a generous people so why can't we be generous with each other? We need to take to heart the words spoken by Thomas Jefferson:

Let us restore to social intercourse that harmony and that affection without which liberty and even life are but dreary things.

A nation is formed by the willingness of each of us to share in the responsibility for upholding the common good.

A government is invigorated when each of us is willing to participate in shaping the future of this nation.

In this election year we must define the common good and begin again to shape a common good and begin again to shape a common future. Let each person do his or her part. If one citizen is unwilling to participate, all of us are going to suffer. For the American idea, though it is shared by all of us, is realized in each one of us.

And now, what are those of us who are elected public officials supposed to do? We call ourselves public servants but I'll tell you this: we public servants must set an example for the rest of the nation. It is hypocritical for the public official to admonish and exhort the people to uphold the common good if we are derelict in upholding the common good. More is required of public officials than slogans and handshakes and press releases. More is required. We must hold ourselves strictly accountable. We must provide the people with a vision of the future.

If we promise as public officials, we must deliver. If we as public officials propose, we must produce. If we say to the American people it is time for you to be sacrificial; sacrifice. If the public official says that, we—public officials—must be the first to give. We must be. And again, if we make mistakes, we must be willing to admit them. We have to do that. What we have to do is strike a balance between the idea that government should do everything and the idea, the belief, that government ought to do nothing. Strike a balance.

Let there be no illusions about the difficulty of forming this kind of a national community. It's tough, difficult, not easy. But a spirit of harmony will survive in America only if each of us remembers that we share a common destiny. If each of us remembers when self-interest and bitterness seem to prevail, that we share a common destiny.

I have confidence that we can form this kind of national community.

I have confidence that the Democratic Party can lead the way. I have that confidence. We cannot improve on the system of government handed down to us by the founders of the Republic, there is no way to improve upon that. But what we can do is to find new ways to implement that system and realize our destiny.

Note effective use of Lincoln quotation

Now, I began this speech by commenting to you on the uniqueness of a Barbara Jordan making the keynote address. Well I am going to close my speech by quoting a Republican President and I ask you that as you listen to these words of Abraham Lincoln, relate them to the concept of a national community in which every last one of us participates: As I would not be a slave, so I would not be a master. This expresses my idea of Democracy. Whatever differs from this, to the extent of the difference is no Democracy.

Steve Wozniak

Why I Shouldn't Be Here

Steve Wozniak, co-founder of Apple Computer, Inc., presented this speech to The Commonwealth Club of California, on Februrary 27, 1987. The student should note that Wozniak's speech is an extended externalization—what might be called an empathy speech. Also, note the absence of traditional speech forms such as outline terms, specific introductory and concluding material, and references. Wozniak's material is strong enough to transcend these omissions. Do you think that you could improve on this speech's structure?

Apple was a Dream, and dreams have no script. No one could have written the story of Apple Computer, Inc. A few years ago, I felt under extreme pressure. I got very tense and anxious, so went to a doctor. The doctor told me to run 10 miles a day. I ran 10 miles the first day—and had aching legs. But I ran 10 miles the next day; and pretty soon, I started feeling good all day long. My spirits were lifted, I had a positive attitude—everything worked. After a month, I called the doctor back, and told him I'd never been so happy. He asked me, "How's work, Steve?" I said, "I don't know; I'm 300 miles away."

Note absence of purpose, statement, and formal introduction

Growing up in Silicon Valley—back then it was called Santa Clara Valley—we read Tom Swift and developed heroes. I read a book called *SOS at Midnight,* about a ham radio operator who builds a special piece of equipment to get out of a kidnapping situation. He was my hero. By sixth grade I had my ham radio license.

Science fairs were a good place to start for those of us who were to become Silicon Valley's electronic entrepreneurs. Fairchild was so generous as to give me 400 transistors and diodes to help me build a small computing project.

Even by high school, we still didn't have computers. They were unheard of; the teachers didn't know anything about them. Even my parents didn't know much—although my father, an engineer, gave me some direction.

Occasionally, a top math student gets involved in electronics. It's really that combination of math and electronics that leads to engineering. Fortunately, I had an electronics teacher who saw that school wasn't enough, that I was playing pranks—miswiring everyone else's radios. He contacted an engineer at a local company and arranged for me to go there once a week to learn how to program a computer.

Relays throughout

I was self-taught. I discovered manuals about mini-computers. It was an internal puzzle for me—I didn't get a grade for it. I started to learn the way zero's and one's added together, and how logic circuits are designed with registers and arithmetic logic units.

I read manuals that described computers: what was inside them, what they did, how they worked. I had access to books that showed components that computers could be built out of—but didn't have the in-between step. I sat down with a piece of paper and started to draw—with only imagination to guide me. I drew designs of the various mini-computers. They would start out 20 pages long, but eventually would shrink to five. Every time a computer company in Silicon Valley would introduce a new set of chip components, I would study them to find out which ones could make my design have fewer components than before.

It became very important to "optimize": very few parts for the same, final result. It's an artistic consideration. Some people assume it's only a matter of defining what you want to build and then implementing it. But there are always the few who try to find an optimal solution.

My best friend in high school and I had posters of computers on our bedroom walls. There were about 20 mini-computers introduced in 1968 and 1969. A mini-computer had 4K memory. It was the minimum machine that could actually run a computer language. We dreamed of owning our own computers—in those days, a mini-computer cost almost as much as a house. But I decided in high school that no matter what, I would someday own one of those machines.

A company called Data General introduced a new computer called the *Nova*. Their brochure—a typical one for those days—would describe the computer, and on the last page, have an "instruction set." Today, computer companies do not send out instructions for processors: what combinations of zero's and one's mean "add the A register to the B register and shift it two places." This computer had only one instruction, while the others had 50.

This intrigued me; I set out to design my own version. I discovered something very shocking: The various components, connected together directly, came out to half as many as other computers. Here was a computer that could do as much as any other, was just as good, but only had half the number of parts. I was impressed. It was an artistic appreciation of the purity of thinking something out, over and over again, until you come out with a concept that can be more easily implemented. This principle of elegant, simple lines became my guiding force.

In my first year of college, those of us interested in computers were still "hackers": trying to read all the manuals, learn as much as we could—"crash" the system. I'm half embarrassed and half proud to look back, because I was put on probation that year for what they called "computer abuse."

I had seven programs to print different mathematical tables. I would submit the seven—all at once—in the morning, come back in the afternoon, and there would be 60 pages of printout for each one, along with punched-out cards to submit the next one. I had to do this, because if your program ran more than a minute, the computer cut you off automatically. So I ran 60 pages times seven programs three times per day. Reams of paper would pile up in my dorm—tables of powers of two, prime numbers—the professor thought I was out to get him.

When you're young, you walk through an orchard, eat a cherry—you don't think you're trespassing. In my computer course, they assigned us a number and said we could run our programs under that number. I thought the school was saying, "Because you're a student, we're providing this tool for you to learn and develop"—not quite. The university leased the computer to certain departments, which in turn allocated time on it to their professors for certain courses. Eventually, they discovered that my professor had $469 of excess billing for me. I wanted my own computer.

That year, I built a little device called a TV-jammer. I sat at the back of the dorm, turned the knob on my jammer, and it fuzzed-up the TV set. This is a thrill for young people who are into electronics, because people don't know where it's coming from. My friend in the front row hits the TV set: the picture becomes perfect. Within a half hour, there would be five people in front of the TV with chairs, pillows, and fists banging the TV set every time it went on the blitz. I never got caught, or I wouldn't be here today.

After two years of college, I worked for a computer company to earn money for my third year. They had a computer that could handle 64 users at once, and had all the mass storage and hardware working. It could run BASIC or FORTRAN programs—it was unbelievable, beautiful, and low-priced for what it did. The company went broke. They only sold two: to the DMV.

After my third year of college, I took advantage of a very special opportunity. I was one of the first to buy the first scientific calculator: the Hewlett-Packard 35. It cost $430 in 1970—but was destined to revolutionize the world. Those of us who knew it—and needed one to calculate our sines, cosines, and logarithm faster and more accurately that with a slide rule—bought one.

I also had the opportunity to work as an engineer, in the calculator division, at Hewlett-Packard. Although I designed calculator chips, this wasn't really the computer background that would lead to Apple Computer. Oddly enough, electronics was still my "hobby."

I designed my own "Pong" game, a "Breakout" game with Atari, systems to put movies in hotel rooms, and organized dozens of Hewlett-Packard engineers to buy the first VCRs. In 1973, a color VCR cost $60—before Sony introduced the Betamax. All of these hobby projects were to ultimately converge on the product Apple was to become. There was no plan, no way to know it.

Chronological organization

Then the Homebrew Computer Club started up, a group for people who had terminals and things. I had just built my first terminal in a friend's basement, after I saw him chunk away on a big, old teletype, to talk to a computer in Boston. I had never realized that all that computer access was available if you had a terminal—so I built one. About this time, magazines came out for those interested in their own low-cost computers. *Byte* was the first.

The major computing companies, that should have spawned the micro-computer revolution, didn't foresee the home computer explosion. They didn't calculate that the market existed, even though they could have, theoretically, from the numbers of people buying computer magazines. The trouble was, the companies putting out hobby computer kits were all losers. There was no way to take advantage of it, even if you knew the market existed.

At the curb, we were all the fringe, technical element. We were in jeans with holes; we were the outcasts—not managers, just people interested in owning our own computers. None of us had much money; we couldn't go out and buy that $400 computer. We saw the tool as revolutionary: Everyone would have a computer to operate their houselights, garage doors, write programs, and do calculations.

Analysis

We came from an environment where the company owned the computer. There was a little door to submit your program through, and they would run it for you. Computers were very foreign territory—off-limits—and we were going to blow that open. For 500 people, every second Wednesday was the most important day of their lives.

Our club didn't even have the vision that Steve Jobs had: masses of people buying already-built personal computers. There was no plan to build a computer and sell it. This was fortunate, because a lot of decisions of what parts to use and how to make it could not have been freely made. The design of the computer was driven not by understanding a market or a need—no market existed yet. The market was essentially myself.

Shortly after this, a microprocessor called the 6502 was introduced in San Francisco; it cost $20. I took advantage of the opportunity, because it was the finest 8-bit microprocessor for the cheapest price. Quite a few Silicon Valley companies used this microprocessor as the heart of their computers.

The question was: What do you do for an input and output device? I decided to use my home TV, because it was the cheapest input/output device I had. This choice determined many of the features of the computer. One of the major decisions was choice of memory. Steve Jobs suggested using the 16 pins from Intel. I couldn't afford it, at $75 a chip. But Steve called them, and got free samples—he wasn't as shy as I was.

Direct externalization

Steve Jobs was a free spirit, unlike myself. He suggested starting a company. He said we could make blank PC boards and sell them for $40. We'd hold them up at the Computer Club and say, "Who wants to buy this?" We figured if we sold 50, we'd break even. I said, "We won't sell 50; we'll lose money."

Jobs said, "Yeah, but we'll have a company for once in our lives." What young person could turn that down? It was a very rare way to start a business. We had a partnership: Steve had 45 percent; I had 45 percent; and a friend of ours had 10 percent.

Steve Jobs started to set up credit. He got an order for already built computers—$50,000 worth—the biggest turning point in Apple's history. We now had to buy parts. A couple of friends loaned us $5000. We even got Atari, who was very friendly to us, to sell us parts—at their cost, out of our warehouse. But we needed credit, and didn't have any assets. I didn't even own a car. But we had a purchase order. Steve managed to get us "30 days net credit": You get the parts, build the computer board, sell it to a computer store, and then take the money from that sale to pay for the parts. We had 30 days to do it. We did it in 10 days. It's amazing what you can do if you only have one level of management.

Apple Computer, Inc. was born out of a rare combination of things. Apple had unique engineering: color, graphics, paddles, and sound—it was truly different. A fundamental decision was to build an "open" rather than a "closed" computer. Whenever you can build in a lot of features that everyone wants, very inexpensively—like color, sound, graphics, amount of memory—you should build them in, but leave room for growth.

When I buy a computer, I want to buy something that takes care of my needs but will be good for at least five years. I want to know that features that aren't even invented yet can be added later.

Apple today is very sensitive to market desires. If the market indicates that more memory or a certain feature is needed, the company shouldn't try to find a reason not to implement it or attempt to switch a customer to another product. Everything should be to the user's expectations. For a while we emphasized the Apple III—every brochure showed it—when the whole world was buying the Apple II. That was the wrong strategy.

We're now into compatible upgrades. You can upgrade your Macintosh to a Macintosh Plus, so Macintosh owners aren't left behind. We have a "one Apple" approach: If you buy a printer, it will be designed to plug into all Apple computers. Not only the employee, but also the customer should love both the product and the company.

Adlai E. Stevenson

Eleanor Roosevelt: A Lady for All Seasons

Among the many tributes and eulogies on behalf of Eleanor Roosevelt is the following, given by Adlai Stevenson (Governor of Illinois and Ambassador to the United Nations). This speech is properly termed a "eulogy" but is closely related to speeches of commemoration and dedication, in that Governor Stevenson expresses thanks on behalf of all the nation for the many good works of Mrs. Roosevelt. Specific strengths of Stevenson's speech include his elegant language and careful organization.

Eleanor Roosevelt was a lady—a lady for all seasons. Like her husband, she left "a name to shine on the entablatures of truth—forever."

Note that Stevenson chooses "four score" instead of "eighty"

It is hard to condense what one can say about this remarkable, brave, warm, practical, and persistent woman who gave herself to her time as no one else in her generation. However, in remembering her on what would have been her eightieth birthday, what comes to mind first is the fact that in nearly fourscore years she never ran out of things that needed doing, and she worked all her days for the realization of a human city embracing all mankind.

When she died on that gray November day in 1962, she was the most respected woman of this century. Some small measure of that respect was evidenced in the score of eulogies delivered in the General Assembly of the United Nations—the first and only time a private citizen was so honored. I recalled then that she gave her faith not only to those who shared the privilege of knowing her and of working by her side, but to countless men, women, and children in every part of the globe who loved her even as she loved them.

For to them she embodied the vision and the will to achieve a world in which all men walk in peace and dignity. And it was to this goal, a better life, that she gave her tireless energy, the strange strength of her extraordinary personality, shining ever with a radiance that displaced darkness, warmed the cold, beckoned to the lost, and kindled hope where none had ever flamed.

Sets up the following paragraph

There is, I believe, a legend in the Talmud telling us that in any period of man's history the heavens themselves are held in place by the virtue, love, and shining integrity of thirty-six just men. They are completely unaware of this function. They go about their daily work, their humble chores—doctors, teachers, workers, farmers (never, alas, lawyers, so

I understand), just ordinary devoted citizens—and meanwhile the roof tree of creation is supported by them alone.

> Note repetitive questions

There are times when nations or movements are similarly sustained in their purposes and being by the pervasive, unconscious influence of a few great men and women. Can we doubt that Eleanor Roosevelt had in some measure the keeping of the era's conscience in her special care? That her standards and integrity steadied our own? That her judgment persuaded the doubters and "too-soon despairers"? That her will stiffened the waverers and encouraged the strong?

I do not suggest some unwordly saint dwelling in remote regions of unsullied idealism. On the contrary, as we all know, Eleanor Roosevelt was a bonny fighter, at her best down in the arena, face to face with opponents and ideas she disapproved, and in ripe old age she took on tasks that might have daunted people half her age.

> Note use of "communist bosses" rather than "communist leaders"

Whether it was Communist bosses in the United Nations where she was the inspired architect of the Declaration of Human Rights, whether it was shoddy politicians, whether it was exploiters of the poor or traducers of the faith of freedom no matter where—she sailed in, tall, courteous, good-tempered, implacable, and thwacked them with the dispassionate energy of a good mother chastising a bad boy.

She was a remarkable person, this great and gallant woman who was known as the First Lady of the World. She was strong but gentle, idealistic but practical, humble as well as proud. She thought of herself as an "ugly duckling," but she walked in beauty in the slums and the ghettos of the world, bringing with her the reminder of her beloved St. Francis, "...it is in the giving that we receive..." And wherever she walked beauty was forever there.

The facts of her restless, fearless life are simple. She was the wife of a President, an author of books, the writer of a daily newspaper column; she was a diplomat, and she was also a gifted and most unusual politician. And because her dedication to the public good—to the world good—grew year by year until she had played a part in most of the great causes of her day, I have discovered that in some standard reference works it is her independent career of "U.S. diplomat and writer" that is listed first and her role as the "wife of F.D. Roosevelt," second.

I don't know if she would approve of this sequence, but I believe Franklin Roosevelt must have been thinking of her when he said, "The only limit to our realization of tomorrow will be our doubts of today."

Surely there was no limit to the tomorrow in Eleanor Roosevelt's life. There were no doubts. She moved all her days with strong and active faith, for to her, as she put is simply and wisely—as she did with all things, "life was meant to be lived and curiosity must be kept alive. One must never, for whatever reason, turn his back on life."

She never did, and we are the richer.

But to measure the impact of her life, or to tabulate the times she turned defeat into a shining victory, would be empty exercise. She was, above all a realist, and she would be the first to object. Her own role in history was not what interested her-only the work to be done and the need.

It was precisely her involvement, too, that gave her such tremendous influence.

Throughout the Depression, her patient journeys brought to the President and dramatized for the nation the misery and neglect of millions.

> Note color metaphor

During the gray days of national peril she heartened the wounded and the weary.

When we emerged from the war, blinking and surprised, to the role of world leadership, there she was at the center of the effort, reminding her countrymen of their duties as citizens in the greater society of man.

And during the affluent Fifties, when misery ran for cover before the national complacency, she never ceased to remind us of the slums, disease, and deprivation that still make up the dark side of this shining American nation.

But perhaps her name a century from now will be remembered above all for her dauntless energy and courage in facing the facts of the social revolution now part of our national folklore.

She saw the fearful implications of racial inequality and social injustice all over the world when most of us were only dimly aware that something was stirring beneath the surface of the old social order. And she set out to do something about it while there was yet time. For she knew the urgency of subduing the prejudice that persists between one kind of men, simply because they are one kind of men, for another kind of men, simply because they are another kind.

These senseless prejudices that have been the root cause of all the most terrible wars—the wars of race, of religion, of nationalities—are now suddenly no longer merely senseless, merely dangerous, they are something far worse. They are, in the most literal sense, the possible destroyer of the world.

But Eleanor Roosevelt had faith that men's hearts could be changed because she had seen them change. Indeed, although she would have been the last to say so, she had seen men change because she changed them herself.

Note repetiton and lists

It is this faith, of course, that now is the rationale of the Eleanor Roosevelt Foundation established as a living memorial to her by an act of Congress. And because it bears her name, it believes that we have no choice but to do something about our troubles—about even the ancient, brutal, ignorant suspicions, jealousies, prejudices, and hatreds that will destroy us unless we do something about them.

The Eleanor Roosevelt Memorial Foundation takes its cue from Mrs. Roosevelt's own life and work, which tell us how to proceed. They tell us it is not by sweetness, not by eloquent words, not by good wishes that human beings can be saved from one another; it is by humanity itself, by enlarging the concept of humanity so that it both contains the ill will and liberates it.

They tell us that in our concern with human rights there must ever be respect, certainly, for law and order, and equally a constantly renewed effort to see that our laws are such as free men can respect.

So, though she has left us—our counselor, our friend, our conscience—there can be no doubt where she would be directing our efforts today.

Effective repetition of "she would"

She would bid us add to the equality we now guarantee by law the extra dimension of opportunity without which even important rights can seem so much emptiness.

She would counsel us that we have done no more than set the framework within which the real struggle must still be fought out.

She would tell us to look at our great cities and ask ourselves whether, in the midst of overwhelming affluence, we can afford such misery, such squalor, such hopelessness.

She would tell us to labor on in the vineyards of the world, to succor the needy, to underpin the rule of law, to check aggression, and, with remorseless purpose, to seek peace among nations.

She would ask us to engage ourselves profoundly in the war on poverty at home and abroad.

She would urge us to build the great society not only for America, but for all God's children, so that all people everywhere are henceforth considered equal in dignity, equal in responsibility, equal in self-respect.

She did her share, more than any of us can do, to turn magnificent promises into even more magnificent facts—facts we must now and ever defend against those in our society who would like to escape history, to evade the fiery trial, to turn back the clock. Eleanor Roosevelt never would and never did.

She had the courage to battle everlastingly for something better and the prescience to "see a world in a grain of sand, and a Heaven in a wild flower." Happily for us, she could share her dream of a better tomorrow with all of us. That was, of course, the key to her greatness, the very reason of her life.

And we will fulfill the rich legacy she has left us only to the extent we make real her dream and press forward even as she in the patient, unspectacular, lonely search for the interests that unite the nations and toward the ultimate victory of reason, racial harmony, and justice in a world ruled by law.

Concludes with rhetorical question

And what finer remembrance could there be for Eleanor Roosevelt?

Photography Credits

- Antonio Navarro: Jack Hilton Incorporated.
- Thomas C. Collins: The Procter and Gamble Company.
- Geraldine Ferraro: © Cheryl Traendly/Jeroboan, Inc.
- Lech Walesa: © UPI/Bettmann Newphotos.
- Dwight D. Eisenhower: © UPI/Bettmann Newsphotos.
- Nicholas Johnson: © UPI/Bettmann Newsphotos.
- Barbara Jordan: © UPI/Bettman Newsphotos.
- Steve Wozniak: Cortesy of Apple Computers, Inc.; Will Mosgrave, Photographer.
- Adlai E. Stevenson: © UPI/Bettmann Newsphotos.

Bibliography

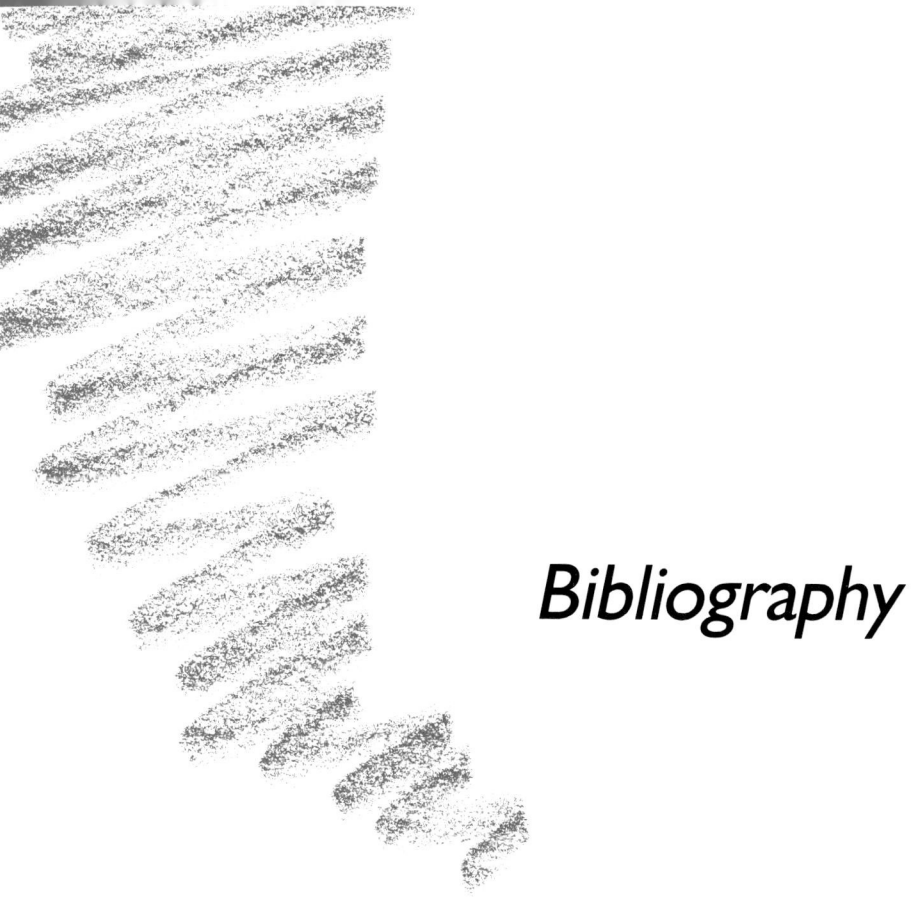

Aiken, E., G. Thomas, and W. Shennum. 1975. Memory for a lecture: Effects of notes, lecture rate, and informational density. *Journal of Educational Psychology* 67: 439–444.

Altheide, D., and J. Johnson. 1980. *Bureaucratic propaganda*. Boston: Allyn and Bacon.

Andersch, E., L. Staats, and R. Bostrom. 1969. *Communication in everyday use*. New York: Holt, Rinehart, & Winston.

Anderson, J. 1966. Equivalence of meaning among statements present through various media. *AV Communication Review* 14: 499–505.

Anderson, J. 1968. More on the equivalence of statements presented in various media. *AV Communication Review* 16: 25–32.

Applegate, J. 1985. The impact of face-saving strategies on listener impressions of interaction partners. Paper presented at the Meeting of the Speech Communication Association, Denver.

Backlund, P., J. Brown, and F. Jandt. 1982. Recommendations for assessing speaking and listening skills. *Communication Education* 31: 9–17.

Baddely, A. 1976. *The psychology of memory*. New York: Basic Books.

Barker, L. 1972. *Listening behavior*. Englewood Cliffs, NJ: Prentice-Hall.

Bavels, A. 1953. Communication patterns in task-oriented groups. In *Group dynamics*, eds. D. Cartwright and A. Zander. Evanston, IL: Row-Peterson.

Becker, S. 1963. Relationships among communication skills. *Central States Speech Journal* 17: 258–264.

Becker, S. 1978. Visual stimuli and the construction of meaning. In *Visual learning, thinking, and communication,* eds. B. Rhandawa and W. Coffman. New York: Academic Press.

Becker, S., and C. Dallinger. 1960. The effect of instructional methods upon achievement and attitudes in communication skills. *Speech Monographs* 27: 70–76.

Berlo, D. 1960. *The process of communication.* New York: Holt, Rinehart, & Winston.

Bettinghaus, E. 1980. *Persuasive communication.* New York: Holt, Rinehart, & Winston.

Bettinghaus, E., G. Miller, and T. Steinfatt. 1970. Source evaluation, syllogistic content, and judgment of logical validity by high and low-dogmatic persons. *Journal of Personality and Social Psychology* 16: 232–244.

Bitzer, L. 1959. Aristotle's enthymeme revisited. *Quarterly Journal of Speech* 45: 399–408.

Booth-Butterfield, S. 1987. Action assembly theory and communication apprehension. *Human Communication Research* 13: 386–398.

Borman, E. 1980. *Communication theory.* New York: Holt, Rinehart, & Winston.

Bostrom, R. 1963. Classroom criticism and speech attitudes. *Central States Speech Journal* 14: 28.

Bostrom, R. 1980. Communicative attitudes and communicative abilities. International Communication, Minneapolis.

Bostrom, R., and C. Bryant. 1980. Factors in the retention of information presented orally: The role of short-term listening. *Western Journal of Speech Communication* 44: 137–145.

Bostrom, R., and E. Waldhart. 1980. Listening abilities, notetaking, and type of response in the retention of information. Paper presented at the International Listening Association, Washington.

Bostrom, R., and E. Waldhart. 1978. Short-term listening as a factor in the acquisition of information. Paper presented at SCA, Minneapolis.

Bostrom, R., and E. Waldhart. 1980. Components in listening behavior: The role of short-term memory. *Human Communication Research* 6: 211–227.

Bostrom, R., E. Waldhart, and M. Brown. 1978. Memory functions in listening behavior. Paper presented at International Communication Association, Philadelphia.

Bowers, J. 1963. Language intensity, social introversion, and attitude change. *Speech Monographs* 30: 350–361.

Bowers, J., and J. Bradac. 1981. Issues in communication theory. In *Communication Yearbook V,* ed. M. Burgoon, 1–28. New Brunswick: Transaction.

Bowers, J., and M. Osborn. 1965. Attitudinal effects of selected types of concluding metaphors in persuasive speeches. *Speech Monographs* 33: 147–157.

Bradley, P. 1978. Power, status, and upward communication in small decision making groups. *Communication Monographs* 45: 33–43.

Brandstatter, H., J. Davis, and H. Schuler. 1978. *The dynamics of group discussion.* Beverly Hills: Sage.

Brigance, W. 1952. *Speech: Its techniques and disciplines in a free society.* New York: Appleton-Century-Crofts.

Brockreide, W. 1972. Arguers as lovers. *Philosophy and Rhetoric* 5: 1–11.

Brown, M. 1985. That reminds me of a story: Speech action in organizational socialization. *Western Journal of Speech Communication,* 49: 27–42.

Buchli, V., and W. Pearce. 1972. Listening behavior in coorientational states. *Journal of Communication* 24: 62–70.

Burgoon, J. 1976. The unwillingness to communicate scale. *Communication Monographs* 43: 60–79.

Burgoon, J. 1977. Unwillingness to communicate as a predictor of small group discussion behaviors and evaluations. *Central States Speech Journal* 28: 122–133.

Burgoon, J., D. Buller, J. Hale, and M. deTurck. 1984. Relational messages associated with nonverbal behaviors. *Human Communication Research* 10: 351–378.

Carmichael, C., and G. Cronkhite. 1965. Frustration and language intensity. *Speech Monographs* 32: 107–112.

Carter, J., and N. VanMatre. 1975. Note taking versus note having. *Journal of Educational Psychology* 67: 900–904.

Cartwright, D., and A. Zander, eds. 1968. *Group dynamics.* New York: Harper & Row.

Cherry, C. 1957. *On human communication.* New York: Science Editions.

Clark, R. 1984. *Persuasive messages.* New York: Harper & Row.

Clevenger, T. 1966. *Audience analysis.* Indianapolis: Bobbs-Merrill.

Combs, J., and M. Mansfield, eds. 1976. *Drama in life: The uses of communication in society.* New York: Hastings House.

Cooper, L., trans. 1960. *Aristotle's rhetoric.* New York: Appleton-Century-Crofts.

Corbett, E. 1965. *Classical rhetoric for the modern student.* New York: Oxford University Press.

Cottrill, T., and R.T. Alciatore. 1974. A comparison of two methods of teaching listening comprehension to college freshmen. *Western Speech* 38: 117–123.

Dittman, A. 1972. *Interpersonal messages of emotion.* New York: Springer.

DiVesta, F., and G. Gray. 1973. Listening and note taking: II. Immediate and delayed recall as functions of variations in thematic continuity, note taking, and length of listening-review intervals. *Journal of Educational Psychology* 64: 278–287.

Dominick, J. 1983. *The dynamics of mass communication.* Reading, MA: Addison-Wesley.

Educational Testing Service. 1957. *Sequential tests of educational progress.* Princeton, NJ: Educational Testing Service.

Ehninger, D., and W. Brockreide. 1963. *Decision by debate.* New York: Harper & Row.

Ehninger, D., A. Monroe, and B. Gronbeck. 1978. *Principles and types of speech communication.* Glenview, IL: Scott, Foresman and Co.

Eisner, S., and K. Rohde. 1959. Note taking during or after the lecture. *Journal of Educational Psychology* 50: 301–304.

Ellis, A., and G. Beattie. 1986. *The Psychology of Language and Communication.* New York: Guilford Press.

Ekman, P., W. Frisen, and P. Ellsworth. 1972. *Emotion in the human face: Guidelines for research and an integration of findings.* New York: Pergamon.

Fairhurst, G., E. Rogers, and R. Sarr. 1987. Manager-subordinate control patterns and judgment about the relationship. In *Communication Yearbook X,* ed. M. McLaughlin, 395–414. Beverly Hills: Sage.

Fishbein, M. 1967. A consideration of beliefs and their role in attitude measurement. In *Readings in attitude theory and measurement,* ed. M. Fishbein. New York: John Wiley and Sons.

Fisher, A. 1987. *Interpersonal communication: The pragmatics of human relationships.* New York: Random House.

Fisher, J., and M. Harris. 1975. Effect of note taking and review on recall. *Journal of Educational Psychology* 65: 321–325.

Fiske, S., and E. Taylor. 1984. *Social cognition.* Reading, MA: Addison-Wesley.

Gallup, G. 1 March 1987. More think drinking a problem. *Los Angeles Times.*

Gibb, J. 1961. Defensive communication. *Journal of Communication* 11: 141–148.

Glanzer, M. 1972. Storage mechanisms in recall. In *The psychology of learning and motivation,* ed. G. Bower. New York: Academic Press.

Goffman, E. 1959. *Presentation of self in everyday life.* Garden City, NY: Doubleday.

Goldhaber, G. 1974. *Organizational communication.* Dubuque: Wm. C. Brown.

Gordon, J. 1923. Last days of the Confederacy. In *Modern Eloquence,* ed. A. Thorndike, vol.5. New York: Modern Eloquence Corportation.

Goss, B. 1982. *Processing communication.* Belmont, CA: Wadsworth.

Gouran, D., and S. Geonetta. 1977. Patterns of interaction as a function of the degree of leadership centralization in decision-making groups. *Central States Speech Journal* 28: 47–53.

Greynolds, M. 1972. Charles Bronson Alcott's Conversations. Paper read at the Annual Meeting of the Speech Communication Association, San Francisco.

HeenWold, A. 1978. *Decoding oral language.* New York: Academic Press.

Hirokawa, R. 1980. A comparative analysis of communication patterns in effective and ineffective decision-making groups. *Communication Monographs* 47: 312–320.

Hirsch, R.O. 1979. *Listening: A way to process information aurally.* Dubuque: Gorsuch Scarisbrick.

Hoar, G. 1923. Eloquence. In *Modern Eloquence,* ed. A. Thorndike, vol. 5. New York: Modern Eloquence Corporation.

Holden, C. 1987. Is alcoholism treatment effective? *Science* 236: 20–22.

Howard, D. 1983. *Cognitive psychology.* New York: Macmillan.

Hunt, E., C. Lunnenborg, and J. Lewis. 1975. What does it mean to be high verbal? *Cognitive Psychology* 7: 197–227.

Institute for Propaganda Analysis. 1937. *Propaganda analysis.* Detroit: Institute for Propaganda Analysis.

Jablin, F. 1979. Superior-subordinate communication: The state of the art. *Psychological Bulletin* 86: 1201–1222.

Jablin, F., D. Siebold, and R. Sorenson. 1977. Potential inhibitory effects of group participation on brainstorming performance. *Central State Speech Journal* 28: 113–121.

Janis, I. 1971. Groupthink. *Psychology Today* 5 (6): 43–46.

Johnson, J., and N. Szczupakiewicsz. 1987 The public speaking course: Is it preparing students with work-related public speaking skills? *Communication Education* 36: 131–137.

Jones, J. E., and L. Mohr. 1976. *The Jones-Mohr listening test.* LaJolla, CA: University Associates.

Jourard, S. 1959. Self disclosure and other-cathexis. *Journal of Abnormal and Social Psychology,* 59: 428–431.

Just, M., and P. Carpenter. 1978. *Cognitive processes in comprehension.* Hillsdale, NJ: Erlbaum.

Katriel, T., and G. Phillipsen. 1981. "What we need is communication:" Communication as a cultural category in some American speech. *Communication Monographs* 48: 301–311.

Kellermann, K., and S. Jarboe. 1987. Conservatism in judgment. In *Communication Yearbook X,* ed. M. McLaughlin, 259–281. Beverly Hills: Sage.

Kelly, C. 1965. An investigation of the construct validity of two commercially published listening tests. *Speech Monographs* 32: 139–143.

Kelly, C. 1967. Listening: A complex of activities—and a unitary skill? *Speech Monographs* 34: 455–466.

Kelly, C. 1970. Empathic listening. In *Small group communication,* eds. R. Cathcart and L. Samovar. Dubuque: Wm. C. Brown.

Kelly, G. 1955. *The psychology of personal constructs,* Vol. 1. New York: Norton.

Kelman, H. 1961 Process of opinion change. *Public Opinion Quarterly* 25: 57–58.

Kemp, J., and D. Dayton. 1985. *Planning and producing instructional media.* 5th ed. New York: Harper & Row.

Koenigswald, G. 1962. *The evolution of man.* Ann Arbor: University of Michigan Press.

LaFrance, M., and C. Mayo. 1979. A review of nonverbal behaviors of women and men. *Western Journal of Speech Communication* 43: 96–107.

Leathers, D. 1972. Quality of group communication as a determinant of group product. *Speech Monographs* 39: 166–193.

Leathers, D., and T. Emigh. 1980. Decoding facial expressions: A new test with decoding norms. *Quarterly Journal of Speech* 66: 418–436.

Levinson, H. 1973. Asinine attitudes toward motivation. *Harvard Business Review* 51: 70–76.

Linkugel, W., R. Allen, and R. Johanneson, eds. 1982. *Contemporary american speeches.* 5th ed. Dubuque: Kendall-Hunt.

Littlejohn, S. 1983. *Theories of human communication.* 2d ed. Belmont, CA: Wadsworth.

Loftus, G. R., and E. F. Loftus. 1976. *Human memory: The processing of information.* New York: John Wiley and Sons.

McCombs, M. 1976. Agenda-setting research. *Political Communication Review* 1: 1–7.

McCroskey, J. 1969. A summary of experimental research on the effect of evidence in persuasive communication. *Quarterly Journal of Speech* 55: 65–72.

McCroskey, J. 1980. On communication competence and communication apprehension. *Communication Education* 29: 109.

McCroskey, J., and V. Richmond. 1982. *The quiet ones.* Dubuque: Gorschuck-Scarisbruck.

Meyer, J., and F. Williams. 1965 Teaching listening at the secondary level: some evaluations. *Speech Teacher* 14: 299–304.

Miller, G. A. 1951. *Language and communication.* New York: Appleton-Century-Crofts.

Miller, G. A., and P. Johnson-Laird. 1976. *Language and perception.* Cambridge: Harvard University Press.

Miller, G. R. 1980. On being persuaded: Some basic distinctions. In *Persuasion: New directions in theory and research,* eds. M. Roloff and G. Miller. Beverly Hills: Sage.

Miller, G. R., and M. Burgoon. 1973. *New techniques of persuasion.* New York: Harper & Row.

Miller, G. R., and M. Steinberg. 1975. *Between people.* Chicago: Science Research Associates.

Motley, M. 1976. Stage fright manipulation by false heart rate feedback. *Central States Speech Journal* 27: 186–191.

Motley, M. 1986. Consciousness and intentionality in communication. *Western Journal of Speech Communication* 50: 3–23.

Motley, M. 1987. On whether one cannot communicate: A sender-oriented perspective. Paper presented at the International Communication Association Meeting, Montreal.

Nichols, R. 1948. Factors in listening comprehension. *Speech Monographs* 15: 154–163.

Norman, D. A., and D. Rumelhart. 1975. *Explorations in cognition.* San Francisco: Wm. H. Freeman.

O'Neill, D., ed. 1971 *Speeches by black americans.* Encino, CA: Dickenson Publishing Co.

Paivo, A., and R. Steeves. 1967. Relations between personal values and imagery and meaningfulness of value words. *Perceptual and Motor Skills* 24: 357–358.

Palmatier, R. A., and G. McNinch. 1972. Source of gains in listening skill: Experimental or pretest experience. *Journal of Communication* 22: 70–76.

Palmgreen, P., and P. Clarke. 1977. Agenda-setting with local and national issues. *Communication Research* 4: 435–452.

Pearson, J. 1985. *Gender and communication.* Dubuque: Wm. C. Brown.

Peterson, L., and S. Peterson. 1959. Short-term retention of individual verbal items. *Journal of Experimental Psychology* 58: 193–198.

Phillips, G. 1968. Reticence: Pathology of the normal speaker. *Speech Monographs* 35: 39–43.

Phillips, G. 1980. On apples and onions. *Communication Education* 29: 107.

Pierce, J. 1961. *Symbols, signals, and noise.* New York: Harper & Row.

Plutchik, R. 1980. A language for the emotions. *Psychology Today* 13 (9): 68–80.

Postman, N. 1979. The technical thesis. *Vital Speeches of the Day* (January): 180–185.

Premack, A., and D. Premack. 1972. Teaching language to an ape. *Scientific American* 227 (October): 92.

Public papers of the presidents. 1953. Washington, D.C.: United States Government Printing Office.

Ray, E. 1983. Identifying job stress in a human service organization. *Journal of Applied Communication Research* 11: 109–119.

Reardon, K. 1981. *Persuasion: Theory and context.* Beverly Hills: Sage.

Reardon, K. 1987. *Interpersonal communication: Where minds meet.* Belmont, CA:Wadsworth.

Reeves, R. 1982. TV is changing the world—for the better. *Television Guide* 30 (July 3): 4.

Reid, L. 1980. *Speaking well.* New York: McGraw-Hill.

Reynolds, R., and M. Burgoon. 1983. Belief processing. In *Communication Yearbook VII,* ed. R. Bostrom, 83–104. Beverly Hills: Sage.

Rokeach, M. 1973. *The nature of human values.* New York: The Free Press.

Rosenfeld, R., and V. Christie. Sex and persuasion revisited. *Western Journal of Speech Communication* 38: 224–231.

Rubin, R. 1982. Assessing speaking and listening competence: The communication competency assessment instrument. *Communication Education* 31: 19–32.

Rubin, R., and C. Roberts. 1987. A comparative analysis of three listening tests. *Communication Education* 36: 142–153.

Salomon, G. 1981. *Communication and education: Social and psychological interactions.* Beverly Hills: Sage.

Sayers, Gale. 1970. *I am third.* New York: Viking Press.

Schwartzman, R. 1987. Competence, expertise, and accountability: Classical foundations of the cult of expertise. Paper presented at the Southern Speech Communication Association, St. Louis.

Scott, W., D. Osgood, and D. Peterson. 1979. *Cognitive structure: Theory and measurement of individual differences.* New York: John Wiley and Sons.

Searle, B. 1984. The effect of medium of transmission, notetaking, sex, ability, and activation level on the comprehension and retention of information. Unpublished Ph.D. dissertation, University of Kentucky.

Shank, R., and R. Abelson. 1977. *Scripts, plans, goals, and understanding.* Hillsdale, NJ: Erlbaum.

Shannon, C., and W. Weaver. 1949. *The mathematical theory of communication.* Urbana: University of Illinois.

Siegel, A., and J. Allik. 1973. A developmental study of visual and auditory short-term memory. *Journal of Verbal Learning and Verbal Behavior* 12: 409–418.

Skinner, B. 1958. *Verbal behavior.* New York: Appleton-Century-Crofts.

Spectra, Speech Communication Association. 1973. (December): 4.

Sperling, G. 1960. The information available in brief visual presentations. *Psychological Monographs* 74: 1–29.

Squire, L. J. 1975. Short-term memory as a biological entity. In *Short-term memory,* eds. D. Deutsch and A. Deutsch. New York: Academic Press.

Staats, A. 1968. *Learning, language, and cognition.* New York: Holt, Rinehart, and Winston.

Sticht, T. G., and D. R. Glassnap. 1972. Effects of speech rate, selection difficulty, association strength, and mental aptitude on learning by listening. *Journal of Communication* 22: 174–188.

Sumner, W. G. 1923. Who pays? In *Modern eloquence,* ed. A. Thorndike, vol. 5. New York: Modern Eloquence Corporation.

Sumner, W. G. 1960. The forgotten man. In *American forum,* eds. E. Wrage and B. Baskerville. New York: Holt, Rinehart, & Winston.

Sypher, B. 1984. Communication competency in large organizations. In *Competency in communication,* ed. R. Bostrom. Beverly Hills: Sage.

Sypher, H., and J. Applegate. 1984. The role of schema in organizing communication. In *Communication Yearbook VIII,* ed. R. Bostrom. Beverly Hills: Sage.

Toulmin, S. 1958. *The uses of argument.* Cambridge: The Cambridge University Press.

Tufte, E. 1983. *The visual display of quantitative information.* Cheshier, CT: The Graphics Press.

Waldhart, E., and R. N. Bostrom. 1980. Listening skills and retention strategies. Paper presented at the International Listening Association, Washington, D. C.

Watzlawick, P., J. Beavin, and D. Jackson. 1967. *Pragmatics of human communication.* New York: Norton.

Weaver, C. 1957. Measuring point of view as a barrier to communication. *Journal of Communication,* 7: 5–11.

Weaver, C. 1972. *Human listening: Processes and behavior.* Indianapolis: Bobbs-Merrill.

Whatmough, J. 1956. *Language: A modern synthesis.* New York: Harper & Row.

Wheeless, L. 1975. An investigation of receiver apprehension and social context dimensions of communication apprehension. *Speech Teacher* 24: 261–268.

Whitman, R., and T. Foster. 1987. *Speaking in public.* New York: MacMillan.

Wicker, T. 15 May 1987. Drugs vs. Alcohol. *San Francisco Chronicle.*

Williams, F. 1983. *The communications revolution.* Beverly Hills: Sage.

Williams, F. 1985. *The new communications.* Belmont, CA: Wadsworth.

Winans, J. 1938. *Speechmaking.* New York: Appleton-Century-Crofts.

Winick, W., and K. Kressel. 1965. Tachistoscopic recognition thresholds, paired associate learning, and free recall as a function of abstractness-concreteness and word frequency. *Journal of Experimental Psychology* 70: 163–171.

Wolvin, A., and C. Coakley. 1985. *Listening.* 2d ed. Dubuque, IA: Wm. C. Brown.

Wood, J. 1982. *Communication: A symbolic interactionalist perspective.* New York: Holt, Rinehart, & Winston.

Work, W. 1978 Listen, my children... *Communication Education* 27: 147–161.

Worthy, M., A. Garay, and G. Kahn. 1969. Self-disclosure as an exchange process. *Journal of Personality and Social Psychology* 13: 59 -63.

Yerby, J. 1975. Attitude, task, and sex composition as variables affecting female leadership of small problem solving groups. *Speech Monographs* 42: 160–168.

Zajonc, R. 1985. Emotion and facial efference: A theory reclaimed. *Science* 228: 15–21.

Glossary

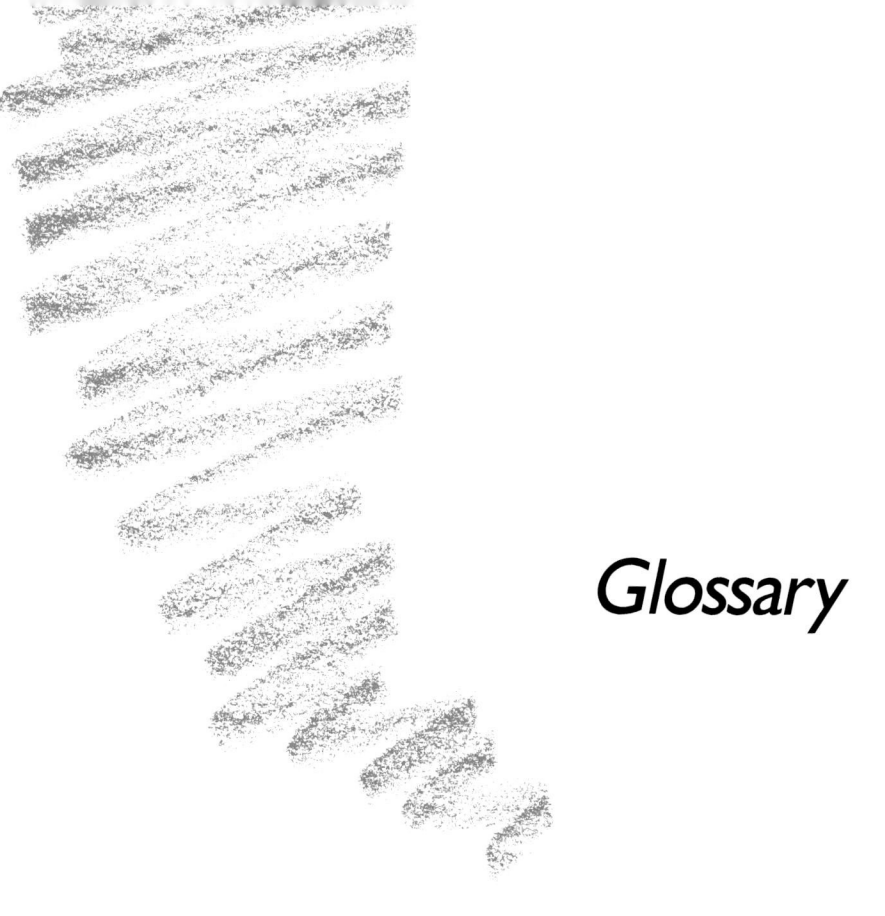

The chapter in which each word can be found appears in parentheses at the end of the definition.

Abstraction is the process of using words to describe large classes of things. (10)

Activate is to communicate in a way that calls for action as well as a change in the internal environment of the listener. (2)

Adaptation is the changing of material to suit a particular audience. (1)

Affects are emotional states typically involving autonomic arousal such as heart rate, breathing rate, and skin conductivity. (2, 14)

Apology is a speech of self-defense; one in which the usual strategy is to explain the circumstances and deny wrong-doing. (16)

Appropriateness refers to making the speech fit the occasion, audience, or situation. (7)

Attention refers to the involuntary ways that humans attend to certain stimuli as opposed to others. (12)

Audience analysis is the process of compiling data on the characteristics of an audience that may influence their response to the speaker's message. Such characteristics include demographic information on age, sex, ethnic background, educational background, and religious orientation, as well as information on their internal environments. (6)

Behavioral intention is a special kind of schema in which *potential* behavior governs the structure of the response. (14)

Beliefs are commonly thought of as "objects plus attributes." (7)

Body usually refers to all speech elements except introduction, thesis, and conclusion. (5)

Body lean refers to the vertical orientation of the torso. Forward usually denotes interest. (11)

Briefing is the act of giving precise instructions or essential information. This form of informative speaking provides information that supplements other information already known. (13)

Card catalog is a common feature of every library, where every book has its own card. (8)

Cause-effect is a type of organization in which one proceeds by analyzing events and their causes. Most cause-effect reasoning is indirect. (9)

Chronological means according to time sequence–the Greek word *chronos* means "time." (9)

Claim is one of the principle elements in the Toulmin Model. The basic idea behind Toulmin's model is that a logical argument begins with evidence, and then proceeds to "claims" by means of a "warrant." The Toulmin model provides explicit limitation on the force of the claim. The qualification of the claim is extremely important in this kind of communication and does not necessarily take place in the syllogistic form. (15)

Cohesiveness refers to the quality of the group that makes it "cling" together. Cohesiveness can be created by a number of factors: common goals, common background, liking for one another, external forces or pressures. (16)

Coercion refers to a physical force as a means to bring about behavioral change. Physical coercion rarely, if ever, changes attitudes and might even reinforce them. Many people confuse persuasion with coercion, even though they have important differences. They both aim at influencing behavior, but the effects are drastically different. Coercion is usually effective only under conditions of surveillance (Kelman, 1961), while persuasion is more permanent. (14)

Code words are a handy organizational device which make useful mnemonic (memory) aids and useful plans. (9)

Commemoration is a type of speech traditionally used to remind us of the importance of a specific event. In this kind of speech, we often refer to the values that a group shares, the importance of the occasion, and the worth of the individuals involved. The most typical examples are commencement addresses, dedication speeches, and the like. (7)

Communication is purposeful interaction between at least two persons, principally through the use of verbal and nonverbal symbols. (1)

Communication apprehension is the fear-like emotional reaction that accompanies many communicative situations. (4)

Comparison involves at least two elements which have striking similarities or differences. (8)

Compliance-dynamism refers to a credibility factor involving the audience's perception of the speaker's power. It is usually not thought of as a characteristic of credibility at all. (14)

Conclusion is a summary of main points or a summarization of a speech by repeating the thesis and the main subheads. (5, 9)

Concreteness refers to highly specific words and phrases. (10)

Condense is the act of cutting elaborate phrases or words to their most essential elements. (5)

Connotative is an emotional meaning, or affect, attached to a word. (10)

Constructive listening involves listener participation from an affirmative or altruistic point of view. (3)

Contrast is similar to comparison, except that differences are stressed. (8)

Convince means to change someone's point of view, primarily beliefs and attributions. (7)

Credibility consists of those characteristics of a source that contribute to a belief. (14)

Dedication refers to the initiatory ceremony of a new facility. (16)

Deduction is one of the two traditional forms of logic (the other being induction) where a specific statement is derived from a broad statement. (15)

Definition is the restating of complex material using simpler terms. (8)

Demographic audience analysis is the identification of such traits, such as ethnic or racial background, religious orientation, or sex, to gain information which will allow a speaker to better empathize with listeners, adapt the message in order to win their attention, understand their frame of reference, and respond to their needs. (6)

Demonstration is usually defined as the presentation of an act or a process without intermediate steps. (13)

Denotative is a type of meaning, often called "historical meaning," acquired through usage. This kind of meaning is typically recorded in dictionaries. (10)

Development involves adding meaning through implications and significance. Extended examples also qualify. (13)

Dissonance is an internal tension which occurs when there are inconsistencies among source evaluations and communication objects. These inconsistencies are usually termed imbalance, dissonance, and incongruity. (14)

Duration refers to the length of time that a stimulus lasts. (12)

Electronic audience is used to describe the differences that technology have created in the behavior of listeners. People are more likely to participate than to simply observe. (6)

Empathy is the ability to see things the way the other person does. (6)

Enthymeme is a form of reasoning used by communicators in which one of the premises is implied. Part of the power of the enthymeme lies in the assumption that the audience agrees with one of the premises; and it is definitely one of the more persuasive forms of reasoning (Bitzer, 1959). (15)

Equivalency is one of two principles involved in constructing the foundation, the heading system, of an outline. When ideas are equivalent, they get the same level headings. Subordinate ideas would be placed under these main heads. (9)

Ethical communication involves the greater good and transcends individual needs and rewards. (3)

Ethics is the formal study of right and wrong, of good and bad. "Morals" are another way of examining ethics. (3)

Evaluation is the assigning of judgment to single stimuli, and usually an interpretive aspect. (3)

Evidence is one of the principle elements in the Toulmin Model.

Examples are generally of two kinds: real and hypothetical. Real examples come from your own experience or from one of your sources. Hypothetical examples are those that you invent. (8)

Expand is similar to development, and typically involves specific instances of more general statements. (5)

Experience is a vital source of the information you gather for speeches and consists of two basic types: *first-hand* (from direct experience) and *secondhand* (from other than direct experience). (8)

Explanation is a form of informative speaking which provides information that supplements other information already known. Often it provides additional schemata than was otherwise known. (13)

Extended messages differ from interpersonal messages in that they are delivered to larger groups in formal situations and are typically aimed at specific social or organizational goals. (1)

Extensity refers to size. (12)

Externalization, or self-disclosure, is quite similar to relaying; the material that is transmitted is composed not only of percepts, but also of at least one schema. (2)

Extemporaneous is a speech in which the outline is carefully prepared, but the specific words are not chosen in advance. (5)

Extrinsic credibility derives from the characteristics of the message; usually it means that the speaker has thoroughly researched the topic. (7)

Eye contact is the contact made visually with the eyes of another person. (11)

Facial expression is the affect display brought about by rearranging the facial muscles. (11)

Fact is any statement that can be verified by the senses. (15)

Focal length refers to the way in which the projector's lens focuses the image and how far the image can reach; the farther the image is projected, the larger it is, but this depends on the particular projector and a particular lens. (12)

Formalistic is the point of view that arrangement and structure is as important as content. (9)

General purpose of a speech is how a speaker intends to affect the inner environment of the audience. (7)

Group dynamics are the unique internal characteristics of a group. Group dynamics usually involve three important characteristics: *cohesiveness*, *structure*, and *identity*. (16)

Group purpose refers to the fact that groups are based on a specific purpose. (16)

Hidden agenda consists of the ulterior motives of the speaker. (7)

Identity is the sense of "belonging" in a small group. (16)

Illustrations are particularly vivid examples. They contain more references to sensory impressions than ordinary examples and serve the same purpose that diagrams or pictures do. (8)

Imbalance is an internal tension that operates in the juxtaposition of a credible source with a novel or attitude-discrepant ideas. This tension, if effective, results in attitude change. Imbalance can also be referred to as incongruity or dissonance. (14)

Implicit responses are private ideas and feelings of which other people are not aware. (14)

Impromptu is a speech given with no preparation. (5)

Incongruity is an internal tension which, if effective, results in attitude change. The name of the process that operates in the juxtaposition of a credible source with a novel or attitude-discrepant idea is called variously imbalance, incongruity, or dissonance. (14)

Induction is the generation of a broad statement based on a number of specific statements. (15)

Inflection is the degree to which a speaker's voice rises and falls during a word or sentence. (11)

Inform means to pass on information, or to *relay*. (7)

Information is the absence of redundancy, or predictability. (13)

Informative communication is the process of combining relays for the purpose of recreating experience, and in some ways it can be the most important communicative activity in your personal or professional life. (13)

Inner environment is a general term for mental events: thoughts, emotions, and language. (2)

Intensity is generally involved with the strength of a stimulus. (10, 12)

Interaction involves interdependent behavior; during true interaction one response follows another in a cyclical, back-and-forth pattern. (2)

Interpersonal communication takes place when the participants are in direct contact, that is, when they can see, hear, or touch each other. (1)

Interpretation is the process of integrating incoming material with existing schemas. (3)

Interpretive listening is the type of listening usually associated with the decoding of affective messages. Most typically the nonverbal signals are involved. (11)

Intrinsic credibility is derived from characteristics of the source, rather than the message. (7)

Introduction is an organizational element used to capture attention and to orient the audience. A speech of introduction usually contains a short personal anecdote, biographical material, or an enhancement of the speaker's credibility. (5, 9, 16)

Invention, as defined by the ancient rhetoricians, is the process of developing thought and ideas for a message. (8)

Language occurs when symbols are formally organized and when they are used to express our thoughts, feelings, and complex ideas. It can be universal or private; spoken, written, or gestural. (2)

Lecture listening includes anything we retain longer than one hour. Information must be transferred from short-term to long-term memory by conscious effort. (3)

Listening is the act of taking in information from an oral stimulus. It involves short-term, intermediate, and long-term storage. (3)

Logic is a formal system involving the acceptable relationships among statements. (9)

Long-term listening is used when we retain something for a long period of time, usually at least five minutes. (3)

Manuscript is a form of speech which involves a word-by-word preparation for delivery and makes use of an actual written manuscript. (5)

Mass communication happens when a very large number of receivers are involved, usually more than a thousand. Today, the "institutions" of mass communication (press and broadcast media) also tend to define the form. (1)

Mediated communication occurs when some device, usually mechanical, is interposed between participants. (1)

Mediated response is a non-immediate response, one affected by internal processes. (10)

Memorized is a manuscript speech without the aid of a manuscript; it is one in which eye contact is maintained, and delivery is more free because the speaker is not chained to the podium. (5)

Metaphor is a figure of speech which compares two items without the use of "like" or "as." (10)

Motivated sequence, invented by Alan H. Monroe, is an organizational plan consisting of five steps (attention, need, satisfaction, visualization, and action) for organizing messages. (9, 14)

Narrowing refers to the process used in developing a speech covering a general topic to fit the interests and expectations of the audience. (7)

Network is a particular communication pattern in a large organization. (16)

Nomination refers to a speech that is a persuasive presentation that aims to enhance the attitude of the audience. A nominating speech should have two basic parts: a description of the qualities needed in the office, and a listing of the candidate's characteristics that fit these qualities. (16)

Nonverbal elements modify communication, usually through affect displays by various elements of the body. (11)

Normative-identificatory is a characteristic of credibility in which the speaker attempts to get an audience to identify with him or her. It is often used in advertising. (14)

Objective listening is the processing of information without comparison to the person's value system. (3)

Outer environment consists of the external stimuli affecting each person from moment to moment. (2)

Outline terms refers to a way of speaking in which a point to point reference directly to the outline is made as the speech proceeds. (9)

Percepts are impressions of objects perceived and formed by the senses and recorded in memory. Percepts do not have direct, exact correspondences with the environmental events; they are created internally by the perceptual system. (2)

Performance refers to skill in the use of voice and body by which actors and speakers "give a show." (1)

Persuade means to move someone to action. (7)

Pitch is the relative frequency at which the basic vocal sounds are produced. (11)

Positional relationships refer to the communicator's and listeners' positions in the organization's hierarchy. (16)

Premise one of the assumed statements in a syllogism. (15)

Problem-solving is a plan of proceeding from the definition of a problem to the proposal and adoption of a solution. (9)

Proposition is the "building block" of logic and is the single statement of a characteristic. (15)

Proximity is the general distance between communicators, intimate, typical, and formal. (11)

Psychophysical refers to the interaction between psychological processes and physical stimuli. The discipline of psychophysics deals with physical characteristics of stimuli, such as loudness, brightness, and duration. (12)

Public speaking is a specialized form of communication. It is not mediated or mass communication, which would seem to place it in the "interpersonal" category. While it usually takes place in a face-to-face setting, it differs from most interpersonal communication in three important ways: in size of group involved, the nature of the message, and in the formality of the occasion. (1)

Purpose is the articulation of individual, group, or organizational goals in a message. (2)

Qualification-expertness is a basic credibility factor which concerns whether the source is able to speak with authority on a particular issue. (14)

Qualifier is an element of the Toulmin Model which is needed to help define a cause-effect relationship when composing a logical argument. It is usually used with *reservations* and *support*. (15)

Quotation is the recitation of someone else's words directly. Attribution is always necessary. (8)

Reader's Guide is an index to subject matter found in popular periodicals. It is published annually and found in most libraries. (8)

Receiver-orientation is sensitivity to the expectations and needs of listeners; consideration of the inner environments of the audience. (6)

Rehearsal listening occurs when you keep something in your mind consciously by repeating it to yourself. You utilize short-term rehearsal when you look up something in the telephone directory and keep repeating the number in your mind. (3)

Reinforcement is the psychological process that explains our tendency to repeat experiences we find pleasant and avoid those we do not. Reinforcement can be verbal and physical. (4)

Reinforcing refers to a type of response to persuasion which occurs when the speaker modifies an existing attitude or behavior. (14)

Relationship is the amount of intimacy, immediacy, and dominance existing between two persons. (11)

Relay is a communicative act in which the source acts as a surrogate stimulus for the receiver. (2, 13)

Repetition is the repeating of words and phrases as a rhetorical device. (8, 12)

Research is the entire process of discovering what has been written or discovered about particular topics. (5)

Reservation is an element of the Toulmin Model which is needed to help define a cause-effect relationship when composing a logical argument. It is usually used with *qualifiers* and *support*. (15)

Retention is the process of retaining information. Retention involves memory, and the types of retention vary with the type of memory used. Basically, there are three types of retention—short-term, short-term with rehearsal, and long-term—that use three different memory functions. (3, 9)

Reticence is the unwillingness to communicate, and is not necessarily the same as communication apprehension (Burgoon, 1976). A reticent person often just doesn't care. (4)

Rhetoritherapy is a method of treatment for communication apprehension. It involves the acquisition of skill rather than the specific treatment of apprehension. (4)

Safety-trustworthiness is the characteristic of credibility that relates to the basic truthfulness of individuals. Since truthful persons are "safe," most researchers use "safety" together with trustworthiness when discussing this factor. (14)

Schemas are groups of concepts and percepts and the systems we use to organize them. (Sypher and Applegate, 1984). (2)

Selection is this process of choosing which stimuli will be perceived. This process of selection depends heavily on our background, our attitude, our age, and our interest (Weaver, 1972). (3)

Selective listening is an individual's propensity to choose only part of a message to hear and remember. (6)

Selective perception is the psychological process of focusing on particular stimuli and ignoring others. Sometimes it is unconscious and automatic. (12)

Self-disclosure is a special form of informative speaking which focuses on the speaker—the revealing of attitudes, background, and experiences that create a person's character. This process is also referred to on occasion as externalization. (13)

Shaping occurs when the audience has no previous experience with, or knowledge about, the topic.

Short-term listening is what we do when we retain the content for less than 90 seconds. (3)

Shyness is a personality trait of persons who avoid social interaction in general, not just communicative situations. (4)

Situational audience analysis is the analysis of a particular audience and its situation, and is an important step in the construction of a speech. (6)

Social signaling involves very basic relationship messages and usually does not utilize symbols. Usually this process is automatic and not processed through thoughts. (10)

Sort is the process of grouping ideas in the body of a speech for further amplification and discussion. (5)

Spatial is a type of organization useful for describing the appearance of objects, especially in a speech that is aimed at developing percepts. It follows spatial principles, such as right to left, or higher to lower.(9)

Specific purpose is a precise statement of what you wish to accomplish. The specific purpose should concentrate on one aspect of a subject. (7)

State apprehension is the apprehension that appears before and during a speech experience but does not persist after the speech is over. (4)

Statistics consist of numerical evidence. (13)

Stimulating means pleasing the audience or invoking other emotional responses, usually through the audience's specific schemata. (7)

Stimulation occurs when the source relays and/or externalizes in such a way that the receiver's affective system is aroused. (2)

Structure is an associative method used to organize and integrate mental events; an internal plan to keep everything straight in order to use knowledge. (9, 16)

Subordination is one of two principles involved in constructing the foundation, the heading system, of an outline. Subordinate ideas are placed under the main, or same level, headings. (9)

Summarize is the reduction of a larger body of words into a smaller one, usually by eliminating support and examples. (5)

Support is an element of the Toulmin Model which is needed to help define a cause-effect relationship when composing a logical argument. It is usually used with *qualifiers* and *reservations*. (15)

Syllogism is a form of deductive reasoning. (15)

Symbol is a sound or action that is associated with a concept or class of stimuli. (10)

Thanks is a speech expressing gratitude to a particular person or organization. (16)

Thesis is the single sentence whereby the "meat" of the speech is expressed. (5)

Topoi are topics. More specifically, they are the "places" of argument, roadways showing where to look for ideas. (8)

Touch is physical contact between communicators. (11)

Toulmin Model represents a logical argument beginning with evidence and then proceeding to claims by meaning of warrant. The Toulmin Model provides for the explicit support of warrants, emphasizing the importance of the warrant in the overall structure of the argument. (15)

Trait apprehension is the fright experienced by apprehensive persons regardless of whether or not a communicative task is imminent. (4)

Transition is the name for a phrase which orients a listener to a change in thought. (9)

Value refers to statements asserting rightness or wrongness of good and bad. (15)

Variety is the process of adding interest through different material and language. (11)

Verbosity is the usage of more words than is necessary or tasteful. (10)

Warrant is one of the principle elements in the Toulmin Model.

Welcome is a speech that establishes relationships between persons normally not attending a particular meeting, such as visitors or the like. (16)

Index

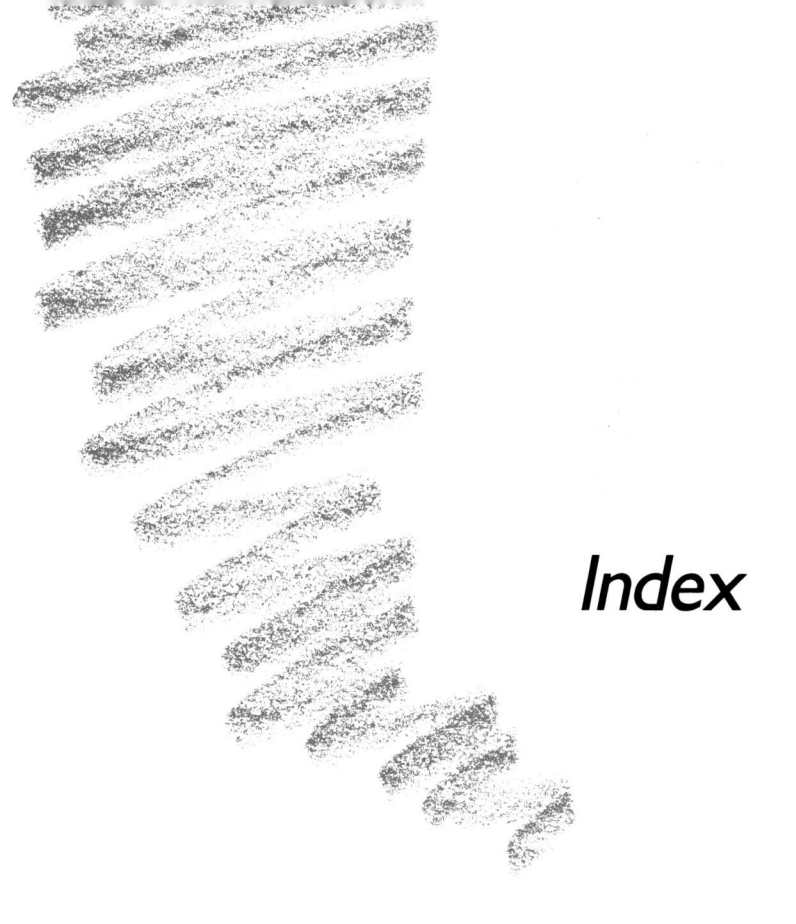

Abelson, R., 138
abstraction, 148–149
activate, 29
adaptations, 15
adjectivals, 150
affect, 25, 38, 212, 222–224
agenda, hidden, 102
Alda, Alan, 150
Allen, R., 36, 150
Andersch, E., 240
Anderson, J., 174
Applegate, J., 23, 217
apprehension, communication, 53–61
  dealing with, 58–60
  nature of, 54
  receiver, 54,
  state, 57
  trait, 57
appropriateness, 101
atmosphere effect, 15–441
attention, 174–176

attitudes, 212–213
audience analysis, 75, 88
  checklist for, 85–86
  demographics and, 81–84
  importance of, 77
  logic and, 213–232
  persuasion and, 217
  situations and, 84–85
audio–visual equipment, 180–184
  audiotape, 181
  film projectors, 183
  listening and, 183
  overhead projectors, 181
  public address systems, 180
  record players, 181
  slide projectors, 182
  videotape, 183

balance, theories of, 214–217
Bavelas, A. 245
Beattie, G. 240

Beavin, J., 19
Becker, S., 138
behavioral intentions, 212–213
belief, 93
Berlo, D., 16
Bettinghaus, E., 138, 231, 240
body, (of a speech), 68
body lean, 162, 164
Booth-Butterfield, S., 56, 61
Borman, E., 16
Bostrom, R., 41, 51, 58, 82, 88, 170, 217, 227
Bowers, J., 19, 150, 157
Bradac, J., 19
Bradley, B., 74, 88
Brandstatter, H., 77
briefing, 196–197
Brigance, W. 184
Brockreide, W., 48, 51, 236
Brown, M. 250
Buller, D., 161, 172
Burgoon, J., 54, 61, 161, 172, 246
Burgoon, M., 227, 240

card catalogue, 114–115
cause–effect, 129
Charmichael, C., 157
Cherry, C. 208
Christie, V., 88
chronological, 128
Cicero, M. T., 13
Clarke, P., 98, 104
Clark, R., 227
Clevenger, T., 88
Coakley, C., 16, 51
coercion, 213–214
comparison, 117
communication, 17–34
  animal, 144–145
  apprehension of, 53–66
  definition of, 18
  forms of, 5–6
  information and, 19, 193–194
  interpersonal, 6
  intrapersonal, 23
  mass, 6
  mechanics of, 25
  mediated, 6
  process and, 11
  public speaking and, 31
  purpose and, 19
  special settings for, 6

symbols and, 19
networks, 246
persuasive, 212–216
compliance–dynamism, 216
conclusion, 69, 129–130
concreteness, 148–149
condense, 70
congruity, 215–217
constructive listening, 46
contrast, 117, 176
conversation, 7, 33
convince, speaking to, 93
Cooper, L., 36
Corbett, E., 108–109, 122
credibility, 9, 212–216
  extrinsic, 102
  intrinsic, 102
Cronkhite, G., 157

Dayton, D. 184
Davis, J., 77
definition, 117
delivery, 163–169
  eye contact and, 165
  gesture and, 164
  listening and, 170
  movement and, 164
  posture and, 164
  voice and, 166–170
demographic audience analysis, 80–84
demonstration, 177–178, 195–196
denotative, 10–28
DeTurck, M., 166, 172
diagrams, 179
dissonance, 215–216
Dittman, A., 172
Dominick, J., 5, 16

Ekman, P., 172
Ehninger, D. 230
Eisenhower, D. 128
electronic audience, 81
Ellis, A. 240
Ellsworth, P., 172
Emigh, T., 163, 172
entertain, 93
environment,
  inner, 20
  outer, 20
ethics, 47, 48, 96
evaluation, and listening, 47

exactness, in language, 152
examples, 116
expand, 70
experience, 109
explanation, 196–197
extemporaneous speeches, 71
extended message, 8
externalizing, 26
eye contact, 165

facial expression, 163
Fairhurst, G., 255
feedback, 32
Fishbein, M., 93
Fisher, B., 16
Fiske, S., 24, 36
formalism, 124
Foster, T., 74
Friesen, W., 172
functions, of public speaking, 8, 9

Garay, A., 199, 208
Garven, M. 130
Geonetta, L. 245
gesture, 165
Gibb, J., 253, 255
Goffman, E., 104
Gouran, D., 245
Greynolds, M., 33
group dynamics, 244–245
　cohesiveness, and, 244
　identity, and, 245
　participation and group influence, 245
　structure, and, 244
group larger, 8
group purpose, 243

Hale, J., 161, 172
Hayakawa, S., 148
headings, (outline), 131
HeenWold, A., 42
Howard, D., 240

ideas, 107
illustrations, 117
implicit responses, 211–213
impromptu speeches, 71–72
induction, 128
inflection, 168
inform, speeches to, 92, 189–207

information, 189–207
　demonstrations and, 196
　first hand, 106–111
　language and, 194
　measurement of, 191–192
　percepts and, 193
　process and reasoning, 232
　redundancy and, 191
　schemas and, 194
　second hand, 111–115
　self-disclosure and, 198–200
Institute for Propaganda Analysis, 227
intensity (of language), 150, 217, 175
　language and, 150
　persuasion and, 217
　stimuli and, 175
interaction, 19
interpretation in listening, 42–44,
introduction, 68, 129–130, 252
invention, 108

Jablin, F., 246
Jackson, D., 19
Jarboe, S., 255
Johanneson, R., 36
Johnson, J., 191
Johnson, W., 80
Jourard, S., 199, 208

Kahn, G., 13–23, 208
Katriel, K., 14
Kelman, H., 213
Kellerman, K., 255
Kelly, C., 79, 88
Kemp, J., 184
Kressel, K., 149, 159
Kroger Corporation, 4

language, 22–23, 38, 143–157
　abstract, 148–149
　adjectivals, 148–149
　animals and, 144–145
　concrete, 148–149
　connotative, 151
　denotative, 150
　intensity and, 150
　listening and, 153–156
　metaphor, 150
　persuasion and, 217
　sexism in, 154
　usage of, 152–154

lecture listening, 41
Leathers, D., 163, 172
Levinson, D., 246
Linkugel, W., 36, 150
listening, 37–51
  aids, 12–20
  audio-visuals and, 183–184
  delivery and, 170
  efficiency in, 46
  evaluation and, 47
  information and, 206
  interpretive, 42–44, 45
  language and, 153–154
  lecture, 41
  nonverbal cues and, 170
  persuasion and, 224–226
  rehearsal, 41
  retention in, 41
  selective, 38, 39
  short-term, 38, 41, 45
Littlejohn, S., 18
logic, 229–240
  atmosphere effect in, 231
  audiences and, 231
  deductive, 234
  enthymeme in, 235
  inductive, 233
  natural, 232
  propositions and, 233
  schemas and, 229
  Toulmin model of, 236–239
loudness, 168

manuscript speeches, 70
McCombs, M., 104
McCroskey, J., 61
meaning, 151–153
  connotative, 152
  denotative, 151
mediated responses, 146
memorized speeches, 70
message, extended, 8
metaphor, 150
Miller, Goerge, 148, 157
Miller, G. R., 7, 211, 227
motion, 175
Motley, M., 19, 56, 61
movement, 175

narrowing, (topics), 100–101
natural logic, 232

networks, 246
Nichols, R., 49–50
nonverbal, 160–171
  body lean and, 162
  delivery and, 163–170
  eye contact and, 162
  facial expression and, 162
  nature of, 161
  proximity and, 161
notetaking, 137

objective listening, 46
opinion, 146, 212
organizations, speaking in, 246
Osborne, M., 150
Osgood, D., 126, 138
overworked words, 153
outlines, 130–135
  delivery and, 134
  heading system in, 131
  outline terms, 130, 135
  sample of, 132–133
  transitions and, 130, 135

Paivio, A., 149, 159
Palmgreen, P., 98, 104
percept, 21, 38
performance, (and speaking), 10
persuasion, 93, 209–227
  attitudes and, 212
  behavioral intentions and, 212–213
  credibility and, 217–220
  compliance–dynamism in, 219
  construction of, 220–221
  evidence and, 220
  factual statements, 220
  listening to, 224–226
  motivated sequence in, 221
  normative–identificatory and, 219
  opinion, 221
  organization of, 221
  problem–solution and, 221
  qualification–exertness and, 219
  safety–trustworthiness and, 218
  stimulating–arousing audiences, 232
Peterson, D., 126, 138
Phillips, G., 58, 61
Phillipsen, G., 14
Pierce, J., 5
pitch, 167

positional relationships, 247
   personal characteristics, 248
   semantic-information distance, 247
   upward influence, and, 248
posture, 164
Premack, A., 145
Premack, D., 145
process of reasoning, 229–231
problem-solving, 128
propaganda, 224–226
   bandwagon effect, 225
   half-truth, 225
   hasty generalization, 225
   name-calling, 226
   plain folks, 226
   transfer, 226
propositions, 233
proximity, 161
psychophysical attention factors, 174–176
public speaking, 3–16
purpose, in communication, 18–19
   general, 91
   methods of classifying, 90
   specific, 92–95
   traditional, 91–93

qualification–expertness, 219
quality, of voice, 168
quotation, 112

rate, of speaking, 169
Reader's Guide, 112
reasoning, see logic
Reardon, K., 138, 227
Reid, L., 104
reinforcement, 58
relay, 25, 13–39
repetition, 118
response, 212–213
retention, 41, 125
reticence, 54
Reynolds, R., 240
rhetoritherapy, 58
Richmond, V., 61
Roberts, C., 172
Rogers, E. 255
Rosenfeld, L., 88
Rubin, R., 172

Sarr, R., 255
Sayers, G., 14

Sawyer, Diane, 12
Schank, R., 126, 138
schema, 23–24
   information and, 194
   logic and, 229
Schwartzman, R., 103
Schuler, H., 77
Scott, W., 138
Seabury, H., 14
selection, in listening, 38–39
selection, and audiences, 78
selective perception, 174
self-disclosure, 198–200
settings, communicative, 6
   intercultural, 6
   international, 6
   organizational, 6
   political, 6
   small group, 243
sexism, (in language), 154
shyness, 54
Siebold, D. 246
situational audience analysis, 84–85
Skinner, B., 36
social signalling, 144–145
sort, 70
spatial, 127
spectra, 54
speeches (special types) 250–254
   apology, 253
   dedication, 251
   introductions, 252
   nominating, 252–253
   welcome, 251
Speech Communication Association, 54
Staats, L., 240
statistics, 200–202
   polls as, 202
   reasoning and, 200
Steeves, R., 149, 159
Steinberg, M., 7
Steinfatt, T., 240
Stevenson, A. 155
stimulate, 27
"success," and speaking, 9
summarize, 70
Sumner, W., 148
symbols, 20
Sypher, B., 43
Sypher, H. 23
Szczupakiewicz, N., 191

Taylor, S., 24, 36
thesis, 68
topic choice, 97–103
   current events and, 98
   ethics and, 96
   great ideas and, 99
   listening, and, 102
   narrowing, and, 100–101
   purpose, and, 102
   sources for, 97
Topoi, 108–109
touch, 162
Toulmin, S., 236
transition, 130, 135
Tufte, R., 184

variety, and voice, 169
visual aids, 173–184
voice, 166–170
   inflection and, 167
   loudness and, 168
   pitch and, 167
   quality and, 168
   rate and, 168
   variety and, 168

Waldhart, E., 41, 51, 170
Watzlawick, P., 19
Weaver, C., 38, 51, 81, 135, 138, 157
Whatmough, J., 148, 157
Wheeless, L., 54
Whitman, R., 74
Williams, F., 122
Winans, J., 7
Winnick, W., 149, 157
Wolvin, A., 16, 51
Worthy, M., 199, 208

Yerby, J., 245, 255

Zajonc, R., 164